CONSTRUCTING HUMAN RIGHTS IN THE AGE OF GLOBALIZATION

International Relations in a Constructed World

Commonsense Constructivism, or
The Making of World Affairs
Ralph Pettman

Constructing International Relations:
The Next Generation
Karen M. Fierke and Knud Erik Jørgensen, editors

Constructing Human Rights in the Age of Globalization
*Mahmood Monshipouri, Neil Englehart, Andrew J. Nathan,
and Kavita Philip, editors*

Constructivism and Comparative Politics
Daniel M. Green

Foreign Policy in a Constructed World
Vendulka Kubálková, editor

International Relations in a Constructed World
Vendulka Kubálková, Nicholas Onuf, and Paul Kowert, editors

Language, Agency, and Politics in a Constructed World
François Debrix

CONSTRUCTING HUMAN RIGHTS IN THE AGE OF GLOBALIZATION

MAHMOOD MONSHIPOURI
NEIL ENGLEHART
ANDREW J. NATHAN
KAVITA PHILIP
EDITORS

Routledge
Taylor & Francis Group

LONDON AND NEW YORK

First published 2003 by M.E. Sharpe

Published 2015 by Routledge
2 Park Square, Milton Park, Abingdon, Oxon OX14 4RN
711 Third Avenue, New York, NY 10017, USA

Routledge is an imprint of the Taylor & Francis Group, an informa business

Library of Congress Cataloging-in-Publication Data

Constructing human rights in the age of globalization / edited by Mahmood Monshipouri
. . . [et al.].
   p. cm. — (International relations in a constructed world)
Includes bibliographical references and index.
ISBN 0-7656-1137-6 (alk. paper); ISBN 0-7656-1138-4 (pbk.; alk. paper)
   1. Civil rights. 2. Human rights. 3. Globalization. I. Monshipouri, Mahmood, 1952– II.
Series.

JC571.C66 2003
323—dc21   2003041563

ISBN 13: 9780765611383 (pbk)
ISBN 13: 9780765611376 (hbk)

Contents

Acknowledgments

This book grew out of a 1999 National Endowment for Humanities, Summer Seminar at Columbia University entitled, "Cultural Differences and Values: Human Rights and the Challenge of Relativism," under the directorship of Professor Andrew J. Nathan. Many of the contributors to this book, who participated in that seminar, would like to express their deep gratitude to Professor Nathan for his genuine efforts, valuable guidance, and enthusiatic drive to complete this project.

Introduction

Observing Human Rights in an Age of Globalization

Neil A. Englehart, Mahmood Monshipouri, Andrew J. Nathan, and Kavita Philip

Globalization breeds universalisms—a multitude of them. Often these universalisms exist in tension with each other, sometimes in explicit contradiction or competition. Yet the very fact that people experience these ideas and practices as universal leads them to assume that they cannot be subject to contradiction, at least not in good faith. How is this possible?

People in many cultures have often constructed their most basic or cherished beliefs as universals. Religious faith or assumptions about human nature, for instance, are often couched in universalist terms, explicitly intended to transcend particular cultures. Such "local" universalisms were easier to sustain prior to the nineteenth century. The difficulties of travel and communication before the invention of the steamship and the telegraph made it easier to relegate difference to the realm of the exotic.

Today difference is omnipresent. New technologies continually drive down the costs of long-distance communication, leading to the intensification of cross-cultural contacts. The burgeoning social and economic integration made possible by increasing transnational networks and flows of capital, finance, information, and ideas represents a growing global interconnectedness that we call globalization. Globalization changes the environment of universalist beliefs. With globalization, universalisms compete before our eyes.

Paradoxically, globalization simultaneously undermines and confirms universalisms. They are undermined when the recognition of other, conflicting universalist claims leads to relativism—the assumption that, since all universalisms cannot simultaneously be true, none can be true—or at least none can have a stronger claim to truth than any other.

Cross-cultural contacts, however, can also confirm universalisms. Globalization draws people into global networks, so that they begin to interact more regularly with others across national and cultural borders. They begin to share ideas, assumptions, and practices necessary for them to cooperate—for instance, assumptions about markets that permit business networks to operate, or technical knowledge and ethical commitments that enable networks of environmental activists to cooperate globally. These ideas and practices are confirmed as having universal validity precisely because they are shared across cultures. They often do not mesh across networks, however, and thus may lead to competing transnational universalisms.

The international human rights movement is one such global network. As the chapters in this volume show, human rights activism joins people across borders in a partially overlapping normative framework. Thus transnational actors and regimes—in contexts such as property rights (Chapter 1), international law (Chapter 3), or U.S. foreign policy (Chapter 6)—may exert influence over local actors, with varying degrees of receptivity. As Neil Englehart argues, accepting universals advanced by transnational actors may create unintended consequences that also have global scope and lead to their own universalisms—such as local movements for rights and democracy.

This is not to suggest that globalization simply promotes human rights activism. For it is equally true that human rights activism advances globalization. Local actors may also have incentives to build globalization from below, by linking with transnational actors—as in Iran (Chapter 5) and Hong Kong (Chapter 8). The relationships within and between these networks are complex and sometimes perverse—as with the phenomenon, noted by Mahmood Monshipouri and Charles Lockhart, that conservatives across borders may echo each other's rhetoric of a cultural tradition hostile to human rights, creating in effect a transnational network of traditionalist cultural nationalists.

The phrase "competing universalisms" is intended to suggest two interlocking ideas. First, globalization and human rights both claim to be universal ideas, but at many levels they place conflicting demands on actors. Second, each of these universalizing processes evokes resistance, but resistance in the modern world is seldom willing to present itself as localistic or particularistic, and may stake a claim to universalist pretensions of its own. This argument suggests that the usual analyses of both human rights and globalization as representing universalizing forces that are arrayed against localist, relativist resistances are false—at least to the subjectivity and rhetorical strategies of the combatants. Instead, the paradoxical processes that we are describing produce a babble of competing ideas that all claim universal validity. Universalism itself becomes the only universal idea—all the rest is contested.

But these processes are not random. They can be analyzed and understood, since the ideologies and identities at stake are constructed in response to one another. Thus our task throughout these chapters is to decipher the sibling relationships among antagonistic worldviews, to see the way in which actors and concepts trying to be different from one another thereby end up mirroring each other. Our analytic vantage point is middle-range. We conduct neither a micro-level analysis in which the dynamics of human rights and globalization are treated as independent, nor a macro-level approach that assumes them to be mechanically interconnected. This level of analysis permits enough scope to render visible the complex interactions between the two without committing us to grand theorizing.

To the globalization literature, we hope to contribute the insight that the debate over human rights illustrates both the dynamics of globalization and the reaction to it, and is itself one integral part of the process of globalization. For those interested in human rights, we hope to help supersede the notion of a single universalism striving to overcome a series of reactive localisms. To the larger public discourse over current trends in world affairs, we would like to contribute an enriched sense of how uncertain and contingent are the processes unfolding in the world around us.

Realizing how crucial interdisciplinary work is to understanding a globalized world, we seek to explore complexities, opportunities, and constraints that globalization poses to the fulfillment of international human rights and shed light on the connecting points of politics, economics, culture, and environment. We hope this can serve as a corrective to the idea that the triumphs of both globalization and human rights are foreordained and easy.

In this introduction, we will first discuss the notion of constructed and competing human rights. We will then apply the idea to the globalization literature, and to the development of the international human rights movement. The final section sketches the organization of this book.

Constructed Universals

Constructed universals is an intentionally paradoxical formulation. We use it to capture an intriguing facet of the interaction between globalization and human rights: that both lend themselves to the construction of multiple, sometimes conflicting sets of institutions, ideas, and practices that reach across borders and become, in a sense, universal. Sometimes these can become so widely accepted that they assume an appearance of inevitability, as for instance property rights (Chapter 1) or the modern state (Chapter 2). In other cases, such as the quest for environmental rights (Chapter 3) or women's rights (Chapter 4), activists explicitly attempt to make their beliefs universal. In the language used by Chenyang Li (Chapter 11), they attempt to persuade others that a belief that is not now universally held ought to be. Globalization in politics, economics, communications, and technology has made this possible on a truly global scale, fostering the development of competing sets of ideas and institutions with worldwide scope. These ideas and institutions claim universal validity, not necessarily because they are ontologically given, but because they are constructed as universals.

Our ordinary understanding of a "universal" is derived from the Enlightenment tradition, best exemplified by Immanuel Kant, who held that some truths were necessary a priori in order for a rational mind to be possible. Such truths were therefore universal, in the sense that they had to be true for all rational minds. From this epistemological position, Kant then developed what he regarded as an equally necessary and universal account of morality, justice, and politics. The universal in this Enlightenment vision is absolute and brooks no competitors.

Yet there was always a tension in this Enlightenment vision of morality. Kant recognized that rights had developed historically, and that the world did not actually conform to his ethical system—implying a process of historical evolution still under way (Beck 1978). Kant responded with a teleological theory of history, in which progress was driven by "asocial sociability"—the need for human beings to invent institutions to protect themselves from other human beings (Kant 1963, 53–68). Thus Kant admits a certain constructivist dimension (Rawls 1980). If human institutions are constructed, then alternative, competing constructions are at least logically possible as well.

This volume is not a theoretical attack on Enlightenment liberalism, but rather a series of empirical observations on the relationship between globalization and human rights. Our chapters are linked less by a common theory than a common problematic: What occurs at the intersection of human rights and globalization? We collectively illustrate how people have constructed multiple universalisms with respect to human rights. This happens in a variety of ways. In some instances, globalization leads to the spread of human rights norms, or to global debates about what norms are most appropriate. In others, local struggles for human rights lead to globalization.

These universalisms are the products of human agency, not philosophical necessity. What makes them universals is not their apodictic certainty, but rather the empirical fact that they have spread around the globe and make universal claims. They are global universals rather than absolutes. This means that they are also intrinsically subject to challenge and dispute.

Multiple universalisms are likely to clash. Transnational networks of people holding different interests and believing in different universalisms are likely to come into conflict. It is one of the features of universalisms that they often seem obvious and natural to those who believe them. When those people encounter competing universalisms, they may therefore view them as perverse and unnatural. Alternatively, they may assume that the people who advance competing universalisms do so in bad faith, for unethical or self-interested reasons.

As globalization increases contact across borders and speeds up the flow of information around the world, people will increasingly be exposed to the ideas and institutions constructed by others. The result of this will not simply be a clash of civilizations or a homogenization of global cultures. It will be a complex mix of responses, with some people adopting or adapting alternative ideas and joining global networks, while others reject competing universalisms in hostile, localizing reactions. We now turn to the globalization literature for guidance in navigating among the possibilities.

Competing Theories of Globalization

Our work draws from, and aims to develop, several competing—but not necessarily incompatible—theories of globalization. We wish to highlight in this section two central issues on which students of globalization disagree. First, what drives globalization? Is it a process driven by autonomous economic forces, by politics, or by cultural diffusion and struggles over identity? Second, is globalization a simple homogenizing process, or does it create complex localizing dynamics as well? Is it a unidirectional syndrome of coordinated changes, or is it a multilayered process of change with significant contradictions, discontinuities, and inconsistencies?

What Drives Globalization?

The sources of globalization can be seen from a variety of perspectives. One common theory holds that it is primarily an economic phenomenon, characterized by the knitting together of markets and firms across borders.

This branch of the globalization literature tends to reproduce a long-standing debate between liberals and their critics on the left.

Thomas Friedman, for instance, sees globalization as a set of trends in politics, society, and culture produced by the functional needs of an increasingly integrated and advanced global economy, and driven by the development of new communications technologies. These changes tend to empower individuals, promote greater openness and transparency in politics, and foster greater democratization of economic life (Friedman 1999). Friedman thus echoes the classical liberals who saw free trade and cosmopolitanism as essentially beneficent forces that would promote world peace, democracy, and global prosperity.

A relatively new, related literature on globalization examines it as an evolutionary process, suggesting that it is made possible by the liberalization of access to information and transmission of ideas via the electronic media, information technology, networking, and the interconnection of economies through international finance and global markets. Unlike past eras of globalization, today massive flows of direct foreign investment in plants and equipment, as well as growing cross-border mergers, are indispensable to global economic interdependence. Globalization has increasingly become central to corporate strategy and actually equals continual restructuring: "Virtually every major corporation in the world is in a constant state of restructuring these days" (Garten 2000, xii). This restructuring is occurring amid growing new risks, including financial volatility, unprecedented corporate competition, and individual market failures. As the integrated global economy expands, however, these new threats to survival will be accompanied by new challenges and opportunities (Garten 2000, xiii).

Not all globalization theorists see economic integration as such a benign process. World systems theorists hold that global markets have long been integrated, with the current era distinguished only by the size and frequency of economic flows. In this world economic system, there have always been distinct winners and losers (Wallerstein 1974; Braudel 1984). Core states or cities have always been able to secure resources from peripheral areas in unequal economic relationships. Contemporary globalization simply represents an intensification of those relationships.

Because neoliberal economic prescriptions take little account of the social and cultural implications of such policies for developing countries, global economic pressures undermine the ability of the developing countries' governments to protect minorities or to preserve important cultural and social elements within communities. Globalization may have increased the possibility of state fragmentation, or may have simply doomed the state to irrelevance. This is precipitated by shifting decisionmaking processes away from governments and people to globalized economic institutions and transnational corporations (TNCs) that have but a meager interest in the sociocultural welfare or human rights of people in the developing world (McCorquodale and Fairbrother 1999, 756–765).

For some critics, however, globalization is not simply an autonomous economic process. It is instead driven by political strategies on the part of those most powerful in the international system. In this argument globalization is a political project that rests on hegemonic powers such as the United States. Seen this way, globalization is defined as a new power game, or a hegemonic system based on "ingraining the idea and practice of neoliberalism" (Mittelman and Falk 2000, 131). Other forms of politico-economic and cultural hegemony proceed from the assumption of cultural imperialism and rationalist hubris. Absent an equitable, just, and democratic system of global governance, it is argued, concerns are raised over the emergence of "global apartheid" and "cultural colonialism" of sorts (Alexander 1996; MacBride and Roach 2000).

Others regard globalization as a site of intersection between power and culture, mediated by the interests of national, transnational, and subnational groups (Sassen 1998; Jameson and Miyoshi 1998). According to this theory, rights norms are seen as a Trojan horse for inserting Western cultural power into non-Western contexts. Chenyang Li (Chapter 11) and John Downey (Chapter 12) both urge the importance of mutual respect and persuasion in cross-cultural dialogue, precisely to circumvent this possibility and safeguard the legitimacy of the idea of human rights.

Blending political and cultural arguments, some theorists maintain that the end of the Cold War has produced a U.S. hegemony that operates partly through soft power. Also known as co-optive behavior, soft power is an indirect exercise of influence in world politics. Soft power can be instrumental in establishing preferences associated with such intangible power resources as culture, ideology, and institutions. This aspect of power refers to "the ability to set the political agenda in a way that shapes the preferences others express" (Nye 2000, 57).

The United States employs a universalist rhetoric in the exercise of soft power, even if its foreign policy often appears highly particularistic. Resistance and reaction to U.S. policies therefore also tend to take the form of universalist claims. Such universalist claims appear to carry more weight than particularistic ones, and are taken more seriously by the international community. Hence even localizing reactions to human rights activism end up framed in universalist terms such as "all peoples have a unique cultural heritage." This tends to convert human rights debates into issues of identity.

Manuel Castells (1997, 243, 307–308) argues forcefully that globalization can be seen as a struggle over identities in which the spread of global cultural elements produces a localist/fundamentalist reaction. Castells points out that inequalities in the international system have caught nation-states in a dilemma between global economic flows and local identity. Nation-states, he explains, must abide by global rules favorable to capital flows if they are to prosper economically. And yet they survive because of the defensive communalism of nations and people in their territories, holding on to their last refuge against the whirlwind of global flows. Castells views the relationship between state politics and transnational politics as paradoxical: "the more states emphasize communalism, the less effective they become as co-agents of a global system of shared power. The more they triumph in the planetary scene, in close partnership with the agents of globalization, the less they represent their national constituencies." The politics of the late twentieth century, Castells warns, was "dominated by this fundamental contradiction" virtually everywhere around the globe (1997, 308).

Homogenizing or Not?

Many theorists influenced by modernization theory argue that globalization is a simple homogenizing process leading to greater respect for political and civil rights. Modernization theory holds that economic development brings a host of cultural and political changes, producing greater political openness as an expanding middle class demand greater respect for their interests. According to this argument, economic development creates a paradigm shift involving fundamental changes in values, lifestyles, and tolerance for diversity (be it ethnic, cultural, or sexual) and individual choice. Ronald Inglehart (1997) argues that an empirically demonstrable shift is occurring in the political, economic, and cultural spheres. Many economists view such a shift as fundamental to effective international economic integration. Accordingly, this paradigm shift reflects the convergence of a multipolar world, global capitalism, and new communications technologies. Globalization is seen as an extension of the effects of modernity to the entire world, and the compression of time and space simultaneously (Giddens 1990; Robertson 1992).

A related theory, offered by Francis Fukuyama (1992), is that liberalism has become the dominant international political theory in the aftermath of the Cold War, offering greater prospects for safeguarding international human rights (see also Forsythe 2000). Accordingly, globalization leads ultimately to a broad consensus on the same values.

The critics of globalization view the pressures to conform to the spreading Western consumer monoculture as destroying traditional societies, undermining local economies, and eradicating regional differences. All over the world, they note, villages, rural communities, and their cultural traditions are being destroyed by such globalizing forces as fast-food chains, Hollywood films, cellular phones, multilane highways, and concrete cities. "In the remotest corners of the planet," argues Helena Norberg-Hodge (1999, 70), "Barbie, Madonna, and the Marlboro Man are familiar icons. From Cleveland to Cairo to Caracas, *Baywatch* is entertainment and CNN news." This pressure of "cultural homogenization," or more accurately "Westernization," is everywhere and is simply becoming unstoppable.

This form of cultural intrusion is likely to deny the individual's own cultural identity as well as to increase personal insecurity, further compounding the struggle to survive amid the euphoria of the "global village" and its vision of togetherness. The Western global monoculture holds severe implications for the 90 percent of people living in the poor countries: "While it destroys traditions, local economies, and sustainable ways of living, it does not even provide the poor with the glittering, wealthy lifestyle it promised them. It provides no replacement for that which it destroys but a fractured, isolated, competitive, and unhappy society" (Norberg-Hodge 1999, 77).

Other analysts view "cultural imperialism" as inexorably linked to the process of cultural globalization. This linkage, according to pessimistic globalizers (Mackay 2000, 65), epitomizes a profound structural cause: "Global media and cultural corporations are massive structures and have become an increasingly significant component of the global economy. They are closely linked with one another and have interests that span the breadth of the information, communication, entertainment and leisure sectors." The West's dominant cultures, critics insist, are swamping minority cultures in processes of homogenization and reducing diversity. This strategy is chiefly designed to safeguard the economic interests of the United States and other Western nations.

On the other hand, some scholars argue that globalization is not a steady and inexorable homogenization of the world. It has complicated relationships to local circumstances. Richard Falk (1999) identifies two forms of globalization that operate simultaneously: "globalization from above" and "globalization from below." While the former is imposed from the outside and is controlled and led by TNCs and international financial institutions

(IFIs), with states facilitating the process, the latter is local, grassroots, and enjoys broader mass support as it mobilizes global civil society. The two levels, Falk notes, are in a dialectical relationship. Increasingly, hegemonic neoliberal globalization is counterbalanced with an emerging global civil society (Wapner 1996). While globalization from above is inherently homogenizing and hegemonic in its tendencies, globalization from below is essentially pluralistic. Whereas globalization from above leads to a hegemonic human rights discourse based on the concepts of universalism and secularism, globalization from below fosters a more holistic and integrated vision of rights. It is the latter that is compatible with the worldwide realization of human rights (Aziz 1999, 34).

The growing activism of nongovernmental organizations (NGOs), according to some analysts, has led to domestic political and social struggles. NGOs are bent on building a culture of human rights from below, and this globalization is a product of local agency rather than global hegemony. Focusing on grassroots empowerment and education, NGOs have become agents of change (Welch 1995). Yet, as many of the chapters in this volume show (most clearly Chapters 5 and 8), local agency often constructs universalisms that mesh well with those advocated by transnational networks.

Many observers have emphasized that globalization can produce either accommodation or resistance. James H. Mittelman maintains that "globalization is a multilevel set of processes with built-in strictures on its power and potential, for it produces resistance against itself. In other words, globalization creates discontents not merely as latent and undeclared resistance, but sometimes crystallized as open countermovements" (2000, 7). Globalization paradoxically breeds localisms and universalisms as part of the same process.

Underscoring the importance of complex and competing trends associated with global changes, James N. Rosenau similarly argues that globalizing dynamics are accompanied by localizing dynamics (1997, 362). The two sets of dynamics are causally linked in that "every increment of globalization gives rise to an increment of localization, and vice versa." Although it is hard to avoid conflict between the localizing and globalizing tendencies, Rosenau posits that there is no inherent contradiction between the two and that both tendencies can develop simultaneously. He nevertheless endorses the idea that the globalizing scenario of change is far more tenable than the localizing one: "some globalizing dynamics are bound, at least in the long run, to prevail" (361).

Globalization thus entails a paradox: "Despite the homogenizing aims of globalization, local situations remain robust in their resistance" (Schreiter 1997, 8). In both technical and cultural senses, globalization does not mean homogenization. In the technical sense, globalization requires strategies and practices that allow for the diversity that exists across countries. Local differentiation and infrastructure is vital for the success of some business processes (Moss Kanter 1999, 42–43). In the cultural sense, globalization has intensified the normative discourse between cosmopolitans and localists (see Chapter 5).

Resistance and Accommodation: Dynamic and Complex Interrelations

The authors of this volume concur that globalization is a complex process. We agree with Robert Keohane and Joseph Nye (2000, 110–111) that globalization is best seen as a set of linked yet distinct dimensions: economic, military, cultural, social, and environmental. These dimensions create a complex context in which the actions of states, multinational corporations (MNCs)/TNCs, and NGOs constantly impinge on each other, resulting in further uncertainty about the ability of governments, market participants, and other actors to comprehend and manage globalization. Furthermore, we agree that globalization is a process full of contradictions, inconsistencies, and localizing reactions.

We also agree with Anthony G. McGrew (1998, 194–196) that globalization may not necessarily foreshadow a new and more progressive era for the promotion of universal human rights. Conversely, its implications for the practice and substantive realization of human rights are "highly ambiguous and contradictory." Contemporary globalization, McGrew notes, is implicated "in a set of growing disjunctures between the global diffusion of the idea of universal human rights and the social, political, and economic conditions necessary for their effective realization." As the conditions of globalization are intensified, the capacity of states and the global human rights regime to ensure compliance with established global norms is significantly eroded. Furthermore, because globalization creates global patterns of hierarchy and stratification, both of which accentuate growing inequalities within and between nations, it contributes to a bifurcation of the global system into "zones of compliance" and "zones of instability." It is in the latter domain that internal strife, poverty, and repressive mechanisms undermine, if not totally eliminate, the basis of compliance with emerging global norms, and hence beget chronic resistance to universal human rights standards.

Recognizing these complexities, we argue that the best way to understand the relationship between human rights and globalization is through a series of case studies, selected to provide insight into key issues. Human rights is an excellent lens through which to study globalization, because it is by definition globalized, itself a universal constructed by transnational networks of actors. It has provoked a complex series of reactions, ranging from resistance to adoption by local activists, depending on local circumstances.

Themes in the Globalization of Human Rights

The modern human rights movement was globalized from its beginnings with the approval of the Universal Declaration of Human Rights (UDHR) by the UN General Assembly on December 10, 1948. Prior to this, human rights was purely a domestic issue, internationalized only when transnational trade was involved—most notably in the nineteenth-century anti-slavery movement.

The contemporary human rights movement was born of the atrocities committed during World War II. The Holocaust experience in Europe and the international reaction against Nazi aggression and genocide fundamentally raised global awareness of and consciousness about the consequences of failure to prevent large-scale human suffering (Korey 1998). Human rights norms spread slowly at first after World War II, more rapidly after the 1975 Helsinki Final Act, and accelerated further after the end of the Cold War. In the course of this evolution, several important geopolitical themes have challenged the salience traditionally attached to political and economic power within a state-centric and realist framework.

In the immediate post–World War II period, much of the promise of the UDHR was obscured by the Cold War. The most active human rights diplomacy in the 1950s and 1960s involved North-South relations, as national self-determination became the rallying cry of the decolonization movement, and economic and social rights became an important issue for the G77 (Vincent 1986, 76–91). These movements focused attention on human rights as a means to achieve social justice rather than as ends in themselves. They introduced the language of "first-wave" civil and political rights, "second-wave" economic rights, and "third-wave" social and cultural rights, to which the authors in this volume generally adhere. In general, the contributors to this volume promote the shared principle that these three "generations" of human rights are interdependent and interactive—not sequential.

However, the bipolar balance of the Cold War dominated world politics and overshadowed the nascent human rights movement. As governments largely ignored the issue, NGOs became the primary advocates of human rights. This period saw the founding of such pioneering human rights

NGOs as Amnesty International, the Fund for Free Expression (which later evolved into Human Rights Watch), and the International League for Human Rights (Korey 1998). These organizations operated across borders to create what Margaret Keck and Kathryn Sikkink (1998) term a "transnational advocacy network." Such networks bring new ideas, norms, and discourses into policy debates. In addition to norm implementation, they serve as communicative structures and create political spaces in which different actors negotiate the social, cultural, and political meanings of their joint enterprise. Such advocacy networks "often involve individuals advocating policy changes that cannot be easily linked to a rationalist understanding of their interests" (Keck and Sikkink 1998, 8–9). Since World War II, such advocacy networks have played a major role in internalizing human rights norms around the world. Hence the indisputable status of these norms today. The upshot has been "a process of a genuine international 'norm cascade' as the influence of international human rights norms spread rapidly" (Risse and Sikkink 1999, 21).

Human rights began to be relegitimated as an intergovernmental issue in the 1970s. The 1975 Helsinki Accords, officially known as the Final Act of the Helsinki Meeting of the Conference on Security and Cooperation in Europe, marked the onset of a new era in East-West relations. Political and economic rights were added to the U.S.-Soviet dialogue over security concerns in Europe. With the rise of Mikhail Gorbachev in the Soviet Union in 1985, the Soviets increasingly conceded human rights components of the Helsinki Accords (known as "Basket Three"), giving the impression that a peaceful and gradual transformation was occurring in the USSR. The Helsinki process helped relegitimate human rights as a diplomatic issue after the long Cold War lull.

Since the end of the Cold War, a number of other important developments amounting to a sea change have framed the contours of moral discourse in the international community more generally. The collapse of the Soviet Union and the end of the Cold War era were perhaps the most significant force behind a burgeoning international human rights movement. Despite the abrupt 1989 upheavals in Eastern and Central Europe, it was clear that the Helsinki Accords established a norm for the spread of democratic governance. At the 1990 Helsinki follow-up convention in Copenhagen, all of the newly established democracies of European states unanimously endorsed political pluralism, independent multiparty systems, independent judiciaries, and the guarantee of minority rights (Poole 1999, 122).

The Helsinki process helped legitimate human rights as an issue in international relations. This very legitimation then posed the problem of how best to achieve the goals of human rights diplomacy—through direct intervention, the United Nations or other international organizations, legal mechanisms, local Truth and Reconciliation Commissions, or local activists.

In the last quarter of the twentieth century, the most controversial patterns of protecting human rights globally assumed the form of humanitarian and military interventions. Nothing has caused divisions among foreign policymaking and academic circles quite so dramatically as the issue of intervention. Since the failed U.S. military intervention in Somalia (1992), such missions have come under increased critical scrutiny. The Kosovo intervention (1999) rekindled debates about the cost and consequences of moral policy. Such interventions, however, have increasingly been couched in human rights terms, creating broader popular favor for taking direct and forceful action. Defenders of this approach (Teson 1998, 40) argue that "illegitimate states and governments are not protected by the principle of state sovereignty." This, however, is not to suggest that intervention is always warranted against such states and governments. As we completed work on this book, President Clinton at the UN Millennium Conference called for greater international intervention in domestic conflicts, while declining to specify the circumstances that would justify such interventions (*New York Times* 2000, A16).

An alternative to intervention is to work within the framework of intergovernmental institutions, most importantly the UN system. Since the UN established the Office of the High Commissioner for Human Rights (OHCHR) in 1993, it has vigorously attempted to expand and enforce human rights protections at the governmental level. A member of the Secretary-General's executive committee, the Commissioner has both elevated her portfolio and enhanced early warning activities. The OHCHR has expanded its activities to monitor the human rights records of member states through public forums and routine reviews. Increasing use of other UN "thematic mechanisms," such as the UN High Commissioner for Refugees (UNHCR), the Committee on the Elimination of All Forms of Discrimination Against Women (1982), and the Committee Against Torture (1987), has refocused considerable attention on assessment and implementation efforts (Poole 1999, 134–137).

International law has also been developed as a human rights tool. In the 1990s, a trend emerged that linked the doctrine of universal jurisdiction with international constitutional features. The plethora of international agreements on the creation and the strengthening of the necessary institutional arrangements to pressure governments into respecting their citizens' rights suggest the internationalization of domestic jurisdiction. The creation by the UN Security Council of two ad hoc international criminal tribunals in the former Yugoslavia and Rwanda in the 1990s signified an era of justice without borders. These draw on the legacy and precedent of the Nuremberg tribunal, largely ignored during the Cold War. The 1993 International Criminal Tribunal for the former Yugoslavia (ICTY) was authorized to investigate ethnic cleansing and genocide perpetrated after the disintegration of that country in 1991. The 1994 International Criminal Tribunal for Rwanda (ICTR) was established to prosecute those responsible for the genocidal massacre of the Tutsi minority at the hands of the Hutu-dominated government. Although there are many questions regarding the effectiveness of such tribunals, their existence has generated burgeoning interest in the notion of an impartial justice system to try those perpetrating war crimes and to bring the offenders to account.

Likewise, the creation of a new, permanent International Criminal Court (ICC) to try cases of international war crimes, aggression, genocide, and crimes against humanity is emblematic of this rising attention. At the Rome Diplomatic Conference of July 17, 1998, UN member countries voted overwhelmingly for a treaty to establish the new international criminal court by a vote of 120 to 7, with 21 abstentions. As in the international movement against the use of land mines, NGOs (especially the Coalition for the Establishment of the ICC) and grassroots groups made great contributions to generating the support for the creation of a strong and independent court.

Spanish magistrate Baltasar Garzon's request to British authorities to arrest General Augusto Pinochet Ugarte on October 16, 1998, for the crimes of the former Chilean dictator's regime was a new test for the viability of international human rights laws. Although British officials ruled against extradition to Spain, and Pinochet was eventually released, the case had profound repercussions for establishing two new precedents in international human rights laws. First, that a former head of the state is not immune from prosecution for acts committed while in office. Second, that people may seek redress of human rights abuses in courts outside the country where crimes have occurred. These precedents indicated both a basic alteration of the international law as well as a wider scope of application beyond the region where the alleged crimes took place.

Another alternative is the use of Truth and Reconciliation Commissions (TRCs). The UN TRCs were empowered to grant amnesty in exchange for public and authoritative acknowledgment of prior abuses, and to perform investigative and advisory functions. Although in some countries, such as Uganda and Rwanda, TRCs were effectively barred from a reliable accounting of the past, they played a significant role in many countries struggling to come to terms with widespread human rights abuses (such as

Chile, El Salvador, Argentina, Bolivia, Uruguay, and South Africa). These commissions have spawned a fruitful debate over how best to deal with past atrocities.

At the same time, economic globalization has highlighted the importance of a transnational approach to economic rights and social justice. The world political economy took a new turn as the 1991 Maastricht summit set forth a framework for achieving greater European unity. The European Union's creation of a Europe-wide central bank and single currency (the euro) was a prelude to an emerging worldwide trade system if not a new global monetary regime. In 1995 the establishment of the World Trade Organization (WTO) inaugurated a new era in the receptivity to global economic standards, as new rules and institutions came to characterize trade relations among nation-states. The purpose of the WTO was to monitor the implementation of trade agreements and settle disputes among trading partners in an increasingly competitive and globalizing world economy. With enforcement mechanisms at its disposal, this new organization represented a watershed in the global management of free trade. These recent striking developments illustrate that global economic interdependence and integration drive the quests for both global economic justice and universal human rights.

Local activists have been able to shape this emerging global economic order to some degree. For instance, the proposed Multilateral Adjustment Mechanism, which would have liberalized financial flows across borders in the same way the General Agreement on Tariffs and Trade (GATT) and the WTO liberalized trade, was successfully opposed by activists employing another product of globalization—the Internet. Until February 1997 the treaty was relatively unknown, with officials of the Organization for Economic Cooperation and Development (OECD) quietly negotiating behind closed doors. After a draft copy was leaked to a public-interest NGO in Washington and posted on its website, it immediately attracted hostile scrutiny from other NGOs and the press. The flood of negative publicity exacerbated existing differences of opinion among the negotiators, and led the OECD to suspend negotiations in 1998 (Kobrin 1998).

The rise of a global epistemic community that uses the same language and pays verbal obeisance to similar values, and a set of institutions that endeavor to promote these values in short, contributed to a "regime." Regimes, according to Stephen D. Krasner, are "sets of implicit or explicit principles, norms, rules, and decision-making procedures around which actors' expectations converge in a given area of international relations" (1983, 2). Regime analysis has a significant if limited and largely heuristic/ organizational utility for the case of human rights, according to Jack Donnelly (1986, 639). Given that the ultimate success of human rights regimes hinges on internal political factors, Donnelly points out that a vision of an international regime does not extend much beyond a politically weak *moral* interdependence. Human rights regimes entail extensive and coherent norms but extremely limited international decisionmaking powers. These strong norms and weak procedures/institutions (i.e., "there is no international enforcement") stem from conscious political decisions, reflecting underlying political perceptions of interests and interdependence (619). Several theoretical insights have informed our understanding of human rights over the years as a growing number of scholars have attempted to explain the trend toward protecting and promoting human rights globally.

But for some experts, to set rhetoric apart from reality, it is fundamentally essential to know the place of human rights in the dynamics of U.S. foreign policy (Forsythe 1989). Since the Carter administration, American policymakers have had to find a moral rationale for foreign policy that appeals to the American public, as a way of combating isolationist tendencies in American political culture after the U.S. defeat in Vietnam. At the same time, a highly interventionist, crusading style of foreign policy may be counterproductive. New policy instruments need to be developed for this new global context.

The contemporary developments cited above have fostered a spreading academic discourse regarding human rights. However, according to David Forsythe, despite the rising prominence of human rights in international relations since 1945, questions about the "origins" and "true" nature of human rights remain unsettled (2000, 28). Establishing international human rights standards as a means to ensuring minimal standards of human dignity is an evolving process, in part because "[t]hreats to human dignity change with time and place" (49). Forsythe maintains that continuity and change will determine what to retain as valid and what to modify in the face of emerging moral and political judgments.

However, transnational networks are hardly the monopoly of human rights activists. Numerous other groups are capable of forming similar networks, or more loosely defined "epistemic communities" (P. Haas 1990; E. Haas 1990). These include groups that are often accused of violating human rights, such as TNCs or the "epistemic community" generated at the U.S. government's infamous "School of the Americas" training camp. They also include groups actively opposed to transnational human rights activism, such as the diplomatic coalition that generated the Bangkok and Cairo declarations on human rights. These competing networks generate their own particular universalist discourses.

It is unclear that any single universal will ever triumph. Globalization has fostered a critical engagement of universalisms, nudging the global moral discourse further along a nonfoundational understanding of human rights between different cultures. Some of the contributors to this book defend a more holistic and integrated vision of rights emanating from cross-cultural dialogue and normative consensus (see Chapters 10–12), an approach described by some analysts as "cosmopolitan pragmatism" (Dunne and Wheeler 1999, 10–11).

The linkage between human rights and globalization is far from obvious and the theories that link them are underdeveloped. We believe that the globalization literature has not adequately explored an important set of processes where globalization and human rights interact—processes that help to explain why both globalization and the spread of human rights norms are more contingent, less predictable, and messier in outcomes than many theories anticipate. We wish to pay attention to how local agents, experiencing globalization on the ground, construct universalisms, or perhaps better, construct competing universalisms—an intentionally paradoxical formulation. Globalization may indeed produce a convergence toward human rights, yet this process is contested and, most importantly, more local and diverse than the literature to date has acknowledged.

Increasing interdependence between countries has made such issues more and more pressing. As communications technology improves our knowledge of events in other places and economic globalization implicates our livelihood with that of people far away, the "global village" (McLuhan and Fiore 1967) is increasingly a reality. As its citizens, we are all responsible for constructing the institutions that govern that village.

Organization of the Book

The book is conceived as a set of explorations of three critical areas in the intersection of human rights and globalization. Part I addresses the struggle to control human rights regimes, while discussing who actually owns culture and how the cultural and political struggles over human rights are shaped around the world. We examine the interactions between human rights and two firmly established universal constructions: property rights regimes and the modern state. The interlocking issues of environment, development, and human rights as well as the case of universal women's rights will be analyzed with a view toward ascertaining whose interests are really served in promoting or resisting globalization. In short, Part I deals with universals that have become so dominant that they are often assumed to be somehow natural, rather than constructed. The chapters in Part I attempt to show how these universals are constructed, and how they may be resisted or limited.

Among the rights that states guarantee are property rights—also taken to be natural and normal universals in the modern world. Yet property turns out to be an ambiguous and contested concept. As both Caren Irr (Chapter 1) and Kavita Philip (Chapter 3) show, economic globalization reveals contradictions between different systems of property rights.

According to Irr, the globalization of human rights regimes entails the forceful institutionalization of private property and its accompanying social relations, while simultaneously provoking a reaction in the name of communal property rights. This leaves us with two competing, universal conceptions of property: one emphasizing private property as an extension of economic globalization, and one privileging communal property as a facet of local culture. The former provides a right to commodify culture, the latter a right to enjoy culture free of the restrictions of commodification. This duality has produced conflicts and court cases, pitting TNCs against NGOs representing local people. Although global institutions more often favor private property in these contests, international law does at least accommodate the conflict and provide an arena for debate.

Neil A. Englehart (Chapter 2) argues that states are social constructions that have become universal in the modern world. They are so dominant that they seem natural and normal, causing both human rights activists and governments to lose sight of their importance in guaranteeing human rights. The globalization of the state has promoted human rights activism indirectly, because states create an institutional framework that makes human rights and democracy possible. Ironically, states are often perceived to be both the primary target of transnational human rights activism and the primary site of resistance to it, yet they are by their very nature the necessary instrument of human rights protections. Indigenous human rights movements require the constructed universal of the modern state as the foundation for their own brand of globalization from below. At the same time, cultural uniqueness is no longer a plausible excuse for authoritarian rule, because states already represent a global monoculture.

International law is itself constructed, and may be vulnerable to reconstruction on the basis of competing universal claims. Kavita Philip argues that human rights advocates operating under international law may foster the construction of a new set of universal human rights: environmental rights. She claims that the right of communities to control their own environments in order to sustain a viable livelihood can be argued as a universal human right. This argument is most effective when couched in universalist rather than localist language. Such environmental rights would have two important theoretical implications for globalization. First, they would curb the right of TNCs to maximize profits by optimizing global economic differentials in their favor. Second, they would threaten to divide human rights advocates on different sides of the question of social and economic rights. Because of these conflicts, it remains an open question whether this reconstruction of international law can succeed.

Ellen Freeberg (Chapter 4) similarly argues that some human beings universally share experiences that can become the foundation of a dialogue across universalist positions. She argues that the universality of patriarchy provides a common basis for theorizing about the experience and agency of women transcending cultural particulars. Women's agency may be different in different places, however. Such theorizing must empower local women to reconstruct local institutions according to their own preferences, or it risks alienating the very people it is intended to protect.

The four chapters in Part I suggest the common view of globalization as an instrument of international actors to exercise power over local communities, which become the major site of resistance. However, it would seriously misrepresent the nature of globalization to present it as a one-sided, top-down phenomenon that always meets local resistance. In fact, local activists often construct globalization from below by linking with transnational networks sympathetic to their cause. In Part II, we examine a variety of cases in which universals are constructed from below.

We look explicitly at the dynamics and counterdynamics of globalization, or transnational networks, and their peculiar, sometimes perverse interactions with local actors. Here the politics of culture in Iran, the pursuit of civil society in China, the situation of workers in China, and localizing dynamics in Hong Kong will be explored.

Even without explicit connections to transnational organizations, activists may construct discourses that conform to the universalist language and standards used by such organizations. Ironically, local activists may even use local materials to construct such discourses. Mahmood Monshipouri (Chapter 5) presents the case of activists in Iran working for women's rights and freedom of the press, who use local cultural resources to claim rights compatible with the standards enshrined in international human rights documents such as the UDHR. These activists see Islam as compatible with cosmopolitan standards for human rights, and they must use Islamic justifications to engage their primary audience: local conservatives opposed to such human rights protections. The conservatives, on the other hand, end up echoing the particularistic claims made by conservatives universally.

Governments may participate in transnational networks and universalist discourses for their own purposes—it would be a mistake to regard such networks as a purely nongovernmental phenomenon. Rebecca Moore (Chapter 6) shows how U.S. policy in China has focused on encouraging globalization from below rather than imposing standards coercively. She points out that the U.S. government's human rights policy toward China has avoided traditional instruments such as trade policy, and instead is supporting indigenous NGOs to build civil society there. The goal is to assist local activists in constructing human rights standards and the rule of law. This assistance meets with approval from the Chinese government, which sees certain benefits flowing from it—although it also regards with some ambivalence the spectacle of a foreign government giving funds to private or semiprivate organizations within its borders.

Dorothy J. Solinger (Chapter 7) points out that "virtual globalization" reproduces the impacts of globalization on citizens and workers that are seen in many other countries more exposed to the global economy. Yet the Chinese government has undertaken these policies without the stimulus of actual competition from abroad, but under the influence of globally dominant ideas about competitiveness that normally come attached to economic globalization. This effectively minimizes the citizenship rights of Chinese workers, exposing them to the same sorts of uncertainties and disadvantages that are normally associated with structural adjustment programs.

Linda Butenhoff (Chapter 8) completes this triptych of views of China by examining the localizing dynamics of change in Hong Kong. Whereas Moore looks at support for civil society NGOs by foreign governments, and Solinger is interested in the Chinese government's spontaneous attempts to conform the country's economy to global standards, Butenhoff examines private linkages made by NGOs in Hong Kong to the international community. She shows how local and international NGOs in Hong Kong demand the implementation of civil, political, economic, as well as social rights, and reject the relativist "Asian values" argument. Local NGOs represent globalization from below, but actively seek outside support for their work. The chapters in Part II all point toward the construction of universals acceptable to free-market liberals in the West. However, it is far from certain that those universals will triumph.

In Part III, which delves into setting the terms of debate and seeking ways to achieve a global consensus, four authors challenge the vision of a triumph of Western liberalism emerging from globalization. These chapters examine regional perspectives and obstacles to overlapping consensus given the existing conflicts between competing rights. Part III underscores the importance of the notion that there is a need to explore possibilities for dialogue across these competing positions.

Regional perspectives on human rights, according to Joanne Bauer (Chapter 9), demonstrate diversity of ideas, institutions, cultural traditions, and practices among non-Westerners. Different regions have varying human rights priorities that stem from their own history and experience, but it is a mistake to interpret the differentiation of priorities as a disagreement over norms. In short, there is room to maneuver and move toward building a global consensus. Charles Lockhart (Chapter 10) draws on the earlier chapters to make a more theoretical argument. He sees attempts to construct universal human rights norms of any kind as futile, given the irreducible differences between cultures. He argues that culture is inherently plural. In the contemporary world there are three cultures—individualistic, egalitarian, and hierarchical—which will always coexist and none of which will ever disappear. They coexist both within and across national boundaries. Each supports different kinds of rights, for which each may claim universal validity. The best that can be hoped for is accommodation, not consensus—and even that depends on favorable political and economic circumstances.

The remaining chapters in Part III pick up Lockhart's challenge by examining the possibilities for dialogue across cultures and between universalisms. They emphasize the need for mutual respect as a starting point, recognizing that people who hold universal ideas cannot be expected to neutrally evaluate competing universalisms. Instead a progressive dialogue is necessary for real progress.

Chenyang Li (Chapter 11) points out that any productive dialogue must be based on mutual respect and willingness to reevaluate one's own beliefs. Given that people have different values, moral persuasion is the best way to create a global normative consensus, rather than coercion or enforced conformity. Genuine dialogue requires us to participate in the construction of universals by reevaluating our own beliefs, as well as advocating them.

One basis of cross-cultural dialogue, cautiously advanced by John Downey (Chapter 12), is the experience and memory of suffering. Suffering is a universal human experience, and can therefore provide one avenue for a dialogue about human rights that can transcend cultural barriers. Because it is based on shared experience, such a dialogue can respect local difference while helping to achieve mutual understanding and constructing a common conception of rights.

The conclusions of the authors in this last section of the book broadly agree with those of the more empirical chapters: that in a world of constructed, competing, and conflicting universals, only dialogue initiated under conditions of mutual respect can preserve and enhance human dignity and promote social justice. It is not obvious how to achieve these ends. Hence a polyphony, or perhaps a cacophony, of voices are represented here. The intent of our book is not to argue the need for a prescriptive formula. Rather, we would argue that in a volume on constructed—even competing—universals, it is only appropriate that what we share is a problem, not a solution: How can social justice and human dignity be promoted at the intersection of human rights and globalization? The solution is not incontestably certain—it must be constructed through debate and dialogue.

References

Alexander, Titus. 1996. *Unraveling Global Apartheid.* London: Polity Press.

Aziz, Nikhil. 1999. "The Human Rights Debate in An Era of Globalization: Hegemony of Discourse." In Peter Van Ness, ed., *Debating Human Rights: Critical Essays from the United States and Asia.* New York: Routledge, 32–55.

Beck, Lewis White. 1978. "Kant and the Right of Revolution." In Lewis White Beck, *Essays on Kant and Hume.* New Haven: Yale University Press: 171-187.

Braudel, Fernand. 1984. *The Perspective of the World: Civilization and Capitalism, Fifteenth–Eighteenth Century.* Vol. 3. Philadelphia: Harper and Row.

Castells, Manuel. 1997. *The Information Age: Economy, Society, and Culture: The Power of Identity.* Vol. 2. Malden, MA: Blackwell.

Donnelly, Jack. 1986. "International Human Rights: A Regime Analysis." *International Organization* 40 (Summer): 599–642.

Dunne, Tim, and Nicholas J. Wheeler, eds. 1999. *Human Rights in Global Politics.* New York: Cambridge University Press. (See "Introduction: Human Rights and the Fifty Years' Crisis," pp. 1–28.)

Falk, Richard A. 1999. *Predatory Globalization: A Critique.* London: Polity Press.

Forsythe, David P. 1989. *Human Rights and World Politics.* 2nd ed. Lincoln: University of Nebraska Press. (See esp. chap. 5.)

———. 2000. *Human Rights in International Relations.* New York: Cambridge University Press.

Friedman, Thomas. 1999. *The Lexus and the Olive Tree.* New York: Farrar, Straus, and Giroux.

Fukuyama, Francis. 1992. *The End of History and the Last Man.* New York: Free Press.

Garten, Jeffrey, ed. 2000. *Worldview: Global Strategies for the New Economy.* Boston: Harvard Business School Press.

Giddens, Anthony. 1990. *The Consequences of Modernity.* Stanford, CA: Stanford University Press.

Haas, Ernst 1990. *When Knowledge Is Power.* Berkeley: University of California Press.

Haas, Peter 1990. *Saving the Mediterranean: The Politics of International Environmental Cooperation.* New York: Columbia University Press.

Inglehart, Ronald. 1997. *Modernization and Post-Modernization: Cultural, Eco-*

nomic, and Political Change in Forty-three Countries. Princeton: Princeton University Press.

Jameson, Fredric, and Masao Miyoshi, eds. 1998. *The Cultures of Globalization.* Durham, NC: Duke University Press.

Kant, Immanuel, 1963. "Conjectural Beginning of Human History." In Lewis White Beck, ed., *Kant on History.* Indianapolis: Bobbs Merrill: 53-68.

Keck, Margaret E., and Kathryn Sikkink, eds. 1998. *Activists Beyond Borders: Advocacy Networks in International Politics.* Ithaca, NY: Cornell University Press.

Keohane, Robert O., and Joseph S. Nye Jr. 2000. "Globalization: What's New? What's Not? (And So What?)." *Foreign Policy* 118 (Spring): 104–119.

Kobrin, Stephen 1998. "The MAI and the Clash of Globalizations." *Foreign Policy* (Fall): 112–124.

Korey, William 1998. *NGOs and the Universal Declaration of Human Rights: "A Curious Grapevine."* New York: St. Martin's Press.

Krasner, Stephen D., ed. 1983. *International Regimes.* Ithaca, NY: Cornell University Press.

MacBride, Sean, and Colleen Roach. 2000. "The New International Information Order." In Frank J. Lechner and John Boli, eds., *The Globalization Reader.* London: Blackwell, 286–292.

Mackay, Hugh. 2000. "The Globalization of Culture?" In David Held, ed., *A Globalizing World? Culture, Economics, Politics.* London: Open University, 47–84.

McCorquodale, Robert, and Richard Fairbrother 1999. "Globalization and Human Rights." *Human Rights Quarterly* 21, no. 3 (August): 735–766.

McGrew, Anthony G. 1998. "Human Rights in a Global Age: Coming to Terms with Globalization." In Tony Evans, ed., *Human Rights Fifty Years On: A Reappraisal.* Manchester: Manchester University Press, 188–210.

McLuhan, Marshall, and Quentin Fiore. 1967. *The Medium Is the Massage.* New York: Random House.

Mittelman, James H., ed. 1996. *Globalization: Critical Reflections.* Boulder, CO: Lynne Rienner.

———. 2000. Introduction to James H. Mittelman and Richard Falk, *The Globalization Syndrome: Transformation and Resistance.* Princeton: Princeton University Press, 3–14.

Mittelman, James H., and Richard Falk. 2000. "Global Hegemony and Regionalism." In James H. Mittelman and Richard Falk, *The Globalization Syndrome: Transformation and Resistance.* Princeton: Princeton University Press, 131–146.

Moss Kanter, Rosabeth. 1999. "Global Competitiveness Revisited." *Washington Quarterly* 22, no. 2 (Spring): 39–58.

New York Times. 2000. "Clinton at the UN: 'Aspirations Pile High.'" September 7, p. A16.

Norberg-Hodge, Helena. 1999. "Consumer Monoculture: The Destruction of Tradition." *Global Dialogue* 1, no. 1 (Summer): 70–77.

Nye, Joseph S., Jr. 2000. *Understanding International Conflict: An Introduction to Theory and History.* 3rd ed. New York: Addison Wesley Longman.

Poole, Hilary, ed. 1999. *Human Rights: The Essential Reference.* Phoenix, AZ: Oryx Press.

Rawls, John. 1980. "Kantian Constructivism in Moral Theory." *Journal of Philosophy* 77, no. 9 (September): 515–572.

Risse, Thomas, and Kathryn Sikkink. 1999. "The Socialization of International Human Rights Norms into Domestic Practices: Introduction." In Thomas Risse, Stephen C. Ropp, and Kathryn Sikkink, eds., *The Power of Human Rights: International Norms and Domestic Change*. Cambridge: Cambridge University Press, 1–38.

Robertson, Roland. 1992. *Globalization: Social Theory and Global Culture*. Newbury Park, CA: Sage.

Rosenau, James N. 1997. "The Complexities and Contradictions of Globalization." *Current History* 96, no. 613 (November): 360–367.

Sassen, Saskia. 1998. *Globalization and Its Discontents: Essays on the New Mobility of People and Money*. New York: New Press.

Schreiter, Robert J. 1997. *The New Catholicity: Theology Between the Global and the Local*. Maryknoll, NY: Orbis Books.

Teson, Fernando R. 1998. *A Philosophy of International Law*. Boulder, CO: Westview Press.

Vincent, R.J. 1986. *Human Rights and International Relations*. Cambridge: Cambridge University Press.

Wallerstein, Immanuel. 1974. *The Modern World System*. 3 vols. New York: Academic Press.

Wapner, Paul. 1996. *Environmentalism and World Civic Politics*. Albany: State University of New York Press.

Welch, Claude E., Jr. 1995. *Protecting Human Rights in Africa: Roles and Strategies of Non-Governmental Organizations*. Philadelphia: University of Pennsylvania Press.

Part I

The Struggle to Control the Human Rights Regime

1

Who Owns Our Culture?

Intellectual Property, Human Rights, and Globalization

Caren Irr

Economic globalization has exacerbated long-standing and serious controversies over the ownership of culture. Such disputes arise when transnational corporations seeking resources to capitalize and commodify lay claim to cultural materials circulating in local economies. Or, when Inuit seamstresses sue Donna Karan for appropriating traditional parka designs, an Amazonian leader contests the Body Shop's use of his image in their advertising campaigns, Indian agriculturalists protest the patenting of turmeric (used in traditional remedies), or the Thai government opposes a Texas company's claim to own the germ of a hybrid form of jasmine and basmati rice, then the ownership of culture is at issue.[1] In each of these instances, economic globalization has heightened anxieties about who may legitimately claim the artistic and scientific traditions of a culture.

Such conflicts are not simply the result, however, of a one-directional global seizure. Similar disputes occur when transnational corporations (or national governments acting on their behalf) seek redress for unauthorized reproductions of cultural products. For example, in the 1970s Hollywood's concern to protect the profitable hit film *Saturday Night Fever* from Turkish reproducers led the U.S. Senate to upgrade film piracy to felony status—an effort the Business Software Alliance seeks to duplicate with respect to information technology. Similarly, the recording industry has famously prosecuted the inventors of file-exchange websites, such as Napster, and even toy companies such as Mattel vigorously protect properties such as Barbie from illicit reuse by struggling artists.[2] Contests over the ownership of culture include challenges to seizures both "from above" and "from below."

In the context of an increasingly integrated global economy supported by mobile populations, the "above" versus "below" opposition does not always correlate to "global" versus "local." In fact, for the purposes of intellectual property disputes, the distinction involves two different but equally historically inflected and conflicted understandings of the relationship between culture and property. On the "below" side are those who defend culture as a way of life belonging to and authenticated by a sustained communal involvement in a set of practices. On the "above" side are those who assert rights to ownership of cultural works based on contractual obligations, especially obligations involving the alienation of authorship in exchange for monetary reward. Culture in this second view rests on individualist forms of production. On one side, then, the right to culture has priority over property rights and perhaps limits the scope of what can be claimed as property; on the other side, culture appears from the start in its guise as property, and the rights of property owners supersede those of users. For both sides of this not entirely symmetrical debate, the claims of the opponent are registered as illicit infringements—hence the necessary redundancy of the question, "Who owns *our* culture?" Culture, for both positions, is already possessed (by a community or an individual), and both Donna Karan and a Turkish video copier thus appear to their respective antagonists as illegitimate pirates attacking the very foundations of cultural vitality.

Both the "above" and "below" positions have long pedigrees in Euro-American law and philosophy, and tensions between them have long remained unresolved within this tradition. Legal instruments—most notably intellectual property legislation and statutes—attempt to balance the competing and equally universalist claims of users and authors/owners of culture. Article 1, Section 8 of the U.S. Constitution, for instance, asserts that the Senate has the right "to promote the Progress of Science and useful Arts, by securing for limited Times to Authors and Inventors the exclusive Right to their respective Writings and Discoveries." In this eighteenth-century model, the social good resulting from progress and public access to valuable works of art and science is balanced against economic incentives deriving from the author's limited monopoly over the work's reproduction and circulation.

The U.S. constitutional solution to competing concepts of rightful ownership of cultural products has not, however, proved universally acceptable. Not only are the terms of the balance regularly contested within the U.S. framework, but also other legal traditions introduce outlying factors. French law, for instance, recognizes authors' noneconomic moral rights; socialist countries have weighted communal concepts of all forms of property (including cultural properties) much more heavily than individualist concepts; and many non-Western legal systems begin with entirely different definitions of culture and property rooted in popular tradition.[3] In the context of increasingly intimate global economic integration, then, these disparities between national laws have become extremely significant. And since many of the most valuable products in the new economy (such as information technology, film, popular music, pharmaceuticals, and genetically modified foods) are intellectual properties, the stakes in these international disputes are high. For this reason, when business groups and international administrative bodies alike call for harmonization of intellectual property rights regimes, conflicts over the ownership of culture become concrete conflicts over the mechanisms of the global economy.

At the same time, these conflicts often have a symbolic register as well—in which conflicts over the ownership of culture allegorize the assertion or distribution of geopolitical power. In particular, as my initial set of examples indicate, the political level of conflicts over ownership of culture often becomes especially intense along North-South axes and this pattern introduces the question of equity in a formation that we might understand as an emergent global empire.[4] At this level, calling into question developmentalist theses associated with the critique of cultural imperialism, disputes over the ownership of culture can help us recognize some of the distinctive opportunities for social justice that accompany economic globalization.

Because the question of the ownership of culture has such powerful resonance for global politics and economy, it has also become entangled with the uniquely twentieth-century phenomenon of human rights, and thus it has become the business of international bodies such as the UN. Since the 1940s, human rights advocates have staked out important positions on intellectual property. The foundational documents of international human rights bodies all recognize intellectual property rights, and the World Intellectual Property Organization (WIPO, initially established in the 1880s to administer the Berne Convention treaties on copyright) was absorbed into the United Nations in the 1960s. In fact, spokespersons for the WIPO and the UN regularly describe intellectual property as a precondition for economic development, which in turn is described as a precondition for human rights.[5]

As demonstrated below, however, the human rights documents fail to resolve the fundamental conflicts over the initial relationship between culture and property. While treating ownership of intellectual property as an individual human right, the human rights documents also rely on a more collective right to culture. In statements from the 1940s, 1950s, and 1960s, this right to culture usually appears as an appeal to a universal cultural heritage, but since the 1970s, appeals to more localized "peoples' rights" have also become common. While both proposals have their merits, neither offers a fully consistent and effective means for synthesizing the communal and individualist ideals.

In short, human rights documents reflect the profound conflict between competing universalist concepts of culture and property, a conflict that has intensified with recent waves of economic globalization. Human rights documents see culture as being both universal and belonging in principle to everyone, as well as alienable and particular and belonging for practical purposes almost exclusively to its individual creator—a definition in which creativity and individuality become the universal norms. Both of these incompatible positions are widely evident in human rights documents.

Human rights documents reveal this philosophical tension for the concrete historical reasons sketched briefly below. Most fundamentally, this conflict occurs because economic globalization does not integrate all national economies on an equal footing but instead allows—and probably requires—the uneven concentration of wealth and resources characteristic of previous phases of capitalism to continue. Philosophical conflicts reflect the conflicts between collective entities with different degrees of economic and political control over the production of the social totality, as well as registering the traces of previous attempts to negotiate such disparities. With this hypothesis to guide us, we can at least begin to see how the current wave of economic globalization reinvigorates historical tensions and reveals fissures in the legal or political instruments designed to negotiate those tensions. Instruments such as the human rights covenants are not in this account treated as universally or historically valid, though their language often presents them this way. Instead, I aim to reveal the way that human rights documents encode geopolitical conflicts even as they attempt to ameliorate those conflicts, and then consider briefly the consequences for practical politics of these theoretical conflicts. Starting with the problem of economic globalization helps us identify and evaluate the human rights conception of intellectual property—including the emergent and critical proposal that all peoples have the right to possess their "own" culture.

Human Rights Documents and Intellectual Property

The consistently principled theoretical documents articulating the basic structures of human rights repeatedly encounter conceptual difficulty on the topic of intellectual property. On the one hand, these documents often describe culture as nonproperty, as a universal common heritage; on the other hand, they also sometimes describe culture as necessarily bolstered by the assertion of individual property rights. However, in the last quarter of the twentieth century, some human rights documents began to describe cultures as communal but nonuniversal. This third emerging conception of culture has become a flashpoint for conflicts over concepts of property rights for tangible and intangible goods. Over the past fifty years, this third position has gained ground relative to the universalist and individualist models, though all the documents I have examined reveal traces of all positions. As a result, each document singly (and perhaps human rights discourse in toto) reveals unresolved contradictions about the universality of property rights. These contradictions are historical in nature and reflect the contradictory development of property relations in the latest phase of the global capitalist economy. From this historicist perspective, to identify contradictions is not to disparage the foundational documents of human rights or their authors. Instead, my goal in tracing contradictory ideas about culture, property, and humanity in human rights texts is to learn how historical contradictions have been encoded and might be redirected—if not resolved—by international organizations and activists. Historicizing supposedly universal positions need not produce the political stalemate of a legitimacy crisis, since this kind of analysis reveals political structures as terrains of human action and opportunity.

The Universal Declaration of Human Rights

To launch this discussion, it is necessary to begin with the Universal Declaration of Human Rights, the document adopted by the General Assembly of the United Nations in 1948 and generally considered the foundational document for the modern conceptions of human rights.[6] Formulated in the wake of World War II, the Universal Declaration reflects efforts by the West—especially by the United States—to establish a balance of power favorable to itself. The document includes major efforts to prevent any resurgence of the race politics and aggressive sovereignty claims of the Axis powers, but it also reflects an emerging opposition to Western colonial powers, such as the UK, France, and Belgium. But perhaps most influential is the fact that the ideological battle lines of the Cold War led U.S. supporters of the United Nations and human rights more particularly to distinguish general principles of the Universal Declaration from concrete and binding methods for their implementation.[7] In the interest of asserting and maintaining a hegemonic status in postwar geopolitics, the United States acted to curtail the most activist interpretations of human rights and of property rights in particular.

The United States found these efforts necessary because the goals of some of the drafters of the Universal Declaration of Human Rights, as individuals and as state representatives, diverged from U.S. interests. John Humphrey, a Canadian social democrat, was the individual responsible for originating much of the language of the Universal Declaration, and he preferred to interpret human rights in terms of human needs—including the needs of developing nations to control and claim ownership to natural resources, for instance. Humphreys was supported in this interpretation by the Latin American members of the drafting committee, but the French representative, along with the U.S. representative, required revisions and limitations to the needs argument.[8] The Soviet influence on the early drafting of the Universal Declaration was reportedly limited; like the United States, the USSR favored nonbinding covenants in the early phases of discussion, although for different reasons. According to one recent analysis of participants' geopolitical motives, the overriding goal of the USSR in the early years of the UN was to delink law from the state and thus to oppose any assertion that property rights derived from state authority alone. The Soviets preferred to minimize any opposition between individual and state—a position that also informed the socialist support for colonial independence movements and self-determination. Specifically with respect to intellectual property, the Soviet agenda during the drafting of the Universal Declaration focused on rejecting state control of nuclear secrets;[9] access to benefits of science and technology should not be national but should be shared by the human populace as a whole, the Soviet representative reportedly argued.

Already in the earliest human rights documents, then, we find at least three "external" factors influencing the formulation of rights: the geopolitical balance of power, struggles for access to the basic means of existence (in the anticolonial and needs-based analyses), and the arms race. The Universal Declaration of Human Rights recodes these political, economic, and technological conflicts by invoking the concept of property in multiple ways. In Article 2, it includes property in a long list of factors that do not justify discrimination or limitations to rights. Then, in Article 17 the Universal Declaration asserts a positive and universal "right to own property alone as well as in association with others." Despite this sweeping statement, the right to be an owner is subsequently qualified by means of acquisition and the nature of the property in question. Article 4 prohibits slavery and servitude in all their forms, Article 12 disallows arbitrary search and seizure, and the second section of Article 17 couples the right to ownership with a ban on arbitrarily depriving another of property. In the Lockean tradition, as filtered by postwar social democratic interpretations, one individual's freedom to own property pertains so long as it does not interfere with another individual's exercise of the same right, in particular the right to own oneself.

This balance of positive and negative freedoms is complicated, however, by the fact that the Universal Declaration also asserts a right to culture. Introducing the concept of "free" or institutionally uninhibited access to employment, education, culture, religion, media, the arts, and science as necessary to the full development of human life, the Universal Declaration provides serious grounds for further qualification of liberal assertions of the right to own property. Drawing on the Soviet interpretation of natural, social, and technological resources as part of "the commons," the Universal Declaration of Human Rights asserts a strong version of individuals' rights to *use* property. As articulated in Article 27, the right to culture states that "everyone has the right freely to *participate* in the cultural life of the community, to *enjoy* the arts and to *share* in scientific advancement and its benefits" (emphasis added). A universal right to participate in, enjoy, and share in culture (which here refers to both the arts and the sciences) explicitly involves a limitation of the property rights of the individual owners of culture. In particular, the assertion of a right to "share in scientific advancement and its benefits" challenges monopolistic understandings of patent or trade-secret laws. The underlying principle here is that insofar as art and science are part of "the cultural life of the community," everyone in the community has a right to benefit from the projects of art and science. The strongly universalist sense of culture as a universal and common heritage thus entails an implicit justification for some form of communal access or ownership.

Since the tendency toward communalism indicated in Article 27, Section 1 clearly contradicts the strong articulation of individuals' property rights asserted in Article 17, it is not surprising to find that Article 27 also includes a second section introducing intellectual property rights. "Everyone has the right," this section reads, "to the protection of the moral and material interests resulting from any scientific, literary or artistic production of which he is the author." Where there is individual authorship, in other words, that individual has the right to protect his or her "moral and material interests." This is the version of property rights preferred by U.S. and French delegates. Leaving aside for a moment the fact that individual authorship is a highly contested category that is far from being universally accepted as a norm for the variety of media in which culture is produced,[10] what is asserted in Article 27, Section 2 is a right to protect, not a right to own. Although the language and context strongly suggest that this section is intended to justify the concepts of patent, copyright, and trademark as fundamental human rights, the actual phrasing universalizes the *goal* of those tools, not the tools themselves.

This equivocation reflects a U.S.-style effort to forestall conceptual tensions in intellectual property law. After all, the goal of intellectual property law is not simply to protect the positive rights of owners of intangible property against any and all infringement. As has been restated any number of times in statutes, legislation, and case law, in the strongly pro-property U.S. tradition, the goal of modern intellectual property law is to balance two positive goods—the incentives for creation *and* the public's right to benefit from works that constitute part of the cultural heritage.[11] Although in the Anglo-American tradition "incentive" is typically understood as being almost entirely constituted by economic factors, other legal traditions (such as that of the majority of European nations, especially France) interpret incentive more broadly—including, for instance, an artist's right to protect the integrity of the work. These two traditions are rhetorically allied in the Universal Declaration in the phrase "moral and material interests," but the concrete differences between these understandings of authors' rights are not addressed. Instead, an appeal to the "balance" so crucial to both Western regimes is made. While clearly placing a high priority on the individualist notion of the individual author and deferring positive defense of public good to the concept of balance, this strategy demonstrates that both individual and communal forms of ownership are vital to intellectual property law. This logical simultaneity suggests that the conflicts between U.S., social democratic, and Soviet property rights in culture need not be absolute even though in the Universal Declaration of Human Rights the three interpretations coexist in an indeterminate relation. Even though the contradictions and tensions among these positions are not resolved in principle in the Universal Declaration, since the document reflects a U.S. Cold War hegemony, the terms introduced in this document allow room for subsequent renegotiations.

The International Covenant on Civil and Political Rights

Once general principles governing human rights had been outlined in the Universal Declaration, the most immediately contentious political questions concerned the establishment of legally binding agreements. To maintain its internationally hegemonic postwar role, the United States affirmed the mission of the Universal Declaration but opposed or stalled the development of binding obligations, withholding concrete support in many instances. This is one significant reason why the drafting of the international covenants took nearly twenty years. Some even argue that U.S. actions during this period have undermined the efficacy of the human rights regime in its entirety.[12]

While the goals and effectiveness of human rights regimes remain controversial, it is clear that for practical purposes the twin sets of civil and political rights and economic, social, and cultural rights developed along separate but parallel tracks, despite their significant conceptual overlap. The International Covenant on Civil and Political Rights (ICCPR) and the International Covenant on Economic, Social, and Cultural Rights (ICESCR) were officially adopted in the UN General Assembly and opened for ratification in 1966, but neither entered into force until at least 1976.[13] Even then, the specific provisions often remained unmet. Both covenants repeat and expand on some of the rights in the Universal Declaration, but each was—predictably—supported by different factions in the international community; the United States and Western Europe preferred the former document, and the socialist and third-world countries the latter. Both documents, though, reflect the major geopolitical development of the twentieth century: the global wave of anticolonial revolutions. After considerable controversy, both covenants included powerful statements affirming a national right to self-determination. This right includes a people's right to "freely dispose of their natural wealth and resources without prejudice to any obligations arising out of international economic co-operation" (Article 1, Section 2). That is, from the start, the civil and political rights established by the ICCPR include, in a broad sense, a people's right to decide for themselves what kind of economic behavior is necessary for their own subsistence. The consequences of such rights for third-world debt payment or property rights of former imperial powers worried the dominant powers for practical reasons, and ideologically as well the Western powers had a stake in separating civil/political and economic rights, the essentially autonomous relation between politics and economy being a core assumption of U.S.-style capitalism. In this sense, the separation of the covenants as well as much of their content reflects the postcolonial situation of the 1960s and 1970s.

That said, many articles of the ICCPR repeat the Universal Declaration of Human Rights verbatim and do not appear particularly conflicted in their relation to economic rights; the ICCPR is, despite postwar geopolitics, also developing the logical possibilities inherent in the Universal Declaration. So, slavery is prohibited, as are arbitrary search and seizure, as well as libel and slander. Also, some other rights implicit in the Universal Declaration are articulated more fully, in much the same spirit, such as the right to freedom of thought, conscience, and religion.

Other rights, however, are restated in a fashion that changes their meaning significantly in response to new developments. Freedom of expression, for instance, appears in the Universal Declaration coupled with freedom of opinion; it also entails freedom to "seek, receive and impart information and ideas" through the media (Article 19). In the ICCPR, however, opinion and expression are separated, and the means of expression are defined more carefully and individualistically. The latter document asserts a right to "seek, receive and impart information and ideas *of all kinds, regardless of frontiers, either orally, in writing or in print, in the form of art, or through any other media of his choice*" (Article 19, Section 2; italics signify added matter). The emphasis in dilemmas over freedom of expression has clearly shifted from matters of content alone to matters of medium. As the culture industries grew in size and influence through the 1950s and 1960s, freedom of expression became even more clearly an economic question. Furthermore, the ICCPR reflects some discomfort about an absolute or universal freedom of expression in the third section of Article 19—a section underlining the individual's responsibility to respect the reputations of others and the state's duty to protect "national security or . . . public order . . . or . . . public health or morals." While specifying the individual's right to use a variety of media, this article also expands the state's right to delimit the individual's exercise of that right in the interest of public goods. McCarthyist and Stalinist censorship in the interest of the state is here legitimated, a position that—all political content aside—again reflects a burgeoning late-capitalist recognition of the systematic and institutional character of culture. The emphases on both media and censorship tend to contradict the strongly monopolistic and neoliberal interpretation of the corporate author as having exclusive rights to its own products and networks, free from all state interference. There are implicit consequences for property rights in these reinterpretations of freedom of expression; a complete separation of political and economic rights proves difficult to sustain, since the separation itself represents an effort to resolve a historical conflict between two versions of political economy.

Thus we should not be surprised to find another qualification of classical Lockean property rights suggested in Article 27; here is articulated a significant statement of the rights of ethnic, religious, or linguistic minorities to "enjoy their own culture, to profess and practise their own religion, or to use their own language" without interference. Although stated negatively (as a right to be free from the denial of a right), this articulation of minority cultural rights significantly modifies the Universal Declaration. The earlier document did not place priority on minority rights (unless women and children are "minorities"); the Soviet and socialist representatives did advocate minority rights as one feature of their strategic anticolonial agenda, but they were opposed by the colonial powers.[14] Thus the more explicit recognition of minority cultural rights in the ICCPR indicates the changed geopolitical climate of the 1960s, suggesting that a positive right to culture might be a necessary feature of self-determination.

In the ICCPR, the right to culture is not counterbalanced by a restatement of the rights of individual authors. Article 27 explicitly asserts that cultural rights are to be defined communally: "in community with the other members of their group." These anticolonial communal rights provide early signs of the rising tide of so-called peoples' rights—rights that are neither individual nor universal, but rather collective and communal in a more limited sense. It is significant (and perhaps tautological) that the right "to enjoy their own culture" is one of the first areas where this kind of legal subject (a "people") appears in the major human rights documents. In this transitional document, the universal right to access the common cultural heritage provides a justification for defending the cultural particularism of ethnic, religious, or linguistic minorities. Because they have "their own culture," these groups are recognizable as peoples, and because they are peoples, they have the special communal right to enjoy, profess, practice, or use their culture. As later developments of peoples' rights indicate, this circular logic of group identification ultimately has consequences for questions of property.

The International Covenant on Economic, Social, and Cultural Rights

Historically motivated conceptual contradictions concerning a right to culture appear even more forcefully in the ICESCR. Developed concomitantly with the ICCPR but with Soviet not U.S. support, the ICESCR has suffered throughout its history from even weaker implementation than its counterpart.[15] The initial committee never received adequate funding, nor were its requests for information widely heeded by the international community. Of course, since the fall of Soviet communism in the late 1980s, the power of the covenant's major supporters has lessened enormously and the political will for economic rights has been relocated to the more numerous but less influential nations of the developing world. Ironically, simultaneous with these geopolitical developments has been a bureaucratic reorganization within the United Nations that offers some promise for improved monitoring of economic rights, even if measures for the active promotion of these rights remains weak.[16] Some NGOs, such as Food First!, have also begun working to resuscitate the language of economic rights. Since some form of activity continues to surround international economic rights, it still matters, even without the Soviet superpower, that the concepts in this covenant are conflicted in nature.

Some of the conflicts in the ICESCR continued those evident in the Universal Declaration, while others are unique to this document and reflect its situation more particularly. Repeating the ICCPR's commitment to the right of self-determination, including economic self-determination with respect to natural wealth and resources, in Article 5 the ICESCR also reiterates a statement to the effect that none of the rights it enumerates should be understood as overturning or contradicting "fundamental human rights" recognized by other conventions, laws, regulations, or customs. Despite this provision, however, several of the specifics of the ICESCR could only be implemented if the right to property (and intellectual property in particular) were radically transformed. The covenant's pragmatic focus on the material conditions of human existence to some extent serves to obscure the profound theoretical contradictions limiting its implementation.

Building from a needs-based analysis, the ICESCR affirms the right of all human beings to enjoy high standards of physical and mental health— including adequate food, clothing, and housing, as well as education. The document outlines many of the institutions necessary for achieving these rights and proposes their graduation codification at national and international levels. Among the basic needs and institutions recognized is

> the right of everyone:
>
> I. To take part in cultural life;
>
> II. To enjoy the benefits of scientific progress and its applications;
>
> III. To benefit from the protection of the moral and material interests resulting from any scientific, literary or artistic production of which he is the author. (Article 15, Section 1)

Although the Universal Declaration's right "to *share* in scientific advancement and its benefits" has been limited here to the right to "*enjoy* the benefits," most of the provisions of the right to culture remain in place (emphasis added). In fact, the right of authors has been enhanced from the Universal Declaration's "right to the protection," becoming the right "to benefit from the protection"; this change in wording suggests that the ICESCR seeks to ensure that authors actually derive profit from the protection of their interests.

Similarly, the second section of Article 15 adds new principles necessary for the "full realization" of the right to culture. These principles include "the conservation, the development and the diffusion of science and culture." Echoing the first article's language regarding a right to development, this section—along with the next two—balances the specifics of intellectual property with general ideals. The following sections appeal to signatories to respect creative freedom and to encourage international exchanges and cooperation in scientific and cultural fields, but they do not propose particular means for ensuring that these goals will be met. Nor, however, do they ground the ideals of freedom and cooperation in a strongly universalist concept of culture. Rather, these additions suggest that culture results from individual authorship, social mechanisms for conservation, and international cooperation. This cornucopia of ideals weakens the right to culture, leaving the expanded provenance of authorship the only clearly articulated portion of the article.

Furthermore, perhaps because the right to culture has generally not been understood as a primary economic right, this incoherent, contradictory conceptual array has persisted. In the more clearly economic struggles against metropolitan empires, that tactic may have had forceful strategic value— papering over cultural conflicts within the anticolonial coalitions, for instance. In the contemporary scene, however, with anticolonial struggles subsiding along with the project of cultural nationalism, those vagaries are once again exposed. In their wake, it matters that a protectionist version of intellectual property may be the only viable or simply the strongest element of the human rights regime's right to culture.

Towards Peoples' Rights—International Cultural Policy

Perhaps because a right to culture has increasingly proved difficult to reconcile with the right to development, since the 1970s human rights discourse has seen the emergence of a "third generation" of peoples' rights. Attempting to move beyond the opposition of economic versus civil or political equality embedded in the first two generations, peoples' rights draw from both sides and seek to ground themselves in various concepts of cultural identity. Many supporters of peoples' rights have been activists on behalf of indigenous groups, but proponents also include representatives from parts of the world previously poorly represented in the UN—mainly Africa and Asia. These proponents are often ranged against strong defenders of earlier versions of human rights, since the later conception has seemed to many to undermine the ideals of individualism and universality so crucial to civil and political rights, as well as the concept of the essentially identical character of basic human needs invoked by proponents of economic rights.[17] In this context, it would certainly be an exaggeration to say that peoples' rights have attained any but the most peripheral presence in national legislatures. It is useful, however, to trace the emergence of the peoples' rights thesis, in part because this effort involves redefining the relationship between intellectual property and human rights. Rather than taking property as a universal and inherent human right in all its forms, the proponents of peoples' rights begin with defenses of cultural diversity and derive from those defenses their positions on property rights, including intellectual property rights. Although unlikely to supersede the more powerful interests of either transnational capital or local property owners, these theses illuminate the sites and shape of an emerging activist agenda that treats culture as an economic human right.

The significance of peoples' rights can best be grasped by examining more closely the concept of cultural cooperation outlined in the ICESCR. In 1966, the same year the ICESCR was adopted, the General Conference of the UN Educational, Scientific, and Cultural Organization (UNESCO) produced a "Declaration of the Principles of International Cultural Cooperation." This idealistic document expands on the ICESCR's Article 15, Section 4 and outlines goals for the organization, its member states, and the peoples of the world. It restates UNESCO's commitment to seek "the intellectual and moral solidarity of mankind" and describes the diffusion of culture and the education of humanity as "a sacred duty."[18] UNESCO's vision, then, is one in which cultures are separate entities capable of diffusion by participants who also enjoy an arm-linking solidarity under the watchful eye of the sacred. Distinctions among cultures are stations along the path toward a universal and transcendent culture: "In their rich variety and diversity, and in the reciprocal influences they exert on one another, all cultures form part of the common heritage belonging to all mankind" (Article 1, Section 3). In this essentially Romantic dialectic, "cooperation" is the mediation, drawing elements from both the particular and the universal phases, and as such it is inherently contradictory.

Perhaps the most obvious tension involved in the UNESCO concept of cooperation is this: on the one hand, the Declaration of Principles asserts that "each culture has a dignity and value which must be respected and preserved" (Article 1, Section 1), while on the other it determines that "any mark of hostility in attitudes and in expression of opinion shall be avoided" (Article 7, Section 2). That is, the purportedly noncultural principles of tolerance and diversity reveal their limits when any attacks on those principles are made. It is not only the form or mode of cultural expression that is being regulated here; it is also the content. "Any mark of hostility" will disqualify a culture or cultural expression from protection by the principle of limited tolerance. As a mediation between particular cultures (often at odds with one another) and a universal culture of peace, justice and friendship, "cooperation" thus disallows the full preservation of cultures that someone (an unnamed party) feels display some element of hostility; protection of culture thus protects universal peace only through perhaps arbitrary exclusions.

To negotiate the terms of this necessary contradiction, the Declaration of Principles calls on social institutions, such as the school, the law, and the church. Because "cultural co-operation is a right and a duty for all peoples and all nations," the development and maintenance of these institutions of cooperation also become rights and duties (Article 5). Thus the form and the content of cultural activity are dictated by the declaration, which apparently regards the modern liberal humanist institutions of cultural transmission as culturally neutral or nonspecific. This is precisely the assumption that contemporary controversies over intellectual property throw into question.

For instance, in 1974 we find the same international body, the General Conference of UNESCO, refining its arguments in the "Recommendation Concerning Education for International Understanding, Co-operation and Peace and Education Relating to Human Rights and Fundamental Freedoms."[19] Prompted by recognition of the small number of students and educators impacted by the activities of UNESCO and by the "wide disparity between proclaimed ideals, declared intentions and the actual situation," the preamble to this recommendation redefines key terms and guiding principles, before outlining plans for national policies, curricular revisions, teacher preparation, educational equipment, research, and international exchanges. Among these detailed recommendations, especially notable is the absence of the vocabulary of "common heritage" that we have observed in so many preceding documents. Taking its place is the concept of the "global." Reflecting the political climate of a post-Vietnam era, this 1974 UNESCO document reformulates the dialectic of universal and particular cultures as a dialectic between adopting an "international dimension and a global perspective" and maintaining "understanding and respect for all peoples" (Paragraph 4, Sections a–b). This is not simply a shift in diction. As the subsequent recommendations make clear, replacing the concept of universal culture with a "global perspective" involves a full conceptual shift and registers a realignment of forces in the larger world shaping these documents, as well as being described or performatively invoked by them.

Rather than regulations concerning the content and forms of cultural expression, this 1974 document addresses the simultaneous development of universal reason and material particulars. In its recommendations, UNESCO promotes a form of education that emphasizes "a sense of social responsibility and of solidarity with less privileged groups"; it encourages individuals "to acquire a critical understanding of problems at the national and international level"; and it proposes that fully educated persons will "observe the elementary rules of procedure" and "base value-judgements and decisions on a rational analysis of relevant facts and factors" (Paragraph 5). That is, in this document, UNESCO takes critical reason as a universally advantageous tool that will illuminate problems "at the national and international level" and enhance presumably privileged students' "solidarity with less privileged groups."

Despite this universalizing strain, however, the consequences for intellectual property of a shift to the "global" become apparent when we examine the content of the desired exercise of critical reason. "Education should include," Paragraph 14 reads,

> critical analysis of the historical and contemporary factors of an economic and political nature underlying the contradictions and tensions between countries, together with study of ways of overcoming these contradictions, which are the real impediments to understanding, true international co-operation and the development of world peace.... Education should emphasize the true interests of peoples and their incompatibility with the interests of monopolistic groups holding economic and political power, which practise exploitation and foment war.

In other words, in this "Recommendation Concerning Education," the critical exercise of a universal reason is understood to involve materialist analysis of the economic and political factors interfering with the emergence of a universal ideal. Prominent among those factors are the "interests of monopolistic groups"; thus an education aiming to foster international cultural cooperation is here understood as involving a critique of property relations. Adopting a "global perspective" therefore means using reason to foreground and explain the concrete "contradictions and tensions between countries," not to obscure them with appeals to hazy pseudo-universal ideals.

That said, this document still betrays some anxiety about the purported cultural neutrality of the tools of analysis. It recommends that all parties "adapt and use the mass media of communication" (Paragraph 3, Section b) and "the entire range of equipment and aids available" (Paragraph 38, Section a). But at the same time, it also urges "teaching to help the pupils to select and analyse the information conveyed by mass media" (Paragraph 38, Section b) and the "reciprocal study and revision of textbooks and other educational material in order to ensure that they are accurate, balanced, up to date and unprejudiced and will enhance mutual knowledge and understanding between different peoples" (Paragraph 45). That is, we see in the UNESCO "Recommendation Concerning Education" the emergence of a sentiment that adopting a global perspective involves not only acquiring international materials, but also critically analyzing the content and production of those materials. "Cooperation" here refers to more than a well-intentioned affirmation of the ideals of peace, justice, and friendship; it involves cross-cultural exchanges of information and ongoing critical revision of the means by which those exchanges occur. Because at present "information" is so often intimately bound up in its content and mode of transmission with commercial relations,[20] the UNESCO document suggests that "cooperation" can be understood to support some analysis of the commodity logic governing intellectual property.

The Rights of Peoples

This foray into educational policy has led us to leap ahead of our story. To chart the emergence of the peoples' rights thesis and a critical approach to intellectual property as a universal human right, we will need to return to the main stream of discourse on human rights. For this purpose, an essential source is the "African [Banjul] Charter on Human and People's Rights," adopted by members of the Organization of African Unity in 1981 and entering into force in 1986.[21] This document is of interest because it explicitly asserts that "respect of peoples' rights should necessarily guarantee human rights" (Preamble). It describes civil, political, economic, social, and cultural rights as inseparable (not irreconcilable), and it takes as its central problem the confrontation of modernity and tradition on a number of topics, including property.

Like the ICESCR, the Banjul Charter has had extremely limited effectiveness in implementation, and it is of course not binding for nonsignatories, unless at some point in the future its principles come to be interpreted as features of international customary law. In 2000, few of the most powerful nations had signed the treaty, and there is little evidence to indicate that the most influential nations will ever become signatories. This charter, however, does signal the presence of new sets of ideals on the international scene and suggests that future innovation in human rights thinking may well begin with regional accords and coalitions (especially where these define themselves against a hegemonic center).

Reiterating much of the structure of the Universal Declaration of Human Rights, the Banjul Charter repudiates slavery and guarantees the individual's right to receive information and to express and disseminate opinions. It also provides for equal access to public property and affirms the right to property in general. In a crucial modification, however, Article 14 of the Banjul Charter allows encroachments on the right to property "in the interest of public need or in the general interest of the community and in accordance with the provisions of appropriate laws." Here, the social democratic/Latin American defense of nationalization is reformulated around neotraditional lines. Similarly, the Banjul Charter provides a right to education and participation in cultural life, though it qualifies these provisions with the statement that "the promotion and protection of morals and traditional values recognized by the community shall be the duty of the State" (Article 17). Another significant change includes a strong restatement of the ICESCR and ICCPR's guarantee of the right of nations to dispose freely of their wealth and natural resources. Here there is special provision made for the "lawful recovery of its property" by a dispossessed people and a charge to eliminate the economic exploitation exercised by "international monopolies" (Article 21). Finally, the right to development is in this document coupled with the rights of "all peoples" to "the equal enjoyment of the common heritage of mankind" (Article 22). The right to culture has here evolved and expanded to become a "people's right" to develop "with due regard to their freedom and identity" and to extract themselves from surveillance and exploitation by other powers.

For the purposes of this essay, it is significant that, in this updated right to culture, we find no restatement of the rights of authors. Where the Universal Declaration and most of its subsequent interpretations balanced the right to enjoy the common heritage against the individual author's right to protect and/or enjoy the material and moral benefits of production, the Banjul Charter understands the central issue differently. In this document, it is not the property rights of the individual that are counterbalanced by the access rights of the community; it is the right of the people to develop and enjoy "their freedom and identity" that opposes and potentially supersedes the exploitative and monopolistic property relations of the international economy. This "global perspective" de-emphasizes the individual and in several places replaces "his" concerns with those of peoples. In this process, a different role emerges for the state. No longer the site of determining a hypothetical balance between positive and negative freedoms, the state here has the responsibility to ensure development, while also protecting and promoting traditional morals and values. Its responsibility is not so much to protect one Hobbesian individual from undue interference on the part of others as it is to ensure that the cultural identity of the people or peoples is not sacrificed to economic modernization. This is neither a laissez-faire nor a welfare state; struggling with tradition and culture, this may be a new form we could call cultural federalism.[22] The consequences of this kind of postcolonial state could be many; insofar as intellectual property is understood (as it has been in the Anglo-American tradition) as an outgrowth of individual property rights, though, it is no longer a primary or "core" human right in this document or the affiliated versions of the state. This is mainly the case because defining culture as an economic and collective right displaces versions of intellectual property premised on the individual as the primary economic unit.

Peoples' Rights and Intellectual Property

The possible consequences of the Banjul Charter's conception of peoples' rights for intellectual property are further sketched in two additional documents specifically addressing indigenous peoples' concerns. In 1994, delegates at a meeting of indigenous national authorities (representing the Crimean Tatars, the Numba People of Sudan, the Six First Nations, the Opethesaht First Nation, and the West Papua Peoples Front, and others) initialed the "International Covenant on the Rights of Indigenous Nations," thereby beginning a process of establishing "minimum standards for the survival and well-being of the indigenous peoples of the world."[23] Although this covenant had not been put into force as of 2002 and does not appear to have generated substantial or widespread public discussion, it establishes important priorities and interpretations of peoples' rights. It begins with an affirmation of the dignity of peoples of indigenous nations, a consideration of the importance of diversity, and an excoriation of "scientifically false, culturally repugnant, legally invalid, morally condemnable and socially unjust" forms of racism (Preamble). From this basis, the "Covenant on the Rights of Indigenous Nations" elaborates its conception of the right of self-determination.

First, it maintains a distinction between "nations" and "states"—recognizing the rights of indigenous nations to participate in the life of a state while also maintaining their sovereignty and cultural distinctiveness as nations. Second, the covenant asserts rights of an indigenous nation to protect itself from genocide, which here includes not only military attack or incarceration, but also relocation from traditional lands, territories or resources, removal of children, recruitment into armed forces, and being made the target of propaganda. These violations of "the inherent collective and individual . . . right [of a people] to identify or define itself" are grouped together as examples of "ethnocide" (Paragraphs 6–7). The third section of this covenant concerns the cultural rights of nations, and it specifically and in great detail enumerates a people's right to cultural property, such as archaeological and historical sites, artifacts, designs, ceremonies, arts, and literature. These rights then entail a subsequent insistence on "the right to establish their own media in their own language and to exercise the right to equal access to all forms of communications media" (Paragraph 16). After affirmations of the people's right to decide priorities for their own communities, we find further application of this right to questions concerning ownership and control of land, the environment, natural and genetic resources, seeds, knowledge of fauna and flora, and many other cultural manifestations. These include the right of indigenous peoples to protect their cultures "as intellectual property" and to demand restitution for seizures of their property that took place without free and informed consent (Paragraphs 26–27).

In other words, this covenant offers a broad definition of culture and cultural rights, and it proposes a strongly protectionist application of the Lockean property rights currently recognized in international law. The most significant innovation is that the "owner" is here almost exclusively understood to be a "people" and not an individual or even a corporate fiction of an individual; thus the effects of this covenant, if it were to be ratified and fully implemented, would likely be much at odds with the practice of individual rights to private property in the global economy. This covenant attempts to take literally the universalist claims that proprietary rights are human rights. But instead of beginning with the assumption that the owners of property determine the rightful content and form of cultural expression, the authors of the "Covenant on the Rights of Indigenous Nations" assert that cultural difference is primary and that property rights should be protected to the extent that they flow from the existence and authority of cultural identity.

Taking this logic a step further, the authors of "A Treaty Between Indigenous Nations on the Protection of Cultural Property and Traditional Resource Rights" (a briefing memorandum prepared by the Center for World Indigenous Studies) argue that intellectual property rights themselves are culturally specific:

> There is a fundamental difference between indigenous peoples' values and cultural concepts and the values espoused by states' governments, corporations and others within the framework of globalization agreements and policies. Cultural properties in particular are not thought in general by indigenous nations as including items that can be bought and sold, "com-

modified" or commercialized. In many cases, the cultural property is thought of as belonging exclusively to the group. . . . In contrast, . . . International laws and the laws of states' governments proclaim the sanctity of individual rights in private property.[24]

Understanding property rights as culturally specific, this memorandum urges indigenous nations to negotiate with states not only for the power to own cultural properties but also for the "power to define rights of ownership" for themselves. Thus for the authors of this document, to fully exercise the human right to self-determination involves redefining or even rejecting the models of authorship and ownership articulated in the Universal Declaration of Human Rights. Because the concept of cultural rights has expanded, the balance between the right to enjoy culture and the right to benefit from works one has authored has shifted dramatically. When authorship is treated as collective or communal, then the rights of access or enjoyment can appear as a cover for monopolistic cross-cultural appropriations. The right to enjoy culture can, on this view, be protected only by divorcing it from culturally specific—though dominant—concepts of benefit. The intent of the 1940s-era views of intellectual property as a human right can only be realized, at this point in the discussion, when intellectual property is not a human right.

Perhaps this has been difficult to realize because it was inherently contradictory from the start. By defining intellectual property as a human right, the authors of the Universal Declaration and related documents established a complicated and unstable tautology. Using the concept of "culture" to validate rights to enjoy the arts and sciences, as well as to establish property rights in certain kinds of intellectual activities, they established a structure in which existing cultural authority legitimated the rights of some claimants to own and control the forms of culture. In this context, the right to culture was exercised as a majority right—that is, by those accepting and participating in the dominant conception of culture. But over the course of the twentieth century, the right to culture became increasingly important to peoples and nations whose identity and survival were under threat because they were less powerful and economically traditional minorities. Thus, not only the content, the form, and the media by which cultures communicate have been the sites of struggle, but also the status of culture as property has increasingly come into question. The contradictions between understanding culture as a set of determinate universal and/or particular values and exchanging culture as a commodity have increasingly come to the forefront of public discussion and political life. As documents concerned with human rights reveal, the mid-twentieth-century preoccupation with correlating particular cultural practices to universal values seems to have given way to a somewhat different later preoccupation with maintaining traditions of cultural diversity in the context of economic modernization. As a result, at this stage, whichever contradiction preoccupies us most (universal/particular or diversity/development), it is now increasingly difficult to sustain the position that either individual authorship or communal access to a common heritage is a universal human right. Despite the efforts of prominent philosophers, such as Martha Nussbaum, to reconcile property generally and human rights on the grounds of a reinvigorated universalism, the contradictions outlined above persist in the central covenants and treaties devoted to human rights.[25] These contradictions and sites of incoherence reflect the material conditions of a struggle over the global economy and political hegemony since the 1940s. Whether or not these contradictions could be resolved in theory, at the practical level they persist because of powerful ongoing conflicts between the owners and users of culture in all its guises—as traditional practices, corporate commodities, and tangible works of individual genius. This situation suggests that equitable implementation of property rights as human rights cannot be achieved without thorough recognition of and changes to the historical and material conditions of capitalist globalization.

Activism and Institutions

Current efforts to redress in practice the conceptual contradictions between intellectual property and human rights take several forms. At the local level, activists and nongovernmental organizations concerned for instance with patents on food and medicine have drawn attention to conflicts between intellectual property and human rights. These efforts have not to date had a significant effect on case law in the United States (where most targeted companies are incorporated), though they accompany revision of national legislation in the developing world toward U.S. standards. At the global level, international negotiation over trade-related intellectual property has fostered the growth of institutions such as the World Intellectual Property Organization (WIPO) and the World Trade Organization (WTO). These institutions have experienced some internal conflicts regarding their mission and have of course been the target of public demonstrations, but in practice they mainly treat intellectual property as an undisputed human right. These actions from "above" seem to ensure that individualist interpretations of intellectual property, supported by U.S. power, will dominate global practices in the near future.

These trends are most visible at the international level. Taking its current shape in 1970, as mandated by the convention that established it, the WIPO is the body primarily responsible for administering the twenty-one major international treaties involving intellectual property. Its predecessors included organizations administering the Berne Convention and other international intellectual property treaties on the European continent. In 1974 the WIPO joined the UN's group of organizations, and in 1996 entered into agreements with the World Trade Organization, so that the two entities could coordinate their influence (especially their influence on the developing countries). With 171 member states and a 2000 budget of 383 million Swiss francs, the WIPO commands considerable resources and power. This influence is primarily directed toward protection of the rights of owners and creators; the organization describes itself as an entity that "oils the wheels of international trade."[26] Among its many efforts, five major areas emerge as priorities: harmonizing intellectual property legislation worldwide, providing international services such as inexpensive patent registry, training administrators in developing countries to implement intellectual property regulations, providing dispute resolution mechanisms, and organizing information relating to intellectual property. Overall, the WIPO serves as a clearinghouse and administrative center for intellectual property regulations. It does so not out of self-consciously regionalist motives, but rather out of a determinist conception of the relationship between law and economy. Its documents regularly refer to U.S.- or European-style intellectual property laws as "an engine for economic, cultural and social development."[27]

The mission of the WIPO is primarily administrative, and—perhaps not surprisingly, given the habits of bureaucracy—it is not always in harmony with other international administrative institutions. Also, when it produces documents considering the role of intellectual property more broadly, we find internal dissension among intellectual property rights experts over the nature, utility, and consequences of these rights. For instance, in *Intellectual Property and Human Rights,* a series of papers presented in Geneva on November 9, 1998, for a panel discussion commemorating the fiftieth anniversary of the Universal Declaration of Human Rights, the specialists from various organizations indicate their serious disagreements with one another. On the one hand, Roberto Castelo, the deputy director-general of the WIPO, reiterates the legal determinist position that intellectual property is an "engine" of global development (3). In a modification of this position, Brian Burdekin—speaking on behalf of Mary Robinson, the UN High Commissioner for Human Rights at the time—presents intellectual property rights as complementary to human rights, although possibly requiring changes in order to protect human rights of traditional communities (5).

On the other end of the spectrum, Peter Drahos, an intellectual property scholar from the University of London, describes global intellectual property rights as the effect of initiatives on the part of sectors of the U.S. business community. Drahos outlines areas in which human rights and intellectual property rights often conflict in practice. He argues that intellectual property rights ought to be treated as merely instrumental, not as foundational and essential. Other discussants address particular human rights in the context of intellectual property: the right to health, to culture, nondiscrimination, and access to the benefits of science. Throughout the discussion, divisions between the perspectives of those representing developed and developing countries emerge, but no matter which regional perspective is adopted, participants consistently posited economic globalization as a threat to human rights. Even though the WIPO's "harmonization" of intellectual property rights "oils the wheels" of the global economy, the global economy is seen as dangerous to human rights. The resulting situation is that disputes over the moral, ethical, and philosophical grounds of intellectual property as a human right seem not to interfere with the operation of the WIPO as an international organization committed to modernization, development, and potential opposition to particular human rights.

The nonresponsiveness of international administrative organizations to their own internal dissent has, however, become the topic of public discussion, in part as a result of first-world protests in 1999 and 2000 targeting the WTO, the World Bank, and the International Monetary Fund. On these occasions, well-established nongovernmental organizations (NGOs, many of which had previously articulated more regional or issue-specific agendas, such as Global Exchange and Food First!) joined with national critics of politics and economy, such as Ralph Nader, and coalitions of environmentalist, labor, and youth organizations to voice opposition to the international institutions. Spotlighting threats to democracy, health, and the environment, these protests aimed to draw public attention to the power of international administrative institutions and to present some positive alternatives to these highly centralized elite operations.[28] Although initially most successful in meeting their first goal (publicity), the antiglobalization protesters have also had some limited success in offering "fair trade" as a substitute for the neoliberal agenda of "free trade."[29]

In addition to these metropolitan attacks on the institutions administering and embodying contradictions between human rights and intellectual property rights, grassroots activists around the world have in some cases drawn attention on the concepts and principles involved. For instance, drawing on important emergent lines of alliance between a cosmopolitan technocratic elite and the politicized fractions of local populations of postcolonial democracies, Indian scientist and activist Vandana Shiva has become a prominent critic of biopiracy, the appropriation of natural resources in one part of the world by nonnationals. Criticizing "intellectual colonization," Shiva has argued that traditional and communal modes of ownership need to be strengthened in order to protect third-world agriculturalists from exploitation by transnational corporations controlling intellectual property in seeds, genetic information, and agricultural techniques.[30] Other similar efforts on the part of regional NGOs involve partially successful movements to make AIDS drugs more widely available in Africa and activities of groups such as Doctors Without Borders (see Chapters 3 and 8).

The potential for legal reform at the international level as a result of sporadic local activities is difficult to evaluate. The likely paradoxes appear, for example, in the Jasmati rice case briefly mentioned in the introduction to this essay. After the Texas corporation Ricetec successfully acquired a U.S. patent on a breed of rice it marketed as "Jasmati" (combining the appeal of traditional breeds of jasmine and basmati), Thai farmers and government protested.[31] The ensuing controversy has raised fundamental questions about what can be claimed as property and by whom, as well as who has the standing to question these fundamental ideas in court. Since the United States is unusual in allowing patents on lifeforms, representatives of other nations quickly grow uneasy when U.S. corporations use these expansive rights to claim patents on seeds and related bioengineered products; unfortunately, the lack of an international civil court for such matters means that decisions on such issues can be made for the purposes of "convenience" by U.S. courts. The likelihood of a U.S. court undertaking a massive overhaul of fundamental principles of U.S. property law on behalf of litigants motivated by alien legal and ethical systems is low.[32] American political and institutional hegemony allows an exclusive and individualist version of property rights to prevail.

A defense of cultural diversity does not necessarily disrupt the trend toward standardization. Private corporations regularly make use of geographical and cultural disparities to establish the "novelty" required for patents in the developed world, even though the techniques under discussion may have been traditional in other parts of the world for hundreds or even thousands of years. Clearly, arguments based on cultural difference are not effective when detached from a more thoroughgoing and practical critique of property law.

Popular support for a critique of culturally specific forms of ownership may, however, be possible. Regardless of the legal specifics, in these disputes one finds much evidence of the feeling that corporations such as Ricetec are stealing from traditional farmers and deceptively passing off their own engineered products as traditional ones. Despite the WTO's efforts to reassure farmers and activists that intellectual property rights are always to be balanced with the public good and interest of the communities involved, in controversies such as the Ricetec case, the conflict seems to derive from a much deeper source than recent regulations.[33] The sense of property-as-theft invoked in accusations of biopiracy reproduces the fundamental conflict between understandings of property voiced by the authors of treaties on indigenous and peoples' rights. Critics such as Shiva who attack the WIPO and the WTO are expressing not only concern about the logistics of "harmonizing" intellectual property regimes around the world; they are attacking the individualist and colonialist assumptions that motivate the drive toward harmonization in the first place. In this sense, we might say that the practical consequences of theoretical contradictions in the "intellectual property as human right" discourse include not only the likely dominance of individualist standards but also a fresh polarization of political confrontation on this issue. While international administrative bodies such as the WIPO gain power in this climate, they also confront vocal and intense opposition to their principles and practices from the inside and the outside.[34] This opposition reflects the material presence and continuation of noncapitalist modes of production; in the context of globalization the disturbance of previous forms of uneven development can result in the rapid and highly politicized formation of new social movements at the local level. At several levels of political action, then, from the international to the local, we find efforts to address the complicated effects of a form of capitalist globalization premised on universal and individualist property rights.

Conclusion

If my sketch of the contradictions underlying contemporary theories of intellectual property as a human right has been accurate, and if the institutional, political, and juridical concerns briefly outlined here are indeed related consequentially to these materially determined theoretical contradictions, then it seems plausible to conclude that issues concerning the ownership of and access to culture will become even more complex in the near future even as the stakes continue to rise. Within the context of economic globalization, individual rights to private property are being more vigorously implemented by powerful interests such as the Business Software Alliance (representing, among others, Microsoft), even as advocates of peoples' rights challenge the foundational premises of intellectual property rights. Critics of biopiracy have complicated the distinction between culture and science assumed in some human rights documents—a critique that may ultimately require rethinking the entire discourse of modernization and development. Finally, in addition to complicating questions of who may own and what may be owned, protests over the actions and structure of international administrative bodies such as the WTO lead the global public increasingly to ask how the rights of owners and users of culture can and ought to be exercised.

These controversies show no signs of abating in the near future. Quite the contrary. Grassroots activists associated with the antiglobalization protests have called explicitly for renewed efforts to formulate alternatives to the regime of private property, and today some of the most dramatic efforts in that direction have appeared in indigenous peoples' movements.[35] What these efforts suggest is that globalization is not simply an inevitable phase in the universalization of one culture or law. It is a complex dialectic in which legal regimes such as private property are forcefully installed around the world as a determinate form of social relations, even as communal or collective forms of ownership and social imagination solidify themselves in reaction to that process and trigger the proposal of subsequent forms of culture and property.

Globalization, in other words, involves a continuing struggle over who is human and what structures and modes of life are necessary to realize one's humanity as an individual and as a group. Because intellectual property is a special kind of "object"—an object embodying the features of culture often taken to be essential to the human condition—it is not surprising that the questions about who and what is human provoked by globalization result in conflicts over intellectual property. What is notable, however (even if it, too, is unsurprising), is that controversies over intellectual property have recursively led to questions about the cultural presumptions of the institutions of human rights themselves. For activists such as Vandana Shiva, politicians such as the authors of the International Covenant on the Rights of Indigenous Nations, and legal scholars such as Peter Drahos, the right to culture guaranteed by the Universal Declaration of Human Rights ultimately provides grounds for critiques of the highly centralized international institutions organized to implement that charter in the first place. Universal human rights justify critiques of specific forms of property relations, even though those property relations ground and limit the institutions claiming to embody that universality. With respect to ownership of culture in a global context, then, it appears that human rights must be and cannot be treated as universal. It will be the task of any utopian political project that treats culture affirmatively to mobilize this contradictory situation—perhaps by redrawing the balance between conflicted notions of individual intellectual property and a more substantive notion of the common good.

Notes

1. See Rick Mofina, "Culture 'Confiscated' for High Fashion: Inuit Women Want to Trademark Tradition to Fend Off Fashion Industry's 'Exploitation,' " *Ottawa Citizen,* November 16, 1999, p. A1; Michael Durham and Jan Rocha, "Amazon Chief Sues Body Shop," *The Observer,* March 3, 1996, p. 5; "Antioxidant Composition from Turmeric," *The Hindu,* February 25, 1999; and "Jasmine Protest," *Bangkok Post,* January 16, 2000.

2. See "The Piracy and Counterfeiting Amendments Act of 1981," Hearing Before the Subcommittee on Criminal Law of the Committee on the Judiciary, U.S. Senate, 97th Congress, 1st sess., June 19, 1981; www.bsa.com; and Norma Meyer, "Taking on Mattel; Company Isn't Toying Around with Artist and Barbie Exhibit," *San Diego Union-Tribune,* November 16, 2000, p. E1.

3. On differences between French and U.S. law, see Brian T. McCartney, "'Creepings' and 'Glimmers' of the Moral Rights of Artists in American Copyright Law," *UCLA Entertainment Law Review* 6 (Fall 1998): 35. On regional disparities in concepts of intellectual property, see Frederick M. Abbott, "TRIPS in Seattle: The Not-So-Surprising Failure and the Future of the TRIPS Agenda," *Berkeley Journal of International Law* 18 (2000): 165. On issues concerning socialist or former socialist countries' intellectual property laws, see, for example, Michael W. Smith, "Bringing Developing Countries' Intellectual Property Laws to TRIPS Standards: Hurdles and Pitfalls Facing Vietnam's Efforts to Normalize an Intellectual Property Regime," *Case Western Reserve Journal of International Law* 31 (Winter 1999): 211.

4. See Michael Hardt and Antonio Negri, *Empire* (Cambridge: Harvard University Press, 2000).

5. Numerous examples of the development discourse linking intellectual property and human rights are available at www.wipo.org, especially in the mission statement.

6. Universal Declaration of Human Rights, available at www.un.org.

7. Here I draw on Tony Evans's regime analysis of human rights in *U.S. Hegemony and the Project of Universal Human Rights* (New York: St. Martin's Press, 1996).

8. An excellent source of in-depth information on the drafting process is Johannes Morsink, *The Universal Declaration of Human Rights: Origins, Drafting, and Intent* (Philadelphia: University of Pennsylvania Press, 1999).

9. Ibid., p. 61.

10. For one influential analysis of the contests surrounding the modern Anglo-American concept of authorship, see Martha Woodmansee, *The Author, Art, and the Market: Rereading the History of Aesthetics* (New York: Columbia University Press, 1994), chap. 2.

11. So argues Pierre N. Leval in "Toward a Fair Use Standard," *Harvard Law Review* 103 (1990): 1105–1136.

12. Evans, *U.S. Hegemony,* p. 8.

13. The full text of both covenants is available at www.unhchr.ch.

14. See Evans's discussion of the "colonial clause" in *U.S. Hegemony,* chap. 5, "The International Covenants on Human Rights."

15. For detailed analysis of the structure and history of this covenant, see Matthew C. R. Craven, *The International Covenant on Economic, Social, and Cultural Rights* (New York: Oxford University Press, 1995).

16. See Philip Alston, "The Committee on Economic, Social, and Cultural Rights," in Philip Alston, ed., *The United Nations and Human Rights: A Critical Appraisal* (New York: Oxford University Press, 1992), pp. 473–508.

17. For a range of typical criticisms of peoples' rights, see James Crawford, ed., *The Rights of Peoples* (New York: Oxford University Press, 1988).

18. "Declaration of the Principles of International Cultural Cooperation," available at www.unhchr.ch.

19. Available at www.unhchr.ch.

20. See Ann Branscomb, *Who Owns Information? From Privacy to Public Access* (New York: Basic Books, 1994).

21. Available at www.umn.edu/humanrts/instree/z1afchar.htm.

22. Here I build on the distinctive and original concept of the role of federalism in midcentury postcolonial situations, as it has been described by Imre Szeman in *Zones of Instability: Literature, Postcolonialism, and the Nation* (Baltimore: Johns Hopkins University Press, forthcoming).

23. "International Covenant on the Rights of Indigenous Nations," Paragraph 45, available at www.cwis.org/fwdp/international/icrin-94.txt. This is the site for the Center for World Indigenous Studies, and it has many useful documents for the study of the rights of peoples.

24. "A Treaty Between Indigenous Nations on the Protection of Cultural Property and Traditional Resource Rights," available at www.cwis.org/260tcptr.html.

25. See Martha Nussbaum, "Human Capabilities, Female Human Beings," in Martha Nussbaum and Jonathan Glover, eds., *Women, Culture, and Development: A Study of Human Capabilities* (New York: Oxford University Press, 1995), p. 85.

26. See *World Intellectual Property Organization: General Information,* p. 3, available at www.wipo.org.

27. See foreword to *Intellectual Property and Human Rights,* panel discussion to commemorate the fiftieth anniversary of the Universal Declaration of Human Rights (Geneva: WIPO, 1998), p. i.

28. See Working Group on the WTO/MAI, *A Citizen's Guide the World Trade Organization: Everything You Need to Know to Fight for Fair Trade,* July 1999 (pamphlet).

29. See Global Exchange website: www.globalexchange.org.

30. See Vandana Shiva, "Bioethics: A Third World Issue," available at www.ratical.org/co-globalize/bioethics.html.

31. Prangtip Daorueng, "Farmers Protest Copycat 'Jasmine' Rice," International Press Service, May 13, 1999, www.oneworld.org/ips2/may98/04_30_007.html.

32. For discussion of international jurisdiction, see Caren Irr, "One Dimensional Symptoms," in Caren Irr and Jeffrey T. Nealon, eds., *Rethinking the Frankfurt School: Alternative Legacies of Cultural Critique* (Albany: State University of New York Press, 2002), pp. 167–186.

33. See the WTO's summary of issues at www.itd.org/issues/india6.htm.

34. For an example of increasingly influential analysis of the concept of the commons as it operates in relation to issues of cyberspace and the Internet, see Lawrence Lessig, *Code and Other Laws of Cyberspace* (New York: Basic Books, 1999).

35. I have assessed the potential of one indigenous people's movement with respect to intellectual property in "How the Zapatistas' Children's Book Is Owned," in Amitava Kumar, ed., *World Bank Literature* (Minneapolis: University of Minnesota Press, 2002: 237–252).

Bibliography

Abbott, Frederick M. "TRIPS in Seattle: The Not-So-Surprising Failure and the Future of the TRIPS Agenda." *Berkeley Journal of International Law* 18 (2000): 165–179.

Alston, Philip. "The Committee on Economic, Social, and Cultural Rights." In Philip Alston, ed., *The United Nations and Human Rights: A Critical Appraisal.* New York: Oxford University Press, 1992, 473–508.

"Antioxidant Composition from Turmeric." *The Hindu,* February 25, 1999.

Branscomb, Ann. *Who Owns Information? From Privacy to Public Access.* New York: Basic Books, 1994.

Business Software Alliance. www.bsa.com.

Craven, Matthew C. R. *The International Covenant on Economic, Social, and Cultural Rights.* New York: Oxford University Press, 1995.

Crawford, James, ed. *The Rights of Peoples.* New York: Oxford University Press, 1988.

Daorueng, Prangtip. "Farmers Protest Copycat 'Jasmine' Rice." International Press Service, May 13, 1999, www.oneworld.org/ips2/may98/04_30_007.html.

Durham, Michael, and Jan Rocha. "Amazon Chief Sues Body Shop." *The Observer,* March 3, 1996, p. 5.

Evans, Tony. *U.S. Hegemony and the Project of Universal Human Rights.* New York: St. Martin's Press, 1996.

Global Exchange. www.globalexchange.org.

Hardt, Michael, and Antonio Negri. *Empire.* Cambridge: Harvard University Press, 2000.

"International Covenant on the Rights of Indigenous Nation." Available at www.cwis.org/fwdp/international/icrin-94.txt.

Irr, Caren. "How the Zapatistas' Children's Book Is Owned." In Amitava Kumar, ed., *World Bank Literature.* Minneapolis: University of Minnesota Press, 2002, pp. 237–252.

———. "One Dimensional Symptoms." In Jeffrey T. Nealon and Caren Irr, eds., *Rethinking the Frankfurt School: Alternative Legacies of Cultural Critique.* Albany: State University of New York Press, 2002, pp. 169–186.

"Jasmine Protest." *Bangkok Post,* January 16, 2000.

Lessig, Lawrence. *Code and Other Laws of Cyberspace.* New York: Basic Books, 1999.

Leval, Pierre N. "Toward a Fair Use Standard." *Harvard Law Review* 103 (1990): 1105–1136.

McCartney, Brian T. "'Creepings' and 'Glimmers' of the Moral Rights of Artists in American Copyright Law." *UCLA Entertainment Law Review* 6 (Fall 1998): 35–72.

Meyer, Norma. "Taking on Mattel; Company Isn't Toying Around with Artist and Barbie Exhibit." *San Diego Union-Tribune,* November 16, 2000, p. E1.

Mofina, Rick. "Culture 'Confiscated' for High Fashion: Inuit Women Want to Trademark Tradition to Fend Off Fashion Industry's 'Exploitation.'" *Ottawa Citizen,* November 16, 1999, p. A1.

Morsink, Johannes. *The Universal Declaration of Human Rights: Origins, Drafting, and Intent.* Philadelphia: Pennsylvania, 1999.

Nussbaum, Martha. "Human Capabilities, Female Human Beings." In Martha Nussbaum and Jonathan Glover, eds., *Women, Culture, and Development: A Study of Human Capabilities.* New York: Oxford University Press, 1995, 61–104.

"The Piracy and Counterfeiting Amendments Act of 1981." Hearing Before the Subcommittee on Criminal Law of the Committee on the Judiciary." U.S. Senate, 97th Congress, 1st sess., June 19, 1981.

Shiva, Vandana. "Bioethics: A Third World Issue." www.ratical.org/co-globalize/bioethics.html.

Smith, Michael W. "Bringing Developing Countries' Intellectual Property Laws to TRIPS Standards: Hurdles and Pitfalls Facing Vietnam's Efforts to Normalize an Intellectual Property Regime." *Case Western Reserve Journal of International Law* 31 (Winter 1999): 211–251.

Szeman, Imre. *Zones of Instability: Literature, Postcolonialism, and the Nation.* Baltimore: Johns Hopkins University Press, forthcoming.

"A Treaty Between Indigenous Nations on the Protection of Cultural Property and Traditional Resource Rights." Available at www.cwis.org/260tcptr.html.

Universal Declaration of Human Rights. Available at www.un.org.

WIPO. *Intellectual Property and Human Rights.* Panel discussion to commemorate the fiftieth anniversary of the Universal Declaration of Human Rights. Geneva: WIPO, 1998.

Woodmansee, Martha. *The Author, Art, and the Market: Rereading the History of Aesthetics.* New York: Columbia University Press, 1994.

Working Group on the WTO/MAI. *A Citizen's Guide the World Trade Organization: Everything You Need to Know to Fight for Fair Trade.* July 1999 (pamphlet).

World Intellectual Property Organization. Mission statement. Available at http://www.wipo.org.

2

The Consequences of a
Constructed Universal

Democracy and Civil Rights in the Modern State

Neil A. Englehart

States remain the most important political actors in the international system. As such, they play a critical role in both globalization and human rights. Yet ironically, both authoritarian governments and human rights activists have misunderstood the relevance of the state to debates over human rights and globalization. Post–Cold War authoritarian governments treat the state as the defender of a culturally unified nation against the forces of a homogenizing globalization—including human rights activists. However, states are in fact already a global monoculture, one that elites around the world actively support. Activists tend to view the state as the enemy of rights, needing to be restrained and weakened with respect to civil society. However, states create the necessary conditions for human rights and democracy. Universal human rights are only possible because states are universal.

This misunderstanding of the state is a function of its own success. Precisely because states have become ubiquitous, they now seem normal, natural, and unremarkable. Their importance is easy to overlook because of their very universality, in the same way that we ordinarily ignore the importance of air or gravity.

States are constructed universals. As discussed in the introduction to this volume, constructed universals are ideas, institutions, and practices created by human agency that assume an aura of inevitability by virtue of their widespread acceptance. Arguably the states system is the most important of such constructed universals, because it creates a foundation for many others that follow—including global markets and international regimes. In this chapter I restrict my attention to two particular consequences of the modern state: democracy and civil rights.

It may well be true that many prestate societies had mechanisms for protecting human dignity, as Jack Donnelly argues, and rights are simply another means suitable for current conditions (1989, 60). However, as I will argue below, states are actually much more effective at securing human dignity on a systematic basis than are any earlier forms of social organization. The structure of the state creates opportunities for the protection of citizens, both from each other and from governments, that cannot be present under other forms of political organization.

Yet human rights activists are typically antistatist (see, for instance, Donnelly 1996, 389; and Pollis 1996, 321–324). Yet the very notion of a right, legalistic construct that it is, presupposes the existence of a regime capable of enforcing its own laws. The worst human rights situations in the post–World War II era have been precisely in those places where state power has collapsed—Cambodia under the Khmer Rouge, Burma, Afghanistan, Somalia, and central Africa. While the Soviet Union may have denied its citizens political rights, or the United States failed to protect economic and social rights, people in both those societies at least enjoyed basic protection from other citizens.

Universal human rights are possible only because states are virtually omnipresent. Even though the economic and social circumstances of countries may vary, as well as their location and influence in the international system, at least on this one dimension of political culture they share something: a commitment to the set of institutions that defines the modern state. I will show below how this homogeneity contrasts sharply with the diverse social constructions of politics prior to the nineteenth century. The spread of the state thus represents an early and important episode of globalization. I will further argue that the globalization of the state represents the globalization of the opportunities for representative democracy and civil rights. The destruction of traditional political cultures—now universally accepted by political elites—and the substitution of bureaucratic systems created conditions ripe for democracy and civil rights. I conclude with some observations about the implications of this argument for human rights activists and states.

The Construction of State Power

The modern state is defined by the monopoly of the legitimate use of force, made possible by bureaucracy, and with territorially defined boundaries (Weber 1978). The state is a cultural construct in the sense that it exists only because the people who staff it and interact with it share certain kinds of ideas and expectations about how they should behave. The set of ideas that makes the state possible is neither obvious nor "natural," although the ubiquity of states today may sometimes lead us to think otherwise. The culturally constructed nature of the state can best be illustrated by contrasting it with some alternative forms of political organization that preceded it.

European polities were territorially organized even prior to the state. Land in medieval Europe was understood as a source of power, and elites therefore competed for it and carefully marked the boundaries of their control. Even for commoners, rights to land conveyed status. Losing such rights was the worst possible social disaster (Mollat 1986, 13). Indeed, the status of a whole class of people could rise with the acquisition of rights to land. Knightly status in England, for instance, was considered lowly and undesirable in the period immediately following the Norman conquest. Most knights were mercenaries or "house knights" of Anglo-Norman magnates, and did not have any land rights of their own. By the end of the twelfth century, however, most knights acquired land as a result of being enfoeffed by the king and his magnates. Their social status rose accordingly (Harvey 1976).

Not all premodern political cultures were territorial, however. Our familiarity with the modern state misleads us into assuming that territory is necessarily a universal feature of political life.[1] However, many Southeast Asian and African kingdoms were based on hierarchical, personalistic ties, to which land was at best incidental (Mair 1977; Adas 1987; Thongchai 1994). There is a clear contrast, for instance, between William the Conqueror's Domesday Book and the manpower roles *(hangwaw)* of Siamese kings. Both recorded the resources of their kingdoms and who controlled those resources, but the Domesday Book recorded the land and ignored the people who worked it, while the *hangwaw* recorded the people but ignored the land (Douglas and Greenaway 1981, 168; Englehart 2001). Territoriality is thus not distinctively modern, but it is also not natural as the basis of political order. It is, however, a key component of the modern state.[2]

Bureaucracy evolved as a part of European political culture much later, and took a form distinctively different from earlier political systems, including non-European "bureaucracies." In medieval Europe, many officials owned their offices as property, acquired either by inheritance or purchase. Even in places where offices were not property, as for instance in imperial China, officials were usually prebendal—they were unsalaried and expected to make their living by extracting fees from people who came under their jurisdiction.

In Medieval Europe authority was radically decentralized, with vassals defining and enforcing justice on their fiefs. They needed this authority to keep people on the land, make them pay taxes, and make them show appropriate deference. Their authority was institutionalized in seigniorial courts, which were independent of royal courts, to which cases could not normally be appealed. Lords had additional liberties on their fiefs that further restricted royal authority. In England, for instance, which was one of the most centralized medieval kingdoms, the king's agents could not serve a royal writ on a baron's land. This legal right recognized the capacity of the barons to resist; in 1276 the sheriff of Lincolnshire estimated that he would need a force of 5,000 men to execute a writ on a fief of the Earl of Warenne (Palmer 1982, 265).

Such decentralization was quite normal prior to the construction of modern states. Japanese *daimyo,* for instance, had similarly independent legal authority within their domains (Haraguchi et al. 1975). Even where rulers might have the power to overcome such privileges, as for instance in Siam, the difficulty of gathering local information meant that it was prudent for them to permit local officials considerable latitude (Englehart 2001). The Chinese imperial government probably came closest to modern bureaucracy, but depended on prebendal officials (some of whom purchased their office), lacked functional specialization at the local level, and was so thinly spread that it could not have functioned without extensive voluntary cooperation from local gentry. Chinese scholar-officials were not specifically trained for administration, and the most "professional" elements of the administration, in a modern sense, were privately hired secretaries who acted as personal assistants to officials (Ch'ü 1962).

Functional bureaucracy provided a radical departure from such conceptualizations of political authority and office. Bureaucrats are members of hierarchical organizations, obliged to follow instructions from above as closely as possible. Their incentives are shaped to make their interests as consonant as possible with following rules and promoting the interests of the organization of which they are a part. Personally free and subject to their superiors only in their official capacity, bureaucrats are appointed and may be dismissed for malfeasance or incompetence. Bureaucratic salary is their main source of income, with salaries graded according to rank, and advancement a function of seniority and merit, as determined by the bureaucrat's superiors. They are trained in skills specific to their role in the organization, and subject to strict standards of conduct, as laid out in written regulations defining their job. All this shapes the incentives of bureaucrats so they will carry out policy according to the rules of the organization and the wishes of their superiors.

European rulers developed bureaucratic organizational techniques through a long period of trial and error. The impetus for the development of bureaucracy came partly from military competition in early modern Europe, which required rulers to extract more resources from the kingdoms they ruled. "Demonstration effects" spread new ideas through the region, as each ruler had to imitate and improve on the developments and innovations of his rivals to succeed militarily (Hintze 1975; Bendix 1978; Tilly 1990). This is only part of the story, however, as military needs were also pressing in other regions that did not develop bureaucracy.

Bureaucratization was also part of a much wider cultural movement toward rationalization in sixteenth-century Europe. During this period new techniques were developed for the control of nature through the systematic collection of data and the use of mathematical analysis. Insurance based on probability was invented (Brewer 1989, 229–230), as were new forms of bookkeeping. In 1689 the English government became the first in Europe to routinely record income and expenditures (Dickson 1967, 46). As rulers began trying to understand the countries they ruled more systematically, they pioneered the collection of statistical information (Hacking 1975). Bureaucrats develop the capacity to gather and use information in highly specialized ways, making new kinds of government action possible (Weber 1978, 973–975; Hintze 1975, chap. 7). The military and fiscal centralization of seventeenth-century Europe was driven in part by military competition, but was fueled by new ideas and cultural attitudes.

The monopolization of the legitimate use of violence was a function of bureaucratization. Because bureaucracy provided rulers with more reliable subordinates, it also enabled them to require that their servants use violence only in ways they approved. This was not the case in either earlier European or non-European politics, where the authority to use violence was usually distributed among many actors and groups.

In medieval Europe, for instance, nobles, guilds, municipalities, and villages had the authority to use violence in various circumstances. Nobles effectively controlled private armies: they were required to do so by kings, so that they could provide military service. It was common, however, for magnates to enfeoff more knights than they were required to provide for the royal host (see, for instance, Douglas and Greenaway 1981, 224–227, 229, 970–984). These nobles had legitimate authority to independently exercise violence on their estates, and in some kingdoms enjoyed the "right of feud," which allowed them to make war independently of the authority of the king. Clergymen could become the vassals of kings and maintain

their own feudal levies (Bloch 1961, 347–350), and the church had authority to use violence on its own account, as for instance when conducting
inquisitions.[3] In the cities, burgesses often raised their own levies, and
guilds exercised legal jurisdiction over their members (Reynolds 1984, 73–
75, 198–200). Peasant communities could exercise violence, especially
against their own members, and in some cases were required to be self-
policing (Reynolds 1984, 114).

In contrast, seventeenth-century European kings used bureaucratized
royal armies to destroy the intermediate political institutions through which
medieval monarchs had ruled (MacNeill 1982, 125–143). The feudal nobility was reduced to royal service, the church lost its independent authority
to use violence, and cities and peasant communities were reduced to col-
lections of individuals who each confronted the state alone.[4] In most of
Europe this in effect required monarchs to reconquer their kingdoms from
the feudal nobility (Tilly 1975, 1990).

The new states restricted the use of violence to their agents, and bound
those agents to use violence only in certain ways under specified circumstances. In Norbert Elias's words, "when a monopoly of force is formed,
pacified social spaces are created which are normally free from acts of
violence. . . . Here the individual is largely protected from sudden attack,
the irruption of physical violence into his life" (1982, 235–236). Whatever
the difficulties with such a system, there is little doubt that it sharply
reduces the overall level of violence to which ordinary citizens are exposed.[5] This tends to make it popular among most citizens, who see it as
proper and legitimate. Citizens accept the monopoly of violence as morally
correct.

Thus by the eighteenth century, European monarchs had evolved a new
set of institutions that enabled them to radically centralize power. In most
places outside of Europe the state was then introduced through colonialism,
although there were a few places where it was the result of indigenous
reform based on European models. The world is now ruled by people who
conceive of power territorially, rule through bureaucracy, and seek to monopolize the legitimate use of violence. Even in those places where governments lack the monopoly of the legitimate use of violence and effective
bureaucratic organization—for instance Burma, Afghanistan, or much of
sub-Saharan Africa—elites still aspire to establish effective states (Jackson
and Rosberg 1982; Jackson 1990). None reject the state as culturally inappropriate and no country abandoned the modern state after decolonization. Despite its clearly colonial origin in most places, the elites who
assumed power after the colonists left preferred the state to traditional
political arrangements (Mamdani 1996; Badie 2000). An important reason

is that modern states had replaced earlier political cultures. Not only had colonial regimes permanently altered the social and economic structure of the places they ruled, they had also altered the cultural information available to their subjects. Today few if any people in a decolonized country would know how to reassemble the traditional polity. Furthermore, the unparalleled capacity of modern states to centralize power is something that rulers universally approve, even though it is very much at odds with most traditional political cultures.

State formation never culminates in a finished product; it is an ongoing process. Rather than a perfect piece of eighteenth-century sculpture to be admired untouched by later ages, the state is like a house, which once constructed requires constant maintenance and improvement. The state must continually renew and renegotiate its relationship with the citizens who staff, defend, and pay for the institutions composing it. States are socially constructed, but the process of social construction never ends.

Modern states have evolved a remarkable degree of power and control over social life. As Joel Migdal puts it,

> Astonishingly, some states have been able to garner from people's yearly earnings a share equivalent to all their work performed through April or May or, sometimes, even June of that year and to sequester their children for 30 or so hours a week in a state institution. Premodern political leaders could not have imagined such audacious goals. (1997, 209)

States are able to do this best where they elicit cooperation from their citizens. This leads to a paradox: the most effective states are often those that place voluntary restraints on their exercise of power. Such states have considerable legitimacy among their citizens, legitimacy that facilitates the execution of state policies.

One common theme in the negotiation of legitimacy in modern states is the restraint of state power. Political rights are an important strategy in such negotiations. Hence even a document like the Magna Carta, written by barons trying to protect their privileges, can be seen as part of the foundation of Anglo-American democracy: the barons were trying to participate in a growing royal power that they could no longer evade (Kriegel 1995, 75). Not all states legitimize their power by granting political rights to their citizens,[6] but it is a powerful strategy and one that has been nearly universal since World War II. As Guillermo O'Donnell and Phillippe Schmitter point out, even authoritarian regimes since 1945 have been forced to justify themselves with the rhetoric of democracy and freedom (1986, 15).

Citizens and the State

The relationship between citizens and the state is complicated by the fact that most people in the modern world are ambivalent about state power. They fear its abuse by government officials or regimes, correctly recognizing that the state can do them serious harm. On the other hand, as Elias points out, most people want the state to exercise its power to maintain order, create a stable, predictable legal environment, and protect them from foreign threats and their fellow citizens (1982, 113–114). The alternative would be to return to a prestate context in which the authority to use violence is more widely distributed and less subject to legal control. Citizens would be forced to find some private means of protection, which would strike most citizens as wrong, a morally indefensible abrogation of the state's responsibilities. Indeed, the protective functions of the state have increased over time. They have been progressively extended, from protecting citizens from violence to providing a stable economy and guaranteeing "second-wave" social and economic rights, as well as "third-wave" cultural rights.[7]

People thus both fear and desire state power. The logical solution to such a dilemma is to allow the state to be powerful, but to attempt to control the circumstances in which that power is used. Most of the figures in the classical political theory "canon" of the seventeenth through nineteenth centuries respond to the question posed by this dilemma: How can we have the state and make it safe too? Thus for Hobbes, the state's ability to protect citizens from each other is supremely important and requires considerable coercive powers. For Locke the primary danger is that the sovereign will violate the social contract by overreaching his legitimate powers, and citizens must be ready and able to check such attempts. For Rousseau it is only through conformity to the general will that the fact of state domination can be made legitimate. For Marx the state must be removed from the control of the capitalist class, and made to advance the interests of the working class. All focus on the proper role and limits of the state, offering new ways to articulate the relationship between the state and its citizens.

Over time activists and philosophers evolved a set of strategies to limit and control state power that have become part of the conceptual apparatus of the state. Although not universally successful, they are universally available and comprehensible, because of the ubiquity of the modern state. They are equally constructed, in response to the emergence of state power, and represent part of the same cultural and institutional package as the state. While a variety of self-limitations on state power can be conceived, here

I am primarily concerned with two of the most important: democracy and civil rights.[8]

Democracy

The democratic strategy for limiting state power seeks to shape the interests of the elites who control state power by forcing them to seek the approval of citizens to remain in power. Elite access to state power thus becomes dependent on conforming policy to what the public can be persuaded to accept.

Representative democracy is possible because bureaucracies are remarkably neutral with respect to the executive that directs them. Because bureaucracies dispense with the highly personalistic ties that structure nonbureaucratic systems, they can serve different kinds of rulers equally well. Absolute monarchies could therefore be replaced by alternative governments, including elected ones. Precisely because of the monopolization of violence by kings, the deposition of one monarch did not necessarily invite the rise of another. It did not create a power vacuum that could only be filled by the rise of another figure who could draw on the personal allegiance of retainers. Instead, the state bureaucracy remained intact and continued to monopolize violence. An absence of executive power could be filled in a variety of ways. By the end of the eighteenth century, after the experiences of the English civil war, the rise of the Dutch leagues and Italian city-states, and the French Revolution, Europeans had developed a number of models for nonmonarchical rule.

Modern representative institutions evolved out of the parliaments of early modern Europe. These parliaments were explicitly designed to limit the activities of monarchs, by requiring them to specify the purposes to which tax revenues would be put (Harriss 1994, 24; Brewer 1989, 144–145). They became institutions that enabled taxpaying citizens to place constraints on rulers (Poggi 1990, 40).

The key practical problem in controlling the behavior of the state was making the bureaucracy subordinate to the political authority of elected representatives. The relationship between elected governments and bureaucracy developed differently in different European countries. In France, for instance, the monarchy created bureaucracy as the foundation of royal absolutism—but that bureaucracy was later employed and expanded during the revolution, ultimately coming to serve a representative government. Prior to 1688, bureaucracy was bitterly resisted by the English parliament, because of fears that it would be used by the monarchy to reduce the authority of parliament. After the Glorious Revolution, however, parliament itself constructed a bureaucracy, confident that it, rather than the monarchy, would control the bureaucrats (Brewer 1989). Nor did all European legislatures necessarily develop effective parliamentary control over the bureaucracy—in Germany, for instance, this was instituted only after World War II, by fiat of the occupying powers. European parliaments, powerful or not, provided models for later parliaments in places with no historical tradition of representative assemblies at all—as in many decolonized countries after World War II.

Rights

Modern notions of rights also developed in conjunction with the rise of the state. The destruction of intermediate authorities reframed political life as a relationship between individuals and the state. Modern theories of rights were first developed to articulate that relationship and create order in a world of "masterless men," beginning most famously with Hobbes and Locke (Shapiro 1986; Herzog 1989).

Rights represent limits that the state should not trespass in dealing with individuals within its borders. In feudal society the idea that people all had the same set of rights vis-à-vis the government would have made no sense at all: the whole point of political order was that people were not equal, and had distinctive privileges that reflected those inequalities (Lovejoy 1936). While the idea that there are claims people can make against larger communities is not new to the modern state,[9] rights can be seen as the modern form of such claims. Rights take on a special and more absolute character because of the more absolute authority of the state, which becomes the ultimate arbiter over all claims, and which reduces all citizens to a state of (theoretically) legal equality.

Neither effective rights protections nor representative democracy are automatic products of the modern state, let alone of some implacable process of modernization—a point amply illustrated by the "peculiarity" of German history, that the bourgeoisie never pressed the Kaiserreich for effective representative institutions (Blackbourn and Eley 1984). Nor are civil rights necessarily granted equitably, as illustrated by the United States prior to the civil rights movement. States do not cause democracy and rights, but they do universally create conditions necessary for them, and give citizens incentives to agitate for them.

Furthermore, the globalization of the state entails the globalization of models for restraining state power. Because the basic institutional structure of states is relatively homogeneous, in contrast to the variety of political models that preceded it, elites and activists have a variety of examples of democratic regimes, transitions, and civil rights legislation to study and mine for ideas.

Activism

Rights activists and democracy movements appear less hostile to state power than the conventional opposition between state and society would lead us to believe.[10] In fact, they assume that state power could not exist without this opposition. State power, democracy, and rights are part of the same cultural complex.

A close examination of democracy movements even in states under the control of the most vocally anti-Western governments shows that the democracy movements in these places have local roots, although they necessarily resemble struggles in other places by other people to tame state power. This is hardly surprising, given that they are responding to the structural context of the state, exactly as their counterparts elsewhere have done. They may accept assistance from sympathetic Western organizations, but even this supposes a prior level of organization that would attract the sort of assistance discussed in Chapter 6.

International nongovernmental organization (NGOs), sometimes labeled as foreign provocateurs by hostile governments, can generally operate in a country only with extensive local cooperation. Amnesty International, for instance, relies on reports of human rights abuses by a country's own citizens. Without such reports it would be impossible for Amnesty International to gather accurate information, and without accurate information the organization's authority would be severely undermined (Power 1981, 21–26; Korey 1998, chap. 7). Human rights NGOs are most effective at shaming: showing an international audience that internal dissent exists where local governments would prefer to hide it. This is possible only with the assistance of preexisting indigenous dissident movements.

Such strategies may not always work, and may well be historically limited to a narrow window of opportunity. Recently some governments have sought solidarity against this kind of shaming, most importantly in the Bangkok Declaration on Human Rights. The NGO community took the declaration as a challenge because it sought to demote civil rights in favor of more ambiguous cultural and communal rights (Korey 1998, chap. 19).[11] But perhaps more significantly, it represented a serious attempt to shift international human rights norms, in order to weaken the strategy of shaming. The signatories to the Bangkok Declaration adopted a relativist position, attempting to undermine the explicit universalism of most international human rights instruments.

In Iran, as discussed in Chapter 5 by Mahmood Monshipouri, local activists—with support from young people, women, and the press—attempt to promote democracy and civil rights as protection against an intrusive revolutionary state. To do this they employ Islamic arguments and justifications—but the structural goal is the same as in movements for democracy and rights elsewhere. Monshipouri identifies such activists with the forces of globalization: despite the fact that their struggle is carried on with purely local resources, they represent a global trend, responding to the same incentives the state presents citizens of other countries.

Furthermore, citizens do not necessarily concur with governmental claims of cultural difference. For instance, the primary opposition to the government of Singapore's antidemocratic "Confucian values" campaign in the 1980s was from the very domestic Chinese constituency they had hoped to sway (Englehart 2000). The government of Singapore hoped to create an explicitly antidemocratic ideology in contrast to an occidental Other through this campaign, one that would exemplify the rhetoric of "Asian values" they were using abroad at the time (see, for instance, Kausikan 1993). Far from being discontinued because of international criticism, it was the failure of the campaign to appeal to English-educated Chinese that led to its demise. Chinese Singaporeans saw the campaign as an attempt to strengthen state power in a regime that was already perceived as highly intrusive (Tremewan 1994).

Both Rebecca Moore and Linda Butenhoff (Chapters 6 and 8) argue that the Chinese democracy movement has domestic roots. Some groups may appeal for foreign assistance for strategic reasons, but they are not created by or beholden to any foreign organization. They represent attempts to moderate the legitimate sphere of action of an authoritarian state—taking advantage of the state's own shifting economic policies to secure greater protections of individual rights.

Even oppressive governments may see the value of granting political rights in the interest of enhancing state effectiveness. The introduction of democracy can enhance state power by securing the confidence and co-operation of citizens. In rural China, for instance, the central government has responded to the erosion of its authority at the village level by permitting more democratic selection of local leaders. Since the end of collectivized agriculture, increasingly corrupt and unreliable party officials have undermined popular support for the government and forced citizens to seek the protection of unofficial patronage networks. Some of these networks are organized around corrupt cadres, others around more traditional social organizations such as lineage groups, mutual aid associations, and secret societies (Perry 1985, 426–438; Yang 1996, 192–201). These

organizations can resist central government policy in the countryside, usually passively but sometimes actively, and even violently. In response to
this challenge, the Chinese Communist Party has decided to encourage
more democratic village self-government as a mechanism to improve state
control over the countryside. Villagers are permitted more liberal nomi-
nation and election procedures for village offices, with the goal of evicting
corrupt and unreliable cadres and replacing them with candidates who enjoy greater local confidence. This provides the central government with
stronger, more effective local leaders with whom to negotiate (Kelliher
1997; Howell 1998; Thurston 1998; see also Chapter 6).

The domestic origins of democracy movements highlight the importance
of Chenyang Li's argument (Chapter 11) that value persuasion is necessary
to secure international human rights regimes. They cannot be imposed from
the outside, short of full-scale military intervention—as in Germany and
Japan after World War II. Yet we should be struck by the universality of
democracy movements in the world today. They are as ubiquitous as modern states. Because democracy movements respond to the same, globalized
political culture, such value consensus may not be so difficult to achieve.[12]

Conversely, the tendency to identify human rights abuses with strong
states should not be taken to the extreme of assuming that state power is
intrinsically abusive. State power is necessary for rights protections to be
effective. In some cases, such as Afghanistan, Burma, or Somalia, the
creation of an effective state may be a necessary first step toward promoting human rights and democracy. At the very least, states universally provide the foundation for activist movements that generate globalization from
below with respect to human rights norms. Without the protection that
states afford their citizens, such organizations would be unable to function,
as citizens would be forced to seek protection from private sources—much
as in medieval European kingdoms, or in contemporary states that are
failing.

State formation is an ongoing process, and legitimacy needs to be pains-
takingly maintained through the activities of the state. Failure to do so
weakens state institutions, leading to a deterioration of the human rights
situation, as the state loses the capacity to effectively protect citizens. Arguably such a process has occurred in India since the mid-1970s. The
Indian civil service and police have become less professional as they have
been progressively "captured" by politicians and influential local patrons
(Rudolph and Rudolph 1987, 75–102). The delivery of services such as
police protection has declined, and in some states people are increasingly
forced to turn to private sources of patronage and protection. Most often
such patronage is provided by the same local elites who have siphoned off

state resources, control the local police, and in some cases even maintain private armies (Human Rights Watch 1999; Heller 2000). Thus the weakening of the state has led to a worsening human rights situation in parts of India.

The ultimate result of the erosion of state power can be complete collapse, as has arguably occurred in Afghanistan, Burma, and Somalia. In these cases, citizens can only be protected from violence by turning to coercive private patronage networks. Leaders remain in power only by using very costly levels of violence, and are constantly under threat of attack from the leaders of other patronage networks. This is surely a situation that benefits no one.

Conclusion

For people interested in advancing the cause of rights in a globalized world, it is clear from the argument above that states must be a central part of the project. In particular, there are two conclusions that follow from the argument I have made here, one pertaining to human rights activists and the other to foreign policy matters.

First, human rights activists should make state capacity a primary issue. Their generally antistatist prejudices will not serve them well in a world where many of the worst human rights emergencies are due to state collapse rather than state oppression. Activists have largely been guilty of accepting the multiculturalist arguments put forth by governments in documents such as the Bangkok Declaration. While this has helped produce a more serious international dialogue, inspired partly by that declaration, about what shape international norms should take and how they should relate to local cultures (see, for instance, Bauer and Bell 1999), it is important to question how much difference of opinion really exists across regions with respect to human rights norms (see Chapter 9).

This dialogue can advance significantly beyond the now stale debate between universalism and relativism by recognizing the socially constructed nature of the state, and the degree to which it is a product of globalization. If states are all cultural products of a similar type, then the issue of relativism can be avoided: they represent a political culture that has become universal.

Contrary to the multicultural claims represented in the Bangkok Declaration, transnational criticism of governments is not equivalent to criticism of a culture. States by definition are a product of a globalized political culture. Multiculturalism cannot be a defense where a monoculture already exists: transnational critiques of human rights abuses are critiques of governments, not states or cultures. States are a necessary part of the solution. Only states can protect rights—no other institutions or actors have the capacity to do this. The state may be constructed, but there is no alternative construction available with more capacity or promise for protecting human dignity.

The second implication of the argument above reflects on foreign policy. While "nation-building" has recently become a term of abuse in American politics, it is difficult to see any alternative to policies designed to remediate weak or collapsed states. Governments need to accept that nation-building is a legitimate activity for the international community. The maintenance of a healthy international system requires the maintenance of strong states that can uphold international agreements and secure the rights of their citizens.

Collapsed states create problems for other states: they generate flows of refugees, their violence can spill over borders, they can become a source of infectious disease. World Health Organization officials, for instance, worry that the Russian state's inability to deliver basic health services may turn it into an enormous "epidemiological pump" for infectious disease (Zuger 2000, F9). They may also become bases for transnational criminal activity, as first Burma and then Afghanistan became the world's largest exporter of opium and heroin as a direct result of state collapse. State collapse may also lead to pressure from NGOs, international organizations or transnational corporations to restore basic security. U.S. intervention in Somalia, for instance, was the result of pressure from NGOs—primarily the International Committee of the Red Cross—on the UN. The employees of these NGOs could no longer safely deliver food relief in the wake of famine and the collapse of the Barre government in 1991 (Clark 1993).

The increasingly homogeneous global legal framework constructed by states undergirds international law, including human rights law. International instruments such as those discussed by Caren Irr and Kavita Philip (Chapters 1 and 3) depend on individual states for enforcement. No international agreement is effective until it has been ratified by states, thereby receiving the imprimatur of domestic law. Far from undermining state sovereignty, such international agreements depend on it. Furthermore, by adhering to such instruments states may be able to strengthen themselves by improving their own domestic legitimacy. They may also be able to construct international regimes that protect their authority from international actors that potentially do threaten sovereignty—such as multinational corporations or increasingly mobile international finance (see, for instance, Vernon 1971; Mittelman 1996; Winters 1996).

Despite the optimistic predictions of modernization theory (Pye 1990), the empirical evidence does not strongly support the argument that democracy is inevitable. What does seem to be inevitable in modern states is democratic opposition and citizen movements to restrain the state, as well as the constant renegotiation of the relationship between the state and its citizens. Although there is no simple causal relationship, the elective affinity between political and civil rights and the state is strong enough to merit recognition and nurture a world where all three are increasingly under assault.

Notes

For comments on this paper I am indebted to Melissa Miller, Mahmood Monshipouri, Andrew J. Nathan, Kavita Philip, and Josh Sanborn.

1. Robert Ardrey (1966) goes so far as to argue that an instinct to territoriality is genetically encoded in human beings.

2. Some scholars have suggested that territoriality is in decline as an organizing principle of political life (e.g., Sassen 1996; Ruggie 1998), and that this indicates the decline of the states system. While I do not wish to engage here the complex literature on the decline of the state, one should note that all sides of the debate acknowledge territoriality as a defining feature of states.

3. While inquisitors had to turn over convicted heretics to secular authorities for punishment (usually execution), they could also impose stiff corporal punishment on their own account in the guise of penances. They also had the authority to imprison heretics in jails maintained and staffed by the church (Hamilton 1981, 49–57).

4. This process is traced for Germany by David Sabean (1984), and for England by Don Herzog (1989).

5. See, for instance, Lawrence Stone's classic account (1965) of how violence became uncouth in England.

6. See, for instance, Garon 1997 for an account of how the Japanese states built legitimacy and penetrated everyday life in similar ways both prior to and after World War II.

7. The language of a first, second, and third wave of rights reflects the order in which they became prominent concerns of the international human rights movement. It is not intended to imply that some are prioritized over others, and in practice all are probably interdependent.

8. For other self-limitations on state power, see Schedler, Diamond, and Plattner 1999. The delicate negotiation of citizen support is the subject of some of the most interesting recent work on the state (for instance, Corrigan and Sayer 1985; Joseph and Nugent 1994; Munro 1998).

9. See, for example, Marc Bloch's discussion of seisin (1961, 115–116).

10. The opposition between state and society is often too rigidly drawn. On the need for approaches that integrate the two, see Mitchell 1991 and Migdal 1997.

11. Interestingly, the language of the Bangkok Declaration itself is quite mild, even bland. The operative clause reads: "the promotion of human rights should be encouraged by cooperation and consensus, and not through confrontation and the

imposition of incompatible values." This mild language was taken as an affront by NGOs and activists because it was the culmination of a campaign led by the government of Singapore to claim that uniquely Asian values made western versions of human rights inappropriate there. See Englehart 2000 for details on the Asian values campaign in Singapore.

12. This is not to say that people in all countries want precisely the same things from their governments, but rather that they respond similarly to similar institutions. The bills of rights of various countries, or the policies of their elected representatives, may well look quite different—but they will always be similar in the sense that rights and representative institutions are used to curb state power.

References

Adas, Michael. 1987. "From Confrontation to Avoidance: Peasant Protest in Precolonial and Colonial Southeast Asia." *Comparative Studies in Society and History* 23, no. 2 (April): 217–247.

Ardrey, Robert. 1966. *The Territorial Imperative*. New York: Atheneum.

Badie, Bertrand. 2000. *The Imported State: The Westernization of the Political Order*. Stanford, CA: Stanford University Press.

Bangkok Declaration. 1993. UN Document A/CONF.157/ASRM/8 or A/CONF. 157/PC/59.

Bauer, Joanne, and Daniel Bell. 1999. *The East Asian Challenge for Human Rights*. New York: Cambridge University Press.

Bendix, Reinhart. 1978. *Kings or People: Power and the Mandate to Rule*. Berkeley: University of California Press.

Blackbourn, David, and Geoff Eley. 1984. *The Peculiarities of German History*. New York: Oxford University Press.

Bloch, Marc. 1961. *Feudal Society*. 2 vols. L. A. Manyan, trans. Chicago: Chicago University Press.

Brewer, John. 1989. *The Sinews of Power: War, Money, and the English State, 1688–1783*. New York: Knopf.

Brown, R. Allen. 1985. *The Normans and the Norman Conquest*. 2nd ed. Woodbridge, Sussex, England: Boydell.

Ch'ü, T'ung-tsu. 1962. *Local Government in China Under the Ch'ing*. Cambridge: Harvard University Press.

Clark, Jeffrey. 1993. "Debacle in Somalia." *Foreign Affairs* 72, no.1: 109–123.

Corrigan, Philip, and Derek Sayer. 1985. *The Great Arch: English State Formation as Cultural Revolution*. New York: Basil Blackwell.

Dickson, P. G. 1967. *The Financial Revolution in England: A Study of the Development of Public Credit, 1688–1756*. New York: Macmillan.

Donnelly, Jack. 1989. *Universal Human Rights in Theory and Practice*. Ithaca, NY: Cornell University Press.

———. 1996. "Rethinking Human Rights." *Current History* 95 (November): 387–391.

Douglas, David and G.W. Greenaway. 1981. *English Historical Documents*. Vol. 2. New York: Oxford.

Ehrenreich, Jeffrey. 1989. "Lifting the Burden of Secrecy: The Emergence of the Awá Biosphere Reserve." *Latin American Anthropology Review* 1, no. 2.

Elias, Norbert. 1982. *The Civilizing Process.* Vol. 2, *Power and Civility.* Edmund Jephcott, trans. New York: Pantheon.

Englehart, Neil. 2000. "Rights and Culture in the Asian Values Argument: The Rise and Fall of Confucian Ethics in Singapore." *Human Rights Quarterly* 22, no. 2 (May): 548–569.

———. 2001. *Culture and Power in Traditional Siamese Government.* Ithaca, NY: Cornell University Southeast Asia Program.

Etzioni-Halevy, Eva. 1983. *Bureaucracy and Democracy: A Political Dilemma.* Rev. ed. Boston: Routledge and Kegan Paul.

Farb, Peter. 1968. *Man's Rise to Civilization, as Shown by the Indians of North America from Primeval Times to the Coming of the Industrial State.* New York: E. P. Dutton.

Fisher, William. 1994. "Megadevelopment, Environmentalism, and Resistance: The Institutional Context of Kayapó Indigenous Politics in Central Brazil." *Human Organization* 53, no. 4 (Fall): 220–233.

Fukuyama, Francis. 1992. *The End of History and the Last Man.* New York: Free Press.

Garon, Sheldon. 1997. *Molding Japanese Minds: The State in Everyday Life.* Princeton: Princeton University Press.

Gramsci, Antonio. 1971. *Selections from the Prison Notebooks.* Quintin Hoare and Geoffrey Nowell-Smith, trans. New York: International Publishers.

Hacking, Ian. 1975. *The Emergence of Probability: A Philosophical Study of Early Ideas About Probability, Induction, and Statistical Inference.* New York: Cambridge University Press.

Hamilton, Bernard. 1981. *The Medieval Inquisition.* New York: Holmes and Meier.

Haraguchi, Tarao, Robert K Sakai, Mitsugu Sakihara, Kazuko Yamada and Marato Matsui. 1975. *The Status System and Social Organization of Satsuma: A Translation of the Shūmon Tefuda Aratame Jomoku.* Honolulu: University of Hawaii Press.

Harriss, G. L. 1994. "The King and His Subjects." In Rosemary Horrox, ed., *Fifteenth-Century Attitudes: Perceptions of Society in Late Medieval England.* New York: Cambridge University Press, 13–28.

Harvey, Sally. 1976. "The Knight and the Knight's Fee in England." In R. H. Hilton, ed., *Peasants, Knights, and Heretics.* New York: Cambridge University Press, 133–173.

Held, David. 1987. *Models of Democracy.* Stanford, CA: Stanford University Press.

Heller, Patrick. 2000. "Degrees of Democracy: Some Comparative Lessons from India." *World Politics* 52 (July): 484–519.

Herzog, Don. 1989. *Happy Slaves: A Critique of Consent Theory.* Chicago: University of Chicago Press.

Hintze, Otto. 1975. *The Historical Essays of Otto Hintze.* Felix Gilbert, trans. New York: Oxford University Press.

Howell, Jude. 1998. "Prospects for Village Self-Governance in China." *Journal of Peasant Studies* 25, no. 3 (April): 86–111.

Human Rights Watch. 1999. *Broken People: Caste Violence Against India's "Untouchables."* New York: Human Rights Watch.

Jackson, Robert. 1990. *Quasi-States: Sovereignty, International Relations, and the Third World.* New York: Cambridge University Press.

Jackson, Robert, and Carl Rosberg. 1982. "Why Africa's Weak States Persist: The Empirical and Juridical in Statehood." *World Politics* 35, no. 1 (October): 1–24.

Jennings, Francis. 1993. *The Founders of America.* New York: W. W. Norton.

Joseph, Gilbert M., and Daniel Nugent, eds. 1994. *Everyday Forms of State Formation.* Durham, NC: Duke University Press.

Kausikan, Bilahari. 1993. "Asia's Different Standard." *Foreign Policy* 92 (Fall): 24–42.

———. 1998. "The 'Asian Values' Debate: A View from Singapore." In Larry Diamond and Mark F. Plattner, eds., *Democracy in East Asia.* Baltimore: Johns Hopkins University Press, 17–27.

Keck, Margaret E., and Kathryn Sikkink, eds. 1998. *Activists Beyond Borders: Advocacy Networks in International Politics.* Ithaca, NY: Cornell University Press.

Kelliher, Daniel. 1997. "The Chinese Debate over Village Self-Government." *China Journal* 37 (January): 31–62.

Korey, William. 1998. *NGOs and the Universal Declaration of Human Rights: "A Curious Grapevine."* New York: St. Martin's Press.

Kriegel, Blandine. 1995. *The State and the Rule of Law.* Marc LePain and Jeffrey C. Cohen, trans. Princeton: Princeton University Press.

Lovejoy, Arthur O. 1936. *The Great Chain of Being.* Cambridge: Harvard University Press.

MacNeill, William. 1982. *The Pursuit of Power.* Chicago: University of Chicago Press.

Mair, Lucy. 1977. *African Kingdoms.* New York: Oxford University Press.

Mamdani, Mahmood. 1996. *Citizen and Subject: Contemporary Africa and the Legacy of Late Colonialism.* Princeton: Princeton University Press.

Mansbridge, Jane. 1983. *Beyond Adversary Democracy.* Chicago: University of Chicago Press.

Migdal, Joel. 1997. "Studying the State." In Mark Lichbach and Alan Zuckerman, eds., *Comparative Politics: Rationality, Culture, and Structure.* New York: Cambridge, 208–236.

Mitchell, Timothy. 1991. "The Limits of the State: Beyond Statist Approaches and Their Critics." *American Political Science Review* 85, no. 1 (March): 77–96.

Mittelman, James H. 1996. "The Dynamics of Globalization." In James Mittelman, ed., *Globalization: Critical Reflections.* Boulder, CO: Lynne Rienner, 1–19.

Mollat, Michel. 1986. *The Poor in the Middle Ages: An Essay in Social History.* Arthur Goldhammer, trans. New Haven, CT: Yale University Press.

Munro, William A. 1998. *The Moral Economy of the State: Conservation, Community and State Making in Zimbabwe.* Athens, OH: Ohio University Center for International Studies.

O'Donnell, Guillermo, and Phillippe C. Schmitter. 1986. *Transitions from Authoritarian Rule: Tentative Conclusions About Uncertain Democracies.* Baltimore: Johns Hopkins University Press.

Palmer, Robert C. 1982. *The County Courts of Medieval England, 1150–1350.* Princeton: Princeton University Press.

Pateman, Carole. 1970. *Participation and Democratic Theory.* New York: Cambridge University Press.

Perry, Elizabeth J. 1985. "Rural Violence in Socialist China." *China Quarterly* 103 (September): 414–440.

Poggi, Gianfranco. 1990. *The State: Its Nature, Development, and Prospects.* Stanford, CA: Stanford University Press.

Pollis, Adamantia. 1996. "Cultural Relativism Revisited: Through a State Prism." *Human Rights Quarterly* 18, no. 2 (May): 316–344.

Power, Jonathan. 1981. *Amnesty International.* New York: McGraw-Hill.

Pye, Lucian W. 1990. "Political Science and the Crisis of Authoritarianism." *American Political Science Review* 84, no. 1 (March): 3–19.

Reynolds, Susan. 1984. *Kingdoms and Communities in Western Europe, 900–1300.* New York: Oxford University Press.

Rudolph, Lloyd I., and Susanne Hoeber Rudolph. 1987. *In Pursuit of Lakshmi: The Political Economy of the Indian State.* Chicago: University of Chicago Press.

Ruggie, John Gerard. 1998. *Constructing the World Polity: Essays on International Institutionalization.* NY: Routledge.

Sabean, David Warren. 1984. *Power in the Blood: Village Discourse in Early Modern Germany.* New York: Cambridge University Press.

Sassen, Saskia. 1996. *Losing Control? Sovereignty in an Age of Globalization.* NY: Columbia University Press.

Schedler Andreas, Larry Diamond, and Marc F. Plattner. 1999. *The Self-Restraining State: Power and Accountability in New Democracies.* Boulder, CO: Lynne Rienner.

Scott, James. 1998. *Seeing Like a State.* New Haven, CT: Yale University Press.

Shapiro, Ian. 1986. *The Evolution of Rights in Liberal Theory.* New York: Cambridge University Press.

Skocpol, Theda. 1979. *States and Social Revolution: A Comparative Analysis of France, Russia, and China.* New York: Cambridge University Press.

Stone, Lawrence. 1965. *The Crisis of the Aristocracy, 1558–1641.* New York: Oxford University Press.

Thongchai, Winichakul. 1994. *Siam Mapped: A History of the Geo-Body of a Nation.* Honolulu: University of Hawaii Press.

Thurston, Anne. 1998. *Muddling Toward Democracy: Political Change in Grassroots China.* Washington, DC: U.S. Institute of Peace.

Tilly, Charles. 1975. *The Formation of National States in Western Europe.* Princeton: Princeton University Press.

———. 1990. *Coercion, Capital, and European States, A.D. 990–1990.* Cambridge: Blackwell.

Tremewan, Christopher. 1994. *The Political Economy of Social Control in Singapore.* New York: St. Martin's Press.

Vernon, Raymond. 1971. *Sovereignty at Bay: The Multinational Spread of U.S. Enterprises.* New York: Basic Books.

Vincent, R. J. 1986. *Human Rights and International Relations.* New York: Cambridge University Press.

Weber, Max. 1978. *Economy and Society.* 2 vols. Guenther Roth and Claus Wittich, eds. Berkeley: University of California Press.

Winters, Jeffrey. 1996. *Power in Motion: Capital Mobility and the Indonesian State.* Ithaca, NY: Cornell University Press.

Yang, Dali L. 1996. *Calamity and Reform in China: State, Rural Rociety, and Institutional Change Since the Great Leap Famine.* Stanford: Stanford University Press.

Zakaria, Fareed. 1994. "Culture Is Destiny: A Conversation with Lee Kuan Yew." *Foreign Affairs* 73, no. 2 (March–April): 109–127.

Zuger, Abigail. 2000. "Russia Has Few Weapons as Infectious Diseases Surge." *New York Times,* December 5, pp. F1, F9.

3

Reflections on the Intersections of Environment, Development, and Human Rights in the Context of Globalization

Kavita Philip

Contrary to the growing polarization in the commentaries on "globalization," the phenomenon is neither all gloom nor all boom; it is neither the creation of a uniform MacDonaldized world nor the advent of a tribalized global jihad.[1] Globalization is characterized by flexible accumulation; increased cross-border outsourcing and the prevalence of multiple, dispersed sites of economic production; increasingly rapid and wide global flows of capital, natural resources, and people; the growing transnationalization of corporations and the apparent denationalization of nation-states. After the end of the Cold War, globalization came to be characterized by the expansion of a free-market model of liberal democracy, and the expanding consumption of commodified "world" culture (which some see as the export of American mass culture). Since globalization involves a complex interlocking system of politics, economy, and culture, in any assessment of its significance or impact we must remember to ask: What is being globalized? Using the case of environmental rights, I argue in this chapter that the globalization of economic production and the globalization of human rights need to be analyzed as related but sometimes mutually opposed phenomena. Rather than seeing one as logically entailing the other, the possibility is raised that they might sometimes be related as action and counteraction, or as part of a dialectic of "competing universalisms."

Globalization is a contradictory phenomenon, driven by the complex logic of geopolitics and capital, but carrying the potential, as in any large change, for lasting gains in the interests of universal human well-being. Mark Janis points out in his textbook on international law that "official state expressions about rules of customary international law are more likely to be generated in situations of conflict and doubt about those rules than when customary rules are well accepted."[2] The similarity to Kuhn's notion of revolutionary paradigm shift is evident: rules are generated as paradigms crumble, and the articulation of those rules in the midst of confusion and conflict contributes to the construction of the new regime of knowledge and practice, which, while eliminating some of the problems and anomalies of the old paradigm, creates its own characteristic new problematic.

The multiplicity of disciplinary approaches to the study of "globalization" are an indication that several fields find urgent or crucial the need to explore analytical frameworks, explanations, and predictions of this paradigmatic shift.[3] Scholars of politics and international relations are familiar with the rise of political and economic "globalization" discourses in the last decades of the twentieth century. A number of complementary globalization discourses—for example, accounts of the changing interpretations of "culture" (incorporating such issues as art, food, music, and fashion), and of "nature" (incorporating concerns about resources, health, technology, and aesthetics)—have accompanied the growth of these political analyses. The global discourses of culture and nature have been recent subjects of cultural and environmental studies respectively. Meanwhile, new interpretations of the duties and rights associated with the globalized dimensions of economics, culture, and nature have spurred changes in international law.

Though scholarship in these fields—political science, cultural studies, environmental studies, and international law—often embodies disparate assumptions, this chapter attempts to make some of their insights portable, using them as a basis from which to speculate about possible future challenges and opportunities for human rights in a globalized world. As a case study, this chapter takes up some competing interpretations of "environmental rights." Recent conflicts at the nexus of trends in international environmental law, human rights law, and globalized economic development necessitate, I suggest, a rethinking of the assumption that globalization is generally espoused by dominant nations or groups (or from the "center") and resisted by developing nations or local groups (or from the "periphery").[4] There are two arguments associated with this assumption. One conventional, homogenization-from-above argument holds that, although many cultures maintain beliefs at variance with the liberal assumptions of human rights regimes, an acceptance of human rights norms will spread in the wake of the homogenizing integrative trends of globalization, as increasing numbers of nations subscribe to the civil and political practices of democratic liberalism. An opposing argument holds that local particularities will prove intransigently resistant to human rights norms, because human rights regimes, bound up as they are with theories of liberalism, are forcing "Western values" into contexts in which they are incommensurable, or simply unwelcome.[5]

The cases surveyed in this chapter suggest that both of these versions need revision, because the underlying model of spreading homogeneity countered by recalcitrant localism is not entirely accurate. These cases suggest, first, that globalization is not associated with a seemingly natural and uniform diffusion of homogeneous economies and cultures from liberal Western contexts to developing nations. Rather, the pattern that emerges is one of global disjunctures, not global homogeneity; of uneven development characterized by disparities, as well as of rapid growth characterized by wealth and influence, both trends cutting across traditional boundaries of state and community.[6] Second, these case studies offer evidence against a simple scenario of globalization versus antiglobalization (or universalism versus particularism). Instead, the evidence suggests a picture of competing versions of globalization (competing universalisms) being advocated by cross-border coalitions of actors from both above and below, located both at the centers and in the peripheries. Most interestingly for human rights advocates, many contemporary environmental conflicts involve economic actors from the West in coalitions with non-Western states, effecting the globalization of production, while actors from below, in coalition with Western institutions, advocate the globalized application of human rights norms.

While human rights advocates might profit by encouraging the transnational, "global" coalitions that challenge rights abuses, they may lose by backing the equally "global" coalitions that sometimes allow or ignore human rights abuses in the interest of enhancing global production. There is no surefire formula, thus, for hitching the success of human rights to the future of "globalization," conceived as a single homogeneous phenomenon. Meeting future challenges and devising strategies for human rights advocacy will require more fine-grained analyses of the multiple, often contradictory, trends in globalization.

Such messy and contradictory trends suggest that human rights advocates cannot simply assume that human rights norms will spread by piggybacking on the trends related with the globalization of economic relations. Rather, we need to ask: What is being globalized, economic production or human rights norms? The first does not entail the second; indeed, they are sometimes at odds with each other. Rather than assuming a necessary entailment, this chapter suggests that we need an improved analytical framework that conjointly enables grounded analyses of economic, environmental, and human rights issues. In the context of globalization, these issues are invariably intertwined.

Causal hypotheses linking the growth or decline of human rights primarily with characteristic cultural values (liberal democracy, Asian traditionalism, hierarchical communitarianism, and so on) sometimes leave unexplained the complex conflicts and surprising coalitions that occur in culturally mixed contexts (such as the increasingly hybridized global situation). Identifying and attempting to analyze some samples of such conflicts, this chapter suggests that the fundamentals for an analytical framework that unites these issues might already be available in the field of political ecology, which can be usefully combined with traditional methods of human rights analysis. The method of political ecology, rather than trying to define "culture" in all its fuzzy complexity as an independent measurable variable, focuses on changing political and economic processes, helping us sort through contradictory but interrelated causes of conflict.

The Growth of Global Environmental Politics

In September 2000 the U.S. Department of State submitted to the UN its initial report on the Convention on the Elimination of All Forms of Racial Discrimination (CERD). Among the various categories of human rights–related harms it listed was "environmental racism." The report included a three–paragraph section on the progress made toward implementing "environmental justice." At the press conference, Bill Lann Lee, assistant attorney general for civil rights, reported that environment-related harm was "our newest [civil rights] concern": "I expect that domestically it will continue to be a concern. And I expect that across the world you'll be seeing the same kind of developments and the same concerns."[7]

There is in multiple fields an emerging awareness of a connection between the environment, international human rights law, and the race- and class-based elements of (under)development. The civil, political, economic, and social rights at the intersection of these fields have translated into states' legal rights and responsibilities at both the domestic and the international level. Internationally, several legally binding declarations conjoin environmental rights and human rights. One legal scholar reports 350 multilateral treaties and 1,000 bilateral treaties between states, and numerous resolutions among intergovernmental organizations, as evidence of an "international law duty not to destroy the environment that is incumbent upon individuals as well as states."[8]

In the Stockholm Declaration on the Human Environment, 114 nations affirmed that "man has the fundamental right to freedom, equality, and adequate conditions of life, in an environment of a quality that permits a life of dignity and well being, and he bears a solemn responsibility to protect and improve the environment for present and future generations." In the Rio Declaration on Environment and Development, 178 states agreed that human beings "are entitled to a healthy and productive life in harmony with nature." At the World Commission on Environment, the first of the proposed principles declared that "[a]ll human beings have the right to an environment adequate for their health and well-being." The African Charter on Human and Peoples' Rights recognizes that "[a]ll peoples shall have the right to a general satisfactory environment favorable to their development." The Hague Declaration on the Environment recognizes "the right to live in dignity in a viable global environment." The Indigenous Peoples' Convention protects indigenous peoples' environments and their ability to control decisions affecting those environments. The Inter-American Commission on Human Rights found that the highway constructed by the government of Brazil through Yanomami lands brought death to the Yanomami in the form of diseases and conflicts introduced by the influx of construction workers, miners, farmers, and settlers. The same commission found similar effects from oil development in the Ecuadorian Amazon. At the World Conference on Human Rights, all 171 states considered cases of illegal dumping of toxic nuclear waste, and concluded that environmental degradation can threaten the right to life.[9] The UN Special Rapporteur for Human Rights and Environment, Fatma Zohra Ksentini, found widespread evidence that environmental degradation can violate the right to life.[10] There is thus evidence of a vast body of evolving international law that already recognizes the link between environmental degradation and the violation of the human right to life.

As recently as 1990, however, observers diagnosed a widespread lack of scholarship on the links among the areas of environment, economic development, and human rights. Reviewing all three fields, Robert Lutz found that commentators tended "to recognize parallel relationships" but not to recognize an "integrated relationship among the three."[11] Calling for more scholarship on the nature of this integrated relationship, Lutz pointed out its significance:

> Many of the legal issues raised by the global problems of technology development, population growth, desertification, famine, global warming, ozone depletion, deforestation, nuclear proliferation, and the miserable poverty besetting a large percentage of our world are arguably at the intersection of ... environment, economic development and human rights. Since many

of these problems threaten our very existence, they deserve greater attention by the international legal community.[12]

Responding to Lutz's call at a panel discussion on the topic, World Bank vice president Ibrahim Shihata concurred: "A safe environment and economic development are inseparable from human rights, the promotion of which becomes the ultimate objective of the development process."[13] The apparent agreement between development advocates and human rights advocates dissolved, however, when, on the same panel, human rights advocate Philip Alston presented a forceful critique of development organizations in general and the Bank in particular for, he alleged, turning a blind eye to the human rights impact of its policies by adopting a functionalist attitude that isolates environment and development (seen as technical agendas) from human rights (seen as a political agenda).[14] Shihata argued, defensively, that social and environmental costs were inevitable in the development process, and that a development organization could only be aware of them and minimize the harm to the extent possible.

This exchange usefully showcases some of the challenges that remain for those (such as the supporters of the "third generation" of human rights) who wish to argue for the inseparability of human rights from the human needs that compose the context for their realization. Third-generation human rights supporters would argue that a universal defense of sustainable environments, basic healthcare, and collective solidarities ought to be considered of equal importance as the first and second generations of human rights. Globalizers of economic production, however, believe that the engine of global free markets can bring its train of liberal rights to all only if all nations—including presently "underdeveloped" ones—begin to participate in the global marketplace. Since economic development is a requirement for participation, development institutions like the World Bank play an important role in this process. Under the model advocated by structural adjustment programs, development institutions advise and guide nations away from large state expenditure on national agendas such as farm subsidies, land reform, healthcare, and education, while encouraging expenditure that enhances international trade, through an export-led growth model. In this model, then, there is bound to be a lag time during which the costs of development might be difficult to bear, but the theory predicts that the overall benefit from development will outweigh these costs.

Another source of confusion as one tacks among the arguments of development experts, rights advocates, and environmentalists, is the incompatibility of assumptions in discourses of environmentalism and human rights. These two discourses have developed along different trajectories.

Their recent intersection is spurred by the phenomenon of globalization, which has cast a spotlight upon issues at the intersection of nation-state sovereignty, world trade, and international cooperation. But this intersection brings into relief not only their shared areas of operation, but also some of their incompatible and conflicting assumptions.

Exploring the nature of the link between environmental rights, economic development, and human rights will require a brief foray into theoretical models of environmentalism. The multiple political valences within this single, seemingly simple field are often elided in popular discourse; sorting through them will help clarify some of the confusion characterizing the relations between and among these three areas.

Linked Concerns About Environment and Development in the Age of Globalization

Global trade in resources has existed since antiquity. It might be argued that dominant global powers have, at least since the industrial revolution, exploited the natural resources of peripheral countries: for example, the timber of New England forests was used to build British ships and Indian-grown cotton fed Manchester's textile mills. What makes contemporary globalization new, and particularly important for human rights advocates, is that it functions simultaneously through an intensification of the speed and scope of multiple processes, including transport and communication systems, international trade and the creation of its civil and political foundations, and the attempt to regulate ecological effects across national boundaries. Cross-border conflict over the environment, like all the other elements of globalization, predates the present period of "globalization." The 1905 Trail Smelter Arbitration (in which air pollution from a smelter in Trail, Canada, damaged the apple crop in U.S. state of Washington) articulated for the first time what later became (in the Stockholm Declaration's Principle 21) an axiom of international environmental law: that a state had the responsibility to ensure that activities within their jurisdiction did not damage the environment of another state.[15] The rapidly increasing pace of global environmental regulation, however, appears to pose a contradiction to the general direction of globalization: while most economic trends associated with globalization appear to oppose regulation, and (according to some commentators) to weaken the role of the nation-state,[16] the trend in global environmental policy has been toward more rather than less regulation, involving the attribution of greater responsibilities and duties to states.

The Earth Summit at Rio might have been, one observer suggests, the

Woodstock of the 1990s.[17] Notwithstanding the shortcomings of that analogy, it is clear that a significant aspect of the zeitgeist of the late twentieth century was on display when heads of state met in 1992 to discuss the state of "the environment," framed as an issue of resource management and conservation, inextricable from the global politics of economic development.[18]

It is undeniable that there has been a spate of international agreements on the use of common natural resources; however, the environment is often seen as a "special" kind of interest, at odds with economic development and urgent human needs. Environmentalism is commonly understood as an argument for the rights of nature qua nature. Environmentalists are envisioned as earthy sorts of people who love animals and organic food, and spend a lot of time hiking in national parks. They seem to have a romanticist faith in the magic of untouched land, and will spend large sums of money flying to lands they believe no human to have trod.[19] Preservationist and biocentrist environmentalists often argue for the rights of nature to exist independent of any relevance or use that nature might have to human beings. Ostensibly concerned with the survival of nonhuman species or with nebulous benefits to "future generations," the notion of "environmental rights" appears to many to be a more metaphysically or aesthetically motivated concern than human rights law, which addresses urgent issues of everyday survival. How, then, did such an issue come to be debated by heads of state at a 1992 summit, and what is the significance of the spate of environmental regulation that has accompanied the human rights and economic globalization trends of the late twentieth century?

Through the 1980s, a decade of the dramatic globalization of environmental concerns,[20] the image of Planet Earth came to dominate both the popular discourse of "nature lovers" and the directions of international environmental policy. By the end of the decade, picking up on this trend, *Time* magazine called 1988 the year that "the Earth spoke," and featured Earth, "Planet of the Year," as its cover model. The same decade saw the rising prominence of "global," or interdisciplinary, integrative modes of inquiry in the natural sciences, such as climatology and biogeochemistry.

In response to the burgeoning global concerns over issues such as carbon dioxide emissions and global warming, stratospheric ozone depletion, and disappearing soil, water, plant, and animal resources, the UN in 1983 created the World Commission on Environment and Development (WCED), chaired by the former prime minister of Norway, Gro Harlem Brundtland. Its report, *Our Common Future* (1987), said:

When the century began, neither human numbers nor technology had the power radically to alter planetary systems. As the century closes, not only do vastly increased human numbers and their activities have that power, but major, unintended changes are occurring in the atmosphere, in soils, in waters, among plants and animals, and in the relationships among all of these. The rate of change is outstripping the ability of scientific disciplines and our current capabilities to assess and advise. It is frustrating the attempts of political and economic institutions, which evolved in a different, more fragmented world, to adapt and cope.

The report of the Brundtland Commission introduced the concept of sustainable development into global discourse in numerous fields—scientific, technical, political, and economic. By the end of the decade, in December 1989, the UN General Assembly made plans to convene a world conference on the subject (this resulted in the June 1992 UN Conference on Environment and Development or UNCED, popularly known as the Earth Summit, in Rio). Meanwhile, Gro Brundtland, with private funds, established the Center for Our Common Future in Geneva. The center's main role was the promotion of a way to rethink politics in the coming age of global ecology.[21]

Versions of Environmentalism in the Age of Globalization

Nongovernmental and intergovernmental organizations quickly grew in importance through the globalization of environmentalist discourses; many of them have come to wield as much power as nation-states in environmental negotiations. Groups such as the Club of Rome and Brundtland's Center for Our Common Future put forward a strong critique of the "standard" environmental management model, whose basic assumptions (with roots in the nineteenth century, when this model had, most famously, influenced models of public health and social work) had long remained unchallenged. The standard view of environmental management assumed a zero sum between economic growth and environmental protection, and saw state intervention as its main tool. The state was expected to intervene to correct an environmental problem only when there was clear evidence of quantifiable damage to the environment and the failure of the market to "fix" it (e.g., acid rain). Several arguments coalesced in a critique that rejected this zero-sum thesis, postulating that economic development causes systematic environmental harm, and that proactive steps were needed, guided by scientific hypotheses (not necessarily scientific certainties or post hoc analyses), and through the participation of nonstate actors. Geographer David

Harvey chronicles the growth of wide support for this view (which he calls "ecological modernization"), tracing it to wider post–World War II trends:

> The rising tide of affluence in the advanced capitalist countries after World War II increased middle-class interest in environmental qualities and amenities, "nature" tourism, and deepened concerns about environmental dangers to health. . . . Systematic environmental concern for everything from landscape despoliation, heritage, and wilderness preservation, control of air and water quality, exposure to toxics, waste disposal, regulation of consumer products, and the like became much easier to voice given middle-class acceptance of such issues as fundamental to its own qualities of life. . . . *The Limits to Growth* (Meadows et al.) published in 1972, which in many respects was a powerful warning shot to say that the standard view was inadequate, was supported by the Club of Rome (an influential group of bankers and industrialists) and the Brundtland Report (WCED) of 1987. (Harvey 1996, 381)

Harvey notes that the move to bring the question of "sustainability" to the forefront of international and domestic politics was initiated and supported by government officials, industrialists, financiers, and scientists; since then some version of this thesis has gained favor among institutions such as the World Bank, corporations such as IBM, and politicians such as Margaret Thatcher and Al Gore.[22] Proponents of this view were often powerful forces in the creation of legally binding declarations such as the ones at Rio and Stockholm.

More "radical" ecologists of all political stripes, however, have challenged the emerging consensus on "ecological modernization." Much of the current work at the nexus of human rights, development, and environment seeks to alter or critique ecological modernization so as to take account of the even newer fields of environmental justice and political ecology. The site of emergence of these fields has most commonly been minority communities in the United States and third-world sites of resistance to large development projects.

Political ecology as a discipline has its origins in university geography departments in the 1970s, but like many of the other trends surveyed in this chapter, it grew rapidly in the period of globalization. As globalization has often had negative consequences for environmental and health standards, political ecology has proved useful as an analytical model not just for environmental geographers but also for scholars of health and human rights.[23] Political ecology holds that environmental problems cannot be addressed simply by bringing currently dominant stakeholders (such as the state, corporations, and international banks) to the table to negotiate a mutually acceptable compromise between growth and environmental quality. Rather, political ecologists wish to examine the historical, political, and economic contexts in which environmental problems have emerged, and to address these problems by acknowledging their political valences rather than by technocratic fiat. Political ecology tends to give greater weight to solutions originating in civil society, and accords importance to the role of environmental nongovernmental organizations (NGOs), indigenous groups, and other grassroots actors, while critiquing the model of state deregulation that often accompanies globalization scenarios. Political ecology tends to see third-world developmental programs as being in crisis, rather than needing slight modification, and to favor bottom-up rather than top-down solutions. The analysis of social and political power, and of its unequal relations on a global and historical scale, are for political ecologists key concepts in sketching "the topography of a politicised environment."[24] This view plays a large role in the cases examined later in this chapter.

There is another "radical" critique of ecological modernization—one that is mistakenly believed to be the most popular form of environmentalism. This is the biocentrist-preservationist view, which challenges mainstream efforts to unite the analysis of economics and the environment. Biocentrists argue that nature should be valued "for itself," and not for any economic benefit to humans.[25] This view uses the notion of "environmental rights" as analogous to human rights, implying that just as humans have an inalienable right to life, so too do animals, plants, and ecosystems. Environmental rights in this sense would be understood as an argument for the rights of nature qua nature. Although this is a historically and culturally specific version (associated with the growth of Euro-American middle-class interest in nature-related leisure activities), it has achieved the status of a near universal picture of environmentalism. This apparent universalization of a culturally specific view of environmental rights is a source of much confusion in the discussion of how to integrate frameworks of human and environmental rights.

Some critics of ecological modernization reject the biocentrist viewpoint too, arguing that integration by analogy is a weaker argument than a more substantive integration of these rights discourses. Rather than understanding environmental rights as the rights *of* the environment (as if the environment were an entity analogous to humans, entitled to its own rights), they argue that "environmental rights" should signify the rights of humans to have access to those elements of their environment that are vital to their survival, including a sustainable environment that supports their livelihood. One early document of the environmental justice movement critiqued biocentric environmentalism:

> If it is discovered that birds have lost their nesting sites, then environmentalists go to great expense and lengths to erect nesting boxes and find alternative breeding sites for them; when whales are stranded, enormous sums are spent to provide them food and shelter; when forests are threatened large numbers of people are mobilized to prevent damage; but we have yet to see an environmental group champion the cause of homelessness in humans or joblessness as issues on which it will spend vast resources. It is a strange paradox that a movement which exhorts the harmonious coexistence of people and nature, and worries about the continued survival of nature (particularly loss of habitat problems), somehow forgets about the survival of humans (especially those who have lost their "habitats" and "food sources").[26]

This critique of biocentrism differentiates environmental justice and political ecology from the other forms of environmental thinking, including "standard" environmental management and ecological modernization. The environmental justice movement (whose principles have now been incorporated into human rights documents such as the CERD) puts the survival of humans (and, in particular, those living on the political and economic margins) at the center of "environmental rights."[27] The combination of political ecology with environmental justice thus delineates a substantive link between environment and human rights.

The Applicability of Environmentalist Theories to Real-World Conflicts in the Global Economy

Consider the following recent instances of litigation, in which alleged abuses include both environmental and human rights issues. The pleadings in these cases appeal to a wide variety of legal precedents, but all link issues of environmental viability with human rights issues of life and health.

Freeport-McMoran's copper and gold mine in the highlands of Indonesia's Irian Jaya had, as of winter 2000, removed 400 feet of a mountain sacred to the local Amungme people, and polluted the surrounding ground and surface water with toxins. Early in the same year, the company continued to dump 160,000 tons per day of untreated toxic mine tailings into local waterways (expected, at the time, to rise to 285,000 tons per day). The massive release of sediment created an artificial floodplain, destroying the river and inundating surrounding rainforests. The Amungme people suffer from chronic starvation, exacerbated by the exposure to toxic chemicals, the pollution of their water, and the destruction of their lands. Two cases have been brought against Freeport-McMoran, alleging the denial of right to life as a result of the destruction of the Amungme's environment and resources.[28]

Between 1972 and 1992, Texaco drilled oil in the Ecuadorian Amazon, cutting 18,000 miles of trail and 300 miles of road through pristine rainforest. Ignoring the standard industry practice of pumping waste back into wells, Texaco dumped toxic by-products of its drilling operations onto local roads, streams, and wetlands. Water resources which had been used by the locals for drinking, fishing, and bathing were rendered toxic. Texaco filled 600 pits with toxic waste; these regularly washed out in heavy rain, causing rashes, flu, and swollen throats in locals, and contaminating farmland and the water supply. *Sequiha v. Texaco, Inc.*, was a suit brought by Ecuadorian residents for damages caused by environmental contamination from Texaco's oil development in the Ecuadorian Oriente region.

After exposure to dibromochloropropane (DBCP), Costa Rican banana plantation workers suffered various forms of physical impairment, including sterility. DBCP is a chemical banned in the United States, but exported to Costa Rica by Dow. In *Dow Chemical v. Castro Alfaro* it was alleged that Dow was responsible for human rights violations, on the basis of the effects of its environmentally hazardous chemical on human workers.

In *Torres v. Southern Peru Copper Corp.*, over 700 Peruvian plaintiffs brought suit against a mining company, alleging that they had been harmed by sulfur dioxide emissions from mining operations run by U.S. and Peruvian companies.

U.S. and Japanese patents on indigenous Indian plant products such as neem, turmeric, "curry," and basmati are being challenged in European courts by a coalition of Indian NGOs, scientists, and the Council for Scientific and Industrial Research (CSIR), a state-funded research organization. U.S. patents awarded on turmeric (to two University of Mississippi researchers), and on a neem-based fungicide (to the U.S. Department of Agriculture and the pharmaceutical corporation W. R. Grace), have been overturned.

In September 1998 a complaint was lodged with the attorney general of California alleging that the Union Oil Company of California (Unocal) had violated international human rights law as well as international and domestic (U.S) laws against environmental degradation. Introducing several pages of allegations of Unocal's harm to the environment in regions of Burma and California, the petitioners claimed: "The company's environmental devastation extends from local to global and is serious enough to describe as ecocide." The list of twenty-seven petitioners included individuals and NGOs, environmentalists and human rights advocates, and third-

and first-worlders, representing diverse elements of Burmese and American civil society. The legal petition incorporated alleged violations of the entire range (first, second, and third generations) of human rights conventions, Agenda 21 (report of the UNCED at the Rio Earth Summit), the UN Framework Convention on Climate Change, and several conventions of the International Labour Organization (ILO) concerning forced labor and indigenous and tribal peoples.

The cases sketched above, and several more like them that have cropped up in the last five years, have in common the overlap of environmental and human rights claims with issues of economic development. Unlike "environmentalist" issues in affluent parts of the first world, the notion of access to the "environment," in nonelite sections of the developing world, is inextricable from demands for economic and social justice.[29] Excessive pollution can kill—it violates individuals' right to life.[30] Less immediate, but just as severe, has been the destruction of life wrought by development projects in areas where residents have had little outside contact. Diseases to which locals have had little immunity are brought in by project workers; the sudden impact of human flows brought by the project's roads and infrastructure is devastating to human lives and environments. Less direct still, but again just as severe, are the effects of patenting on the prices of drugs and pharmaceuticals.[31] Multinational control of patented drugs tends to price medicines outside the affordable range for working and middle-class people in the developing world, often excluding them from life-saving medications and resulting in their untimely and avoidable death.[32]

Environmental rights in this sense are different in kind from biocentric "rights of nature," or from legislation protecting the right of "the environment" to be protected from human harm. In each of the cases mentioned above, the human right to life cannot be defended without intervening in the process by which privatization and degradation of a resource base occur at the hands of an institution that has no local accountability.

The link between human and environmental rights is simple: the degradation of a resource base takes human lives. That degradation can happen in a number of ways, including excessive local use. Local or indigenous users are not inherently more eco-friendly than distant or global actors.[33] However, this has happened most dramatically, as in the cases above, when a domain once held in public trust by the state, or by a community with common rights, is transferred to private multinational control.[34] This process offers us a conceptual link between seemingly disparate concerns such as toxic dumping and intellectual property rights. Just as chemical pollutants in lakes can deprive a population of water, chemical patents have caused locally used common resources (such as neem leaves) to be priced out of the reach of local people. The neem tree, for instance, is integral to the life of a villager, from brushing his teeth to keeping his cows and crops healthy. When a product patent raises the price of a resource that was formerly free,[35] the villager's life is compromised. In understanding the mode of this compromise, political ecologists would argue that we cannot detach economic rights from environmental rights, nor analyze human rights in a manner that ignores the global power differentials that facilitate the functioning of transnationals in dispersed locations and with diffused accountability.

Legal redress for the entire range of harms in cases such as these cannot be supported by environmental law alone, narrowly conceived. On the other hand, the full range of protection needed to protect the victims' capacity to survive is not available under the International Covenant on Civil and Political Rights (ICCPR) and the International Covenant on Economic, Social, and Cultural Rights (ICESCR) alone, strictly interpreted. However, several legal scholars have proposed that a combination of existing environmental law and the three "generations" of human rights law can constitute a convincing legal argument for the defense of the human right to immediate and continued survival, in cases like these. Legal scholar Richard Herz argues that "international law recognizes a right to a healthy environment based on, although independent from, the rights to life, health, and security of the person. The right to a healthy environment is universal and obligatory. Moreover, it has a definable core of prohibited behavior."[36] As evidence, Herz invokes the combination of environmental and human rights law, listing the numerous international conventions on the environment (such as the Stockholm and Rio declarations), in conjunction with Article 1 of the ICCPR and the ICESCR ("All peoples may, for their own ends, freely dispose of their natural wealth and resources"), and the Indigenous Peoples' Convention, which "contains a variety of provisions protecting indigenous peoples' environments and their ability to retain control over decisions affecting those environments."[37] In support of this legislation is the widespread recognition of the key role played by health factors in human rights promotion. Herz strengthens the argument for environmental rights as human rights by noting that the right to health implies freedom from pollution, from the illicit dumping of toxic waste, and even from nonpolluting factors—such as the penetration of Yanomani lands by road development, which caused the degradation of Yanomani health and environments.

Herz argues that international law (in the areas of environmental, health, civil, political, economic, social, and cultural human rights) offers strong support for seeking redress in U.S. courts, under the Alien Tort Claims

Act, for environment-related human rights abuses facilitated by transnational corporations (TNCs) around the globe. Because the areas of health and environment belong to the third generation of human rights agreements, and because they are relatively new areas in the legal arenas, this argument bears analysis from both a practical as well as a theoretical standpoint.[38]

Although Herz makes a strong legal argument for the conjoining of environmental and human rights issues based on the existence of conventions, treaties, custom, scholarship, and precedent, there are nevertheless many practical obstacles that can and do present themselves to this still novel approach to the implementation of international and domestic law. Some of the cases cited above are under appeal; some have been dismissed under concerns of international comity or forum non conveniens;[39] still others have been dismissed because the plaintiff used environmental law in isolation from human rights law, or because of "judicial hostility" to international law claims and "general misgivings about the domestic applicability of international law."[40] Actions that violate the law of nations can allow parties to be sued in court even if they are private (rather than purely state) actors, if they satisfy the tests applied under U.S. Code Title 42 Section 1983, "Civil action for deprivation of rights," (to determine state involvement in private action or private involvement in state action).[41] Herz points out a related obstacle to litigation: when "the suit involves development supported by a repressive regime, litigation may present grave risks to plaintiffs' and witnesses' lives." [42] Further, in cases where indigenous groups have opposed development projects, TNCs have been known to engineer support with the help of local leaders, both military and indigenous.[43] In a 1999 report on human rights violations in Nigeria's oil-producing communities, Human Rights Watch (HRW), a U.S. NGO, listed recommendations to three kinds of parties—state, corporate, and international agencies. Among HRW's recommendations to the Nigerian government were to "[c]ease harassment of individuals and organizations that engage in research into oil industry compliance with environmental and other international and industry standards, and of activists seeking to hold oil operators and their contractors to these standards."[44] The HRW report recognizes the need for conjoining human and environmental rights advocacy, using the metaphor of environmental protection to advocate human rights protections:

> To carry out a "human rights impact assessment," identifying in particular problems related to security provision and conflict resolution, in addition to the already required "environmental impact assessment," to develop plans to

avoid the problems identified by such assessments, and to cancel the project if they cannot be avoided.[45]

The HRW report also calls on international oil companies to abide by human rights conventions, and to monitor the operation of state security forces working with them:

> Include in written agreements with the Nigerian government relating to the regulation of the oil industry, especially any agreements relating specifically to security, provisions requiring state security forces operating in the area of company operations to conform to the human rights obligations the government has assumed under the International Covenant on Civil and Political Rights, the African Charter on Human and Peoples' Rights and other international human rights and humanitarian norms.[46]

Also addressed to international corporations is this recommendation:

> Insist on screening security force members assigned for their protection, to ensure that no member of the military or police credibly implicated in past human rights abuses is engaged in protecting oil facilities. Companies should similarly screen security staff in their direct employment.[47]

HRW's final category of recommendations, addressed to the "international community," calls for the development of guidelines to oversee the conduct of multinational companies with respect to human rights and environmental rights.

Reports from both legal observers, such as Herz, and NGOs, such as Human Rights Watch, seem to indicate that there is a growing class of situations in which human rights and environmental rights are tangled, and in which actors include not just states but also international agencies, individuals, and TNCs whose activities are entwined in global webs of interdependence. This situation embodies the characteristic complexity of many globalization scenarios. It would be premature to carry a practical analysis of the policy implications further at this point, since the relationship of these multifarious actors to international human rights law and in turn to domestic law is still being negotiated. As Saskia Sassen notes, the global economy is still a work in progress, not reducible to simple inversions of prior relationships between states, transnational corporations, and the legal and financial systems they take part in. It is still in the process of being "produced, reproduced, serviced, financed."[48] How these relations will be worked out remains to be seen.

Although it is not easy to predict the practical resolutions of this question, it is useful to step back and ask which analytical model best fits the growing trend of integration of these multiple issues. This chapter moves, then, back to the question of analytical frameworks of environmentalism, development, and human rights. What models are likely to be the most useful as globalization's multifarious actors struggle to negotiate their modes of integration into the new order?

At first glance, the familiar opposition between "globalization by dominant cultures" and "resistance from peripheral cultures" seems evident in the last two decades of environmental politics. On the one hand, we see an institutional consensus on "sustainable development" emerging among the developed world's major political and financial institutions, and being extended to the developing world via trade agreements and multilateral treaties. On the other hand, we see resistance to this model (with its normative "limits to growth" and curbs on certain kinds of development) on the part of many developing states.[49] On a closer look, however, we also see a growing "grassroots" resistance to dominant models of environment and development, opposing the universalisms espoused by both developed and developing states. Yet it would be incorrect to label these as purely local, particularist, or necessarily antistatist positions. Many grassroots groups actively participate in the construction of "competing" universalisms intended to correct or replace dominant universalisms. Conceptually, these models attempt to construct an alternative theory of development, in opposition to the dominant "new world order," by critically reworking "top-down" discourses of environmental sustainability. Practically, local actors work to "universalize" this alternative vision by working in conjunction with diverse global networks of NGOs, lawyers, academics, and activists. Their critiques are not entirely antistatist, calling often for revising (sometimes increasing) the role of the state in national and international development.

Thus, in an increasingly interlinked, "globalized" world, what we see cannot accurately be described as a binary conflict between globalizing and localizing tendencies, or between modernity and tribalism. Rather we see multivalent globalized webs, composed of theoretical and practical conjunctures within and across developed and developing nations, linking the emerging definitions of globalized society with competing models of local articulation. Actors in these multivalent webs articulate not just two opposed positions on the environment (pro- versus anticonservationist, or sustainable versus unsustainable), but several, more nuanced versions of "environmentalism."

The local and global import of these versions of "environmentalism" and associated rights cannot be understood in isolation from a historical and political analysis of power relations. As in the case of the Unocal petition, we see that both sides in the conflict attempt to use the power of global networks in order to advance their own conceptions of what a globalized society ought to look like. While oil corporations and their consumers believe that globalized production must serve the needs of a growing consumer economy, indigenous resisters believe that globalized human rights regimes must serve the needs of democratic governance, and build coalitions with first-world groups in order to press that claim. A sampling of the twenty-seven groups involved in filing the Unocal complaint indicates its global scope, and its grounding in elements of an emerging "global" civil society: petitioners included the Free Burma Coalition, the National Lawyers Guild of U.S.A., the Burma Forum, the Transnational Resource and Action Center, the Program on Corporations, Law, and Democracy, and even "distantly" interested groups such as the National Organization for Women and the Surfer's Environmental Alliance. [50] The body of the petition includes the text of a letter written by Burmese Karen high school students to Unocal:

> [Y]ou said that if you give your western values and culture to the people in Burma then it will be interesting and good for them. But personally, we think that our ethnic groups in Burma are not interested in your culture. They want to keep and develop their own culture and live in freedom and peace. Your culture is a very big culture, and so we are afraid [for] our small culture. Our small culture could be lost easily, because of your big culture. So, although you may think you have found the way to save our people in Burma from oppression it is actually the way to encourage the SLORC to push us down.

Although statements such as these, in defense of local cultures, are often construed as being "antiglobalization," or as opposing the global spread of human rights regimes, it is important to note that the contexts in which they are produced and disseminated are irreducibly global. The coalition that carries this Karen statement to a California court is a fundamentally global alliance, although rooted in the specificities of local politics and economics. The combining of local interests and global efficacy is not an impossible paradox, but a constitutive feature of the global order. In this case, the group that challenges the effects of globalized production, a coalition involving a diversity of actors from California surfers to Karen children, supports rather than rejects the globalization of human rights regimes, as is apparent from the list of human rights conventions to which the petition appeals.

The formation of such alliances, and the arguments they employ, suggest further that both biocentrism and the "ecological modernization" version of sustainable development are being eschewed in favor of a model of global politics that appears closer to the tenets of political ecology and environmental justice. The biocentrist argument is not invoked in any of these instances of litigation. Indeed, biocentrism is opposed to the very idea of construing nature as a resource. Biocentric arguments in favor of a forest's inherent right to exist would probably militate against any kind of use, whether by indigenous peoples or TNCs. From a policymaker's perspective, this enhances neither the survival of the locals nor the economic needs of the global actors. In fact, the biocentrist argument could conceivably create the context for human rights violations, as in the case of state parks or national forests from which, in the interest of preserving natural elements, indigenous peoples are expelled despite the threat to their survival created by separating them from their traditional sources of food, shelter, and livelihood.[51]

Both the older "standard" model of environmental management and the ecological modernization argument for sustainable development would suggest that the environment and economic development are both "goods" worth pursuing, but that difficult decisions sometimes have to be made in the interest of increased productivity and growth. The destruction or degradation of human lives then becomes the unfortunate by-product of a technocratic decision to favor one side of a binary choice. Policymakers are cast onto the horns of a dilemma when the question of environmentalism is cast in this binary mode, and good faith decisions have been made by development organizations based on such reasoning, leading to a trade-off between "environment" and "development."

The environmental justice model as articulated by one of its major U.S. advocates, Robert Bullard, is clearly differentiated from technicist management models, and its primary purpose is defined as the correction of environment-related inequities:

> The question of environmental justice is not anchored in a debate about whether decision makers should tinker with risk-based management. The environmental justice framework rests upon an ethical analysis of strategies to eliminate unfair, unjust, and inequitable conditions and decisions. . . . The environmental justice framework incorporates other social movements that seek to eliminate harmful practices (discrimination harms the victim) in housing, land use, industrial planning, health care, and sanitation.[52]

"Environmental justice," as used by Bullard (and by institutions such as the U.S. Environmental Protection Agency), is akin to social justice: the word "environmental," substituting for "social," indicates that the human condition is analyzed in conjunction with its surroundings, including its physical, natural, and historical contexts. Similarly, "political ecology" evokes a kinship with "political economy"; the word "ecology" suggesting, once again, an attention to the natural and physical contexts that were often absent in traditional political economy. The political ecology perspective is useful to both local and global contexts involving humans and the environment, because it begins with the dual recognition of the economic and political constitution of ecological problems, and the ecological constitution of human rights problems.

Using the framework of political ecology for the analysis of environmental conflict shows why and how globalized production can often work separately from the interests of human rights advocates, sometimes leading to human rights abuses. These cases show that economic globalization does not always entail the diffusion of liberal democracy. As the HRW report on Nigeria notes, globalized production often facilitates coalitions between TNCs and oppressive state apparatus, enhancing illiberal actions such as coercion, torture, imprisonment, and the degradation of the environment, rather than bringing in its wake the liberal rights to life and dignity, or the civil and political practices of liberal democracy. The responses to these situations show that locals do not resist globalization per se. They are more accurately understood, in the cases surveyed above, as resisting threats to their survival by appealing to legal systems in dominant nations on the basis of human rights claims. In other words, they respond to the "TNC–oppressive state" coalition by building an equally global coalition among victims (in developing countries), lawyers (in developed countries, with legal institutions that incorporate precedents in the defense of environmental conditions and human rights), and international human rights advocacy groups. The response from "local" contexts is not a "particularist" opposition to "universalist" globalization. Nor is this response ever purely local. It is in itself an instance of the globalization of the effort to protect human rights to life and a healthy environment, in resistance to the globalization of production (and its accompanying political ecological effects). Thus we see competing universalisms rather than universalism versus particularism.

Political Ecology and Its Implications for Three Generations of Human Rights

The conjoining of environmental rights with human rights brings the theories of political ecology to life in a practical sense: they go from being scholarly arguments to being a political philosophy for environmentalists, human rights advocates, and legal practitioners. Globalization is rapidly changing the meanings, implications, and consequences of everyday actions, and human rights often suffer because we do not yet have rights-monitoring institutions or analytical frameworks that have kept up with the changes. There is a growing dialogue in many disciplines and professions about how to forge a globalized society that is committed to human rights and is able to respond to globalization's many challenges to humans' economic, social, cultural, and collective needs.

Many of the most publicized cases of resource depletion or destruction—from dumping to patenting—have occurred in the developing world. The weakness of environmental regulation in the developing world was one reason multinationals chose to locate production facilities there. However, as the General Agreement on Tariffs and Trade (GATT)/Trade-Related Intellectual Property (TRIPS) and other agreements under the World Trade Organization are implemented in more and more national contexts, trends indicate a diminution rather than an increase in environmental and economic regulation. This raises a well known "paradox" of globalization: human rights violations that follow in the wake of offshore production siting, and less dramatic but debilitating erosions of social services (such as health and education), resulting from structural adjustment measures, are justified by states in the name of economic growth and the establishment of a global marketplace. Although globalization creates a global consumer class who are indeed finding themselves wealthier and more globally "wired," marginalized populations across the globe bear the brunt of the effects of deregulation, suffering from economic, social, and cultural displacement.

Scholars of political ecology challenge the ideological separation of politics from economics, and suggest that neither humans nor their nonhuman environments are viable in the absence of economic, political, civil, and social equity. They argue that this equity must be procedural as well as substantive. It must, they suggest, simultaneously decentralize political decisionmaking power (as, for example, in the rights of indigenous peoples and local communities to make independent decisions regarding the use and control of their resources) and level the playing field economically. Political ecological studies conclude that making economically and socially disadvantaged people better off and giving them control over the use of their resources will render them better able to prevent the environment from being taken hostage by dominant financial powers, and in turn allow the continued survival of locals who subsist on that environment.[53]

The world's most biodiversity-rich regions house the most economically disadvantaged populations, who are also the most nature-dependent for their livelihood.[54] These populations are rarely players at the table when their lands are handed over for the use of multinational corporations, nor can they easily gain redress in their domestic judiciaries when their lakes are filled with oil-field waste or their trees are harvested for distant markets. Political ecology revises the meaning of "environmentalism" to analyze these interlinked phenomena. The dominant interpretation of environmentalism as referring to the domain of biocentric preservation then appears to be a particular, culturally specific view,[55] and one that Northern activists may not be successful in "universalizing."

Understanding environmental rights as human rights in the context of political ecology thus implies a notion of environmentalism fundamentally different from the one propounded by mainstream environmentalist organizations such as the Sierra Club, and from radical environmental groups such as Earth First! The political ecological notion does commonly characterize environmentalism in the developing world, but is also closely tied to understandings of environmentalism in the pockets of "third worlds" within the first world.[56] This analytical approach to environmentalism adopts a global outlook that attempts to understand different local conflicts in one integrated framework, rather than as particularist holdouts against one universalism.

As an analogy to the growth of environmental rights, one might look at the campaign for health as a human right. Although health issues began as a marginal and seemingly secondary concern for human rights advocates, they have increasingly come to the fore in international human rights discussions. One particularly interesting feature of this discussion is the ways the growth of the "right to health" argument has been propelled not by large institutions such as the UN, nor by "hard" international law and state policy. The case of Doctors Without Borders is instructive. As a nongovernmental organization with humanitarian objectives, Doctors Without Borders drew its early power from people who put the immediate needs of the afflicted above political interests. Its bottom-up strategy placed an emphasis on doctors rather than politicians, suffering people (and peoples)[57] rather than nation-states. The movement, explicitly challenging the sovereignty of states and the nationalism produced by it, asserted the right to interfere in national activities if people were suffering. Antagonistic though it might be to states and international institutions' respect for traditional notions of sovereignty, Doctors Without Borders has seen its positions steadily gain acceptance at the level of "soft" international law. Many of its concepts have become institutionalized—for example, they were adopted into the policies of the French government under the presidency of François Mitterand. The UN General Assembly has incorporated Doctors Without Borders' concept of "the right to interfere, in spite of frontiers and in spite of States, if suffering persons need aid."[58]

Nevertheless, Doctors Without Borders has had to contend with some of the contradictions of operating globally across cultural and national differences. Despite avowing a pacifist attitude toward weapons, it has had to reverse its position on militarization, as it has been impossible sometimes to gain access to conflict situations without the protection of armed forces. It has also repeatedly crossed the traditional boundary between human rights advocacy and politics, as for instance in its campaign against TRIPS in developing countries. Humanitarian crimes often admit to no purely humanitarian or apolitical solution. Health workers have had to contend with the politics of conflict situations when they are on the ground in the midst of them.[59] This is also the case with a recent HRW report (*Broken People*, March 1999) on caste violence in India. Caste violence cannot be understood, or combated, HRW learned, if we adopt a neutral or relativist position with respect to economic status and cultural norms. Although violence is often perpetrated by both upper and lower castes upon each other, *Broken People* effectively took a political position in seeing the violence as based in economic and cultural oppression of Dalits by upper castes. Just as the force of arms that protects Doctors Without Borders is explained as a protective measure against illegitimate violence, *Broken People* allows us to see Dalits' oppression as explaining their need for self-defense in the absence of state protection. This kind of argument links all three generations of human rights into one analytical framework, and thus has policy implications that are different from arguments stemming purely from the first generation of human rights.

The conjoint analysis of political ecology and international environmental law in the context of indigenous communities who are dependent on the integrity of their ecologies suggests, finally, a further extension of the study of globalization and human rights. Scholars of globalization who subscribe to a "competing universalisms" model are likely to next ask whether the ratification of "third-generation" rights (to healthy selves and environments/collective rights) might raise the vision of a globalized world that looks radically different, culturally and politically, from the one in which TNCs and states forge the motor of globalization through capitalist production. The global futures associated with the globalization of production and the globalization of human rights are not necessarily convergent scenarios. It is in this sense that we are faced with a choice, not between a universalist and a particularist world, but between two competing universalist models of a global world.

Herein perhaps lies the core of the "competing universalism" of political ecology. It is a universalism that holds that the struggle for civil and political rights cannot be dissociated from the struggle for economic rights and solidarity rights. Such a universalist claim might evoke fears among advocates of the "first generation" of human rights (civil and political rights) that straying into the second generation (economic and social rights) and the third generation (collective rights to health, heritage, and environment) can take "human rights" too far, until it is indistinguishable from "social justice."

Some first-world human rights advocates indeed hold that the issues of economic, social, and cultural rights, and of rights to environment, health, and heritage, are concerns outside the purview of human rights, or that enforcing these second- and third-generation rights might possibly undermine the competitive force and globalizing drive of capitalism. Questions about the future directions of human rights and the nature of the globalized society being constructed are thus bound up together.

The work of legal scholar Anthony Anghie emphasizes the rift between these competing models of globalization and rights.[60] He raises substantive questions about the political future of human rights work, arguing that competing models of human rights accompany these competing views of the foundations of globalized society. Anghie diagnoses an intensifying division in human rights between the principles of human dignity and well-being as they are embodied in the ICCPR and the ICESCR, on the one hand, and the "marketized" version of human rights, on the other. Human rights has been historically, he reminds us, "an area of contestation, a means of protecting property and preserving inequalities on the one hand, and a liberating force that insists on human dignity on the other."[61] Globalization exacerbates this divide, while privileging the marketized version over the more substantive combination of the ICCPR and the ICESCR. By ignoring the politics of economic power, human rights advocates are effectively ceding human rights turf to the most powerful actor, which is currently the multinational corporation. The ideological separation of politics from economics, then, may well cause traditional notions of human rights to be superseded by newer, slicker, marketized versions, which are at best ambivalent about the economic disparities perpetuated by international financial institutions (IFIs), multinational corporations, and Northern states.

Anghie argues, in a detailed review of post–World War II economic development of the third world directed by IFIs, that the development of the third world as a source of cheap resources and labor, and as a source of untapped markets for consumer goods, perpetuates a colonial model of development that is disadvantageous to developing countries, especially their poorer populations.[62]

> The assumption . . . that the economic development and structural adjustment programs fostered by the IFIs with the aim of improving living standards will in themselves better human welfare, and hence human rights, is highly questionable.[63]

Moreover, the conflict between the multiple interpretations of human rights (Substantive or procedural? Traditional or marketized? Civil or economic or both?) is masked, rather than articulated, by the positivist tendency that seeks to remove politics from these discussions. The effort to "remove" politics simply masks dominant actors' political stakes, rendering the free hand of the market the de facto agent of human rights.

> Within the new human rights discourse proposed by the [World] Bank, however, the tensions between civil and political rights on the one hand, and economic and social rights on the other, appear to have been resolved. The market provides the answer, for the market calls into being the "good government," one which protects civil and political rights and provides the economic growth that is essential to securing economic and social goods. . . . The market becomes the ultimate good.[64]

No clear answers have yet emerged to the question of which version of human rights will prevail in a globalized economy. However, the dominant trends indicate the growing ability of the market (involving TNCs and IFIs in coalition with nation-states) to define political and economic outcomes. Caren Irr (Chapter 1) suggests, analogously, that a globalized marketplace will prove fundamentally incompatible with collective rights to culture. If a global free market proves incompatible, similarly, with group rights to a common heritage based on resource use, or with rights to health, dependent on the preservation of a nontoxic environment, it is likely that political ecology will be fundamental to the debates over "third-generation" human rights. That encounter, too, should be understood not as a standoff between a modernizing vision of globalized markets and a traditionalist vision of customary communities, but as a negotiation between competing versions of a globalized world, each based on an assertion of its own universalizable worth and validity.

Notes

1. The metaphor is paraphrased from Barber 1995, "Jihad vs. McWorld."
2. Janis 1999, 47.
3. See Kuhn 1970. During the paradigm shift from classical to quantum mechanical world views, multiple disciplines, including chemistry, physics, and other basic sciences, attempted to explore similar questions at the foundations of quantum mechanics. When a paradigm shifts, it affects multiple fields, which appear to converge upon the central new problematic; when it settles down, the fields once again shift back into their autonomous and possibly diverging/unrelated programs of research.
4. See Jameson and Miyoshi 1998; Lowe and Lloyd 1997; and Huntington 1996 for different versions of this assumption.
5. See Chapter 10.
6. This more complex picture of globalization is fleshed out in studies by Saskia Sassen (1998), Fredric Jameson and Masao Miyoshi (1998), and Lisa Lowe and David Lloyd (1997).
7. On-the-Record Briefing on the Release of the Initial Report of the United States of America to the United Nations Committee on the Elimination of Racial Discrimination, Washington, DC, September 21, 2000, available at www.state.gov/www/global/human_rights/cerd_report/cerd_index.html
8. Herz 2000, p. 586, citing the UN's Ksentini Report.
9. UN World Conference on Human Rights: Vienna Declaration and Programme of Action, June 25, 1993.
10. This list of international declarations draws on Herz 2000 and Rosencranz and Campbell 1999. See http://fletcher.tufts.edu/multilaterals.html for the full text of many of these declarations, and for the major human rights conventions. On the Yanomani case, Richard Herz cites 1985 Inter-American Yearbook on Human Rights (Dordrecht: Martinus Nihoff) and an article by William Shutkin, "International Human Rights Law and the Earth: The Protection of Indigenous Peoples and the Environment," *Virginia Journal of International Law* 31, no. 479 (1991): 496–497. On the Beanal case, Herz cites *Beanal v. Freeport-McMoran, Inc.*, 969 F. Supp. 362, 382–384 (E.D. La 997), aff'd no. 98–30235, 999 U.S. App. LEXIS 31356 (5th Cir., November 29, 1999). In affirming the district court, the Fifth Circuit only considered "sources of international environmental law."
11. Robert Lutz, professor of law, Southwestern University School of Law.
12. Lutz et al. 1988, p. 41.
13. Ibid..
14. Contrary to the Bank's attitude, Alston suggested, the Bank did not have a real choice about whether it should or should not take account of human rights. At stake was the honoring or violation of UN Charter provisions "obligating all member states, and surely all U.N. organizations, to promote respect for human rights," treaty obligations under the international covenants on human rights, and "clearly enunciated principles of customary international law, principles emphasized in various cases decided since the 1960s by which time the Bank already had gone almost irrevocably into its shell on human rights issues." To debate whether or not the Bank should take account of human rights was thus like debating

whether the Bank had the option of being "an accomplice in the violation of those treaty obligations" Ibid., 52–53.

15. Weintraub 1992, 5 (online version, www.elj.org/archives/nyuelj173t.html).

16. Saskia Sassen points out the error in the oft-posited zero-sum duality between global system and nation-state. Rather than weakening the significance of nation-states, globalization reconfigures their territoriality so that they are able to produce, service, and finance the new global economy, often through strengthening certain components of national states, even such "traditional" ones as ministries of finance. She views deregulation "not simply as a loss of control by the state but as a crucial mechanism to negotiate the juxtaposition of the inter-state consensus to pursue globalization and the fact that national legal systems remain as the major, or crucial instantiation through which guarantees of contract and property rights are enforced" (1999, 24).

17. Brown et al. 1997.

18. Few remember that U.S. President George Bush kept the participants wondering, until the last minute, whether he would attend at all. If the notion of the "environment" was a marginal item on the presidential agenda in 1992, the fact that all presidential candidates in 2000 had to articulate some position on the environment is a measure of the issue's rapid move to a more central position. Political theorists Michael Renner (1997) and Norman Myers (1993) have argued that environmental stability is crucial to global political security. Renner redefines post–Cold War security issues as having moved from "national security" to "human security." His definition of the latter notion sounds much like the combined concepts of human rights and human dignity (Renner 1997, 116).

19. This phenomenon has been studied by environmental economists. See, for example, Gardner Brown Jr. and Robert Mendelsohn, "The Hedonic Travel Cost Method," *The Review of Economics & Statistics* 66, no. 427 (1984): 427–433; and Richard G. Walsh et al., "Valuing Option, Existence, and Request Demands for Wilderness," *Land Economics* 60, 14 (1984): 14–29. Citing these studies, Bernard Weintraub (1992) explains: "The hedonic travel cost method calculates the value of resources, such as national parks, based on a demand curve extrapolated from consumers' willingness to travel various distances to enjoy them. Existence value is a measure of value attached to those experiences that a consumer enjoys (i.e., is willing to pay for) simply because she knows they exist, even though he may never experience them first hand" (202 n.115).

20. The roots of modern environmentalism can of course be traced back through twentieth-century American defenders of nature such as John Muir and Rachel Carson, to eighteenth-century New World settlers (see Nash 1967). For older and more global histories, see Grove 1995 and Glacken 1967.

21. Finger, in Sachs 1993.

22. Harvey 1996, 381.

23. See, for example, Kim et al. 2000, a collection of essays on health and human rights that explicitly invoke political ecology as an analytical framework (e.g., chap. 5 is titled "Theoretical Therapies, Remote Remedies: SAPs and the Political Ecology of Poverty and Health in Africa").

24. Bryant and Bailey 1997, 39.

25. See, for example, Devall and Sessions 1985. Although very few active groups can sustain a purely biocentric argument (as it is constituted by inherent

internal contradictions), the notions of "protecting nature," "defending the environment," "saving the planet," and so on, are used widely in popular environmental discourse, perpetuating the impression that campaigners are fighting for the rights of "the earth" to exist in and of itself. See James Lovelock's "Gaia Hypothesis" (Lovelock 1988) for another source of the belief that the earth is a self-aware system with an inherent right to dignity and preservation.

26. Taylor 1992, cited in Harvey 1996, 386.

27. Biocentrism comes in many versions, both religious and secular. Some versions are part of legal campaigns to accord rights to elements of nature (e.g., forests, apes) understood as persons in their own right, rather than as property. Although many of these legal efforts use the analogy of human rights (see, for example, the Great Ape Legal Project, www.aldf.org/chimp.htm), they must be understood as separate from the (anthropocentric) issue of human survival. Whether or not the biocentric legal argument is successful in the courts, it will be important for human rights advocates to understand this view, and to understand the structure of its argument by analogy with human rights. In the event that this form of argument is dismissed from legal purview, it will be important for us to ensure that the human rights baby is not thrown out with the biocentric bath water. That is, we can advocate the protection of human survival in the context of individuals' and communities' environmental needs even if we do not hold the elements of nature, understood as legal persons, to have inalienable rights. In fact, the sustainable use of natural resources (rather than their preservation, in and for themselves, in a pristine state) is essential to the survival of many indigenous groups. The environmentalist positions surveyed here do not compose an exhaustive list. For examples of the seemingly endless variety of disciplines and positions under the umbrella of environmentalism, see Harvey 1996, chap. 6, chap. 8; and Redclift and Benton 1994, 12.

28. *Alomang v. Freeport-McMoran, Inc.*, and *Beanal v. Freeport.* In the former case, Freeport has employed many of the standard strategies to dismiss foreign-party litigation, but has so far failed. Alomang's attorney has indicated plans to make the lawsuit a class action to include 10,000 Indonesians, and take the case to a jury trial. See Rosencranz and Campbell 1999.

29. Linkages between environment and social justice in the developing world are similar to the issues raised by the environmental justice movement in the United States, which began in Warren County, South Carolina, and spread rapidly to other marginalized and exploited neighborhoods across the country. It articulated "environmentalism" in a mode that distinguished itself, often critically, from the middle-class "nature-loving" narrative more common in mainstream America. It voiced the resource needs—including water, housing, and nontoxic air—of African American and Latino populations, who experience environmental racism across the United States. See Bullard 1994.

30. This is most famously seen in the case of the methyl isocyanate leak from the Union Carbide factory in Bhopal.

31. This rise in prices is most dramatic in contexts in which agricultural and pharmaceutical inventions have previously been specifically excluded from patentability, as was the case in most developing nations before the implementation of the TRIPS provisions of the GATT. See, for instance, the 1970 Patents Act of India (reproduced in Sinnot 1991). It excludes from patenting "any process for the

medicinal, surgical, curative, prophylactic, or other treatment of human beings or any process for a similar treatment of animals or plants to render them free of disease or to increase their economic value or that of their products" (§ 3[h] and § 3[i]).

32. See the Medecins sans Frontiers website, www.msf.org, for examples of inescapably politicized situations at the intersection of health and human rights.

33. Historical evidence shows, however, that small self-sustainable communities with little demand for "outside" commodities have reached an equilibrium with their environments more often than have global extractive systems. However, this is not due to a biological or essential indigenous closeness to nature. Rather, it is contingent on socially reproduced modes of resource use, which are rapidly breaking down in the globalized world as communities are increasingly denied the choice of being purely local.

34. This explanation reverses the neoclassical claim of the inevitable "tragedy of the commons." For an overview of the legal implications of the tragedy of the "anticommons," see Aoki 1998. Needless to say, the debate over whether privatization or common holdings inevitably lead to degradation is extensive, and would take me far afield. My claim is not one of determinism or inevitability. In this chapter I simply identify a trend in recent litigation, and correlate it with a number of simultaneous developments in globalization and human rights advocacy. I am, however, interested in the underlying political philosophies that promote certain kinds of development and encourage certain narratives of human rights. The politics of human rights and globalization, I would argue, speak to a fascinating complexity that is rife with contradictions, rather than supporting either the corporate or nationalistic predictions of inevitable progress or collapse of civilizations.

35. Neem's Latin name is *Azadirachta indica,* which translates roughly as "free tree of India."

36. Herz 2000, 545–632.

37. Ibid., 582.

38. A detailed practical analysis would take this chapter too far afield in the area of specific cases and litigation. Legal scholarship in this area is beginning to grow rapidly. See, for instance, Fowler 1995; and Rosencranz and Campbell 1999.

39. Beanal v. Freeport-McMoran was dismissed by a district court that based its decision on the "precautionary principles" of international environmental law. However, Herz argues that the plaintiff's arguments would have had far greater weight if argued from a human rights approach (2000, 581).

40. Herz 2000, 563.

41. The Alien Tort Claims Act (ATCA) directs courts to apply customary international law within the United States. The tests in the case of private actors (with respect to states) are for joint action, symbiotic relationship, eminent domain, coercion, and/or encouragement (Herz 2000, 561–562).

42. Herz 2000, 637.

43. In Burma and Nigeria, TNCs have worked under the protection of state military personnel. Herz documents that "TNCs often incite disagreement among group leaders. Maxus and Petroecuador bribed individual leaders, involved themselves in elections, and divided villages against one other in order to secure an agreement from the Huaorani people of Ecuador to allow oil development to pro-

ceed. Defendants may use such disagreements to argue that the group accepted development voluntarily" (2000, 637).

44. Human Rights Watch 1999, 19.

45. Ibid., 20.

46. Ibid., 21.

47. Ibid.

48. Sassen 1999, 2.

49. Ranee Panjabi (1997) gives a detailed account of developing countries' critiques of the environmentalist agenda at Rio. Bernard Weintraub (1992) notes that the U.S. "did not initiate comprehensive domestic environmental legislation until more than a century after the beginning of its industrial revolution. See National Environmental Policy Act of 1969, 42 U.S.C. § 4321 (1988)." Several developing states assert the right to develop with disregard for environmental effects, based on this model. Weintraub references "Brazil's criticism of the United States and other industrialized states with respect to their position on the Amazonian rainforests. . . . The United States and Canada act hypocritically when they continue to clearcut forests across North America while discouraging deforestation in Brazil" (1992, p. 175 nn.15–16).

50. The entire petition is available from the International Law Project for Human, Economic, and Environmental Defense (HEED), at www.heed.net.

51. See, for example, West and Brechin 1991.

52. Bullard 1994, 118–119.

53. For instance, in the legal dumping of waste in China, Larry Summer's infamous memo, or the World Bank's "mortgaging of the earth" (see Harvey 1996; and Rich 1995).

54. See, for example, Gupta 1996; and Kloppenburg 1988.

55. That is, one that is specific to an economically privileged society with a cultural history of romanticism and primitivism. For a critique of this form of environmentalism, see Guha 1989.

56. As, for instance, in the environmental justice movement, particularly in the southern United States. See Bullard 1994.

57. The distinction between individual and group rights is a contentious one. While the African Charter on Human and Peoples' Rights recognizes the latter, the United States has usually recognized only the former.

58. Mann et al. 1999, 422.

59. Ibid., 426.

60. Anghie's work is inspired in part by the legal work of Christopher Weeramantry, who is currently vice president of the International Court of Justice. Work that supports Anghie's thesis, and that is cited by him, includes Bhagwati 1998; Mutua 1996; Said 1978, 1993; and Baxi 1998. His argument is rooted in the field of international law, but draws extensively on development critiques, global (especially colonial) political economy, and postcolonial studies.

61. Anghie 2000, 272.

62. Anghie quotes Lord Lugard's *The Dual Mandate in British Tropical Africa* (1922): "The democracies of today claim the right to work, and the satisfaction of that claim is impossible without the raw materials of the tropics on the one hand and their markets on the other" (Anghie 2000, 290).

63. Anghie 2000, 253.
64. Ibid., 254.

References

Alston, Philip. 1990. "U.S. Ratification of the Covenant on Economic, Social, and Cultural Rights: The Need for an Entirely New Strategy." *American Journal of International Law* 84, no. 2 (April): 365–393.
Anghie, Anthony. 2000. "Time Present and Time Past: Globalization, International Financial Institutions, and the Third World." *New York University Journal of International Law and Politics* 32, no. 243 (Winter): 243–290.
Aoki, Keith. 1998. "Neocolonialism, Anticommons Property, and Biopiracy in the (Not-So-Brave) New World Order of International Intellectual Property Protection." *Indiana Journal of Global Legal Studies* 6, no. 11 (Fall): 11–58.
Barber, Benjamin R. 1995. *Jihad vs. McWorld.* New York: Times Books.
Baxi, Upendra. 1998. "Voices of Suffering and the Future of Human Rights." *Transnational Law and Contemporary Problems* 8, no. 125.
Benvenisti, Eyal. 2000. "Exit and Voice in the Age of Globalisation." *Michigan Law Review* 98, no. 167 (October).
Bhagwati, Jagdish. 1998. "The Capital Myth: The Difference Between Trade in Widgets and Dollars." *Foreign Affairs* 77, no. 3 (May–June): 7–12.
Biehl, Janet, and Peter Staudenmaier. 1996. *Ecofascism: Lessons from the German Experience.* Edinburgh: A. K. Press Distribution.
Brown, Gardner, Jr., and Robert Mendelsohn. 1984. "The Hedonic Travel Cost Method." *The Review of Economics and Statistics* 66, no. 3 (August): 427–433.
Brown, Lester, Christopher Flavin, and Hilary French. 1997. *State of the World: A Worldwatch Institute Report on Progress Toward a Sustainable Society.* New York: W. W. Norton.
Bryant, Raymond, and Sinead Bailey. 1997. *Third World Political Ecology.* London: Routledge.
Bullard, Robert. 1994. *Dumping in Dixie.* Boulder, CO: Westview Press.
Devall, Bill, and George Sessions. *Deep Ecology.* Salt Lake City, UT: G. M. Smith.
Duffield, Mark. 1999. "Globalization and War Economies: Promoting Order or the Return of History?" *Fletcher Forum of World Affairs* 23, no. 21 (Fall).
Ferry, Luc. 1995. *The New Ecological Order.* Carol Volk, trans. Chicago: University of Chicago Press.
Foucault, Michel. 1980. *Power/Knowledge: Selected Interviews and Other Writing, 1972–1977.* New York: Pantheon Books.
Fowler, Robert. 1995. "International Environmental Standards for Transnational Corporations." *Environmental Law* 25, no. 1 (Winter).
Jameson, Fredric, and Masao Miyoshi, eds. 1998. *The Cultures of Globalization.* Durham, NC: Duke University Press.
Glacken, Clarence J. 1967. *Traces on the Rhodian Shore: Nature and Culture in Western Thought from Ancient Times to the End of the Eighteenth Century.* Berkeley: University of California Press.
Grove, Richard. 1995. *Green Imperialism: Colonial Expansion, Tropical Island Edens, and the Origins of Environmentalism, 1600–1860.* Cambridge: Cambridge University Press.

Guha, Ramachandra. 1989. "Radical American Environmentalism and Wilderness Preservation: A Third World Critique." *Environmental Ethics* 11, no. 1.

Gupta, Anil K. 1996. "Nature, Agriculture, and Nurturing Societies: Learning from Those Who Care and Conserve." In *CEDIA Conference on "World Market for Agronomists."* Copenhagen, Denmark: N.p.

Harvey, David. 1996. *Justice, Nature, and the Geography of Difference.* London: Blackwell.

Herz, Richard. 2000. "Litigating Environmental Abuses Under the Alien Tort Claims Act: A Practical Assessment." *Virginia Journal of International Law* 40 (Winter): 545–632.

Human Rights Watch. 1999. *The Price of Oil: Corporate Responsibility and Human Rights Violations in Nigeria's Oil Producing Communities.* New York: Human Rights Watch, January.

Huntington, Samuel P. 1996. *The Clash of Civilizations and the Remaking of World Order.* New York: Simon & Schuster.

Janis, Mark. 1999. *An Introduction to International Law.* 3rd ed. New York: Aspen.

Kausikan, Bilahari. 1998. "The 'Asian Values' Debate: A View from Singapore." In Larry Diamond and Mark Plattner, eds., *Democracy in East Asia.* Baltimore: Johns Hopkins University Press, 17–28.

Kim, Jim Yong, Joyce V. Millen, Alec Irwin, and John Gershman. 2000. *Dying for Growth: Global Inequality and the Health of the Poor.* Monroe, ME: Common Courage Press.

Kloppenburg, Jack. 1988. *First the Seed: The Political Economy of Biotechnology.* Cambridge: Cambridge University Press.

Krasner, Stephen. 2000. "International Law and International Relations: Together, Apart, Together?" *Chicago Journal of International Law* 1, no. 93.

Kuhn, Thomas S. 1970. *The Structure of Scientific Revolutions.* 2nd ed. Chicago, University of Chicago Press.

Lovelock, James. 1988. *The Ages of Gaia: A Biography of Our Living Earth.* Oxford: Oxford University Press.

Lowe, Lisa, and David Lloyd, eds. 1997. *The Politics of Culture in the Shadow of Capital.* Durham, NC: Duke University Press.

Lutz, Robert E. 1988. "Environment, Economic Development and Human Rights: A Triangular Relationship?" *American Society of International Law, Proceedings* no. 82, pp. 40–63.

Mann, Jonathan, Sofia Gruskin, Michael Grodin, and George Annas, eds. 1999. *Health and Human Rights: A Reader.* New York: Routledge.

Mutua, Makau. 1996. "The Ideology of Human Rights." *Virginia Journal of International Law* 36, no. 589.

Myers, Norman. 1993. *Ultimate Security: The Environmental Basis of Political Stability.* New York: W. W. Norton.

Nash, Roderick. 1967. *Wilderness and the American Mind.* New Haven, CT: Yale University Press.

Newman, Frank, and David Weissbrodt. 1996. *International Human Rights: Law, Policy, and Process.* 2nd ed. Cincinnati, OH: Anderson Publishing.

Panjabi, Ranee. 1997. *The Earth Summit at Rio: Politics, Economics, and the Environment.* Boston: Northeastern University Press.

Redclift, Michael, and Ted Benton. 1994. *Social Theory and the Global Environment.* London: Routledge.

Renner, Michael. 1997. "Transforming Security." In Lester R. Brown, Christopher Flavin, and Hilary F. French, *State of the World: A Worldwatch Institute Report on Progress Toward a Sustainable Society.* New York: W. W. Norton, chapter 7.

Rich, Bruce. 1995. *Mortgaging the Earth: The World Bank, Environmental Impoverishment, and the Crisis of Development.* Boston: Beacon Press.

Rosencranz, Armin, and Richard Campbell. 1999. "Foreign Environmental and Human Rights Suits Against U.S. Corporations in U.S. Courts." *Stanford Environmental Law Journal* 18, no. 145 (June).

Sachs, Wolfgang, ed. 1993. *Global Ecology: A New Arena of Political Conflict.* Atlantic Highlands, NJ: Zed Books.

Said, Edward W. 1978. *Orientalism.* New York: Pantheon Books.

———. 1993. *Culture and Imperialism.* New York: Knopf. Distributed by Random House.

Sassen, Saskia. 1998. *The Mobility of Labor Capital: A Study in International Investment and Labor Flow.* New York: Cambridge University Press.

———. 1999. "Territory and Territoriality in the Global Economy." Paper presented at the Carnegie Council on Ethics and International Affairs, New York, June.

Sen, Sunanda. 2000. *Trade and Dependence: Essays on the Indian Economy.* New Delhi: Sage.

Sinnot, John P., and William Joseph Cotreau, comp. 1974. *World Patent Law and Practice: Patent Statutes, Regulations, and Treaties.* New York: M. Bender.

Stark, Barbara. 1992. "Economic Rights in the United States and International Human Rights Law: Toward an 'Entirely New Strategy.'" *Hastings Law Journal* 44, no. 79 (November).

Taylor, Dorceta. 1992. "Can the Environmental Movement Attract and Maintain the Support of Minorities?" In B. Bryant and P. Mohai, eds., *Race and the Incidence of Environmental Hazards.* Boulder, CO: Westview Press.

Walsh, Richard G., John B Loomis, and Richard A. Gillman. 1984. "Valuing Option, Existence, and Bequest Demands for Wilderness." *Land Economics* 60, no. 1 (February): 14–29.

Weintraub, Bernard. 1992. "Science, International Environmental Regulation, and the Precautionary Principle: Setting Standards and Defining Terms." *New York University Environmental Law Journal* 1, no. 1: 173–223.

West, Patrick C., and Steven R. Brechin, eds. 1991. *Resident Peoples and National Parks: Social Dilemmas and Strategies in International Conservation.* Tucson: University of Arizona Press.

4

Translating a Liberal Feminism

Revisiting Susan Okin on Freedom, Culture, and Women's Rights

Ellen M. Freeberg

Feminists supportive of women's international rights have often embraced the "first generation" of human rights with caution (Charlesworth 1994). As the political rights of the UN declaration, these remain most closely associated with liberal assumptions about individuals and seem insensitive to the economic and family-center forms of oppression that historically have hindered women's choices (Charlesworth 1994; Romany 1994). The UN declaration has changed over time, adding rights and promoting institutions that now attempt to overcome social and economic disadvantages based on gender (Donnolly 1989). While resistance to acknowledging economic rights (especially from the United States) has not always been encouraging, many now say that the current commitment to women's rights looks more promising (Coomaraswamy 1999). As a result, today's practical advances should eliminate earlier theoretical quibbles (Henkin 1990), and contentious charges that rights operate with a "masculine," Western bias need not prove terribly damaging.

Encouraging as this perspective sounds, battles certainly persist over how to alter practices affecting women's lives and whether rights talk makes sense across the globe. The goals cherished in the UN declaration do seem to require ongoing justification. Some associated with "traditional" cultures decry universalist UN efforts as arrogant and false. They declare such general efforts blind to how ancient customs protect women, and they charge many as too dismissive of how women themselves may choose to change their lives slowly based on their own piecemeal initiatives within a traditional community. Alongside more conservative voices, representatives of so-called left-of-center politics compound the skepticism. Committed to social justice, many offer ongoing critiques of rights talk (Young 1990), challenge efforts to establish commonalities through a universal category of "women" (for example, see Riley 1988 and Mohanty 1984), and aim to expose an altered declaration of rights as elitist and deeply biased again non-Western standards (for example, Flax 1995). Moreover, in a globalizing economy, one linked to free-market capitalism, more radical demands are often declared necessary in order to protect individuals and empower women to enter economic arenas without becoming exploited bodies (see the many citations in Meyer 1995).

If we take such criticisms seriously (whether based on concerns about identity politics, the limits of liberalism, or preservation of cultural diversity), difficult questions emerge. How do we identify, let alone respond to, oppressive norms commonly faced by many (even if not all) women living in cultures constructed around deeply limiting, gender-based restrictions? Even if we seriously engage critics of women's universal rights (from left or right), it seems troublesome in the end to eschew all efforts to rethink common values and to turn away from declaring that no matter our gender, we humans remain purposive beings who deserve the opportunity to participate in and help shape the rules that govern our actions. As I see it, efforts to sensitively sustain cultural diversity and difference need not eviscerate such demands.

This chapter begins with the cautious hope, then, that appreciation for women's diversity and sensitivity to cultural differences can stand alongside efforts to imagine a set of common assumptions about freedom, and that this idea can be effectively used to support and extend women's rights. I am specifically interested in defending a common recognition that women (and all persons) stand as *agents* in need of freedom-enhancing protections. My vision of agency (defined as purposive yet situated action) should sound modest, as it draws from several eclectic thinkers. My hope is that it can support general principles demanding civility, the prevention of degradation, and access to the mechanisms and material goods needed for improved participation by women in the specific practices that shape their life plans. As a starting point, a conception of agency and regard for agency can and should support a set of broad principles and rights; it should do so while resisting claims that the "foundation" of such ideas looks simply biased and therefore unhelpful when trying to address a global vision of justice for women. The difficult balancing act comes when trying to suggest that my assumptions provide a degree of critical leverage over culture while still respecting local efforts to develop choice-enhancing initiatives by and for women who have distinct needs and particular perspectives.

As a starting point, the discussion here engages the liberal feminism of Susan Moller Okin. Her ideas provide a helpful contrast to my own. Okin has relied upon broad support for shared understandings about freedom as autonomy; and she couples these with her expectations about the value of John Rawls's original position for reducing oppressive practices associated with gender hierarchies and especially hierarchies in family units (Okin 1989b). Initially targeting her ideas to women in Western democracies, Okin has argued of late that her ideas can support liberation from patriarchal norms in Western *and* non-Western societies (Okin 1995a, 1998a). While often more intensely damaging to women in poorer, third-world countries, certain harms only differ in degree, as Okin sees it. "Women" may not be exactly "the same" everywhere (certainly they are influenced by diverse cultural traditions), but they do face similar damaging institutions. By extension, the Rawlsian solution (the original position and its assumptions about autonomy) so prominent as a mechanism for checking unfair practices can remain reasonable as a global imperative for promoting right conduct and grounding a universal set of women's rights.

Okin also responds to those concerned about cultural rights and to many aligned with a kind of postmodern feminism at odds with her ideas (see especially Okin 1995b, 1998a, 1999). The question is whether her assumptions about freedom and women's choice could provide an effective critique of cultural practices as well as the grounds for arguing for universal women's rights. I argue that Okin's ideas are promising, but fall short in considering the ambiguous legacy of certain liberal ideals about freedom, and consequently they often seem unable to maintain enough attentiveness to local needs or to arguments pressing for greater recognition of cultural diversity. The position I offer tries to compensate for this, even as it sustains talk of cross-cultural comparability and a minimal set of conditions for enhancing individual freedom. I do not support the arguments of thinkers like Jane Flax (1995) in toto, for example. But problems with important assumptions that Okin retains from Rawls in particular are noted and highlighted as a way to rethink the basis for constructing a global feminism.

How does Susan Okin's "humanist liberalism" (1989a) justify itself—how does it provide a legitimate basis for criticizing traditional practices and supporting a notion of women's international rights? First, Okin believes that her work establishes supportive policies and rights for women worldwide because it effectively justifies a universal basis for fair family and workplace relations reliant on Rawls's hypothetical device for fair representation, the original position (Rawls 1971). Rawls's significant contribution to contemporary political theory centered on his argument that fair principles could emerge from a moral yet reasonable set of constraints on deliberation between autonomous individuals. Most notably, reasonable individuals should come to see that veiling aspects of their identity before constructing public principles to govern their society was absolutely essential. By now this story is familiar: if individuals know nothing about their class or race or age or overall psychological makeup, if they have no idea what they will have or who they will be in their particular society (but they do know that everyone has a life plan and the capacity to cooperate for just purposes), the most neutral, fair-minded public principles of justice would be chosen by such individuals as they considered how they wished to live, and whatever they chose together as self-legislating beings would naturally be embraced by all. Okin's significant contribution to feminism has centered on a co-optation of Rawls's device for moral thinking as a way to expose and rectify injustices promoted within the family (and, by extension, injustices in the workplace). No one would choose anything other than the most egalitarian public policies related to raising children and the treatment of women if they knew nothing about where they would fall in a gender hierarchy, in the family or elsewhere, Okin claims. "What pre-revolutionary Chinese man would have cast his vote for the breaking of toes and hobbling through life, if he well might be the one with the toes and the crippled life? What man would endorse gross genital mutilation, not knowing *whose* genitals" (Okin 1995a, 293–294)? The answer for Okin is clear.

Second, Okin insists that her expectations about the original position can accommodate modifications. True, Rawls limits his most weighty liberal assumptions about freedom to the shared values of Western citizens (Rawls 1996), but Okin believes individuals everywhere are capable of universalizing and acting as self-legislating moral beings using the veil of ignorance. The commonsense logic of the original position should be noted, and no woman should be said incapable of its requests. (So feminist liberals indebted to Rawls need not go the way of "political liberalism"[1] [Okin 1994; see also Exdell 1994 and Ackerman 1994].) Moreover, the idea of "women" as a group still holds weight, and since women worldwide face similar "patriarchal practices" (Okin 1995a), albeit to a greater or lesser degree, women's group identification can also help feminism take an internationalist turn. More than ever, evidence today suggests that a myriad of fundamentalisms threaten women's lives and that we need the power of a modified liberalism to help demand women's basic rights.

As for the first point, it is reinforced by Okin's reconstruction of an original position. Essentially, Okin claims that one may endorse Rawls's universalizing as it insists on a test of moral rightness for political, social, and economic practices; but one should see that what drives individuals to act rightly and veil their differences in the original position (where the goal is reasonable consensus about just principles) is not simply a sense of "mutual disinterestedness" as Rawls claims, but a series of more complex emotions and feelings that Rawls (and any Kantian-based political theory) needs to acknowledge more fully (Okin 1990a).

In her earlier article "Reason and Feeling" (1990a), Okin carefully laid out these modifications of Rawls's argument, critiquing and then supplementing early Rawlsian dependence upon rational choice theory. She illustrated how Rawls could not easily stay true to rational choice assumptions and how gaps in liberal theory indicated a need for more complex expectations about moral motivation in an original position (1990a, 26–32). Moreover, since Rawls, from *A Theory of Justice* (1971) onward, had insisted that the original position did not depend upon individuals exercising egotistical motives (nor were individuals as such expected to remain divorced from all information about human conduct), this social contract model for constructing fairness did not need to acknowledge humans' capacity for empathy or benevolence. Without care and connection between persons, Okin wrote, without expecting individuals to think "from the position of everybody" (rather than nobody) (1990a, 30), there would be no way to ensure equal concern and respect leading to just dealings. Rawls appears to reject reliance on emotions such as empathy, claiming that they are too complex and ultimately require too much knowledge in the original position (Okin 1990a, 30). And Rawls might reinforce his point, in Kantianlike fashion, by illustrating how duty and right conduct should never rely upon empathy (Rawls 1971). But Okin shows quite cleverly how any such use of Kant would present problems given what she adeptly identifies as Kant's misguided descriptions of love and empathy (especially in the *Doctrine of Virtue*) (Okin 1990a, 17–20). Replacing the rational choice expectations with a more ambiguous debt to Kant would still leave liberalism in need of modification.

So Okin tries to answer key feminist objections to Rawls and reconstructs his assumptions about moral personality and freedom before using them for her own purposes. In addition, Okin sees her challenges to Rawls spilling over into a balanced refutation of those feminists who seem to reject the moral weight of liberal autonomy and social contract theory in toto. Work by Carol Gilligan, for all its importance, remains problematic if it fails to explore an integration of empathy and benevolence with liberal universalist tendencies supporting a general moral viewpoint. In fact, thinkers like Gilligan harbor their own debts to liberal expectations for fairness even as they claim to resist such approaches, or so Okin has argued (1990b; 1990a, 33–34).

To complete the refinement of this feminism, Okin goes on to say that private life cannot be shielded from norms of fairness. If one values the capacity to veil irrelevant moral facts and uses this capacity to show equal concern and care for others, one has to imagine how this capacity gets developed. Values fundamental to moral decisionmaking are generally nurtured early within families. So efforts to promote just families and to rethink the public/ private distinction need sustained attention. Rawls hints at this by identifying the family as part of the "basic structure" of a society (1971, 128). But like many liberals, he fails to tease out the implications of his own gestures. Okin addresses the problem by deftly exploring how the early logic of *A Theory of Justice* (unlike its contemporary competitors) implicitly acknowledged families as primary schools of justice (Okin 1989b) and how citizens *learn* to universalize within fair family exchanges. But Rawls never suggested *how* to restructure gender roles (a priori) in accordance with a morally acceptable division of family labor. (A restructuring of such roles should have included talk of alterations in the workplace to accommodate parental leave for care-taking [Okin 1989b, 176], government-subsidized on-site daycare, school-based programs that support male and female equity [177], equal legal entitlement to all earnings coming into the household with payment from a job going to an unpaid worker at home [180], and divorce laws that ensure that both postdivorce households maintain the same standard of living [183].) Ultimately, liberalism has potential, but it must be reworked to advance women's freedom.

What about global acceptance of such ideas? Okin has addressed this question in more recent articles (1995a, 1998a, 1998b, 1999). Here she insists that, with oppressive patriarchal patterns identifiable everywhere, liberalism must establish the common language of rights in a postcolonial era and challenge dangerous relativistic efforts to secure "cultural rights" that impede women's liberation.

A globally relevant feminist liberalism makes sense from a theoretical and practical perspective for the following reasons. First, no theoretical positions contending with her own, Okin suggests, remain as effective at condemning unfair practices. Backing away from liberalism has become fashionable among political theorists in the wake of multiculturalism and antiessentialist theorizing. But these trends lead to untenable relativism or an inappropriate valorization of cultural difference and group rights (1999) as well as to a disconnection between academic talk and actual activism (1998b). Thinkers like Jane Flax (1995) or Will Kymlicka perpetuate such trends; they rarely tackle the oppressive side of "culture," which so frequently exerts dangerous controls over women's reproduction, the education of female children, women's earning capacity, and the like (Okin 1999, 1995a). Moreover, those who would share Okin's concerns but adopt dialogical models of justice from critical theory should be eschewed. These alternative feminist visions too thoroughly reject the power of an original position and talk of an "interactive feminism" (a vision they see as more attentive to women speaking from their own standpoint). With supposed emphasis on greater respect for the "concrete other" and "the multiplicity of voices of distress" (Okin 1995a on Ruth Anna Putnam), dialogical models nonetheless fail to note how older women (or men) will often "rationalize the cruelties" (Okin 1995a, 293) and oppressive practices they have been born into. "People may be seriously deprived yet relatively cheerful," as Okin puts it (1995a, 292). Instead,

> the aim of this endeavor, in cases where serious inequalities exist, should not be simply to understand, but rather to do so with a view to politicizing the deprived so that they can begin to ask new questions about their cultural norms with a view to improving their situation. Given this proviso, then, committed outsiders may often be better analysts and critics of social injustice than those who live within the relevant culture. . . . In essence, then, after engaging in dialogue in order to understand the practices as well as possible, they [any properly constructive critics] would encourage those within the culture to engage in Rawlsian theorizing—to try to imagine themselves in the original position, not knowing who in the social order they were to be once the veil of ignorance were lifted. (1995a, 293)

To reiterate, this plan does not commit one to distinctly Western expectations based on imperialistic assumptions; it pulls together commonsense understandings about right conduct and freedom that all humans would have to acknowledge, Okin argues. One need only review questions like the following to see the necessity of the Rawlsian liberal thought experiment as it puts aside all irrelevant information that could corrupt or prejudice a set of fair principles: "What Muslim man is likely to take the chance of spending his life in seclusion and dependency, sweltering head to toe a solid black clothing, or being forbidden to earn a living by the rules of purdah?" (1995a, 293–294). Only a Rawlsian original position can imagine the proper level of critical moral thinking; and only a feminism demanding autonomous moral decisionmaking from men and women will make fairness a reality.

The practical necessity of such ideas finds empirical support, Okin claims, when one studies worldwide patterns of injustice toward women and female children. And such patterns appear to result from similar situations. Women in "third-world" countries face dramatic disadvantages compared to men. But around the globe, women are disproportionately poorer than men; the gendered division of labor in families disproportionately impacts on the opportunities for women from any country; women generally lack pay for family work, leaving them more vulnerable than men to abuse and significant economic challenges; and no matter where one lives, the practitioners concerned to rectify injustice, whether associated with development studies or so-called western models of justice, often obscure intrahousehold inequalities and neither encourage women's work to "count" nor alter the idea that the male head of household is anything but natural and unproblematic (Okin 1995a).

Women are not the same; but individuals socially constructed as "women" remain marked by diminished opportunities compounded by conditions or efforts to ignore their demands for institutional change within and outside the family. A liberalism modified using feminist sensibilities can demand effective, even dramatic changes. No other theoretical position can make such demands as forcefully; and women everywhere deserve to draw from the moral force of such a reenvisioned liberalism.

So the question is: Do I support these ideas? The answer is yes and no. I agree with Okin on the following: first, that hierarchical patterns established throughout institutions worldwide, especially within the family, tend to limit the opportunity and freedom of those identified as "women"; and second, that we may challenge such hierarchies and justify limits on action and modes of human conduct through the recognition that some shared capacity for freedom (not necessarily freedom defined as autonomy) is possessed by all (including those marked as women). But I would qualify Okin's ideas by claiming that certain limits on action need not flow from an "original position" or from a set of presumptions about autonomy. As an alternative, I would formulate a position declaring the importance of a common conception of agency and suggest ways in which this general claim can provide the basis for an inclusive feminism still sensitive to the diversity of women's lives and voices.

Before exploring these points further, we should highlight how Okin's assumptions do continue to draw sharp rebuke. Jane Flax formulates her notable critiques against Okin by claiming that such a liberalism speaks to a white, middle-class, Western audience exclusively. Flax also finds Okin presumptuous in her characterization of "gender" as being constituted "through what women share, especially their differences from, and domination by, men" (Flax 1995, 500). More thoroughly put, Flax believes Okin

TRANSLATING A LIBERAL FEMINISM 97

inadequately interrogates (1) the dangers of assuming that all can exercise autonomy as demanded by the original position and the dangers of not admitting that this exercise is shaped by a distinct cultural experience; (2) the presumptuousness of a position that emphasizes the commonality of women's experience yet still "enable[s] white women to ignore their complicity in and privileges obtained from their situatedness within relations of race, sexuality (if straight), and geographic location" (Flax 1995, 503); and (3) the dangers of a theory that when extended internationally frequently sees "women" as common only because it presupposes that "third-world" women are "an unresisting homogeneous category" positioned "exclusively as objects of the discourses and practices of others" (504). Reinforced by thinkers like Chandra Mohanty (1984), this last point might support the suggestion that a liberal ethic inevitably will be reconstructed without consulting individuals within particular cultures, thereby reinstating colonizing preferences and damaging the choices of those whom thinkers like Okin claim to liberate.

Well aware of such charges, Okin has concerned herself with the second and third points especially. She spends significant effort addressing the second point about how she works with a biased theoretical framework—and she looks closely at the charge that her own personal vantage point remains biased. Imagining her critics to include a range of "antiessentialists," Okin suggests, for example, that we can acknowledge how many earlier feminists "seemed to have assumed . . . that the women they were liberating would have recourse to servants or (as is so often euphemistically and impersonally put) 'household help'" (Okin 1995a, 275), and how, in the United States, this usually meant black women. But she believes that "few contemporary feminist theorists are neglectful of differences of class and race when these are relevant to their arguments" (although she does believe that sexual orientation has been another matter) (1995a, 275). She notes how her claims have relied upon empirical data that were "decidedly not focused on middle or upper class housewives or professional women" (1995a, 277). And Okin also charges her critics with doing little to prove their claims by examining different women's lives. Hence the third point looks disingenuous. ("[T]hose who charge 'essentialism' at every turn should take on some of the burden of proof—should provide evidence that the differences among the situations of women are so much greater than the similarities so that no meaningful generalizations can be made" [1995b, 511–512].) Okin then claims that she has made better use of empirical data and that no one should apologize for remaining a "committed outsider" in reviewing information about women's well-being. She believes theorists can reflect upon social discourse and practices in cultures outside their own.

Many important activists benefit from being "partly inside and partly outside of the cultural contexts they describe" (1995b, 515, n. 2) and she takes issue with the implication that her own efforts will be so subjective as to remain offensive. Antiessentialists, as well as others, have pressed us hard to attend to the claims of traditionally disadvantaged groups, but they go too far. They either give up altogether on constructing a common moral vantage point from which to gain critical leverage over oppressive practices; or they hint at their own generalized ethic of justice without defending it effectively. (Flax gestures toward several tactics for overcoming domination, but Okin finds the language vague and the theoretical questions unanswered [1995b, 514].)

Although in many instances Okin forcefully tackles objections, my claim at this point would be that we need to explore options in contrast to both Okin's liberal feminism and her antiessentialist critics. More compelling to me is an effort to shift from the "either/or" framework in this debate. I would aim to make a shift on two fronts. First, I consider it valuable to adopt a conception of "women" from a more pragmatic perspective, as discussed by Iris Marion Young, who creatively imagines women as a "serialized" social collectivity. Young has suggested that women can be identified with a practical collective without "implying that all women have a common identity" or a unified relation based on common projects and goals (1995, 714). Second, I would stress how this alternative conception of women as a serialized group actually remains compatible with a notion of freedom based on our capacity as practice-bound actors. And I would borrow here from a rather eclectic reading of freedom from work by Richard Flathman (1987). As situated actors or agents, we may share a capacity for freedom (defined below). But freedom as agency should look different from freedom defined as autonomy exercised through construction of an original position. An alternative notion of freedom as agency should find itself recognizable and more readily embraced by women from different cultures even as it supports certain general limits on the degrading actions that impede individual freedom. To reach for a feminism that recognizes and values "women's" liberation should not be completely dangerous or unthinkable. And it may be assisted by the possibility that we all share the capacity for agency. Women as a (serialized) group may wrongly be deprived of agency in various practices and rightly demand changes based on their claims to exercise agency, but local and particular voices need not be lost as certain rights and demands are formulated based on this claim.

Iris Young, in "Gender as Seriality" (1995), writes of the practical dilemmas feminism faces if it cannot characterize "women" as a group. She wants to acknowledge how thinkers like Elizabeth Spelman and Judith Butler have repeatedly challenged "the subject" for feminism and the category of women (or gender) as a rhetorical move that can devalue or "freeze contingent social relations into a false necessity" (Young 1995, 717). But while avoiding certain systematic explanations of "[t]he way things are in some universal sense," Young nevertheless rejects the implication that "it makes no sense and is morally wrong . . . to talk about women as a group." As she effectively puts it:

> Feminist politics evaporates, that is, without some conception of women as a social collective. Radical politics may remain as a commitment to social justice for all people, among those called women. Yet the claim that feminism expresses a distinct politics allied with anti-imperialism, anti-racism, and gay liberation but asking a unique set of enlightening questions about the distinct acts of social oppression cannot be sustained without some means of conceptualizing women and gender as social structures. (719)

In searching for a middle ground, Young reaches for a pragmatic way to characterize women without providing an entire, self-enclosed theory. Co-opting Sartre's distinctions between levels of social collectivity, including a distinction between group and series, Young presses for a nonfoundational, nonexclusive characterization of women as serialized. A group (in contrast to a series) means "a collection of persons who recognize themselves and one another as in a unified relation with one another. . . . [They] mutually acknowledge that together they undertake a common project. . . . In acknowledging oneself as a member of the group, an individual acknowledges oneself as oriented toward the same goals as the others. . . . [T]his acknowledging usually becomes explicit at some point in the pledge, contract, constitution, set of bylaws, or statement of purpose" (1995, 724). On the other hand, a series is derived "from the way that individuals pursue their own individual ends with respect to the same objects conditioned by a continuous material environment, in response to structures that have been created by the unintended collective result of past actions" (724). A series constructs relations through rule-bound, social structures that constitute similar limits and constraints as individuals try to accomplish distinctive purposes. A series would not define a person's identity "in the sense of forming his or her individual purposes, projects, and sense of self in relation to others" (727). "Women" relate as individuals, then, because they are often produced and organized by a certain set of common structures and objects. Institutionalized practices and assumptions about heterosexuality establish the way women are constituted in relation to men; numerous visual and verbal representations inscribe norms and divide labor or create a "milieu for actions" even if they do not determine it (730). Certain reactions to women's bodies create a range of "meanings and possibilities." For example, "Menstruation is a regular biological event occurring in most female bodies within a certain age range. It is not this biological process alone, however, that locates individuals in the series of women. Rather the social rules of menstruation along with the material objects associated with menstrual practices, constitute the activity within which the women live as serialized" (729). We can agree that "women" should not be reduced to an a priori set of essential attributes or identity (again, when identity refers to deeply held psychological attributes or self-consciously shared values). But this need not dismiss acknowledgment of the structures that position individuals in relation to one another and enable or constrain their action.

Young offers more than a way to start critically exploring women's commonalities, more than a discussion of how rules and "language games" may shape conduct yet allow goals to differ (a well-known Wittgenstein observation). Young indirectly highlights how individuals shaped by practices remain agents—expressing and pursuing individual purposes and goals—and they exercise freedom even when serially situated. To my mind, an appreciation for freedom as agency could provide a basis for expanding expectations about what women (or any serially rule-governed actors) share as equals. Formulations of this kind are what Okin's critics want to destabilize or defer. But one could simultaneously explore how acknowledgment of agency is limited in its virtuous expectations even as it provides protections for action that offer a desirable set of parameters through which to empower women to challenge norms.

What do I mean by agency and how does this differ from autonomy? Recall that Okin's commitments to Rawls's original position imply the following about human beings' capacity for freedom: (1) when one fails to exercise a higher-order (transcendent) moral check on behavior, one is not only failing to pursue justice, but one is failing to act freely *as a self-legislating moral being;* (2) when one fails to act freely in this way, one is not so much restrained by external impediments, but is unwilling to acquire the *moral traits* associated with allowing oneself to overcome certain enslaving desires and parochial perspectives; and by extension, (3) when acting unfree, one may require *internal correction* (for the sake of freedom itself), something that can justify readily overriding local customs. Okin's notion of freedom here is a moralized one, even with its variations on Rawls's theme.

Most visions of autonomy retain demanding, often controversial expectations for our capacity to reason and to control desire. Yet they simultaneously may fail to acknowledge that these expectations are contestable and that freedom itself is a contestable concept. Freedom has been justified as a state reached when our physical movements are unhindered; as a condition reached only when certain physical and psychological obstacles are limited; or as an achievement that individuals as reasoning, thinking beings can and should attain only when exercising higher-order capacities to determine right from wrong.

The moralized conception that Okin supports is a view identified less with the basic removal of physical obstacles to movement and more with the pursuit of distinctive virtues and the acquiescence to (fair) higher-order norms; it implies that freedom is properly tied to characterological demands on a self, demands that must be fulfilled before one is considered a reasonable participant in public life. Beyond simply charging Okin with holding parochial "Western" values, then, important questions should emerge about whether any society could effectively use transcendentally determined virtuous expectations to stand as benchmarks for qualifying individuals as free and equal citizens and supporting women's rights. One may admire the capacity for autonomy (involving efforts to distance oneself from traditions, exercise benevolence leading to reciprocal recognition, and the use of these to assess right conduct), but should an unwillingness or inability to reach this state exclude one as a participant in public life? If yes, descriptive as well as normative dilemmas need to be tackled.

Descriptively positive notions of freedom work with a strong dichotomy between individual desire and higher-order values; they assume a kind of warring, unruly self. A positive freedom response like Okin's often tries to insist that because of such rapacious parochialism, individuals need to be fully contained by higher-order transcendent guidelines. Some political theorists (Flathman 1987) have argued against making such initial assumptions about the self, illustrating how both negative or positive freedom positions alike can end up with an incoherent description of individual desires or goal formation. Richard Flathman, for example, details how autonomy-oriented supporters often fall into the same traps as their negative freedom opponents, and his work has been particularly helpful in reminding thinkers of key dangers associated with positive freedom virtues and their potentially ambiguous role in establishing a relationship to state authority.

More specifically, positive and negative freedom positions often share assumptions about the rapacious quality of desires that give behaviorism too much clout. Negative freedom positions (Hobbes's, for example), insist that freedom exists only when movement propelled by inner states is externally unimpeded. On this view, the self's inner desires, passions, or interests are discussed as mental or physical states, but never as complex expectations, forms of reflection, deliberation, or interests in a particular object (Flathman 1987, 46–47). This view also fails to see anything within the self moderated by rules, norms, or shared principles. Furthermore, this view not only starts with incoherent assumptions about human desires, but it cannot distinguish between movement that just "happens" to a self with or without consent, and movement impelled intentionally or with reason.[2] The Hobbesian view fails to support agency as we can and should understand it; it fails to describe movement that looks "freedom evaluable" (Flathman 1987, chap. 5).

Autonomy-oriented positions often take their opponent's assumptions about desires for granted. They (tacitly or otherwise) talk of desires as brute urges that compel or "enslave." Freedom becomes possible only if the self can rationally order and control its base heteronomous demands. But desires only "enslave" if viewed reductively. Must the free self attune him- or herself to the rationality and morality of collective norms or transcendental rules? Humans do demonstrate a capacity for rationality and self-assessment. And many political theories, rightfully influential in our society, prize ongoing reflection about political (and other kinds of) authority. Yet it remains a serious question whether autonomy and strong rationality should be valued but also serve as the necessary requirements for agency and participation especially within a diverse polity.

While autonomy and rationality (the former always presupposing a high level of the latter) can be worthy achievements, it is not clear that we require rationality in a strong critical sense in order to qualify as agents. On most construals, autonomous action involves a very strong capacity for reason. But numerous habitual, potentially "irrational" behaviors can prove unfortunate, perhaps self-destructive, often unfathomable, but should not be disqualifying of agency. A host of "irrational" behaviors often involve degrees of choice and action (Flathman 1987, chap. 4). Note the religious individual who may fail to exercise strong rationality and/or critical reflection, but who could not plausibly be labeled unfree or in need of internal correction. While "it is true," Flathman writes, "that the rest of us often must assess A's performances, including her claims and laments about coercions" and "it is also true that we cannot do so without employing some standard of judgment" (1987, 213), general standards for reasoning need not "require rationality of the agents and actions they are used to assess."[3] Intentional action can be associated with agency; rationality only more or less.

So there are problems with autonomy as it relates to desires and a weighty notion of rationality. In addition, while cultivation of autonomy may seem consistent with freedom, efforts to make individuals more self-conscious or critically reflective often lead to compulsory programs and possibly undesirable interferences. It is not completely obvious that all such programs are to be applauded or seen as wholly consonant with freedom (see Flathman's examples, 219–220). And autonomy is usually considered an "ideal of character" (297), not easily distributed or protected with assurance. This is not to say that freedoms could never aim to protect autonomy. Or that, at times, we may be "justified in promoting autonomy at the expense of freedoms of action" (298). But a person could enjoy numerous rights and privileges as the equal of others in his or her society, yet never attain autonomy. Moreover, freedoms of action concern most humans as purposive actors while autonomy does not (297). Some who rightly wish to promote a "self-reflective and self-justifying political society" (thinkers such as James Fishkin) incline quickly to establish conditions for an autonomous citizenry that then remain insulated from debate (301–302), and this last move can be troublesome,[4] since it suggests that positions placing extraordinary value on self-rule and self-justification can often undermine the very things they prize.[5]

Okin tries to resist fear of feelings and emotions found in many classic autonomy models; she emphasizes connecting to others through reason supplemented by benevolence in order to engage in the original position. However, her conception of autonomy enhanced by benevolence is set up to ensure the maximum level of critical reflection at a perfected level. Okin considers her virtues untouched by bias and she positions the reflections checked by autonomy as directly opposed to the parochial desires shaped by culture (or by a self-interested set of life plans conditioned by local norms or practices). In other words, her position seems to still face the descriptive trap of mirroring those she may find objectionable. She works with the dramatic expectation that numerous locally constructed understandings remain tainted and unruly. The desire to highlight the dangers of the conditioned, practically situated self is underscored by Okin's ongoing concerns about multiculturalism and her emphasis on the need for the critical observer who can assist women in other cultures, even when such individuals remain unaware of their oppression.

But shouldn't freedom enhancement include attention to the quality of our desires? Shouldn't we want to evaluate how choices are shaped by degrading practices, psychological harm, hierarchies in the value of work, and so forth? If positive freedom as autonomy demands too much, what remains good ground for a common critique and a solid basis for supporting common, even international rights or limits on local customs and behaviors?

As noted, one answer could be that both strong positive and negative freedom assumptions need revisiting—and that a more acceptable starting point for establishing rights, limits, duties, and the like, would revolve around a conception of freedom that sees all individuals as purposive creatures with goals that remain practice bound (conditioned by the rules and norms of a practice). All individuals are situated agents and a practice-bound conception of the self acknowledges that the web of "goings-on" remains deeply shaped and reshaped by the eccentricities of whoever uses them. But it also indicates that no individual is capable of distance from rules and norms through a fully transcendental capacity for critical reflection. To use an example from Wittgenstein, there may be a stop sign in front of us, a rule that frames our choices, but we still have a choice as to how to proceed, whether to turn right or left, go through it, disobey it. Rules need not choke off individual choice and action, as Young has also pointed out; they may provide a set of "adverbial considerations" (Oakeshott 1975) as to how we may proceed. Individuals as conditioned actors remain capable of choice.

Valuing practice-bound agency also could have the following implications. The position need not demand an extraordinary capacity for rational critical distance and should not assume that all women as agents are free only when enslaving desires are radically contained. Achieving freedom would not be the exclusive domain of those associated with extraordinary rational distinctiveness or self-reflection. The religious or more culturally bound individual would not be held immediately in disdain or seen in need of outside correction as a result. But acknowledging and valuing practice-bound agency could lead to demands and protections such as the following:

1. A practice and its rules cannot be conceived as authoritative or legitimate if agency remains unrecognized as necessary to a rule's use.

2. Practices must be scrutinized to assess the room they accord to agency and they should be judged as legitimate guides in part based on the opportunity they give to allow practitioners to voice their concerns and participate in mechanisms that can alter the rules that govern their lives.

3. An evolving set of general limits on the degradation of agency and ways to promote agency development can be envisioned using a shared commitment to agency freedom, though the shape of such limits will depend upon the specific practices of concern.

The expectations above may be influenced by, but cannot be eliminated in the name of, adherence to a tradition or culture. But how do such expectations expect to support basic protections (even certain global rights for women) and yet remain attentive to local norms and interpretations of practices?

Certainly the first point above helps emphasize how even religious rules are affected by human conduct. Religious expectations, while attributed to divine command, remain interpreted by humans; and agency remains a component of any practice. To claim otherwise suggests that humans are nothing other than automatons. Some would add that ample evidence exists from religious texts themselves for supporting agency freedom alongside the need to bend one's will toward God. However, the second point would imply that traditional expectations/norms, such as veiling based on religious command or tradition, would not be readily dismissed through mechanisms like universalizing in an original position. Women joined serially in any specific culture would need to be consulted first before eliminating a practice altogether. For Okin, there seems no question that veiling, female genital mutilation, and many other norms are completely unacceptable, and such assessment can be made from outsiders. We need not talk to anyone to get this right. No man acting autonomously would ever agree to join a society where men as well as women would be the recipients of such demands or physical alterations. Women who fail to recognize this are simply incapable of recognizing their oppression; they are diminished and likely lack an adequate level of critical reflection. But as an alternative, the expectations associated with practice-bound agency would require that we ask whether sufficient mechanisms exist within existing institutions to hear the complaints and questions posed by individuals serially joined and affected by a potentially oppressive practice; and whether procedures exist for instigating change based on the reactions of those most affected by a set of rules. Specific participatory rights relevant to a practice could emerge in order to demonstrate sufficient commitment to agency freedom. And women in local communities must be given the chance to construct those as well. A "council of elders" completely unwilling to listen to those who reject a series of practices and who cannot sustain tactics that allow a broader community, including women, to hear and evaluate whether a practice should continue, remains suspect. Extraordinarily pressing reasons would have to exist for undermining participatory mechanisms that ensure the statement and exercise of agency.[6]

But won't older women in a community continually indoctrinate youth into oppressive expectations and behaviors? Giving some individuals more voice does not guarantee a proper critique of local norms. But I would add, then, that valuing agency should supplement a more cautious approach to criticizing norms while still helping us search for obvious general limits on degradation of agency that come via violence and killing. Such general limits are necessary for basic agency flourishing. So honor killing, for example, as part of a tradition, would remain unacceptable, deeply suspect from the outset of a discussion; and it is hard to imagine that those who support such killing could garner consent *by those affected by the rule.* Moreover, veiling or arranged marriages, while harmful too, could be justifiable but start out suspect. Do these practices value the agency of those involved and can they evolve via processes that consult women as well as men about their exercise of agency? The test for eliminating these less violent but potentially undesirable practices would not involve dismissing them outright since they don't meet the standards in an original position, but would involve asking if attention is paid to the way practices incorporate multiple perspectives, whether those identified as women are grouped as such to exclude them from participation, why exclusions exist, and whether women can participate in discussing the exclusions and shaping the practices over time. Again, this last point is critical—the expectation is that we not ask this question once, but envision *ongoing* mechanisms that allow women's voices to shape and reshape, argue and struggle over their futures in their particular situations.

Many could still say that this approach to the individual and freedom is too biased—and that it might garner support more broadly only if we recognize its limited applicability. The family as private, with its intimacy and distinctive relations shaped by love and responsibility, hierarchy and tradition, must be allowed to interpret a conception of freedom, especially for women, in its own way. This shielding of the private finds voice among many keen to maintain the integrity of "their" culture (as with those who sign but fail to implement the Convention on the Elimination of All Forms of Discrimination Against Women [CEDAW]); or it finds expression in Rawls's later political liberalism, which seeks to avoid imposing a "comprehensive" moral doctrine on others and to establish legitimacy among an array of individuals, especially religious and nonreligious persons, who wish to form consensus around just principles. But while familiar to say that such separation of public and private looks troublesome, the problem is worth noting. And we may add that the dismissal of the broader applicability or translatability of my assumptions may rely on an unconvincing view of culture as uniform and apolitical. This uniformity assumption can be challenged; and such apolitical expectations can be found wanting when one reads about the way so many religious movements shape their views in order to engage in power struggles against failed modernization efforts by emerging nation-states (see, for example, Fanon 1963; and Moghadam 1994). Moreover, no one is suggesting here that we eliminate religious law, but that we should insist that Sharia, or anything akin to it, not supersede altogether agency choice and conditions enhancing it. As for Rawls, I see no need to go as far as he does to protect consensus about public principles, in large part because Rawls continues to rely on a more controversial notion of autonomy than the view of agency discussed here. Rawls may fear that in a multicultural society, consensus will not result easily; but this may be because his echoes of Kant remain controversial (Freeberg 2002, chap. 2), whereas an ethic based on the value of agency should look much less wedded to a "comprehensive" moral doctrine.

Broad formulations about women's rights or general protections for women as a collectivity do face challenges. Of course, many engaged in the practice of implementing human rights and formulating women's international rights might wonder about this preoccupation with the justification of such ideas. Is this simply idle philosophical banter? Why the fuss and struggle when much talk emerges in diplomatic circles about women's rights; why worry when political watchdog groups or nongovernmental organizations now concern themselves with such matters, or when international courts, for example, take on cases about rape in wartime? The problem has been that even with such efforts, high-level initiatives to make women's needs a central concern remain limited; enforcement of existing declarations (such as CEDAW) stalls even in the United States and elsewhere; and too often propagandistic ways of talking about women's subordination occur, making it hard to see women's lives taken seriously (hence First Lady Laura Bush's brief entry into the discussion of women's subordination under the Taliban at a critical time when the Bush White House marshaled efforts to send troops into Afghanistan and declare war on terrorism). The expectations here acknowledge that we share a common capacity for freedom and that "women" are often grouped together and denied freedom based on gender. But the gestures hope to start to formulate assumptions in general terms with room to respond to the most trenchant critics.

The claims of agency are difficult to ignore. They outline chastened assumptions about freedom. Not even the religious individual is generally said to lack agency as defined above. If this is so, then there are protections worth building from this capacity. But if a key value here is that we need to imagine ways to let rule-following, embedded humans have the opportunity to imagine meaningful protections for themselves within the practices they inhabit, then the relation between any general protections or demands must be formulated with a level of particularistic involvement from those living the practices that shape them. Existing rights or demands as outlined by the UN could end up altered given this set of expectations; or they might grow tremendously if we took seriously the need for enhanced participatory mechanisms for collecting information and letting women debate locally and more fully about their expectations. On all fronts, tactics pressing to enhance women's voices, their lives, expectations, needs, and the like, must be explored—and such tactics unquestionably demand the sustained attention of those engaged in practical and theoretical discussions alike.

Notes

1. This shift toward embracing Kant becomes more pronounced in Rawls's Dewey Lectures, of course, and fades in *Political Liberalism*. It is a shift that Okin finds untenable (1994), as noted.

2. You catch your heel in the pavement and fall. Is this a "free" act? I stop you because I happen to be in front of you. Have I made you unfree? Supporters of pure negative freedom say yes. Flathman rightly assumes an ordinary user of language may say no.

3. Flathman continues here: "In general, human beings are coerced if threatened with death, severe pain, bondage, and so forth. It is therefore rational to employ such threats when trying to coerce someone and reasonable to treat such threats as excusing the performance of those subjected to them. But some people are indifferent to or welcome death; pain thresholds and the capacity to tolerate pain vary; prison has been said to be the just person's proper place in an unjust regime; on a cold night jail may be the preferred abode of derelicts" (1987, 213).

4. "There is a paradox lurking here that can be put in the form of a question: how can a society committed unqualifiedly to freedom of political discussion (and autonomy) exclude any remotely political beliefs or arrangements from such a discussion, let alone what on Fishkin's account is its most fundamental political arrangement? Fishkin's liberties are among the basic institutions or arrangements of the society; as such his own argument would seem to forbid (on pain of loss of legitimacy) regarding them as beyond criticism" (Flathman 1987, 301).

5. For an extension of this discussion of Flathman's views on freedom and its implications for other positive freedom positions, see Freeberg 2002, chap. 1.

6. One might question whether this position sounds like a feminism simply adopting a deliberate democratic framework, much like Seyla Benhabib's, for example. I'm sympathetic to deliberate democratic efforts (see Freeberg 2002, chap. 3). But the position does start by assuming that individuals must demonstrate participatory virtuousness, and of a kind that can be hard to identify in a multiplicity of cultures. As a result, I would build from a notion of agency—hoping that it is more likely to receive widespread support than the deliberative democratic view of autonomy. And then I would expect to construct rights or protections from here. Agency may support more limited protections than those proposed by deliberative democrats—and certainly a lesser degree of civic virtue immediately. But my focus would still rest on encouraging rules and procedures within practices that stimulate the argumentation and engagement that the deliberative democratic position values.

References

Ackerman, Bruce. 1994. "Political Liberalism." *Journal of Philosophy* 91, no. 7: 364–386.
Charlesworth, Hillary. 1994. "What Are 'Women's International Human Rights'?" In Rebecca Cook, ed., *Human Rights of Women*. Philadelphia: University of Pennsylvania Press, 58–84.
Coomaraswamy, Radhika. 1999. "Reinventing International Law: Women's Rights as Human Rights in the International Community." In Peter Van Ness, ed., *Debating Human Rights: Critical Essays from the United States and Asia*. New York: Routledge, 167–183.
Donnolly, Jack. 1989. *Universal Human Rights in Theory and Practice*. Ithaca, NY: Cornell University Press.
Exdell, John. 1994. "Feminism, Fundamentalism, and Liberal Legitimacy." *Canadian Journal of Philosophy* 24, no. 3: 441–464.
Fanon, Frantz. 1963. *The Wretched of the Earth*. Constance Farrington, trans. New York: Grove Press.
Flathman, Richard. 1987. *The Philosophy and Politics of Freedom*. Chicago: University of Chicago Press.
———. 1993. *Thomas Hobbes: Skepticism, Individuality, and Chastened Politics*. Newbury Park, CA: Sage.
Flax, Jane. 1995. "Race/Gender and the Ethics of Difference: A Reply to Okin's 'Gender Inequality and Cultural Differences.'" *Political Theory* 23, no. 3: 500–510.
Freeberg, Ellen. 2002. *Regarding Equality: Rethinking Contemporary Theories of Citizenship, Freedom, and the Limits of Moral Pluralism*. Lanham, MD: Lexington Books.
Henkin, Louis. 1990. *The Age of Rights*. New York: Columbia University Press.
Meyer, Ann Elizabeth. 1995. "Rhetorical Strategies and Official Policies on Women's Rights: The Merits and Drawbacks of the New World Hypocrisy." In Mahnaz Afkhami, ed., *Faith And Freedom: Women's Human Rights in the Muslim World*. Syracuse, NY: Syracuse University Press, 135–159.
Moghadam, Valentine M., ed. 1994. *Identity Politics and Women. Cultural Reassertion and Feminism in International Perspective*. Boulder, CO: Westview Press.
Mohanty, Chandra. 1984. "Under Western Eyes: Feminist Scholarship and Colonial Discourse." In Susan Moller Okin and Jane Mansbridge, eds., *Feminism*, Volume II. Aldershot, UK: Edward Elgar, 79–106.
Oakeshott, Michael. 1975. *On Human Conduct*. London: Clarendon Press.
Okin, Susan Moller. 1989a. "Humanist Liberalism." In Nancy Rosenblum, ed., *Liberalism and the Moral Life*. Cambridge: Harvard University Press, 39–53.
———. 1989b. *Justice, Gender, and the Family*. New York: Basic Books.
———. 1990a. "Reason and Feeling in Thinking About Justice." In Cass Sunstein, ed., *Feminism and Political Theory*. Chicago: University of Chicago Press, 15–35.
———. 1990b. "Thinking Like a Woman." In Debra Rhode, ed., *Theoretical Per-*

spectives on Sexual Difference. New Haven, CT: Yale University Press, 145–159, 288–291.

———. 1994. "Political Liberalism, Justice, and Gender." *Ethics* 105, no. 1 (October): 23–43.

———. 1995a. "Inequality Between the Sexes in Different Cultural Contexts." In Martha Nussbaum and Jonathan Glover, eds., *Women, Culture, and Development.* Oxford: Oxford University Press, 274–297.

———. 1995b. "Response to Jane Flax." *Political Theory* 23, no. 1 (August): 511–516.

———. 1998a. "Feminism and Multiculturalism: Some Tensions." *Ethics* 108 (July): 661–684.

———. 1998b. "Feminism, Women's Human Rights, and Cultural Differences." *Hypatia* 13, no. 1 (Spring): 32–52.

———. 1999. *Is Multiculturalism Bad for Women?* Joshua Cohen and Matthew Howard, eds. Princeton: Princeton University Press.

Rawls, John. 1971. *A Theory of Justice.* Cambridge: Harvard University Press.

———. 1993. "The Law of Peoples." In Stephen Shute and Susan Hurley, eds., *Human Rights.* New York: Basic Books.

———. 1996. *Political Liberalism.* New York: Columbia University Press.

Riley, Denise. 1988. *"Am I That Name?" Feminism and the Category of "Women" in History.* Minneapolis: University of Minnesota Press.

Romany, Celina. 1994. "State Responsibility Goes Private: The Feminist Critique of the Public/Private." In Rebecca Cook, ed., *Human Rights of Women.* Philadelphia: University of Pennsylvania Press, 85–115.

Young, Iris Marion. 1990. *Justice and the Politics of Difference.* Princeton: Princeton University Press.

———. 1995. "Gender as Seriality: Thinking About Women as a Social Collective." In Linda Nicholson and Steven Seidman, eds., *Social Postmodernism: Beyond Identity Politics.* Cambridge: Cambridge University Press, 187–215.

Part II

The Dynamics and Counterdynamics of Globalization

5

The Politics of Culture and Human Rights in Iran

Globalizing and Localizing Dynamics

Mahmood Monshipouri

Globalization has spurred a rigorous debate among Iranians over what interpretation of Islam should shape their community's destiny at the dawn of a new millennium.[1] Reform is now more than an idea; it is an essential part of a public discourse in Iran as the theocratic foundations underpinning national politics have become the subject of a nationwide debate. In recent years, the country's moral and political divide has further deepened, with the ruling clerics facing a critical normative and institutional challenge. There can be no doubt, as Richard W. Bulliet (1999, 195) has noted, that "the era of the Shaykh in the classroom instilling wisdom and devotion in his students is gone; the era of the religious quester, male or female, logging onto the Internet in search of answers to moral and political questions—regardless of the formal qualifications of the answer—has arrived." Increasingly, Iran's ruling elites, cultural elites, and public at large have been drawn into a debate over the globalizing and localizing dynamics of change, with some edging toward a convergence with the rest of the global community while others maintain the more traditional Islamic stance against the intrusion of "alien values and ideals" into their local cultural traditions.

Following a brief overview of the internal political dynamics of Iran since the 1979 Islamic Revolution, this chapter addresses the question of how globalization is affecting Iranian society and polity. Powerful ideas and norms such as democracy and human rights have reached different segments of the Iranian population because of the globalization process, resulting in the social construction—in both cultural and political senses—

of new identities and interests as well as shared meanings that Iranians assign to themselves and others. Two related claims shape the discussions in this chapter: (1) that globalization has simultaneously produced globalizing and localizing dynamics in Iran, paradoxically strengthening both sides of the competing forces in the struggle for Iran's cultural direction; and (2) that the interaction of internal and external dynamics in the evolution of Iran's cultural situation tends to reinforce the country's reform movement. I next examine the impact of globalization on the fluid and unstable internal struggle among Iranian ruling elite—that is, the locals and the cosmopolitans. Finally, I explore the implications of globalization for the state of human rights discourse in Iran, with special focus on women's rights and the free press as two areas where the views of the conservatives and reformists continue to be at loggerheads.

Globalization: Interfactional Disputes

Globalization is frequently defined as an evolutionary process and a sociopolitical paradigm shift. The global evolutionary process refers to a trajectory that moves from economic and technological globalization to sociopolitical changes, culminating in cultural adjustments. Thus conceived, globalization involves shifts in values, lifestyles, tolerance for diversity, and respect for individual choice and freedoms. Globalization can also be viewed as a new hegemonic system upheld by the world's major capitalist economies to promote their own political and economic interests. Seen from this perspective, globalization is regarded by the conservative Muslims (as in Iran) as a threat to their cultural authenticity and political solidarity. This explains the conservatives' aversion toward not necessarily everything global but only those aspects of globalization that would threaten their grip over political and cultural status quo. Paradoxically, yet understandably, this perception of threat, coupled with myriad economic and political uncertainties associated with globalization, has intensified interfactional disputes and prolonged the conservatives' political longevity.

The forces of globalization have nevertheless thrust dramatic changes upon Iran's national politics. Twenty years after the Islamic Revolution, a young generation now asks what the revolution was all about. Yearning for basic freedoms, social tolerance, and political pluralism, Iranian youth are not content with what their parents have achieved through revolution.[2] They see in the globalized world a hopeful sign of change, and are keen to exploit technological opportunities to support their favored political candidates. Today's youth in Iran show a heightened concern for human rights, pressing their claims for universal rights and democratic governance.

In addition to the youth, two other groups that have been greatly influenced by the dynamics of globalization are women and the press. Not surprisingly, these are the same groups whose support proved instrumental in
electing President Mohammad Khatami. The public followed the lead of the
intellectuals, scholars, and the press. To many Iranian journalists (Abdi
1999, 139), this movement was consistent with the global resurgence of democracy. Nowhere, however, is the impact of globalization so drastically felt
and visible than in the country's cultural domains, where the divisions between different clerics have led to an internal cultural conflict over how to interpret Islamic values. The analysis of cultural politics has indeed become
pivotal to any understanding of the globalizing and localizing dynamics
within Iran's domestic politics. Before assessing how cultural politics has
played out, a brief overview of Iran's cultural transformation during the
revolutionary and postrevolutionary periods is essential.

Islamic Revolution: From Radicalism to Pragmatism

Spearheaded by Ayatollah Ruhollah Khomeini (1902–1989), the 1979 Islamic Revolution toppled the regime of Mohammad Reza Shah Pahlavi,
ending 2,500 years of monarchy. Of the many grievances that led to the
revolution, the most widely pronounced included the Pahlavi regime's
repressive measures against political dissent and traditional conservative
Islamic culture, distracting as well as alienating the shah from civilian
politics; its mismanagement of the economy, contributing mightily to the
widening gap between the rich and the poor; and most important, the shah's
unrelenting drive toward Westernization and modernization, undermining
a sense of national and cultural identity. In the end, as William Spencer
(1998, 59) writes, "The shah's Great Civilization lay in ruins. Like a trans-
plant, it had been an attempt to impose a foreign model of life on the
Iranian community, a surgical attachment that has been rejected."

Khomeini's ascendancy to power was followed by the prolonged crisis
over the holding of U.S. hostages (1979–1981), the Iran-Iraq war (1980–
1988), the dismantling of opposition groups, both at home and abroad, the
issuance of a fatwa (death decree) for Salman Rushdie, the author of the
novel *The Satanic Verses* (1989), and the Islamization of all facets of life.
Khomeini's death in 1989 left behind disruptive interfactional disputes and
the lack of a credible successor to maintain his agenda with the same
commitment and tenacity. Ever since, many of Iran's 70 million people
have become vastly disillusioned with the clerics' reign of power. The
government has incarcerated tens of thousands of its opponents without

due process and has "systematically tortured prisoners to extract false confessions and public recantations" (Abrahamian 2000, 647). In its foreign policy expressions, the Iranian government has shared with its Asian partners a general disapproval of the West's continued use of human rights as a means of pursuing normative hegemony and power politics (Monshipouri 1998b, 106–107).

Khomeini's death, as John Limber (1995, 51) wrote, left Iran a "theocracy without a chief theocrat," in which the populist fervor of the early years of the Islamic Revolution—with its street demonstrations and popular display of support—was gone. The post-Khomeini era has given way to an Islamic pragmatism in both Iran's foreign policy and its domestic reforms. Factional disputes and the primacy of the economy over ideological issues have emerged as the key developments in Iranian politics in the post-Khomeini era.

A national referendum abolished the post of prime minister and replaced it with a popularly elected president as head of the government—a head of the government who did not need to be approved by the Majles (parliament). This significant move toward popular democracy was construed by some analysts as the beginning of rising powers of the president. Mohsen Milani (1993, 359) argued that this transformation marked the "transition from the consolidation phase to the reconstruction phase of the Islamic Revolution." The changes also enabled President Ali Akbar Hashemi Rafsanjani to implement his reforms while relying on a platform of moderation and pragmatism. Much power was transferred from the clergy to the state, making it the dominant political and economic actor in Iran's political scene (Milani 1993, 371–373).

Although the Majles was important in promoting popular sovereignty in the post-Khomeini era, it failed to provide genuinely broad political participation. Parliamentary elections were manipulated by an oversight committee that controlled access to the Majles (Bill 1993, 404–405) and interfactional disputes continued to present problems for the executive branch. Rafsanjani's liberalization program (1989–1997), however, faced many obstacles, including low levels of private investment, low growth rates, budget bottlenecks, and mounting foreign debt. Corruption and mismanagement further complicated the state's liberalization programs (Wright 1996, 163–164).

Rafsanjani's first term (1989–1993) brought only slight relaxation of the strict enforcement of Islamic social codes by the so-called morals squads and security police. During his second term (1993–1997), however, his wife (Effat Marashi) and daughter (Faezeh Hashemi) actively campaigned for more liberal social planning, eventually obtaining beneficial legislation for families. Their political engagement brought about further relaxation of the strict Islamic codes of behavior. Meanwhile, an emerging debate surrounding civil society brought the discussion of the common standards of moral decency and human rights to the country's domestic forefront. The protection and promotion of women's rights entered a new phase when Zahra Mostafavi founded the Association of Muslim Women to fight for greater access to higher education. In 1992, President Rafsanjani created the Bureau of Women's Affairs and appointed Shahla Habibi as his adviser on women's affairs (Monshipouri 1998b, 191).

Although no such momentous progress toward the creation of a vibrant civil society was made under President Rafsanjani, and although no major reform program was initiated to challenge the conservatives' platform, the terms of debate over civil society, governance, and democracy began to slowly shape public discourse. It was not until the election of Rafsanjani's successor, Mohammad Khatami, who removed cultural restrictions on the printing of books and magazines previously banned, that the real discourse about the reform took place. Since that time, a riveting national debate about cultural conformity, continuity, and change has energized the country. In some respects, globalization has brought back the same old debate that Iranians encountered during the shah's era: How to absorb the shocks of modernization?

Khatami and Cultural Politics

In a decisive electoral victory on May 23, 1997, Mohammad Khatami became Iran's new president. Khatami's landslide victory—he received almost 70 percent of the popular vote—was a firm rebuke to hard-line clerics who had dominated Iranian politics since the 1979 revolution. Khatami's supporters—mainly youth, women, intellectuals, left-wing political activists, and ethnic minorities—demanded greater social and political freedom and more political pluralism. Support for Khatami was impressive not only in urban areas but also in village and rural outposts; he also won strong support in Iran's heavily Kurdish western regions.

In keeping with modern notions of rights and the rule of law, the civil society discourse has fostered the idea of adjusting to the zeitgeist of today's dominant standards of national and international legitimacy. There have emerged sharp disagreements among the ruling elite as to how to respond to the civil society's growing demands on the political regime, with the conservatives favoring the all-too-familiar mode of social control and reformists calling for an open society. Supporters of President Khatami's reformist agenda have advocated a regional détente and improved ties with the West, especially with the United States, on both economic and political grounds. Public opinion has grown increasingly supportive of such foreign policy initiatives, challenging the conservative camp and their allied Islamic radicals to put forth a credible foreign policy agenda. The conservatives, who in response have increasingly turned to state-authorized repression against civil society, especially the secular intelligentsia, have so far failed to offer a viable alternative.

On the domestic front, Khatami brought greater freedom and tolerance not just to the political regime but to the social sphere as well. As a direct result of his policies, freedom of the press reasonably upheld, at least up until the beginning of 2000. Since February 2000 the conservative judiciary has shut down more than thirty reformist newspapers and magazines and has jailed more than twenty-five reformist journalists, intellectuals, and political activists. Almost all of the sixteen reformist writers and activists who attended the Berlin Conference—organized and sponsored by the Heinrich Böll Foundation, an arm of the German Greens Party, during April 7–8, 2000—were put on trial.

On June 8, 2001, Khatami swept his way into the presidency for the second term by winning 78.3 percent of the vote. This victory, along with the reformers' electoral triumph in the Sixth Majles elections, held on February 18, 2000, and subsequently on May 5, 2000, in which reformists won 189 seats of the parliament's total 290 seats, pointed to a national mandate of the sort.[3] Although these victories emboldened ordinary people to speak more openly about public policies and their shortcomings, the reformers' initiative in parliament were repeatedly blocked. On August 6, 2000, when reformers prepared legislation to ease the press law, Khamenei blocked it. In the ensuing months, several reformist newspapers were closed and many reformist leaders were arrested. One observer characterized this situation as a de facto coup (Gasiorowski 2001, 15–16).

Conservatives seemed poised to block any reformist measure, as the power struggle between the two factions reached a new deadlock during the summer of 2002. The conservative clergy became divided and disagreed among themselves as to the pace and direction of change. All indications pointed to the fact that they had failed to run a modern country, while alienating large segments of society (Hardy 2002). As the pressure and popular discontent steadily mounted, one BBC correspondent noted, people began to talk increasingly about an implosion within the regime, rather than an explosion from without (Muir, 2002). Meanwhile Khatami remained in office and the parliament remained in reformist hands, but the conservatives used extensive control over other branches of the state apparatus to prevent the president and parliament from materializing their reform agenda. In recent years, Khatami's popularity has decreased noticeably as the reform process has stalled. During November 2002, Tehran students protested the blasphemy sentence against reformist professor Hashem Aghajari, who gave a speech in August 2002 in which he challenged the rule of hard-line clerics. Using this occasion, the students tapped into deepening frustration with the slow pace of change pledged by President Khatami, whose powers and broad mandate have been constantly opposed by unelected conservatives (Peterson 2002, 6). During his first term, Khatami's policies arguably led to improved gender relations in society at large. He bolstered women's freedom in many areas and appointed several female deputy vice presidents for technical affairs and sports. As a result, female students now compete equally with male students for university seats in all engineering fields previously reserved solely for male students.

Khatami greatly contributed to the strength of civil society in Iran by opening up the political arena, by espousing the formation of new political parties by civil groups, and by supporting the rule of law. He laid the groundwork for introducing transparency into the political texture of society via the institutionalization of law and multiparty system. He abolished the president's slush fund, spoke favorably of all aspects of a civil society, and publicly acknowledged both the negative and positive achievements of Western civilization. Khatami frequently referred to the "dialogue among civilizations and cultures" as the most effective way to achieve global détente. Under his administration, Iran has accepted the UN Chemical Weapons Convention, and many restrictions have been placed on religious vigilantes and militia who spy on people's private lives to enforce Islamic social codes—that is, codes of dress and behavior.

Despite his significant progress toward liberalization, the decisive question remained: How would Khatami's mandate translate into political capital and power in the second term? One measure of Khatami's success, therefore, was how far his government was prepared to go to limit the authority of the supreme leader. The fact remains that Khatami was unable to implement concrete policy reforms during his first term. Given Khatami's inability to convert his popularity into real reforms and given that popular frustration and dismal economic conditions have proven incapable of dethroning the conservatives, the question arises as to whether the democratic gains for which the Iranian people have fought so tenaciously in recent years can be rolled back.

Under the Iranian constitution, the ultimate authority rests with the supreme leader, Ayatollah Sayyed Ali Khamenei, who currently controls many powerful institutions, including the military, the Ministry of Intelligence, the basij paramilitary forces, the national police, the Ministry of Information and Intelligence, and the Revolutionary Guard. Moreover, he maintains control of the judiciary and national broadcasting—that is, state radio and television—and names the key members of the Council of Guardians (Showray-e Neghahban), which serves as a watchdog body capable of blocking any legislation that it sees as unfit according to Islamic ideals. Such wide-ranging powers surely affect the viability of civil society in Iran.

Civil Society: Reality or Farce?

Civil society–state relations in Iran are shaped in a politically fractured setting that calls for the simultaneous leadership of a nonelected permanent supreme leader (*velayat-e faqih*) and an elected president. Theocracy in Iran, as defined solely in terms of jurist's guardianship, has become coterminous with the rule by allegiance. The steering mechanism of this guardianship is controlled by the supreme leader, who has been granted wide-ranging authority by the constitution.

There can be no doubt that Ayatollah Ruhollah Khomeini's charismatic power made the tolerance of such a modern theocracy possible. The post-Khomeini era, however, has seen the emergence of a divided state, part Islamism and part republicanism, a mixture of theocracy and electoral democracy (Abrahamian 2000, 632–634). This division of authority raises the basic question of whether it is possible to have a civil society in a theocracy such as Iran.

The Islamic Republic's political contradictions have stemmed largely from the lack of clarity about who actually heads the state and who controls the levers of power. Although conducted within certain limits, elections are held regularly in Iran. The public elects the president, the Majles, and the Assembly of Experts (Majles-e Khebregan). But the *velayat-e faqih* and the clerically dominated Council of Guardians determine who can compete in these elections. The power of the Council of Guardians to vet parliamentary candidates remains a big obstacle to the enactment of a reform agenda. The Council of Guardians, according to a new rule, must now give written justification for its decision to disqualify parliamentary candidates if the rejected candidate so desires.

The absolute powers of the *velayat-e faqih* also pose a major hindrance to the effective operation of democracy and civil society. He is elected by the Assembly of Experts, which is made up of eighty-six seats. This body has the power to suspend the supreme leader, should it decide to do so. Candidates for the Assembly of Experts, however, are screened by the

Council of Guardians, a twelve–member clerical body composed half of clerics and half of lay jurists, who are knowledgeable in Islamic law (Sharia). It is the role of the Council of Guardians to interpret the constitution, as well as to review and confirm the compatibility of its laws with the tenets of Islamic law. The members of the Council of Guardians are appointed by the *velayat-e faqih* himself. This form of restricted democracy within a fractured political structure is bound to run into periodic dead ends.

Because President Khatami is a member of the clergy and very observant of the Iranian constitution, it is unrealistic to anticipate a drastic move toward any form of liberal democracy in the near future. Ironically, however, President Khatami's policies favoring wide-ranging civil liberties and social reform have raised a basic question: Can the advocacy of and movement toward social reform lead to the demise of theocracy in Iran? Some observers respond to this question with a resounding no, arguing that given the conservatives' hold on power, the power structure in the Iranian constitution practically curbs the outcome of electoral democracy and social reforms. Consider, for example, the most recent elections for the Assembly of Experts (October 23, 1998), in which the conservatives gained fifty-four seats and President Khatami's supporters won only thirteen seats; sixteen seats went to independents.

Those who believe that advocacy of and movement toward social reform can lead to the demise of theocracy in Iran argue that a nascent civil society has emerged, and that its gradual growth must not be underestimated. They call attention to the February 26, 1999, municipal elections, in which virtually 60 percent of the qualified voters participated; voters picked 111,000 council members in 720 cities, 240 towns, and almost 34,000 villages in the first municipal elections ever. Reformists made a clean sweep in the Tehran city council elections and won in the 28 provincial capitals.[4] Moreover, 4,000 female candidates participated in these elections, winning all of the seats in some cities.[5] The victories of Abdullah Nouri, Saeed Atrianfard, Saeed Hajarian, and Jamileh Kadiver, all reformists whose candidacies the conservatives failed to bar prior to city council elections, suggested that civil society is vibrant and bent on strengthening the democratization process in Iran. The results of the February 18, 2000, legislative elections (the Sixth Majles), in which hard-liners lost control of the parliament and reformists won a landslide victory, pointed to yet another nationwide reaffirmation of the reform movement.

President Khatami's efforts to foster the rule of law and to promote social reforms, including depoliticizing the civil society, ensuring equality of access to political channels, and protecting civil rights for all segments of the population, have all fueled a new debate among journalists, intellectuals, and academics: Should the clergy enjoy necessarily superior rights and privileges over the laity? Increasingly, objections are raised to the notion that the state belongs to the clergy and that rule by allegiance should prevail over rule by a publicly elected leader. These objections have multiplied as the globalizing dynamics have struck a chord in Iranian society, raising the level of public awareness of democratic rights and individual freedoms. The interaction of external influences, such as global trends of democratization and human rights, and internal dynamics, such as calls for open society and economic growth, has reinforced an enormous need for change, intensifying in the process the internal cultural clash between localism and cosmopolitanism.

The Politics of Cultural Claims and Counterclaims

Some social theorists (Inglehart 1997, 26) argue that modernization is an unfinished project and that it must be built on rather than rejected. Others (Anderson, Seibert, and Wagner 1998, 145) point out that tradition is likewise a perpetually unfinished project—that is, how people understand their traditions and apply them to practical situations is subject to dynamic change and constant negotiation. In juxtaposing these positions, the key question of who interprets traditional and modern norms—that is to say, what group is in possession of culture—arises. Are cultural norms, over whose formation and interpretation competing interests and claims assert themselves, simply tools of the ruling elite?[6]

At present, Iran is embroiled in a power struggle over what some scholars have aptly described as authoritative definitions of cultural meaning: "In the arena of cultural politics, power interests assert competing claims to the labels, ideals, and symbols that a community holds in high esteem" (Anderson, Seibert, and Wagner 1998, 145). The assertion that culture is intimately linked with power is crucial to understanding politics in the Muslim world. Ronald Inglehart (1997, 26–27) writes, "It would be naïve to believe that culture is neutral: in virtually every society, it legitimates the established social order—partly because the dominant elite try to shape it to help perpetuate their rights." But he also adds that culture does many things, including integrating society in terms of common goals, satisfying intellectual and aesthetic needs, and placing some restraints on the ruling elite. "What leads to cultural change," Inglehart continues "is that life experiences of a new generation give rise to new perceptions of reality."

As noted above, Iranian politics has been witness to a growing power struggle between the conservatives and the reformists, or "the locals" and "the cosmopolitans" respectively. Some scholars (Jacobsen and Lawson 1996, 217) have cautioned against such dichotomies, contending that it is wrong to assume that the relationship between the universals and the particulars is inevitably antithetical. Rather than dichotomizing these dynamics and assuming a negative view of the tensions they create, these scholars insist, they should be viewed as positive elements in a dynamic process by which distinct communities around the world retain important elements of specificity without shielding themselves in a sealed world of cultural differences. This chapter proceeds from the same assumption, while at the same time revealing an existing political conflict over cultural rights to determine how Iranian society should adapt to the forces of globalization.

Perhaps the most daunting challenge facing clerical establishment in Iran at the dawn of the twenty-first century is whose vision of an Islamic society will prevail: that of the reformists or that of the conservatives? There are powerful forces and voices of change at work, and there remain many uncertainties about how to accelerate these changes in the face of a conservative backlash. The central conflict that characterizes Iranian cultural politics today is the perceived incompatibility between global and local paradigms. This conflict has brought about an acrimonious national debate over the direction of social change that Iran next assumes. A report in *The Economist* (July 31, 1999, 38) best captured Iran's reformist-conservative feud within the establishment: "Two decades after a revolution fought in the name of freedom and cultural authenticity, the Islamic establishment is tearing itself apart over those very issues." The voices of change have largely come from the press, women's organizations, student organizations, workers' unions, and ethnic minority movements, all of whom have pushed for reforms that open Iran to a sustainable democracy with fully realized civil-political rights. These groups, who are in part the product of globalization, have become in some sense sources of globalization. At the same time, as noted above, the paradoxes and uncertainties associated with globalization have given rise to localism as a force. Fearing that their autonomy, power, interests, and values would be compromised—or more accurately, undermined—in a globalized world, localizers have tightened their grips over society.

The Locals

Islamic localizers are not a homogeneous group. They pursue different tactics, with some pushing for further purification of social and political practices and others resorting to violence in their pursuit to maintain the status quo. Nevertheless, they both value and embrace cultural conformity around which the Iranian society has historically been shaped. They view aspects of globalization, especially those that relate to the spread of Western values and standards worldwide, as a part of the West's hegemonic push and cultural imperialism.

Deeply suspicious of the global human rights discourse, the locals deny the validity of the universality of civil and political rights, arguing that these rights are culturally specific Western values. The localizers fear that the growing economic globalization, with its ability to shape political conditions as well as to penetrate local economic foundations, as suggested by both Caren Irr and Kavita Philip (Chapters 1 and 3), would pose a serious threat to collective rights to culture. They see the individual as part of the community, to which he or she owes certain obligations. Guided by hierarchical tenets, as Charles Lockhart's grid-group theory's portrayal of hierarchists suggests (Chapter 10), the locals tend to support social rights only to foster national solidarity in the face of the zeitgeist known as globalization.

The localizers argue that Sharia is the Islamic constitution and that the Islamic community paradigm, which is based on towhid (the unity of God, human beings, and universe), provides meaning and spirit to life and action. As such, towhid cannot be subordinated to the notion of the information society paradigm and the emerging global information community. The Islamic notion of community, or ummah, is a society with inclusive membership but binding commitment to Islam. The ummah respects diversity, but at the same time stresses unity (Mowlana 1993, 398–407).

Localizers tend to take an approach that is widely known as the "value dominance critique": human rights are a Western creation rooted in Western values imposed on the non-Western world. This perspective dovetails with the "clash of civilizations" paradigm developed by Samuel Huntington, which argues that in the post–Cold War era, wars of politics and ideology have yielded to a war of cultures and that Western insistence on the universality of its culture and values "is false, it is immoral and it is dangerous" (1996, 310). Some Asian experts, in contrast, have critically noted that the value dominance critique reinforces, and indeed rationalizes, the Orientalist prejudice that Asian culture is inadequate for human rights and democracy (Tatsuo 1999, 41). Propagating the value dominance critique renders it possible for the conservatives to defend a strong version of cultural relativism.

Riding an old wave of anti-Western sentiment, localizers see globalization not just as a threat to the intricate social fabric of Muslim communities, but also as intimately linked to larger Western political and commercial interests. Globalization, they argue, is synonymous with Western global hegemony and represents a new form of "Westoxification" aimed at provoking political and cultural conflicts in the Muslim world (Ayubi 1999, 71–73). Seen this way, globalization is a form of cultural and economic incursion that is meant to destabilize their internal politics. Because globalization promotes, and is itself based on, a system of international capital that includes an impoverished and fragmented periphery, the economically marginalized masses are open to solutions rooted in the new religiously based appeals (Randall 1999, 50).

Some observers have even gone beyond this simple core-periphery division in the latest global system. Saskia Sassen (2000, 71) notes that cities that are strategic sites in the global economy tend to become somewhat disconnected from their region or nation. Likewise, inside global cities we can see a new geography of centrality and marginality. "Alongside these new global and regional hierarchies of cities and high-tech industrial districts," Sassen writes, "lies a vast territory that has become increasingly peripheral, increasingly excluded from the major economic processes that fuel economic growth in the new global economy."

The locals control most of the levers of power, including the army, the police, the national television station (Sedai-e Iran), the judiciary, and the Revolutionary Guard. They have forged an alliance with the traditional business sector, known as Bazzaris; bureaucrats tied to the regime; and conservative religious overlords. Their combative members have regularly resorted to ruthless violence to maintain cultural conformity and the political status quo, carving out a place for themselves in the debate to determine the extent to which "Islamic" societies, such as Iran's, should undergo change (Spencer 1998, 64). In yet another judicial crackdown during 2002, forty-one members of the Freedom Movement of Iran (FMI), a nongovernmental organization founded by the late prime minister Mehdi Bazargan, were convicted and the movement itself was declared illegal. The conservative establishment feared that the FMI was gaining more appeal among young people and that it was forging significant ties with the country's reform movement, which operates within the regime's legal boundary.[7]

The Cosmopolitans

Also known as reformers, the cosmopolitans are both the product and the source of globalization. Over the past two decades, the cosmopolitans have emerged in the context of an interdependent world characterized by the increasing interaction of internal behavior and external values. In recent years, communications and information technology has also fostered such interactive dynamics. Informed by global ideas and ideals, reformers have in turn become an agent of globalization, distancing themselves from the revolutionary zeal while advocating change in response to new information and experiences.

The cosmopolitans are composed of two groups: economic constructionists and political constructionists. While the former group stresses economic liberalization and market globalization, the latter underscores the importance of political liberalization and democratic governance. Economic constructionists, who were associated with President Rafsanjani's regime (1989–1997), came to be known as the Servants of Reconstruction. They viewed the country's economic reconstruction after the war with Iraq as their main task. The political constructionists, who support President Khatami, consist of journalists, intelligentsia, the revived Society of the Militant Clergy, the Islamic Association of Students, and the Islamic Women's Association. They are intent on constructing a new Islamic image worldwide, meeting the requirements of change in this new era of democratization.

These differences aside, the cosmopolitans generally argue the need to modify Islamic practices and principles so as to reconstruct cultural traditions, reconciling the traditional with the modern of the global environment. To them, modernity is a historical reality from which there is no escape. While benefiting from other civilizations' achievements, they note, one must keep open ways of revising one's traditions (Zaimaran and Ebadi 1996, 262). Abdulkareem Soroush, an Iranian philosopher who fits the description of the cosmopolitans, advocates a paradigm shift in Islamic thinking by defining culture as a process subject to constant currents of change (1999, 7).

Iranian news media and universities are the hotbed of cosmopolitan thinkers.[8] Some experts take the victory of Mohammad Khatami in the 1997 presidential elections as the turning point in a move toward globalization. In some ways, this was equivalent to a victory for the globalizers— and a victory of popular mass media over the official media, especially state-run radio and television (Tajzadeh 1999, 40). Khatami's supporters in the Majles have emphasized their interest in stripping the Council of Guardians of the power to vet electoral candidates.

As the reform process takes shape under President Khatami, the cosmopolitans are certain to grow in both strength and influence over time. At present, the cosmopolitans control the parliament and presidency, relying on public support and what is called "social" power. The locals, in contrast, continue to have a firm grip over the most effective levers of power, namely the military, intelligence, judiciary, and broadcasting media.

The continuing demand for reform, both sociopolitically and economically, will propel the struggle between the locals and the cosmopolitans for years to come. Although some globalizing dynamics will ultimately prevail, it is my contention that these two tendencies, as James N. Rosenau (1997) aptly notes, will contradictorily, unevenly, and simultaneously accommodate each other. As the results of the Sixth Majles elections made evident, Iran's reformers are likely to win the struggle over how to cast the national narrative. Whether they can effectively pursue their reform agenda remains the key question. To put into perspective the diversity of views between the locals and the cosmopolitans, the next remaining sections deal specifically with the issues of women's rights and the free press.

The Islamist Ideology and Women's Rights

It seems clear that the status of women during the revolutionary era has deteriorated considerably; it is also evident that their basic opportunities in heathcare, educational attainment, and access to economic resources have noticeably increased during the postrevolutionary period. The globalizing dynamics of the 1990s, prompted by the international conventions held in Rio (1992), Vienna (1993), Cairo (1994), Copenhagen (1995), Beijing (1995), and the Hague (1999), have had important implications for women's rights all over the world, intensifying the pressure on the Islamic Republic of Iran to take necessary measures to improve women's situations in the legal, socioeconomic, political, and educational domains. This form of globalization from below has helped forged shared meanings and identities as well as local structures such as women's rights groups in addition to becoming an effective vehicle for voicing transnational demands for the promotion of gender equality. In this latter sense, globalization has empowered women, making it possible for them to gain access to information, organize local activism, run for the public office, and challenge unfair local norms and traditions. As a process, globalization has also induced the social construction of identity. Sympathy and activism for women's human rights causes know no boundaries. Increasingly, elements of Islamic feminists and secular feminists are converging in their attempts to change gender-biased laws with regard to divorce, custody rights over children, inheritance, alimony, and a whole host of other issues (Bayes and Tohidi 2001).

In the early years of the Islamic Republic, women were pushed out of public life and back into the home. Shortly after he returned to Iran in March of 1979, Ayatollah Ruhollah Khomeini issued a decree dismissing all women judges and barring female students from attending law schools.

He also closed the Law Association (Kanouneh Vokala) and replaced secular courts by religious ones, often presided over by poorly prepared theological students (Afshar 1997, 318). Islamic language and symbolism shaped the new identity of Iranian women. "Islamic concepts and institutions," Parvin Paidar (1995, 220) writes, "were reconstructed in relation to current definitions of modernity and progress to provide the basis for a viable rejection of the West." While the discourse clearly revolved around modernization, the solution to women's rights and responsibilities was sought in some form of conservative Islamic modernity.

The conservative clerics promote an Islamic vision in which political and socioeconomic equality of the sexes is unnatural and emphasize equivalency—not equality—of the duties and functions that male and female members perform. Some Islamic theologians, including Hujjat ul-Islam Nuri, have claimed that women's inferior status is caused by inherent physical and intellectual differences between women and men (Neshat 1983, 201). Others, such as Supreme Leader Ali Khamenei, have argued that although women may be weaker physically than men, they are stronger intellectually in some respects: "In terms of intelligence . . . not only are they not weaker than men, but they are stronger than men in some matters, including the management of the affairs of life—so much so that it is possible to regard women as life's true managers" (quoted in Monshipouri 1998b, 189).

Still others, such as Ayatollah Mutahhari, a conservative cleric, have referred to men's allegedly unlimited sexual needs as a basis for polygamy and have argued that the social and psychological advantages of polygamy far outweigh its drawbacks. Mutahhari has defended the Shia practice of temporary marriage, muta or siqeh, on the grounds that it prevents the spread of prostitution by offering men a legitimate method of satisfying their "unlimited" sexual urges (quoted in Monshipouri 1998b, 189).

The conservatives object to the UN Universal Declaration of Human Rights (UDHR), especially Articles 16 and 18, which contain references to the equality of gender roles and the right to change one's religion, respectively.[9] These articles, according to the conservatives, run counter to Islamic legal traditions. Apostasy (ridda), they say, poses a danger of falling away from Islamic guidance, and according to Sharia, constitutes a capital offense, punishable by death.

In the earlier years of the Islamic Revolution, three aspects of the Islamist ideology on women were expressed in legislation and policy: domesticity, difference, and danger. Domesticity referred to the notion that women should be primarily mothers and wives. Their domestic responsibility included motherhood, the raising of children, and running the internal affairs of the family. Throughout the twentieth century, modernization and urbanization resulted in the gradual replacement of the traditional extended family system by the nuclear family as the basic unit of society. This transformation has enabled women to play a much more significant role in decisionmaking and management of family matters than has been the case in the past.[10]

As the most fundamental building block of the society in the early years of the Islamic Republic, family became the province of females. Women, Paidar (1995, 262) notes, were regarded as "transmitters of communal and national values" to the next generation. The state took on the task of creating "Muslim mothers" and placing them in the service of the Islamic nation. Paidar continues: "The rights and responsibilities of 'Muslim mothers,' however, were left to be determined by the Islamic state in conformity with an unspecified Islamic law." Although the Islamic state gave its female supporters opportunities, a sense of righteousness, and self-worth for the sacrifices they have made for the former to come to power, it certainly did not improve their rights (355).

The "difference" dimension of the Islamist ideology for women referred to their different roles and responsibilities in both the institution of family and society at large. The "danger" side of this political ideology viewed women as the specific vector of globalization's attack on the Islamic culture. This perspective also reflected the prevailing view that cultural imperialism manifested itself through female attitudes and behavior and that excessively Westernized codes adopted by women posed cultural danger. Women's liberation movement as such was viewed as an explicit attempt to pursue hedonism and individualism—two Western influences seen as propelled by the forces of globalization so disdained by the conservatives. To shield women from alien and unwanted influences, the conservatives argue, it is necessary to closely monitor women's public appearance, sexuality, and social activities. Women's sexuality must be limited to their husbands, their bodies to home, and their role to trustee of the family (Mahdi 2000, 9). In response, for example, veiling was made compulsory and has ever since been strictly enforced (Moghadam 1993, 175).

Contradictions of State Policies and Women's Resistance

The Islamist discourse on women's rights has entailed many contradictions, including the notion of gender equality. The Iranian constitution asserts that men and women are equal, but Islamic law fails to treat them equally, particularly in cases of divorce, child custody, polygamy, inheritance, and court testimony (Moghadam 1993, 177). Article 21 of the Iranian constitution (Mayer 1999, 70) restricts women's rights in culturally relativistic terms: "The government must ensure the rights of women in all respects in conformity with Islamic criteria *[mavazin-e eslami]*." In short, Iranian women were, during the early years of the revolution, reduced to second-class citizens isolated from the public arena.

By the late 1980s, the Islamic state found it practically impossible to justify its political and ideological construction of women and was forced to modify it for a number of reasons. First, the Islamic state had to face the country's economic imperatives. This meant that socioeconomic change, which has led to women's "real" life experiences such as an increase in female literacy rate, has come in the form of women exercising their choices. Second, the sociodemographic shifts have resulted in women's participation and representation in public life. Third, women's resistance to the strictly conservative policies of the clerics played a vital role in facilitating such a policy shift.

In the aftermath of Iran-Iraq war, women began to play an important role in the socioeconomic construction of the country. From 1980 to 1988, with large segments of the male population mobilized for the war with Iraq, employers and government agencies turned to women to fill in for the loss of male workers. The imperative of economic development also helped women make some inroads into the economic sphere. Valentine Moghadam (1993, 200) correctly describes this as a shift in the regime's gender policy: "Challenges to a strictly defined gender system (such as that envisioned by the early Islamist ideologues in Iran) may derive from economic imperatives and/or from the growth of the ranks of educated women who reject domestication." Thus the challenges of economic development and demographic changes, such as the growth of an educated female population, have helped to dislodge the previous gender-oriented system.

In the 1990s, declining oil revenues and state income, growing poverty, and indebtedness from the huge expenditures of war with Iraq compelled the government to alter the course of socioeconomic development. In the second five-year national development plan (1995–1999), adopted in February 1995, the state changed its priorities—from ideological purity to pragmatic economic development and from growth through oil exports to human resource development. This shift held significant implications for women. The cumulative effect of the economic imperatives and the postwar sociodemographic realities was to force a number of significant policy changes in the areas of women's access to education and to family planning. Consequently, some restrictions, such as limiting female enrollment in a number of fields of study, were removed. The state's population policy was converted from pronatalist to pro–population stabilization through family planning (Moghadam 1998, 153–162).

This policy shift can be explained in several ways. Neil Englehart (Chapter 2), for example, argues that the state has effectively replaced traditional political cultures and that its power has become indispensable for the effective protection of human rights. This line of reasoning suggests that giving women an opportunity to become active and contributing citizens in the market and other domains (academic and otherwise) was critical for the ruling elites, who were counting on sufficient support from at least some sectors of the society. Other observers have noted that such policy change was, to some degree, a response to resistance by women themselves. Despite the regime's pronatalist policies banning abortion and discouraging contraception, in 1983 some 23 percent of married women of childbearing age used contraceptives (Moghadam 1993, 179). This practice was indeed a form of resistance to conservative state policies. In June 1989 the government formally lifted the ban on contraceptives at state hospitals and clinics. The government also altered its policy on women and the legal profession, and during the 1990s the law allowed for the employment of "women legal consultants" in the Special Civil Courts (Moghadam 1998, 163).

Women's resistance stemmed, in large part, from the inherent contradictions of a theocracy that tried to accommodate modern economic realities without tampering with Islamic traditions. By imposing the burden of the veil on women in the name of protecting Islamic values, as Haleh Afshar rightly points out, the Islamic state had to pay the price of giving them access to the public sphere under the rubric of the same creed. As the public emblem of Islamification, the veiled women have become intellectually and politically active, no longer constrained by harassment and objectification (1998, 15). As Ellen Freeberg discusses (Chapter 4), any normative analysis of a practice should also raise the basic question of whether those who bear the burden of restrictions have had a voice and can continue to have a voice in shaping the rules that govern their lives. Increasingly, Iranian women have used local cultural means, resources, and institutions to defend general principles of preventing degrading social conditions, economic policies, and political practices.

The traditional gender segregation could no longer be strictly observed in the service and industry sectors. A bulk of this resistance came from the ranks of reformist Muslim female elites, who pushed for progressive reading of the Sharia. They have emphasized exploring and extrapolating humane concepts embedded in religious texts. Some female reformists see the roots of the lack of progress toward women's human rights in patriarchy and male-centered culture, both of which are often expressed in Islamic terms (Kar 1999, 45). If, as Mehranghiz Kar points out, Iranian women uncritically accept the traditional religious definition of women's rights, they will remain in a closed circle, and their religious heritage will become a closed collection that not only cannot engage them in a dialogue with other cultures and civilizations, but also will deprive them from absorbing new human experiences in scientific, cultural, and legal domains (1999, 46–47).

A new strand of cosmopolitanism even embraces the idea that the independent understanding of women's rights, based on *ijtihad* (autonomous reasoning), is compatible with the provisions of the UN Convention on the Elimination of All Forms of Discrimination Against Women (CEDAW, passed on December 18, 1979), to which Iran has yet to commit itself. The most obvious discrepancies between Islamic laws and CEDAW relate to adulthood age, blood money *(diyah),* and witnessing rule, which equates two female witnesses with one male witness in the courts.

According to Iranian civil law, men reach puberty at age fifteen and women at age nine. Thus there is considerable age difference between males and females in determining legal eligibility for marriage. This runs counter to the universal standards of human rights, which specify equality in all matters relating to marriage and family relations (Kar 1999, 334). Similarly, this definition of puberty entails different criminal responsibilities for the same criminal act. If a fourteen-year-old boy commits a crime, he will be exonerated from any criminal responsibility. But if the same crime is committed by a ten-year-old girl, she will be held accountable (Zaimaran and Ebadi 1996, 247.) Marriage before reaching the age of puberty is possible through legal means. According to Iranian civil law, the father or his side of the family has the right to enter into a marriage contract regarding a baby daughter or baby son. Only the father and his side of the family will be in a legal position to cancel such a marriage if they decide that such a marriage compromises the boy's or the girl's welfare. The girl or the boy will have no say in confirming or denying the choice of her husband or his wife in the future.

Some Iranian lawyers (Ebadi 1994, 101–102, 119) have likened this practice to a form of slavery. Since the Iranian government, they note, has joined the Treaties to Abolish Slavery (1904, 1926, and 1956), it is obligated, both formally and legally, to determine a minimum age for marriage, and to require, before either a state official or a religious authority, both the husband's and the wife's consent prior to marriage. The current practice is also incompatible with Article 11(a) of the Cairo Declaration on Human Rights in Islam: "Human beings are born free, and no one has the right to enslave, humiliate, oppress or exploit them, and there can be no subjugation but to God the Most-High" (*Twenty-four Human Rights Documents* 1992, 181).

"Blood money," or *diyah,* is the payment for the injury inflicted by a murderer to the victim's family in return for the family waiving its right to insist on the death penalty; *diyah* for women is set at only half that for men. Also, according to current Iranian civil law, two female witnesses equal one male witness. These criminal and judicial rules clearly contradict modern standards of gender equality and human rights.

With respect to acquiring, changing, and retaining nationality of women and that of their children, Iranian laws are incompatible with today's modern standards. Regarding the right to participate in recreational activities and sports, too often the existing limitations for women's active participation are couched in Islamic terms. This is especially true of women's soccer in light of its heightened popularity all over the world. Iranian physical education authorities have instead argued that the Islamic experts must review the sport and decide whether it would be consonant with Islamic culture (Kar 1999, 234).[11] This attitude contradicts international standards, which specify for men and women "the same opportunities to participate actively in sports and physical education" (*Twenty-four Human Rights Documents* 1992, 52).

One can also find in Iran's laws other examples of incompatibility with the universal standards. The inheritance share of a female is half that of a male. Divorce is the man's absolute and unilateral right. The two widely seen, critically reviewed, and talked about movies in Iran during the summer of 1999 were *Two Women* and *Red,* both of which display, albeit in a somewhat exaggerated manner, injustices as well as difficulties surrounding the man's unilateral right of divorce. These cases clearly contradict gender equality with men before the law.

Freedom of movement provides another example of gender discrimination in Iran. Women cannot leave the country without their husband's written consent. Unless mentioned as a marriage condition, women's freedom to choose the place of their residence is limited. These laws run counter to the law relating to the free movement of persons and the freedom to choose their residence and domicile.

Quoting Ayatollah Mossavi Bojnordi, Kar (1999, 340) writes, "What is in the fiqh [Islamic jurisprudence] may not be in the religion." This means that *fiqh,* which has evolved through the efforts of Muslim jurists and scholars, is not eternal and universally valid; it is subject to change and adaptation.[12] It follows that those areas of *fiqh* that are regarded as discriminatory acts against women by today's standards can be revised. This type of change is equally warranted in both civil and criminal jurisprudence.

Women have also resisted the segregation of knowledge and educational opportunities in the form of restricted areas of specialization in universities (Moghissi 1995, 253–254). Under pressure from the Muslim female reformists, the High Planning Council of the Ministry of Culture and Higher Education removed the ban on integration. The influence of modern and reformist thinkers, particularly Ali Shariati, was drastically visible in the ideological and practical activities of the reformist Muslim female elites. Following Shariati, these women have relentlessly maneuvered within the cultural, religious, and political limits of Islamic tradition, seeking a different interpretation to that provided by the clergy. This activism has resulted in an increased autonomy for women vis-à-vis the policies and practices of the state (261). Hence the Islamic Republic's shifting gender politics. Arguably, the clerics have failed to organize the conservative Islamic state to reassert cultural identity in a society far removed from its traditional context. Relying on force and coercion to resolve sociocultural contradictions has proven counterproductive (265).

Increasingly, women in Iran have called family planning "a basic human right." Azam Taleghani, in an article on family planning in *Payam-e Hajar*, wrote that "the right of a woman to control her body and thus her own fertility is central to any discussion of human rights" (quoted in Moghadam 1993, 203). Since the reformists' electoral victories of the late 1990s, some observers have argued that emphasis has shifted away from reforms in women's status to strengthening civil liberties and political rights—that is, rights that many women regard as necessary for the expansion of women's rights (Keddie 2000).

The theme of the historical identity of woman has come to dominate the literature on Iranian women's rights. Hamid Dabashi (1993, 57) captures this notion best: "The birth of 'the people,' 'the individual,' the historical 'man' and the historical 'woman' are all irreversible. Historical 'men' and 'woman' massively participated in the revolution on all sides, Islamic and other." The conservative Islamic establishment can no longer determine what Iranian women's rights or responsibilities are or should be. A new culture is in the making. Its formation may ultimately owe more to socioeconomic changes of the last two decades in Iran than to the religious indoctrination espoused by the regime during the same time (64).

Women's Educational Participation and Attainment

Between 1956 and 1966 the female literacy rate in Iran increased from 8 percent to 17.9 percent. In 1971, some 25.5 percent of women were literate.

Before the revolution, 35 percent were literate, and by the late twentieth century the rate had reached 74 percent (Montaigne 1999, 18). Today, Iranian women are among the most educated and accomplished in the Muslim world. The relative share of females in total primary-level enrollment increased from 38.4 percent in 1976–1977 to 47.2 percent in 1993–1994 (United Nations 1998, 16). In the same period, the junior secondary-level enrollment increased from 36 percent to 43.5 percent, and the senior secondary-level soared from 39.6 percent to 45.4 percent (United Nations 1998, 17). Iranian women still lag behind their male counterparts. The UN data suggest that educational enrollments, particularly at secondary and tertiary levels, continue to be in favor of males, and that the illiteracy rate is considerably higher among females than males (United Nations 1998, 4).

Under the shah's regime, about a third of university students were female; by 1999 women made up fully half of new admissions. Educational opportunities in the 1980s and 1990s have surely paid professional dividends for women. In 1999, one in three Iranian physicians was a woman. In the postrevolutionary era, many women gained access to higher education, making it possible for them to enter public domains. This "coming-out-of-the-kitchen" phenomenon has resulted in the emergence of women as social as well as economic agents in public life; no longer can they be oppressed (Montaigne 1999, 18).

Although an increasing number of women have been nominated as political candidates, and an increasing percentage of eligible women have participated in elections, women are still noticeably underrepresented in the national legislative bodies. While women constitute about a third of all public-sector employees, they hold less than 5 percent of decisionmaking and managerial positions. The number of women parliamentarians increased from four in the first parliament to nine in the fourth parliament, but women constitute only 3.3 percent of the total number of parliamentarians (277). Several occupations still restrict the employment of women, who cannot be appointed as judges or recruited into the armed forces.

The Battle of the Pen: The Media on Trial?

It is evident that a free press and a free society have a natural affinity, and that the world has become more democratic over the last two decades partly because of open technologies and economies, and in part because of the media's enhanced capacity to educate and guide civil society, as well as to expose repressive regimes' ineffectual policies and practices. The media in Iran have no doubt played a major role in generating further transnational channels of contact with other societies, making interactions between internal and external dynamics meaningful.

In the aftermath of the revolution, the power struggle among Iran's ruling clerics played a critical role in defining how journalists and writers can express their views publicly on issues of personal and professional significance. To contain the legal scope of permissible dissent, the Press Law was ratified in 1985. According to this law, the press is prohibited from engaging in discourse "harmful" to the principles and mandates of Islam and public rights. This and similar prohibitions have ever since been subject to manipulation and arbitrary use by governments officials (Human Rights Watch 1993, 25).

The Press Law requires that press offenses be prosecuted before a jury in the courts of general jurisdiction (Article 34). Every two years, a council composed of the head of the judiciary, the head of the city council or alternatively the mayor, and a representative from the Ministry of Culture and Islamic Guidance meets to select the press jury. The council selects fourteen people from different professions, with seven serving as the original jury and the other seven placed on reserve. Harassment of the press and the prosecution of editors, writers, and cartoonists have continued unabatedly since the revolution. In addition, the government has invoked the jurisdiction of the Revolutionary Courts in offenses committed by journalists, writers, and intellectuals, in situations where the earlier punishments have not been severe enough (Human Rights Watch 1993, 25–27).

Since the 1990s, the fight for control of the media has intensified the power struggle between the conservatives and reformers. The press has become the political battleground for the opposing viewpoints within the country's evolving ideological spectrum, reflecting the critical battle between Iran's conservative hierarchy and the burgeoning reform movement. Since Khatami's presidency, many newspapers and magazines have been shut down, and many more have become the target of violent attacks by right-wing vigilantes, known as *ansar-e-hezbollah* ("vigilante friends of the party of God"). Additionally, the Press Law has sought ways of controlling and punishing the unruly media. Judges have been empowered to overrule jury verdicts on the press. Individual journalists, and not just their directors, have been held accountable.[13]

But perhaps none of the previous bans against the media has had a more profound impact than the closure of the reform-minded dailies *Salaam* and *Khordad.* While the closure of *Salaam* resulted in student protests, the banning of *Khordad* was followed by the jailing of its editor, Abdullah Nouri—one of the most outspoken and courageous reformist leaders of postrevolutionary Iran. Nouri, who dominated Tehran's first municipal elections of February 1999, became another victim of the power struggle between the conservatives and reformists when he was convicted in 1999 by the Special Court for Clergy, which is controlled by conservative clerics, on charges of apostasy and spreading anti-Islamic propaganda through *Khordad.*[14] The burgeoning rise in Nouri's popularity after the trial, however, reflected the popular will for change. The trial also demonstrated that the changes sweeping the rest of the world could not be halted at Iran's borders when Nouri's defense and counterarguments against the court appeared on the Internet (Burns 1999, 6).

Two decades after it was shut down, the Writers' Association of Iran was reconstituted very quietly in the late 1990s. One prominent female member, Simin Behbahani, and an active supporter of the association, Monireh Baradaran (who presently lives in exile in Germany), were given the Carl von Ossietzky Medal on December 12, 1999, an annual award presented in Berlin, Germany, to writers who have championed civil and political rights.[15]

President Khatami's attempts to loosen the social, political, and cultural restrictions were particularly welcomed by the press, which embraced the free flow of information and ideas. The conservatives' backlash was uncivil and violent. Since February 18, 2000, when the reformist victory in the Majles became obvious, more than twenty reformist newspapers were ordered shut down by the hard-line judiciary. Several leading reformers were arrested and jailed after appearing at a convention in Germany regarding the future of reform in Iran after the Sixth Majles.

Student Protests and the Free Press

University student associations have often been at the heart of activism in Iran, and have traditionally played a major part in uprisings against the state's repressive measures. Student associations, albeit divided and not entirely independent as they once were under the shah, became an agent of change, demanding economic reforms and press freedom. In the most open act of political defiance since the 1979 Iranian Revolution, the July 1999 student protests, driven mainly by a protest against the closure of the daily *Salaam*—a reformist and left-leaning Islamic newspaper that had begun to release vitally important information regarding the fall 1998 serial killings of secular reformists, including writers and journalists—made clear that students were willing to voice their dissent over the suppression of the news media (Monshipouri 1999, 107).

Controlled by the conservatives, the press court banned several proreform dailies, including *Tous, Jame'h, Neshat, Salaam, Khordad,* and *No-*

rouz. In one issue, *Neshat* called for an end to the death penalty, while questioning Iran's law of retribution *(qasas).* The daily suggested that Iranian law replace "using violence" against criminals with the "modern" approach of reforming rather than punishing criminals. It also published an open letter from Yadollah Sahabi, an opposition leader and one of the founders of the Freedom Movement of Iran, urging Iran's supreme leader, Ali Khamenei, to stay above the political fray, to refrain from showing any favoritism toward conservatives, and to dissociate himself from the so-called pressure groups—that is, the bands of street thugs who invoke violence against their opponents.[16] The closure of *Neshat* set off a new battle between the reformers and the conservatives, with the former arguing that the closure lacked a legal basis.

In the absence of legitimate political parties, and given the myriad obstacles it faced, the press became not only a bastion of the struggle against the conservatives but also a driving force behind the country's political development. In many respects, the press—especially those supporting reform—took the place of political parties in Iran, a prospect that frightened the right-wing clergy and their supporters. The conservatives, who still control the major levers of official political power, had good reason to fear the loss of "soft" or "social" power to the reformists in an emerging civil society.[17]

There were several ways one could interpret the July 8–14, 1999, student protests in Iran. Many experts on Iranian politics (Bina 1999, 52; Mahdi 1999, 25) held that students' demands were more broadly political in nature, and that they signified the cumulative resentment of the public against the suppression of the press and the restriction of other fundamental civil liberties and universal rights—and as such, were by no means particular to the university students alone. As is often the case, the students' demands—transparency, accountability, integrity, and fairness in the government—reflected broader societal demands. The protests demonstrated a pent-up frustration over the fact that President Khatami lacked the necessary authority to implement social reforms and to instill the kind of political democracy and cultural tolerance he had vowed since his ascendancy to power. Supporters of this view argued that the student rally was organized by proreform and socially progressive groups. The rally was, according to this view, a channel to voice widespread social discontent.[18]

Another perspective that was regularly featured in some press reports was that Iranian politics, highly complex and evolving, had to come to terms with the country's new political realities. Aware of such unpleasant realities, the conservatives used such excuses as the foreign-led demonstrations and the country's imminent political chaos to stop rallies, sabotaging in the process the trend toward political development and social reform. By employing the rhetoric pointing to civil unrest and giving the impression that foreign hands were involved, the conservatives raised the question of whether this type of demonstration posed a major threat to Iran's political stability.[19]

The most widely accepted view in Iran stressed the point that the student protests, which revolved around the curbs on press freedoms, "were hijacked by hard-liners determined to foment violence in order to prove [President] Khatami was incapable of controlling the country."[20] Perhaps the most obvious message to emerge from these protests was the existence of a crisis of legitimacy and a crisis of confidence in the ruling conservative establishment. Proregime demonstrations, organized by the conservative establishment to counter student protests, however widespread and organized they were, failed to restore the lost confidence.

Conclusion

Since the 1979 Islamic Revolution, Iranian politics have straddled theocratic and democratic features of the political system. Iranian society, in contrast, has become broadly imbued with modern, global notions of civil society, the rule of law, and human rights. It has become virtually impossible to politicize human rights—as in the past—behind the mask of the sovereignty of the Islamic Republic as a fledgling but active civil society has formed. Increasingly, the social and political changes of the last quarter of the twentieth century have fueled a cultural clash between the forces of globalization and the forces of localization.

This chapter has shown that Iranians' reactions to globalization are varied. The message of the locals is that globalization is a modern-day ploy to homogenize the world's diverse cultures by imposing a near uniformity of values and socioeconomic models on non-Western societies. The cosmopolitans respond that the globalizing dynamics have heralded an era of change, requiring cultural and religious reformation. The youth, the women, the intelligentsia, and the media have all advocated reform of the culture. Unlike the shah's modernization plan, which was imposed from above and lacked domestic constituency, the globalizers' drive toward social change is largely fueled by grassroots support and an internal reform movement. Today, for instance, some Iranian feminists have even called for adjusting domestic laws to the universal standards embodied in the Convention on the Elimination of All Forms of Discrimination Against Women, raising both ethical and legal questions concerning the nation's traditional male-dominated gender formula.[21] Moreover, many local and national women's movements actively support gender equality around the globe, redefining the meanings of identities and interests.

Afraid of globalization from above, the localizers attack the "globalized vision of society" as detrimental to Islamic values. They question the market-oriented values of globalization and its cultural intrusions in societies where the state is held accountable as the main guarantor of economic and social rights. Not surprisingly, the locals have capitalized on confusions and contradictions resulting from globalization in a country where religion and high-context culture continue to play a central role in people's lives. While human rights are an integral part of the national discourse, fears and uncertainties associated with globalization inexorably generate resistance, keeping the conservatives in the thick of the political fray. As the debate rages on whether to embrace or reject globalization, reformers and their allies represent the best hope for change—a change that might be a distant dream but not unthinkable.

Notes

I am grateful to Andrew Nathan, Neil Englehart, and Kavita Philip for providing repeated, detailed comments on the earlier versions of this chapter.

1. Shia Islam is the dominant religion of Iran. With virtually 95 percent of Iranians adhering to this brand of Islam, it is safe to say that over the years, a noticeable degree of social and political stability has characterized Iranian society.

2. See Sadeq Zibakalam's comments as quoted in the *Christian Science Monitor,* February 5, 1999, p. 6. Zibakalam is a political historian at the University of Tehran.

3. More information is available at www.electionworld.org/election/iran.htm.

4. For a detailed analysis of Tehran's city council elections, see *International Iran Times,* March 12, 1999, pp. 4–7.

5. For further information on female candidates' participation in Tehran's city council elections, see *International Iran Times,* March 12, 1999, p. 7.

6. I have borrowed these questions from Inglehart 1997, 26.

7. The FMI was founded in 1961 by Mehdi Bazargan and Ayatollah Mahmood Taleghani after it splintered from the National Front, founded by Mohammad Mossadeq. The FMI's leaders, who called into question the secular tendencies of the National Front, attempted to blend nationalism and religious beliefs. See *International Iran Times,* August 2, 2002, pp. 1–2.

8. I interviewed Saeed Atrianfard, Hamid Reza Jalaeepour, Hadi Semati, and Hadi Khaniki in Tehran in August 1999. Atrianfard, the managing editor of *Hamshahri,* a liberal newspaper, argued that the press was a tool of cultural and political development, and that maintaining connections with international networks was a critical aspect of the function of the media. Jalaeepour, the editor of the banned daily *Neshat,* echoed the same sentiment, arguing that the globalizers were growing in number, although they remained a minority. Jalaeepour also noted that it was only a matter of time before conservatives were swept away from the political

scene, pointing out that we must begin to regard Islam as a religion, not as an ideological school. Semati, a political scientist at the University of Tehran, argued that competing ideologies, accelerated by globalization, have left an indelible mark on the local consciousness to the point that globalization has actually become a local phenomenon. Fluid identities among the young generation have actually provided a bridge point between the globalizing and localizing dynamics. Khaniki, vice president for social and cultural affairs of the Ministry of Sciences, pointed out that no custom has remained traditional for a long time insofar as change was a constant. Some of today's groups, he added, have evolved from their traditional counterparts. Consider, for example, student councils in the universities, which used to be a study group for Islamic tradition, but now have become a voice of change. Some developments have also demonstrated drastic changes and departure from the past. In a not too distant past, he argued, "family and the clergy were the two widely cited and known cultural reference groups in the society. Today, students and the press, which reflect the country's new social and demographic realities, compete with those traditional reference groups."

9. Article 16(1) reads: "Men and women of full age, without any limitation due to race, nationality or religion, have the right to marry and to found a family. They are entitled to equal rights as to marriage, during marriage and at its dissolution." Article 18 reads: "Everyone has the right to freedom of thought, conscience and religion; this right includes freedom to change his religion or belief, and freedom, either alone or in community with others and in public or private, to manifest his religion or belief in teaching, practice, worship and observance." See *Twenty-four Human Rights Documents* 1992, 7–8.

10. United Nations 1998, 6.

11. See a quotation from Tahereh Taherian, the deputy minister of the Organization of Physical Education, in Kar 1999, 234.

12. For more information on fiqh, see Abdul Rashid Moten, *Political Science: An Islamic Perspective* (New York: St. Martin's Press, 1996), pp. 48–49.

13. For an interesting report on Iran's press, see Scott Peterson, "The Battle of the Pen in Iran," *Christian Science Monitor,* November 8, 1999, p. 6.

14. Since the daily *Khordah* has been banned, Nouri's supporters have published the newspaper under a different name, *Fatth* (Victory). The latter was shut down before the first meeting of the Sixth Majles.

15. For more details, see *International Iran Times,* December 24, 1999, p. 1.

16. For further information on this, see *International Iran Times,* September 17, 1999, p. 4.

17. Hamid Reza Jalaeepour, the former editor of *Neshat,* best captures this reality: "The conservatives hold the levers of power within the political order. The reformists, in contrast, enjoy social power, but their power within the political order is woefully inadequate." Author interview, Tehran, August 1999.

18. What began as a purely student-driven peaceful demonstration was clearly infiltrated by so-called saboteurs and students' enemies, some of whom reportedly belonged to the Mojahedeen Khalq Organization (MKO, an opposition group based in Iraq), as beatings of protesters and other violence broke out. Other participants may simply have been thugs, security and intelligence agents, and partisans of the orthodox clerical establishment who were pretending to come from the students' ranks. To date, the extent to which the MKO and other security forces engaged in

these protests remains unclear. But some, like Ayatollah Hossain-Ali Montazari, the cleric once named to succeed Ayatollah Rohullah Khomeini as the supreme leader, accused the regime's security forces as masquerading as civilians in order to beat student protesters in their dorms. These pressure groups, or *ansar-e hez-bollah,* Montazari notes, were in fact official forces trained in suppression tactics. Dressed in civilian clothes, these forces have in the past been accused of attacking people in the name of public good. For more on this, see *International Iran Times,* July 16, 1999, p. 2.

19. Throughout the six-day event of the student demonstrations, the Office for Fostering Solidarity (Daftar-e Tahkim-e Vahdat), the major student alliance, called on students to restrain themselves from pushing President Khatami beyond certain limits, knowing that requesting prompt and unconditional support for students would plunge the country into more confusion.

20. See the interview with Shirin Ebadi by Michael Theodoulou, "A Tough Place to Be a Woman with a Cause," *Christian Science Monitor,* October 15, 1999, pp. 1, 8.

21. For more on this subject, see the interview with Mehranghiz Kar in *Zanan* no. 56 (September 1999): 18–19.

References

Abdi, Abbas. 1999. "An Interview with Abbas Abdi." In Mohsen Armin and Hojjat Razzaghi, eds., *Fears and Expectations: Experts' Opinions on Khatami Government.* Tehran: Hamshahri, 137–144.

Abrahamian, Ervand. 2000. "The Making of the Modern Iranian State." In Mark Kesselman, Joel Krieger, and William A. Joseph, eds., *Introduction to Comparative Politics: Political Challenges and Changing Agendas.* New York: Houghton Mifflin, 607–654.

Afshar, Haleh. 1997. "Women, Marriage, and the State in Iran." In Nalini Visvanathan, Lynn Duggan, Lauri Nisonoff, and Nan Wiegersma, eds., *The Women, Gender, and Development Reader.* London: Zed Books, 317–325.

———. 1998. *Islam and Feminism: An Iranian Case-Study.* New York: St. Martin's Press.

Anderson, Roy R., Robert F. Seibert, and Jon G. Wagner, eds. 1998. *Politics and Change in the Middle East: Sources of Conflict and Accommodation.* 5th ed. Upper Saddle River, NJ: Prentice Hall.

Ayubi, Nazih. 1999. "The Politics of Islam in the Middle East With Special Reference to Egypt, Iran, and Saudi Arabia." In Jeff Haynes, ed., *Religion, Globalization, and Political Culture.* New York: St. Martin's Press, 71–92.

Bayes, Jane H. and Nayereh Tohidi, eds., 2001. *Globalization, Gender, and Religion: The Politics of Women's Rights in Catholic and Muslim Contexts.* New York: Palgrave. See chapters 1, 2, and 8.

Bill, James A. 1993. "The Challenge of Institutionalization: Revolutionary Iran." *Iranian Studies* 26, nos. 3–4 (summer-fall): 403–406.

Bina, Cyrus. 1999. "The Hot Summer of Defiance: Student Protests in Iran." *Journal of Iranian Research and Analysis* 15, no. 2: 47–62.

Bulliet, Richard W. 1999. "Twenty Years of Islamic Politics." *Middle East Journal* 53, no. 2: 189–200.

Burns, John F. 1999. "Order in the Court! A Revolution Is on Trial." *New York Times,* November 7, p. 6.

Dabashi, Hamid. 1993. "The Shattering of the Wor(l)d: Theocracy, Human Rights, and Women in Iran." In *Proceedings of a One-Day Conference: Theocracy, Human Rights, and Women: The Iranian Experience.* Upper Montclair, NJ: Montclair State University, 49–70.

Ebadi, Shirin. 1994. *History and Documentation of Human Rights in Iran.* Tehran: Roshangaran.

Gasiorowski, Mark J. 2001. "Iran Under Khatami: Deadlock or Change?" *Global Dialogue* 3, nos. 2–3 (Spring–Summer): 9–18.

Hardy, Roger. 2002. "Iran: The Pressure for Change." July 29, http:// news.bbc.co.uk/1/hi/in depth/world/2002/islamic world/2159316.stm.

Human Rights Watch. 1993. *Guardians of Thought: Limits on Freedom of Expression in Iran.* New York: Human Rights Watch.

Huntington, Samuel P. 1996. *The Clash of Civilizations and the Remaking of World Order.* New York: Simon and Schuster.

Inglehart, Ronald. 1997. *Modernization and Postmodernization: Cultural, Economic, and Political Change in Forty-three Societies.* Princeton: Princeton University Press.

Jacobsen, Michael, and Stephanie Lawson. 1996. "Between Globalization and Localization: A Case Study of Human Rights Versus State Sovereignty." *Global Governance* 5, no. 2: 203–219.

Kar, Mehranghiz. 1999. *Eliminating Discrimination Against Women: A Comparison of the Convention on Elimination of All Forms of Discrimination Against Women with the Iran's Domestic Laws.* Tehran: Parvin.

Keddie, Nikkie R. 2000, "Women in Iran Since 1979." *Social Research* 67, no. 2: 405–438.

Limbert, John W. 1995. "Islamic Republic of Iran." In David E. Long and Bernard Reich, eds., *The Governments and Politics of the Middle East and North Africa,* 3rd ed. Boulder, CO: Westview Press, 41–61.

Mahdi, Ali Akbar. 1999. "The Student Movement in the Islamic Republic of Iran." *Journal of Iranian Research and Analysis* 15, no. 2: 5–46.

———. 2000. "Caught Between Local and Global: Iranian Women's Struggle for a Civil Society." Paper presented at the Annual Meeting of the Center for Iranian Research and Analysis, Maryland, April 28–29.

Mayer, Ann Elizabeth. 1999. *Islam and Human Rights: Tradition and Politics.* Boulder, CO: Westview Press.

Milani, Mohsen. 1993. "Power Shifts in Revolutionary Iran." *Iranian Studies* 26, nos. 3–4: 359–374.

Moghadam, Valentine M. 1993. *Modernizing Women: Gender and Social Change in the Middle East.* Boulder, CO: Lynne Rienner.

———. 1998. *Women, Work, and Economic Reform in the Middle East and North Africa.* Boulder, CO: Lynne Rienner.

Moghissi, Haideh. 1995. "Public Life and Women's Resistance." In Saeed Rahnema and Sohrab Behdad, eds., *Iran After the Revolution: Crisis of an Islamic State.* London: I. B. Tauris, 251–267.

Monshipouri, Mahmood. 1998a. "Iran's Search for the New Pragmatism." *Middle East Policy* 5, no. 2: 95–112.

————. 1998b. *Islamism, Secularism, and Human Rights in the Middle East*. Boulder, CO: Lynne Rienner.

————. 1999. "Civil Society, Velayat-e-faqih, and the Rule of Law." *Journal of Iranian Research and Analysis* 15, no. 2: 106–110.

Montaigne, Fen. 1999. "Iran: Testing the Waters of Reform." *National Geographic* 196, no. 1: 1–33.

Mowlana, Hamid. 1993. "New Global Order and Cultural Ecology." In Kaarle Nordenstreng and Herbert I. Schiller, eds., *Beyond National Sovereignty: International Communication in the 1990s*. Norwood, NJ: Ablex, 397–417.

Muir, Jim. 2002. "Iran Rifts Deepen as Tension Mounts." July 29, http://news.bbc.co.uk/1/hi/world/middle east/2158274.stm.

Neshat, Guity. 1983. "Women in the Ideology of the Islamic Republic." In Guity Neshat, ed., *Women and Revolution in Iran*. Boulder, CO: Westview Press, 195–216 .

Paidar, Parvin. 1995. *Women and the Political Process in Twentieth-century Iran*. New York: Cambridge University Press.

Peterson, Scott. 2002. "In Iran, a Challenge to Hardliners," *The Christian Science Monitor* (November 14): 6.

Randall, Vicky. 1999. "The Media and Religion in Third World Politics." In Jeff Haynes, ed., *Religion, Globalization, and Political Culture*. New York: St. Martin's Press, 45–68.

Rosenau, James N. 1997. "The Complexities and Contradictions of Globalization." *Current History* 96, no. 613 (November): 360–364.

Sassen, Saskia. 2000. "Whose City Is It? Globalization and the Formation of New Claims." In Frank J. Lechner and John Boli, eds., *The Globalization Reader*. London: Blackwell, 70–76.

Soroush, Abdol Kareem. 1999. "Evolution of Prophetic Experience: A Debate: Khorramshahi and Soroush." *Kiyan* 9, no. 47: 4–11.

Spencer, William, ed. 1998. "The Islamic Republic of Iran." In *Global Studies: The Middle East,* 7th ed. Guilford, CT: Dushkin/McGraw-Hill, 54–64.

Tajzadeh, Mostapha. 1999. "An Interview with Mostapha Tajzadeh." In Mohsen Armin and Hojjat Razzaghi, eds., *Fears and Expectations: Experts' Opinions on Khatami Government*. Tehran: Hamshahri, 37–62.

Tatsuo, Inoue. 1999. "Liberal Democracy and Asian Orientalism." In Joanne R. Bauer and Daniel A. Bell, eds., *The East Asian Challenge for Human Rights*. New York: Cambridge University Press, 27–59.

Twenty-four Human Rights Documents. 1992. Ithaca, NY: Center for Human Rights Study, Columbia University.

United Nations. 1998. *Women in the Islamic Republic of Iran: A Country Profile*. Statistical Profiles no. 15. New York: Economic and Social Commission for Asia and the Pacific.

Wright, Robin. 1996. "Dateline Tehran: A Revolution Implodes." *Foreign Policy* 103: 161–174.

Zairmaran, Mohammad, and Shirin Ebadi. 1996. *Modernity and Tradition in the Iranian Legal System*. Tehran: Gangedanesh.

6

Outside Actors and the Pursuit of Civil Society in China

Harnessing the Forces of Globalization

Rebecca R. Moore

For those who accept that the promotion of human rights is a legitimate concern for state and nonstate actors alike, the relevant question is not whether but how to encourage greater respect for human rights. Historically, the human rights efforts of the United States and other members of the international community have tended to be state-centric. In other words, states have targeted their human rights efforts directly at the state, utilizing an assortment of essentially punitive means, including economic sanctions, public and private criticism, and the termination of economic and military assistance to enforce compliance with international human rights norms. Such efforts have traditionally been directed at the state because states— at least within the context of the Westphalian states system—are understood to bear primary responsibility for the preservation of rights. As traditionally understood, rights have to do with the relationship between a state and its citizens. They are claims that individuals make against the state, imposing on it certain duties and, at the same time, constraining its authority.

Yet as numerous commentators have suggested, globalization in the form of global markets and information technology may be transforming the relationship between the state and its citizens by empowering various nonstate actors at the expense of the state. Indeed, Jessica Mathews has argued that globalization has triggered a "redistribution of power among states, markets, and civil society," which she characterizes as a "power shift."[1] Arguably, these trends also have important implications for the promotion of human rights in any given society.

The Clinton administration even argued that globalization carries with it certain advantages for U.S. human rights policy. Globalization is not only creating new channels for democratic values and ideas; it is also empowering indigenous actors who, through various grassroots-level efforts, seek ultimately to advance economic and political reforms at the state level. The United States, the Clinton administration therefore argued, should avail itself of opportunities to assist these local actors, thereby improving prospects for indigenous political reform and empowering those who must ultimately hold the state accountable for evolving global norms of democracy and human rights.

These arguments were particularly evident in the context of the Clinton administration's China policy. Indeed, in defending his decision to delink human rights from the annual review of China's most-favored-nation trade status in 1994, Bill Clinton argued that he was not abandoning human rights and promised "a new and vigorous American program to support those in China working to advance the cause of human rights and democracy."[2] The Clinton administration later proposed to work with Congress to develop a democracy program for China that would utilize U.S. nongovernmental organizations (NGOs) "to strengthen both civil society and the rule of law." China's economic reforms and the opening of Chinese society to the outside world," the administration observed, "had given rise to "new social organizations," which in turn offered opportunities for the United States and others "to support the development of civil society in China."[3]

The notion that the United States should address its human rights concerns through a proactive democracy program was not a new one. President Ronald Reagan had called publicly for a worldwide campaign "to foster the infrastructure of democracy" as early as 1982, and his administration supported the establishment of the National Endowment for Democracy (NED)—a quasi-autonomous NGO that Congress authorized in 1983 to promote freedom and democracy around the globe—in addition to implementing a number of democracy-building programs through various government agencies. Democracy-building as an explicit component of U.S. human rights policy has been adopted by all subsequent administrations.

For its part, the Clinton administration argued repeatedly that democracy is not simply a desired end, but also a means in the struggle for human rights. As U.S. Secretary of State Madeleine Albright put it before the UN Human Rights Commission in March 2000: "Democracy is the single surest path to the preservation and promotion of human rights."[4] Notably, Albright made this declaration in conjunction with the commission's passage of a resolution that effectively affirmed a 1999 resolution stating that "democracy fosters the full realization of human rights and vice versa."[5]

More so than previous administrations, however, the Clinton administration emphasized the importance of civil society, identifying it as an "essential component" of democracy and declaring the development of "politically active civil society" to be a distinct focus of its human rights and democracy promotion strategy.[6] This focus on civil society represented a sort of tactical shift in the pursuit of democracy and respect for human rights. Many of the democracy programs initiated during the 1980s and early 1990s centered on promoting free elections and democratic political institutions. The Clinton administration did not reject such efforts, but rather characterized its attention to civil society promotion as a shift in emphasis—from creating the supply side of democracy to fueling the demand side.[7] The administration of George W. Bush has continued to support civil society initiatives as part of its own democracy promotion strategy for China.

In championing the opportunities for civil society promotion, the U.S. government has had plenty of company, especially with respect to China. Among many of the international NGOs working in China today, civil society initiatives have demonstrated enormous popularity. Their appeal appears to rest at least in part on an assumption, confirmed for many by events in Poland in 1989, that a strong civil society can act as a powerful vehicle for democratization by exerting pressure against the state from below. Programs designed to assist in the development of a vigorous civil society are thus often construed as a bottom-up versus top-down strategy for promoting democracy and respect for human rights.

Characterizing civil society initiatives for China in this way, however, is troublesome, largely because the emergence of civil society in China has not been a purely grassroots development. Moreover, China's NGOs are linked to the state in a way that makes it difficult to reconcile China's nascent civil society with the prevailing Western paradigm of civil society—that is, an autonomous sphere of voluntary associations capable of bringing pressure to bear against the state. Due in part to concerns about the nature of China's emerging civil society, the Clinton administration initially found little enthusiasm in Congress for its proposed civil society initiative. Many members of Congress, in fact, considered the very notion of a Chinese "NGO" to be an "oxymoron."[8]

China's "NGOs" do look different from most Western NGOs. However, as I will argue below, the unique nature of China's civil society does not necessarily render civil society initiatives a flawed approach to democracy promotion.[9] Indeed, China's civil society is still evolving, and neither its future nor the merits of outside efforts to foster its development should be assessed apart from the forces of globalization at work in China today. Continued economic liberalization, legal reform, and global communications technology have been strengthening Chinese society vis-à-vis the state and connecting it to the outside world in unprecedented ways. Globalization is, in effect, providing outside actors with new opportunities to encourage the development of a civil society that is not only capable of creating pressure for political reform, but equally important, capable of anchoring political and legal reform deep in Chinese society. The evolution of China's civil society may ultimately not fit the Western paradigm, but if China is to democratize, reform must occur at the societal level as well as at the top. Democratic principles and a commitment to human rights must be rooted in Chinese society—in its institutions, practices, and values.

Civil society initiatives constitute an important means of encouraging the societal reforms necessary to support the evolution of a political system that is more democratic and more respectful of human rights. Such initiatives serve as a channel for spreading international human rights norms, but they also offer a means of empowering local actors who seek to advance in theory and in practice a conception of rights that may differ from that espoused by the Chinese regime. In assessing the potential impact of civil society initiatives conducted by outside actors, I first examine both the nature of China's civil society and its potential to act as a force for democratization. Importantly, however, China's emerging civil society does not exist in a vacuum. Given that globalization is creating new links between Chinese society and the outside world, the discussion that follows also explores ways in which these new connections may be influencing China's emerging civil society and benefiting outside actors who seek to encourage its development.

Civil Society as a Consequence of Economic Reform

Recent changes in the relationship between state and society in China, including the emergence of new social associations or organizations (she-hui tuanti) are largely a product of economic reforms initiated by Chinese leader Deng Xiaoping beginning in the late 1970s. Widespread agreement exists that China's gradual adoption of market economic reforms since then has altered the relationship between the state and society by redistributing economic resources in society's favor. As the state has pulled back, it has also created space for the emergence of new social groups with economic resources at their disposal.[10] A top-down initiated process of economic liberalization thus triggered at the grassroots level the rapid formation of new social groups, which comprise now a fledgling civil society.[11]

New associations have not been the only consequence of the transition to a market economy. Economic reforms have produced a host of new social problems, paralleled by a decline in the resources available to the state to address these various problems. Consequently, the state has increasingly found itself looking to social organizations to develop solutions to new problems and to provide the necessary resources. As a group of U.S. foundation executives concluded following a visit to China in 1993: "Chinese government officials, from top to bottom, now concede that society itself must play a larger role in devising solutions to emerging problems—and paying for them."[12]

Economic reforms have also provided the impetus for legal reform, which has in turn assisted the emergence of civil society. A market economy requires that legal protections be extended to independent economic activity. In regulating and protecting such activity, the state effectively recognizes one particular segment of civil society.[13] Moreover, maintaining a viable market economy demands that the state honor and enforce the new laws, thereby accepting limits on its own power.[14] Reforms undertaken to provide the legal foundation for a market economy might therefore also be encouraging progress toward the rule of law.

Although reform of China's legal system has proceeded at a gradual and frequently uneven pace, the reforms that have occurred do appear to be empowering Chinese society and engendering a new understanding of law and rights among the Chinese people. Over the past decade, with the assistance of outside actors like the Ford and Asia Foundations, China has promulgated a number of new laws that serve to limit the discretionary power of the state. These include an Administrative Procedure Law (1990) and a State Compensation Law (1992), which allow citizens to sue the state for a variety of infractions and perceived excesses. An Administrative Penalties Law (1996) limits the power of Chinese officials by outlining principles of transparency, legitimacy, and due process for the administration of punishments and penalties. This legislation also sets forth penalties for officials who violate the new rules. A Lawyer's Law (1997) mandates the provision of free legal aid and assistance to those found to be indigent or "socially disadvantaged," and a new civil code now regulates transactions between nonstate parties in China.[15] In conjunction with the new laws, China's professional legal community has grown substantially since 1979. This growth includes rapid increases in both the number of law schools and the number of lawyers in China. Private law firms also emerged in

1991 and their numbers have since increased rapidly while the number of state firms has in relative terms declined.[16]

These changes have prompted an enormous increase in litigation, including lawsuits filed against the government by private citizens and entities. According to Minxin Pei, the number of commercial disputes adjudicated by the courts rose from about 15,000 a year in the early 1980s to 1.5 million a year in the mid-1990s. The number of civil cases also increased from approximately 300,000 in 1978 to 3 million in 1996. Perhaps most remarkably, as a result of legislation allowing citizens to sue the government, the number of lawsuits filed against the government rose from approximately 600 in 1986 to nearly 80,000 in 1996.[17] Enforcement of the new laws remains uneven, especially in rural areas where reforms have yet to take hold among police, prosecutors, and judges.[18] Still, a growing number of Chinese have been willing to use the legal system to protect their rights and to challenge the state. Minxin Pei has predicted, based on these trends, that the legal system "will continue to grow as an institutional rival to the CCP [Chinese Communist Party]."[19]

Importantly, the emergence of civil society, itself a consequence of legal reform, has in circular fashion necessitated further legal reforms. New laws are required not only to provide recognition of the legal status of China's new NGOs, but also to ensure their accountability to the public. A 1994 report of the National Committee on U.S. China Relations, in fact, concluded that legal system development was "way behind the emerging reality of social organizations" and that the lack of certainty about the legal status of Chinese NGOs was "an impediment to both domestic and foreign confidence" in them.[20] The group further observed that the "infrastructure necessary to sustain a tolerably ordered pluralistic society" was nonexistent at the time.[21]

Coupled with global markets and information technology, China's economic reforms have also amplified the impact of external actors on China's internal development. Indeed, the democracy promotion strategy the Clinton administration articulated for Asia, including China, hinged directly on the region's rapid economic growth and a perceived opportunity to lend active support to the new social organizations generated by that growth. Testifying before Congress in September 1997, then–Assistant Secretary of State for Democracy, Human Rights, and Labor John Shattuck argued that "economic development can gradually undermine authoritarianism because it can create social forces that seek to develop autonomy from the state." Shattuck emphasized that the administration was not subscribing to a theory of "economic determinism," but rather sought to ally itself with these new social forces, recognizing that "democratization is caused by the hard work on the ground by those who promote elements of civil society."[22]

Shattuck's successor, Harold Koh, later defended the administration's policy of engagement with China by arguing that "human rights changes [sic] more frequently from inside, bottom-up, than outside, top-down."[23] Koh also characterized the administration's human rights strategy for China as an "outside-inside" approach, coupling "vigorous support for change from outside China with vigorous support for internal reform within China."[24]

The Western Paradigm of Civil Society

As noted earlier, the interest in China's nascent civil society demonstrated by the Clinton administration and other outside actors was undoubtedly encouraged by events in Eastern Europe in 1989, especially in Poland. There, civil society in the form of an alliance between the independent labor movement Solidarity, the Catholic Church, and the intellectuals emerged in opposition to the state, ultimately generating sufficient political pressure against the state to make possible a negotiated transition to democracy. Current Western notions of "civil society" and its potential as a force for democratization in China are closely associated with the Polish experience. Many outside actors envision China's new social organizations as comprising a place for dissent and opposition—a vehicle through which ordinary citizens can assert their rights against the state.[25] Understood in this way, civil society stands in opposition to rather than in harmony with the state. The notion that "NGO advocacy is critical to democratization" was in fact the premise of a project undertaken by the New York–based group Human Rights in China in collaboration with several Asian NGOs, beginning in 1996.[26] Titled "The Three Freedoms," the project sought to promote freedom of association, assembly, and expression—three freedoms viewed by the participating NGOs as "critical to the well-being of NGOs."[27]

The above conception of civil society is in essence a Western paradigm rooted in the unique historical experience of eighteenth- and nineteenth-century Europe. During this period, the rise of capitalism in Europe produced new private economic associations through which individuals could assert their own interests, which then came to be understood as civil society.[28] This experience produced an assumption that "the market dynamic contains the potential for creating new institutions and shifting the balance of power between state and society in the latter's favor."[29] The historical relationship between capitalism and the emergence of constitutional government has also fostered an assumption that civil society carries with it the potential for political liberalization.[30] As Baogang He has put it: "The idea of 'civil society' and the notions of escaping from, controlling, and democratizing the state are . . . closely interlinked."[31]

Civil Society Chinese-Style?

Applying this particular conception of civil society in the Chinese context is problematic, however. Although China's economic reforms have empowered Chinese society by precipitating a redistribution of China's social and economic resources away from the state and toward the society, these same developments have posed substantial challenges to the authority of the state, to which the state has actively responded. Among the consequences of economic reform are a host of new social problems (e.g., unemployment, corruption, a widening gap between rich and poor, and serious environmental problems), which the regime regards as potential sources of social unrest or disorder.

At the same time, economic reform has diminished the capacity of the state to assemble the resources necessary to address these various problems. Hence the government has been forced not only to tolerate but actually to rely on China's new "nongovernmental" sector to provide the social services it can no longer afford, and to address a variety of other social problems such as environmental degradation.[32] Additionally, the government has recognized a need for NGO activity in regulating the market and promoting science and technology.[33] The state's own acknowledgment of its growing reliance on the NGO community is perhaps most vividly illustrated by the Chinese Communist Party's decision in September 1997 to issue a platform calling for "small government, big society," although the actual intent underlying this slogan remains unclear. Indeed, Sophia Woodman of Human Rights in China has expressed a less sanguine view of the government's motives, arguing that one factor underlying the government's tolerance of NGO activity is a recognition of the value of NGOs "in improving China's image overseas and in attracting funding from international donors."[34]

For the Chinese regime, however, NGO activity is not an unmitigated good. The state fears the potential of China's new social organizations to generate pressure for reform from below, thereby triggering social unrest and a further erosion of its political control. Indeed, one consequence of economic reform has been a deterioration of the state's traditional methods of social control. The government once relied heavily on "work units" *(danwei)* to exercise direct control over the populace, but as large sections of the work force have moved from the public to the private sector, the state's ability to dominate Chinese society has also diminished.[35] Consequently, the government is at once both fearful of NGOs and conscious of its dependence on them. This ambivalence has prompted the regime to permit NGO activity, while at the same time extending its own tentacles into the "nongovernmental" sector in an effort to reassert its control. In so doing, the regime has effectively blurred the thick line that most Westerners imagine between the state and civil society.

The government's effort to use the nongovernmental sector to reestablish its own control over Chinese society has taken two basic forms. First, the government has established what have been termed "GONGOs" (government-organized NGOs), "NGOs" effectively created by the government and typically staffed by state or party officials.[36] Many of China's most prominent NGOs, such as the China Charities Federation (CCF) and the China Youth Development Foundation are in fact "GONGOs."[37] The government envisions these organizations as "bridges" designed to reconnect the state with the society, or as "transmission belts" for government policy.[38] The fact that many of China's leading NGOs are government constructions is certainly one of the difficulties scholars confront in trying to assess the likely political implications of China's emerging civil society. China's nongovernmental sector does contain numerous organizations developed as a result of individual initiative at the grassroots level, but the presence of government-created NGOs means that, unlike in the West, civil society in China has evolved from the top down as well as from the bottom up.[39]

China has also sought to co-opt and constrain the NGO community through a series of administrative regulations. Between 1980 and 1989, China's State Council and Ministry of Civil Affairs issued various rules intended to regulate the rapidly expanding number of social organizations. Not until 1989, however, did the state enact a centralized, comprehensive set of regulations for the registration and management of social groups. The 1989 regulations, which were part of a much larger effort by the government to reassert control in the wake of Tiananmen Square, require that all social organizations register with the Ministry of Civil Affairs after first obtaining a state or party sponsor, often referred to as a "mother-in-law."[40] This provision was designed to prohibit similar associations from forming within the same administrative jurisdiction, and thereby limit the total number of legally recognized organizations.[41]

Then, in 1998, the State Council issued two new sets of regulations covering all nonprofit groups. While similar to the 1989 regulations, the new rules appear to be somewhat more restrictive. Groups are still required to register with the Ministry of Civil Affairs or its departments, and only one social organization in a particular issue area is permitted at each administrative level.[42] The 1998 rules, however, also extend the registration system to cover a new category of associations—"people-run, non-enterprise units" *(minban feiqiye danwei)*—which includes private charitable groups, small-scale service providers, and public-benefit institutions.[43] The previous regulations applied only to "social organizations" *(shehui tuanti),* which are defined as membership organizations.[44]

Reactions to the new rules varied. Many international NGO advocacy and human rights groups expressed disappointment, arguing that the new regulations effectively deny freedom of association.[45] On the other hand, a straw poll of registered Chinese social organizations conducted by *chinabrief,* a Beijing-based, English-language publication that focuses on China's NGO community, found the Chinese organizations "generally less concerned about the new rules than their Western counterparts." *Chinabrief* acknowledged that the new rules reflect a government torn between the desire to release private initiative and the need to retain control, but also noted that the new rules "do at least begin to build a regulatory framework for the nonprofit sector."[46] Though the long-term impact of the 1998 regulations on China's civil society remains unclear, the regulations are indicative of an effort by the state, not only to constrain the NGO community, but also to extend its own reach.

The regime has also shown little tolerance for NGOs engaged in public advocacy.[47] Rather, it appears most comfortable with organizations whose missions are narrowly focused on the provision of charity, relief assistance, or education.[48] Student-led environmental groups that sponsor activities such as awareness classes and field trips also appear to enjoy a fair amount of tolerance. That said, a 1997 report on environmental NGOs issued by the U.S. embassy in Beijing observed that individuals or groups that openly questioned existing government policies had attracted government disfavor, although no individual members were being arrested or openly harassed at that time.[49]

The government's crackdown on the Falun Gong spiritual movement beginning in July 1999 also demonstrates that its promotion of the NGO sector is generally not based on an appreciation of the virtues of freedom of association. Economic and legal reforms have unleashed a variety of new grassroots social forces throughout China, but the potential for these forces to exert pressure for political reform from below has motivated the regime to rein in NGOs even while it looks to them to help it address a growing array of social problems. Gordon White, Jude Howell, and Shang Xiaoyuan have captured the situation well:

While we have argued that there has been a decline in the legitimacy and capacity of the official political institutions and ideology, the reaction of both political leaders and state officials to the reforms has been far from passive. At all levels, they have actively sought to come to terms with social changes, co-opt and co-operate with new social forces, ameliorate or rein in growing tensions between state and society, channel growing pressure for access and participation, and avert the political danger posed by a decline in government ability and control. This has meant a powerful *state impetus* towards reshaping patterns of social association, partly reinforcing and partly countervailing the societal impetus.[50] (emphasis in original)

Even China's village elections, which have frequently been heralded as a manifestation of emerging civil society, and a harbinger of democracy, reflect the regime's efforts to co-opt grassroots movements to serve its own political ends. The village committees, which were recognized by the 1982 constitution as a legitimate form of grassroots political organization, first emerged as a peasant response to Deng Xiaoping's early economic reforms.[51] Then in November 1987, following considerable debate within the Chinese leadership, the National People's Congress passed the experimental Organic Law of Village Communities, officially recognizing the village committees and requiring that their members be elected by village residents.[52] However, as Anne Thurston, an observer of the village elections, has noted, the new law was not necessarily driven by popular demand. Peng Zhen, a conservative party official and former head of the National People's Congress, first advocated recognizing the elections as a means of preventing the villagers, who had become increasingly estranged from local leaders, from revolting. The regime understood that the village elections could also serve as "transmission belts between the government and the villagers."[53] However, the village elections process also attracted support from younger, more reform-oriented party members who had "been influenced both by Western political values and by the success of democratic reform in Taiwan."[54] Tianjian Shi thus concluded in his study of the village elections: "The case study of the implementation process of the Organic Law of the Village Committees shows that just as institutional settings can be used by conservatives to resist reform they can also be used by reformers to promote political change."[55]

In fact, a number of outside actors regard the village elections process as a vehicle for local political participation and an opportunity to extend democratic elections to higher levels of government. The Ford Foundation, the Asia Foundation, the UN Development Program (UNDP) and the International Republican Institute (IRI)—one of NED's four core grantees—

have all provided assistance in support of the village elections to the Ministry of Civil Affairs, which continues to oversee the process.[56] Given that the members of the village committees are not considered government officials, the committees themselves might be viewed as a local form of association and therefore a manifestation of civil society. Ultimately, however, the process surrounding China's village elections reflects the same contradictory impulses the state has demonstrated with respect to the NGO community as a whole. Although the state has encouraged the development of a social sector, it has also intervened in that sector in a manner that is not necessarily compatible with the Western paradigm of civil society. Yet it is the Western paradigm that is closely associated with democratization and therefore underpins many of the assumptions surrounding civil society initiatives. Might China's emerging civil society differ so fundamentally from the Western paradigm that those assumptions are untenable in the Chinese context?

Civil Society as a Force for Democratization?

Indeed, understanding the nature of China's civil society is important to assessing whether civil society in the Chinese context should be viewed as a force for democratization, and thus whether civil society initiatives constitute a viable means of furthering political reform in China. The state's penetration of China's newly emerging social sector raises the question of whether it is even appropriate to characterize this sector as "civil society" or use the term "NGO" to describe China's social organizations. The title of White, Howell, and Shang's study, *In Search of Civil Society,* captures well the difficulties scholars confront in locating the Western paradigm of civil society in today's China.[57] As one observer of China's NGO community noted: "If held up to the lens of commonly held Western definitions of NGOs, China's social organizations appear flawed, particularly in terms of their relative autonomy from the state."[58] Even Yan Ming Fu, president of the China Charities Federation—a government-created NGO— when asked whether there were any "real" NGOs in China, responded: "[W]e need to use Chinese standards to measure whether or not NGOs in this period are real. The 'pure' kind of Western NGO is very difficult to find in China. Because if you don't have government support, it is very difficult to get anything done."[59] The fact that most Chinese NGOs lack genuine independence from the state has led some scholars to employ such terms as "state-led civil society" and "semi-civil society" to characterize China's social sector.[60] Others have noted that, because of the close connections that exist between the state and NGOs, civil society in China appears to embody elements of "corporatism."[61]

If China's civil society does not fit the dominant Western model, must we then also question the virtue of civil society initiatives as a means of fostering democracy in China? Are such initiatives based on false assumptions about the nature of China's civil society and its potential as a force for democratization? Sophia Woodman, a vocal critic of the rush by outside actors to embrace China's fledgling NGO community, has argued that common characterizations of China's civil society are overly optimistic and reflect "certain misperceptions about what kind of change is occurring in China and the agents of that change." In her view, "the Chinese authorities have gradually appropriated the discourse of 'NGOs' for their own purposes, obscuring the fact that they have no intention of allowing the formation of autonomous organizations."[62] Even Barnett Baron, executive vice president of the Asia Foundation, has suggested that "the dominant but overly simplistic 'civil society' paradigm . . . is a real obstacle to understanding the context in which non-profit organizations are emerging in China today. . . . [I]f China has an embryonic 'civil society' . . . it is surely not developing in opposition to the State."[63] Yet the Asia Foundation, along with other international and U.S.-based NGOs and foreign governments, has been actively engaged in the promotion of civil society in China.

In fact, a *Directory of International NGOs Supporting Work in China,* published by China Development Research Services in late 1999, observed that civil society initiatives appear "set to become a significant trend among large donor organisations in the coming decade."[64] The directory lists a total of 120 international organizations from the United States, Canada, Europe, and Asia currently working in China, many of which have implemented programs that directly or indirectly support China's "nongovernmental" sector. These may be the "most active groups with sizeable programs," but the directory also estimates that they represent "probably no more than a quarter of the total number of organisations engaging with China at some level."[65] Indeed, the number of international NGOs currently working in China is large enough that the directory's publisher has since 1996 also produced a quarterly English-language publication titled *chinabrief,* whose stated mission is "to increase the flow of information to and between international agencies funding or implementing development projects in China."[66] In addition to the Asia Foundation, U.S.-based NGOs currently working in China include the Ford Foundation, the American Bar Association, the National Committee on U.S.-China Relations, and the Rockefeller Foundation.[67]

Beginning as early as the late 1970s, China's economic and legal reforms provided an opening for these and other organizations seeking to influence China's internal development. Both the Ford Foundation and the Asia Foundation began implementation of various legal reform initiatives nearly two decades ago. In fact, rule of law initiatives have served as the centerpiece of the Asia Foundation's programming in China since 1979. The foundation has worked directly with China's Bureau of Legislative Affairs and Ministry of Justice to implement programs in the areas of administrative law and procedure, civil law, legal education, judicial training and exchanges, and the distribution of legal texts and journals.[68] The Asia Foundation has also sought to promote China's nonprofit sector through a variety of initiatives, including assisting the work of the China Charities Foundation, the Chinese Academy of Social Sciences, and the China NGO Research Society. According to Asia Foundation officials, such programming is intended to increase popular participation in society, devolve authority, and promote pluralism.[69]

The Ford Foundation's legal reform initiatives date back to 1983, when the organization began sponsoring legal exchanges between the United States and China. More recent programs have centered on judicial reform and facilitating more effective use of law to protect citizens rights and curb the arbitrary exercise of state power. Programs designed to fulfill the latter objective have included implementation of law and legal aid initiatives as well as support for research in administrative law, constitutional law, and human rights law.[70] The Ford Foundation has also expanded funding for programs designed to make government more responsive to citizens and to increase popular input into government decisionmaking. Such programs include an initiative designed to support China's village elections.

Not all legal and civil society programming, however, has been carried out by private foundations. Temple University in Philadelphia, for example, recently launched an unprecedented experiment to train Chinese lawyers, judges, and prosecutors in U.S. law. In response to a request made by the Chinese Ministry of Justice in the mid-1990s, the university established an LL.M. program at the Chinese University of Political Science and Law in Beijing. According to the program's Beijing director, Zhang Mo, the university's intent was not to impose the U.S. legal system on China, but rather to offer the Chinese "information about how America has chosen to handle the legal problems that it has faced in the development of a legal system."[71] The American Bar Association (ABA) has also supported legal training and the development of both the legal aid system and business law through the creation of an Asia Law Initiative in 1998. As part of that initiative, the ABA conducted a trial demonstration program in China in

1998, hosted by the National Judges College of the Supreme People's Court in Beijing.[72]

U.S. Democracy Assistance

Despite the popularity of civil society initiatives within the NGO community and among some foreign governments, the Clinton administration had only limited success in achieving the congressional support necessary to conduct the civil society and rule of law initiatives it had proposed. The provision of assistance to the Chinese government in any form has constituted an extremely sensitive topic on Capitol Hill, where human rights policy still tends in some quarters to be identified with withholding assistance from rights abusive regimes. Indeed, assistance to the Chinese government is currently illegal under legislation Congress passed in the 1970s, specifically prohibiting economic and security assistance to governments engaged "in a consistent pattern of gross violations of internationally recognized human rights."[73] Moreover, as noted earlier, the Chinese government's involvement in China's social sector has led many members of Congress to question whether there are any "real" NGOs in China and whether civil society initiatives can be expected to assist in the development of a more democratic political system and greater respect for human rights.

That said, beginning in the fall of 1998, Congress did take a small step in the direction of a democracy program for China by passing legislation, in conjunction with the FY1999 appropriations process, authorizing the State Department to set aside a portion of its "economic support funds" to provide assistance to "nongovernmental organizations located outside of the People's Republic of China" for the purpose of "fostering democracy" in China.

Congress again authorized such assistance in its FY2000 and FY2001 Foreign Operations appropriations bills. However, all of these bills specify that "none of the funds made available for activities to foster democracy in the People's Republic of China may be made available for assistance to the government of that country."[74] The one entity exempted from this rule was the National Endowment for Democracy. In making appropriations for both FY2000 and FY2001, Congress specified that funds may be made available for NED or its grantees to carry out democracy programs in China "notwithstanding" the proviso that no funds "be made available for assistance to the government of that country." The exception was made to allow NED grantees currently working in China on programs involving local government officials to continue their projects.

The Clinton administration encountered even greater difficulties in gaining support for a China rule of law program, for which it had requested $6 million in FY1999. The initiative stemmed from an agreement reached by President Clinton and Chinese resident Jiang Zemin during their 1997 summit in Washington, D.C. At that time, the two leaders pledged to cooperate on legal reform and the development of the rule of law in China. Following the 1998 Beijing summit, the two sides produced a more detailed document outlining five areas for rule of law cooperation: judicial and lawyer training, legal protection of human rights, administrative law, legal aid for the poor, and commercial law and arbitration. Although the Chinese government has been eager to cooperate with the United States on rule of law programs, in making its FY1999 appropriation Congress stated explicitly that the democracy assistance provisions could not be used to support funding for the rule of law initiative.[75] The lack of congressional support forced the State Department to rely on funding from private sources and the cooperation of U.S. NGOs to conduct even a limited number of the programs planned under the initiative.[76]

During its final year in office, the Clinton administration made greater progress in the area of rule of law programming. In its FY2001 Foreign Operations bill, Congress for the first time authorized the State Department to make funds available to nongovernmental organizations "located outside of China" engaged in activities intended to "foster rule of law" in China. Support for this measure was ultimately bipartisan and came from both those opposing and those supporting permanent normal trade status for China.

Democracy assistance for China has fared better during the Bush administration. In its FY2002 Foreign Operations bill, Congress appropriated "not less than $10,000,000 . . . for activities to support democracy, human rights, and the rule of law in the People's Republic of China." Not only did this figure represent a substantial increase over the funds appropriated for democracy programs for China in previous years, but the 2002 legislation was also less restrictive in terms of whether these funds could be made available to assist the government of China.[77]

Congress has also indirectly supported proactive programs aimed at fostering democracy and human rights in China through its annual appropriation to the National Endowment for Democracy,[78] which in turn has supported prodemocracy activities in China through two of its grantees. One of those grantees, the International Republican Institute, has been working with the Chinese Ministry of Civil Affairs and other government agencies and academic institutions on village elections, legal reform, and other projects. Another grantee, the Center for International Private Enterprise, has conducted policy forums with Chinese scholars and government officials on reforming various aspects of China's economic policy.

Still, at least some members of Congress have remained reluctant to support initiatives involving direct U.S. cooperation with the Chinese government. No doubt this reluctance is at least partly rooted in concerns about the political palatability of such programs rather than serious doubts about whether China's emerging civil society is truly conducive to long-term democratization. Many members of Congress are simply more comfortable with supporting dissident activities through NED and Radio Free Asia (RFA) than they are with authorizing U.S. assistance that they fear might somehow benefit the Chinese government. Nevertheless, legitimate questions as to whether China's civil society can ever truly serve as a force for democratization do exist. Moreover, such concerns should inform the debate over the merits of civil society initiatives conducted by outside actors.

General agreement presently exists that, at least in its current form, China's civil society lacks both the strength and the independence necessary to pressure the state to move in a more democratic direction.[79] Not only is Chinese civil society lacking in autonomy, but key segments of society, including workers and intellectuals, currently appear to have few connections with one another. This points to another important difference between the Chinese and Polish cases. In Poland, the success of civil society in bringing about a negotiated transition to democratic rule is typically attributed to the strong alliance that formed between the Catholic Church, the workers, and the intellectuals. No such alliance currently exists in China.[80]

That said, China's NGOs possess at least the potential to gravitate gradually away from the state, thereby unleashing a more autonomous social sphere. Already, the degree to which China's NGOs are controlled by the state clearly varies, and some do appear to be attaining greater independence.[81] Indeed, Tony Saich has suggested that analyses of China's social sector that focus exclusively on the "top-down" control of the state "risk obscuring the dynamics of change in China and the capacity of the 'co-opted groups' to influence the policy-making process or to pursue the interest of their members." Despite state efforts to control the emerging social sector, Saich explains, "social practice reveals a pattern of negotiation that minimizes state penetration and allows such organizations to reconfigure the relationship with the state" in ways that allow them to advance their own interests.[82]

Moreover, continued economic reform is likely to increase the government's reliance on NGOs, but as *chinabrief* editor Nick Young has noted, the ability of NGOs to engage in the innovation and problem solving that will be required of them may "correlate strongly with how 'bottom up' these organizations are."[83] In fact, president of the China Charities Federation and former Vice Minister of Civil Affairs Yan Ming Fu has said that the state's current dominance is only "natural given that China is still in transition from a planned economy, but he has also stressed that China's reforms are 'irreversible' and will necessarily require devolution of state functions to "progressively more autonomous NGOs."[84] Given China's rapidly changing economic and social environment, informal forms of association such as those that have sprung up around China's growing number of labor migrants, are also likely to expand.[85]

China's civil society, however, is also unlikely to enjoy the autonomy assumed by the Western paradigm of civil society without a further commitment to political reform at the top. Yet even if this proves to be the case, any future political reform will need to be rooted in society if China is to experience a smooth transition to democracy. China's civil society, though still constrained, should therefore be understood as laying the groundwork for future political reforms by fostering the participation, pluralism, and decentralization generally associated with liberal democracy. As Anne Thurston has observed: "Longer-term development of basic-level democracy in China will require significant changes at both the bottom and the top. At the grassroots, democracy will remain stunted without the development of a more pluralistic civil society. And the development of democracy will ultimately require a major commitment at the highest reaches of Chinese political power."[86] Outside efforts to assist in the development of civil society in China are perhaps thus better conceived as serving to build a sort of infrastructure for democracy rather than a force capable of opposing the state.

Given the nature of China's civil society, however, many opportunities to assist in its development do entail working with the Chinese government. Generally speaking, international NGOs working in China have found it necessary to define their individual missions carefully, and to take care not to antagonize the Chinese government. Failing to do so might mean losing their access altogether. For example, a German foundation—the Friedrich Naumann Stiftung—was forced to leave China in 1996 after it refused to revoke funding for a conference in Germany that involved the participation of groups supporting Tibet.[87] Unlike NGOs working from outside China, NGOs working in China typically choose not to characterize their missions in terms of democracy-building or human rights and are often quick to disavow any connection to the U.S. government. Indeed, the vast majority of international NGOs hoping to influence China's future have had to choose between working from within the system or working from outside the system. Interestingly, NED emerges as one exception to this rule. It is unique in that its structure encompasses both dissident-led organizations such as Human Rights in China and organizations like the International Republican Institute, which has been working with the Chinese government on various projects.

To some extent the issue here is the age-old question of whether it is morally permissible to work from within the system in an effort to reform it. For some, this practice is simply unacceptable and those who engage in it are little more than collaborationists. No doubt this is a sentiment shared by some in Congress who continue to oppose various forms of engagement with China. Others, however, believe strongly that there are plenty of "closet democrats" in China and that institution-building at all levels must also occur if China is to experience a peaceful transition to democracy. As one NGO official offered, working with the Chinese government allows outside actors to propose "liberal" remedies to a growing array of social problems for which Chinese officials are actively seeking solutions.[88]

International NGOs working in China are also increasingly responding to growing grassroots demands for legal redress and services.[89] For example, a number of NGOs have initiated what the Ford Foundation describes as "law in action" programs. The objective underlying such initiatives, according to the Ford Foundation, is to alter understandings of law at the societal level so that it comes to be recognized as a set of rules to which citizens can turn for protection of their rights rather than as a mere instrument of coercion.[90]

Harnessing the Forces of Globalization

As suggested earlier, the fact that China's civil society is evolving in an era of globalization is significant. Any assessment of its potential to serve as a vehicle for democratization and greater respect for human rights must consider ways in which globalization is both informing the direction of China's civil society and assisting those outside actors who aspire to encourage it. Indeed, global markets and information technology associated with globalization are multiplying the channels through which outside actors can influence Chinese society, and simultaneously undermining the regime's strict control. China's leaders appear to have gambled that they could continue economic liberalization without jeopardizing their political authority. In doing so, however, they have unleashed forces in Chinese society that, especially in an age of globalization, will be extremely difficult, if not impossible, to control over the long term. Hence any effort to assess the virtue of civil society initiatives must take note of the forces of globalization at work in the world today and the impact of such forces on both China's emerging civil society and efforts by outside actors to assist its development.

New information technologies, including the Internet and e-mail, have greatly facilitated the ability of overseas dissidents and international NGOs to circumvent the Chinese government and make direct contact with Chinese society. These technologies have not only expanded the information and ideas to which individuals in China have access; they have also created a proreform community that transcends political borders. The Internet, for example, constitutes a sort of forum for free association, but it also expands the community in which one can exercise freedom of association. As *chinabrief* editor Nick Young has observed: "Who you associate with is largely a function of who you can communicate with, and modern technologies have, famously, opened completely new horizons."[91] Perhaps it is not unreasonable then to question whether the very concept of civil society is becoming a borderless one.

The growing ease of communication is facilitating the formation of global networks of NGOs, as international NGOs seek to promote democracy and human rights through collaboration with indigenous social groups. The "Three Freedoms" project was itself inspired by a perceived need to build coalitions among Asian NGOs in the aftermath of the 1993 UN World Conference on Human Rights, during which Asian governments challenged the universality of human rights in the name of culture and Asian values.[92] The Asia Foundation has also sponsored initiatives aimed at fostering cooperation among local and international NGOs, including an International Conference on the Nonprofit Sector and Development at Tsinghua University in Beijing in late July 1999 involving 131 participants. According to Barnett Baron, executive vice president of the Asia Foundation: "The candour with which different perspectives on the current nature of the non-profit sector in China were discussed, and the wide range of international delegates invited to participate, were remarkable."[93]

Asian NGOs are also organizing forums for discussion and cooperation. For example, an NED-supported Mongolian NGO that calls itself LEOS (Liberal Women's Brain Pool) has hosted meetings of the East Asian Women's Forum in which groups from both China and Taiwan have participated. Collaboration among Chinese NGOs has also been growing, as evidenced by the formation of a Chinese network of nonprofit organizations, initially funded by the World Bank and the Asia Foundation. The network, which publishes a newsletter and has its own website, is not itself a formal organization, but hopes to represent its members by relaying their concerns to the Ministry of Civil Affairs and other government entities.[94]

Such cooperation among NGOs coupled with and indeed facilitated by information-age technology will make it increasingly difficult for the Chinese government to isolate and constrain civil society.

International radio broadcasts, including Radio Free Asia's weekly call-in programs, also serve to increase access to information and provide an opportunity for discussion that is outside the reach of state authorities.[95] Programs such as "Listener Hotline," "Democracy Salon," and "Voices of the People" take listener calls from mainland China, and thereby provide a forum for open and anonymous discussion of sensitive political issues. Discussions typically reflect a diverse assortment of views, and cover a wide range of issues, including the rule of law, democracy, police harassment, the Chinese Communist Party, and Jiang Zemin. Another call-in program—"Labor Corner"—is mediated by labor activist Han Dongfang, who relocated to Hong Kong after serving a three-year prison term in China for activities surrounding the 1989 demonstrations at Tiananmen Square. Han takes listener calls in Hong Kong from mainland China on a wide range of labor and workers' rights issues.[96] Additionally, RFA broadcasts commentary by some of China's most prominent dissidents, including Wei Jingsheng, Liu Binyan, and Wang Dan.[97]

As is true of many actors engaged in democracy and human rights promotion, RFA has also harnessed the power of the Internet, offering visitors to its website news and transcripts of its programming in a total of nine languages. Seven of the nine language services also provide for feedback through a bulletin board system to which visitors can post and respond to messages. It is not clear how many mainland Chinese regularly access the RFA website. Web traffic data for September 1999, for example, confirmed only 0.0018 percent of RFA's website visitors to be mainland Chinese. These data may be misleading, however, because they cannot account for Chinese visitors who use U.S.-based proxy servers or U.S. Internet service providers.[98]

Human Rights in China, the New York–based dissident organization whose mission is "to encourage and empower the nascent grassroots human rights movement in China" also relies on the Internet and RFA to transmit information to China, including documents for reform originally drafted in China. The organization's own tracking data as of mid-1999 suggested that its website was receiving as many as 2,000 hits per week.[99] In fact, Human Rights in China claims to be "in touch with more than 100,000 students and scholars worldwide" via the Internet. "With mainland access to the Internet exploding," the organization has observed, "the potential for conducting human rights advocacy and education electronically is enormous."[100]

Indeed, the Internet is increasingly regarded by outside actors as a powerful tool for breaking through government censorship and, because of the anonymity it offers, for empowering Chinese society. The NED has supported a number of reform-oriented Internet publications based outside China, including *China News Digest* and *The Press Guardian Freedom.* Yet another NED-supported publication, *Democratic China,* went from printing 6,000 copies per monthly issue to registering 1.7 million hits per month when it switched to an online format.[101]

E-mail is also proving to be an important tool for publishing news and other information inside China. For example, a magazine titled *Tunnel* is distributed in China entirely via e-mail. The magazine's articles are written and edited in China and then forwarded to a website in the United States, which e-mails the magazine back to its readers in China. When first launched in June 1997, *Tunnel* claimed to be the first online magazine published in China intended to break the government's information monopoly and control of opinion.[102]

Of course, access to the Internet in China remains limited for a variety of reasons. One factor is simply cost. The price of a computer is prohibitively expensive for most Chinese, as is the cost of Internet access at the growing number of Internet cafes springing up in China's cities. A lack of Chinese-language material on the Web also limits the Internet's capacity as an important source of information for most Chinese.[103] That said, Internet use in China has been increasing rapidly. Figures vary, but according to the state-sponsored China Internet Information Center, China had nearly 9 million Internet users as of January 2000, up from just 2 million the previous year.[104] Chinese-language sites are becoming more common as well. And China's own NGO community has also tapped into the power of the Internet. Larger NGOs are acquiring their own websites, through which some are even taking donations.

From the regime's perspective, however, the Internet poses a serious dilemma. As evidenced by the release of a variety of regulations intended to restrict Internet use, Chinese authorities perceive the Internet to be at once vital to continued economic growth and a serious threat to their ability to control Chinese society. The latest rules, issued in January 2000, forbid organizations and individuals "from releasing, discussing or transferring state secrets on bulletin boards, chat rooms or in Internet news groups."[105] Determinations as to what constitutes a "state secret" are largely left to the discretion of the regime. Additionally, companies and individuals using software intended to protect transfers of sensitive information are required to register that software and the names of those using it with the government.[106]

Chinese authorities have also attempted to block access to websites they have deemed dangerous, such as those of overseas Chinese dissident organizations and other Western sources of news and information. At best, this is proving to be an extremely difficult task. New websites appear every week, and Internet users can circumvent the firewalls the government has erected through various means. One strategy entails the use of a proxy server. Chinese users can bypass blocks or filters by setting their browsers to proxy servers, available free on the Internet, which allows them to obtain and relay material from blocked sites without revealing its origin. Users can protect their e-mail by taking advantage of encryption technologies, which the government is loathe to ban because of the role of this technology in protecting commercial transactions. They can also obtain free, Web-based e-mail accounts like Hotmail that allow for frequent address changes.[107] As Judy Chen of Human Rights in China has observed, the task of achieving comprehensive control over the Internet will become ever more difficult as Internet use expands and websites proliferate. "The Chinese authorities success in censoring the Net," she concludes, "will depend on whether they are willing to invest the increasing amounts of time, money, personnel and technology necessary to keep up with Internet growth."[108]

Restrictions on foreign investment in Chinese Internet service providers were also set to end upon China's entry into the World Trade Organization (WTO). The 1999 U.S.-China trade agreement, which paved the way for China's accession to the WTO in late 2001, required that China initially allow up to 49 percent foreign ownership of telecom service providers, including Internet service providers. That percentage was scheduled to rise to 50 percent two years after China's accession to the WTO.[109]

Implications for Outside Actors

China's entry into the WTO also serves as an example of how the forces of globalization are transforming from above and below the very shape of Chinese society and its relationship with the regime in ways that may ultimately benefit the status of human rights in China. During a press conference following the release of the U.S. State Department's 1999 human rights report, Harold Koh, in fact, said of the 1999 U.S.-China trade agreement:

> That agreement will benefit both countries economically, but it will also require China to follow international trading rules, open its regulations to public scrutiny, and reduce the role of state-owned enterprises. This should

expand the rule of law and hasten the development of a more open society. The human rights situation in China will not be transformed overnight, but joining the WTO will add to the pressures welling up from within China for greater personal and political freedom.[110]

Interestingly, some human rights advocates, who once favored withdrawal of China's most-favored-nation status as a means of protesting continued human rights abuse, ultimately came to favor China's entry into the WTO on human rights grounds. Even before the United States and China finalized the 1999 trade agreement, Human Rights Watch released a statement suggesting that "China's membership in the WTO could increase pressure for greater openness, more press freedom, enhanced rights for workers and an independent judiciary."[111] Globalization in no way guarantees China's peaceful transition to democracy or greater respect for human rights. The forces associated with it, however, are connecting Chinese society to the outside world in unprecedented ways, in the process improving prospects for a more autonomous civil society and providing outside actors with opportunities to encourage its development.

Civil society is unlikely ever to play the sort of role in China that it did in Poland in 1989. Rather, many scholars and NGO advocates currently engaged in China believe that China is likely to democratize in an evolutionary rather than revolutionary way. The course of China's democratization "may be slow and gradual rather than swift and sudden," as Liu Binyan put it in 1991. In the interim China would need "a flowering of all kinds of independent organizations, especially free trade unions, and a strengthening of civil society. The resulting pressures should help force the Communist regime to carry economic reforms through to the end and gradually expand democratic political rights."[112] Indeed, if genuine liberal democracy is to evolve in China, reform must occur from the bottom up as well as from the top down—at the societal as well as the state level. A strengthened and increasingly autonomous civil society will serve not only to encourage reform at the top, but also to ensure that reforms are firmly rooted in Chinese society—in its habits, institutions, and values.

Conclusion

The once closed nature of Chinese society allowed few opportunities for outside actors to engage in proactive efforts to foster democracy and respect for human rights. Deng Xiaoping's decision to initiate economic reform and open China's doors to trade in the late 1970s, however, effectively opened up Chinese society to outside influences as well. As

China's economic liberalization proceeds and its society becomes ever more connected to the outside world, opportunities for the United States to promote democracy will continue to multiply. Already the opportunities exceed available funds. Louisa Coan, NED's senior program officer for Asia, for example, has noted that NED is unable to fund many of the worthy grantee requests it receives for democracy programs related to China.[113]

The United States should, where possible, take advantage of opportunities to assist the development of both civil society and the rule of law in China, even if in some cases it means cooperating with the Chinese government. Numerous opportunities also exist to work with U.S.-based NGOs, some of which have a long history of engagement in China. As Anne Thurston has observed, many of these NGOs possess certain advantages over the U.S. government when it comes to implementing democracy programs. In her words: "At present U.S. NGOs may be better structured to cooperate with China than are government agencies, both because of NGOs longtime expertise at the grassroots level and because they are better cushioned against Washington's changing and often powerful, political winds." Thurston adds, however, that "cooperative efforts could benefit greatly from an infusion of funding, both governmental and private."[114]

The United States must recognize that it can no longer rely on punitive measures (e.g., economic sanctions, and public and private criticism), traditionally targeted at the state, if it truly wishes to foster democracy and respect for human rights in China. These essentially state-centric measures are simply inadequate in that they fail to assist in the development of democratic institutions, practices, and values at both the state and the societal levels. The virtue of civil society and rule of law initiatives lies in their implicit recognition that, if China is to democratize, the relationship between the state and society must change in a way that enables the Chinese people not only to claim but actually to enforce their rights against the state. Such initiatives serve to empower those local actors who ultimately must play a central role in holding the Chinese government accountable for evolving global norms of democracy and human rights. China needs an indigenous civil society that can act from below to restrain the arbitrary exercise of power by the state.

Notes

An abbreviated and modified version of this chapter was published in *World Policy Journal* 18, no. 1 (Spring 2001): 56–66.

1. Jessica Mathews, "Power Shift," *Foreign Affairs* 76, no.1 (January–February 1997): 50.

2. Text of Press Conference of President Clinton, May 26, 1994. Clinton suggested that such a program would include "increased support for nongovernmental organizations working on human rights in China."

3. See testimony of John Shattuck, "U.S. Democracy Promotion Programs in Asia," Hearing Before the House Subcommittee on Asia and the Pacific of the Committee on International Relations, 105th Congress, 1st sess., September 17, 1997, p. 9.

4. Madeleine Albright, Address to the UN Human Rights Commission, Geneva, Switzerland, March 23, 2000,http://secretary.state.gov/www/statements/2000/000323.html

5. See Commission on Human Rights Resolution 1999/57, Released by the Commission on Human Rights, United Nations, New York, April 27, 1999, www.state.gov/www/global/human   rights/democracy/9957   unresolution.html. Three years earlier in his *Agenda for Democratization,* then UN Secretary-General Boutros Boutros-Ghali also observed that democracy was "increasingly being recognized as a response to a wide range of human rights concerns and as essential to the promotion of human rights." See Boutros Boutros-Ghali, *An Agenda for Democratization* (New York: United Nations, 1996), p. 6.

6. See Shattuck, "U.S. Democracy Promotion Programs in Asia," pp. 6, 40.

7. Rebecca R. Moore, "Globalization and the Future of U.S. Human Rights Policy," *The Washington Quarterly* 21, no. 4 (August 1998): 205.

8. Author interview with Department of State official, December 1999.

9. The term "NGO" is problematic in the Chinese context insofar as it implies a degree of autonomy that most social organizations in China do not presently enjoy. However, I use it here to refer to Chinese social organizations or associations in a way that is generally consistent with existing literature on the topic.

10. See, for example, Yijiang Ding, "Corporatism and Civil Society in China: An Overview of the Debate in Recent Years," *China Information* 12, no. 4 (Spring 1998): 49; and Baogang He, *The Democratic Implications of Civil Society in China* (New York: St. Martin's Press, 1997), p. 2.

11. China scholar Minxin Pei has identified two phases of rapid growth in what he terms "civic associations" between 1979 and 1992. During the initial phase, which lasted from 1979 until 1981, a renewed emphasis on science, technology, and basic research prompted the formation of numerous scholarly associations. Deepening economic reform triggered the second phase of growth, which was driven largely by the emergence of new business and trade associations and lasted from 1984 until 1989. Minxin Pei, "Chinese Civic Associations: An Empirical Analysis," *Modern China* 24, no. 3 (July 1998): 299–303.

12. *The Rise of Nongovernmental Organizations in China: Implications for Americans,* report on a project of the National Committee on U.S.-China Relations, Inc., National Committee China Policy Series no. 8, May 1994, pp. i–ii.

13. He, *Democratic Implications,* p. 23.

14. Yet another factor currently driving legal reform in China is a growing corruption problem. Abuses of power by party/state officials throughout China have inspired public anger and protest, providing further incentive for the state to adopt

rules and procedures designed to limit the discretionary power of government officials.

15. Testimony of Allen Choate, "U.S. Policy Options Toward China," p. 66.

16. See testimony of Minxin Pei, ibid., p. 91.

17. Ibid., p. 92.

18. See, for example, Elisabeth Rosenthal, "In China's Legal Evolution, the Lawyers Are Handcuffed," *New York Times,* January 6, 2000.

19. Minxin Pei, "Is China Democratizing?" *Foreign Affairs* 77, no. 1 (January–February 1998): 76–77.

20. *Rise of Nongovernmental Organizations in China,* pp. 24–25.

21. Ibid., p. ii.

22. Shattuck, "U.S. Democracy Promotion Programs in Asia," pp. 5, 9.

23. Harold Koh, U.S. Department of State On-the-Record Briefing upon Release of 1999 Human Rights Report, February 25, 2000.

24. See testimony of Harold Koh before the House Committee on International Relations, January 20, 1999.

25. Michael Frolic, "State Led Civil Society," in Timothy Brook and B. Michael Frolic, eds., *Civil Society in China* (Armonk, NY: M. E. Sharpe, 1997), p. 46.

26. The NGOs participating in the "Three Freedoms" project are the Cambodian Association for Human Rights and Development (ADHOC); the Alternative Law and Development Center, Inc. (ALTERLAW), the Philippines; the Institute for Policy Research & Advocacy (ELSAM), Indonesia; Hong Kong Human Rights Monitor (HKHRM); Human Rights in China (HRIC); and the Law & Society Trust (LST), Sri Lanka.

27. Sidney Jones, "The Three Freedoms in Asia: An Overview," in *Promoting Three Basic Freedoms: Towards Greater Freedom of Association, Assembly and Expression in Asia* (Human Rights Watch/Asia, September 1997), www.three freedoms.org. The "Three Freedoms" project defines civil society as "all those social organizations and networks operating outside the official sphere, including professional associations, trade unions, charitable groups, political parties, the press, cause-oriented movements, social clubs and NGOs."

28. This understanding is essentially a Hegelian one in which the birth of the institutions of civil society is closely connected with the recognition of a right of private property.

29. Gordon White, Jude Howell, and Shang Xiaoyuan, *In Search of Civil Society: Market Reform and Social Change in Contemporary China* (Oxford: Clarendon Press, 1996), p. 8.

30. Larry Diamond is just one scholar of democratization who has recognized a positive link between the emergence of civil society and the process of democratization. Diamond has identified ten democratic functions of civil society, including limiting state power, supporting economic reform, and disseminating new information and ideas. See Larry Diamond, "Rethinking Civil Society," *Journal of Democracy* 5, no. 3 (1994): 7–11.

31. He, *Democratic Implications,* p. 1.

32. For a useful account of the emergence of NGOs in the environmental sector, see Elizabeth Knup, "Environmental NGOs in China: An Overview," China

Environment Series, Working Group on Environment in U.S.-China Relations (Washington, DC: Woodrow Wilson Center), pp. 9–15.

33. Sophia Woodman, "Less Dressed Up as More? Promoting Non-Profit-Making Organizations by Regulating Away Freedom of Association," *China Perspectives* no. 22 (March–April 1999): 18.

34. Ibid.

35. Ding, "Corporatism and Civil Society in China" p. 49.

36. See, for example, White, Howell, and Shang, *In Search of Civil Society,* p. 112; and Pei, "Chinese Civic Associations," p. 295.

37. Nick Young, "A Million Flowers Bloom; One Is Weeded Out," *chinabrief* 2, no. 4, (December 1999–March 2000): 11; and Yan Mingfu, "NGOs Are 'Inevitable Trend of the Times,'" *chinabrief* 2, no. 3 (August–November 1999): 21.

38. Jonathan Unger, "'Bridges': Private Business, the Chinese Government, and the Rise of New Associations," *China Quarterly* no. 147 (September 1996): 795; and Frolic, "State Led Civil Society," p. 57.

39. Ding, "Corporatism and Civil Society in China," p. 49.

40. Knup, "Environmental NGOs in China," p. 10; and Woodman, "Less Dressed Up as More?" p. 18. The 1989 regulations also specified that social organizations must not act contrary to the interests of the state and must submit information concerning their mission statement, members, source of funding, and organizational structure.

41. According to Minxin Pei, the 1989 regulations did produce a drastic reduction in the number of new associations formed in 1990. Pei, "Chinese Civic Associations," pp. 299–303.

42. "New Rules for the Nonprofit Sector," *chinabrief* 2, no. 1 (February 1999), http://www.chinadevelopmentbrief.com.

43. Young, "A Million Flowers Bloom," p. 12.

44. "New Rules for the Nonprofit Sector."

45. Human Rights in China criticized two U.S. foundations—the Asia Foundation and the Washington, D.C.–based International Center for Not-for-Profit Law (ICNL) for allegedly assisting the Ministry of Civil Affairs (MOCA) in drafting the new regulations, and thereby "supporting efforts to regulate away citizens' rights in the name of 'legal reform,' promoting civil society or assisting the development of the non-profit sector." See "Bound and Gagged: Freedom of Association in China Further Curtailed Under New Regulations," released by Human Rights in China, November 13, 1998, p. 7. However, the Asia Foundation maintains that, while it did sponsor a study tour to the United States and Australia in December 1997 for a small group of MOCA officials, it never provided any advisory support or assistance to the MOCA with respect to the actual drafting of the new regulations. Author interview with Asia Foundation official, March 2000.

46. "New Rules for the Nonprofit Sector."

47. Woodman, "Less Dressed Up as More?" pp. 17–18.

48. *Rise of Nongovernmental Organizations in China,* p. 10.

49. Knup, "Environmental NGOs in China."

50. White, Howell, and Shang, *In Search of Civil Society,* p. 26.

51. Paul Grove, "Challenges and Obstacles to Village Elections in China," speech before the Council on Foreign Relations, February 9, 1999.

52. Implementation of the Organic Law of Village Communities began in

1989. For an excellent account of the evolution of the village elections, see Tianjian Shi, "Village Committee Elections in China: Institutionalist Tactics for Democracy," *World Politics* 51, no. 3 (April 1999): 385–412.

53. Anne Thurston, *Muddling Toward Democracy: Political Change in Grassroots China,* Peaceworks no. 23 (Washington, DC: U.S. Institute of Peace, August 1998), p. 11. Michael Frolic has also noted that the "law was not designed to dismantle the state at the village level. Rather a strong state presence was deemed crucial to stop parochialism and the growth of 'independent kingdoms.'" Frolic, "State Led Civil Society," p. 64.

54. Thurston, *Muddling Toward Democracy,* p. iii.

55. Shi, "Village Committee Elections in China," p. 410.

56. Ibid., pp. 406–407. During a visit to Fujian province in 1994, the IRI became the first international organization to observe the village elections. The IRI continues to work with the Ministry of Civil Affairs to improve and possibly expand the elections. See, for example, the testimony of Lorne W. Craner, president of the IRI, "U.S. Policy Options Toward China: Rule of Law and Democracy Programs," pp. 84–85

57. White, Howell, and Shang, *In Search of Civil Society,* 26.

58. Knup, "Environmental NGOs in China," p. 14.

59. Yan Mingfu, "NGOs Are 'Inevitable Trend of the Times.'" Ming Fu added, though, that "as China's reforms advance, NGOs will inevitably become more independent" (http://www.chinadevelopmentbrief.com).

60. Baogang He has used the term "semi-civil society" to reflect the fact that Chinese social organizations are "neither completely autonomous nor completely dependent on the state." He, *Democratic Implications,* p. 8. Frolic has employed the term "state-led civil society" to refer to the organizations and groups created by the state "principally to help it govern, but also to co-opt and socialize potentially politically active elements in the population." Frolic, "State Led Civil Society," p. 56.

61. See, for example, Ding, "Corporatism and Civil Society in China."

62. Woodman, "Less Dressed Up as More?" p. 25.

63. Barnett Baron, "Some Reflections on NGOs and Civil Society," speech at Yonsei University, Seoul, Korea, September 1999.

64. Introduction to Fong Ku, ed., *2000 Directory of International NGOs Supporting Work in China* (Hong Kong: China Development Research Services, October 1999), p. vi.

65. Ibid., pp. i–ii.

66. *Chinabrief* was formerly published as *China Development Briefing.* A Chinese-language companion to *chinabrief* is also distributed free on request to mainland Chinese organizations. Its readership reportedly includes Chinese government agencies, research institutes, and nonprofit organizations. The publication is funded in part by grants from Action Aid India, the Kadoorie Charitable Foundations, the Ford Foundation, Save the Children (UK), and the Trace Foundation.

67. This represents only a small sample of the U.S. NGOs currently working in China.

68. Testimony of Choate, "U.S. Policy Options Toward China"; and author interview with Asia Foundation official, December 1999.

69. Author interview with Asia Foundation official, December 1999.

70. Ibid.; and *The Ford Foundation in China* (brochure).

71. "Beijing Trial for U.S. Law Studies," *Hong Kong Standard,* September 25, 1999. www.thestandard.com.hk.

72. Ku, *2000 Directory,* p. 4.

73. In 1974 Congress amended Section 116 of the 1961 Foreign Assistance Act to prohibit economic or development assistance to "the government of any country which engages in a consistent pattern of gross violations of internationally recognized human rights." In 1978 Congress also amended Section 502B of the 1961 Foreign Assistance Act to make legally binding a prohibition on security assistance to "any country the government of which engages in a consistent pattern of gross violations of internationally recognized human rights." For a detailed discussion of this legislation, see David Forsythe, *Human Rights and U.S. Foreign Policy: Congress Reconsidered* (Gainsville: University of Florida Press, 1988).

74. See Sec. 527, Conference Report on H.R. 4328, Making Omnibus Consolidated and Emergency Supplemental Appropriations for FY1999; and Sec. 526, Conference Report on H.R. 3194, Consolidated Appropriations Act 2000, November 17, 1999.

75. See Sec. 527 (Democracy in China), Section 101(d), Foreign Operations, Export Financing, and Related Programs Appropriations Act 1999 (Report).

76. Author interviews with Department of State officials, December 1999. Thus far, the United States and China have conducted programs on reforming arbitration and administrative law and have held several rule of law conferences, including one on the legal protection of human rights. A program concerning the provision of legal aid to the poor originally scheduled for June 1999 was canceled due to the bombing of the Chinese embassy in Belgrade by the North Atlantic Treaty Organization (NATO) during the 1999 Kosovo war.

77. See Sec. 526 (Democracy Programs), Foreign Operations, Export Financing, and Related Programs Appropriations Act 2002 (Reported in Senate).

78. Although the NED receives annual appropriations from Congress and is subject to congressional oversight and review, an independent, bipartisan board of directors makes all policy and programming decisions.

79. See, for example, Jude Howell, "An Unholy Trinity? Civil Society, Economic Liberalization, and Democratization in Post-Mao China," *Government and Opposition* 33, no. 1 (Winter 1998): 79–80.

80. Frolic, "State Led Civil Society," p. 67.

81. See Knup, "Environmental NGOs in China," p. 11.

82. Tony Saich, "Negotiating the State: The Development of Social Organizations in China," *China Quarterly* no. 161 (March 2000): 124–125.

83. Young, "A Million Flowers Bloom," p. 13.

84. Quoted in Barnett Baron, "International Conference in Beijing Hails Emergence of Chinese NGOs," *Alliance* 4, no. 4 (December 1999), http://www.asiafoundation.org/new/news-high28.htm.

85. Young, "A Million Flowers Bloom," p. 14.

86. Thurston, *Muddling Toward Democracy,* p. xi.

87. The "Three Freedoms" project mentions this particular incident in its report.

88. Here the term "liberal remedies" should be understood as approaches that are consistent with the classical liberalism of theorists such as John Locke—in

other words, approaches that recognize the virtues of limited government and respect for individual liberties. Author interview, October 1999.

89. "Promoting the Rule of Law," *chinabrief*, 2, no.1 (February 1999), www.chinadevelopmentbrief.com.

90. *Ford Foundation in China.*

91. Young, "A Million Flowers Bloom," p. 17.

92. Author interview with Human Rights in China official, July 1999.

93. Baron, "International Conference in Beijing."

94. Young, "A Million Flowers Bloom," p. 12.

95. Congress established Radio Free Asia in 1994 as a private corporation, for which it makes an annual appropriation.

96. Author interview with Radio Free Asia official, October 1999.

97. Approximately fifteen high-profile dissidents currently offer commentary for Radio Free Asia.

98. Author interview with Radio Free Asia official, October 1999.

99. Author interview with Human Rights in China official, July 1999.

100. See website of Human Rights in China, http://www.HRIChina.org.

101. Testimony of Louisa Coan, "Human Rights in China," Hearing Before the House Committee on International Relations, January 20, 1999.

102. Zhang Weiguo, "Evading State Censorship: From the Bible to New Century Net," *China Rights Forum* (October 1998): 24.

103. Judy Chen, "China On-Line: Surfing into the Future," *China Rights Forum* (Fall 1998): 30.

104. Elisabeth Rosenthal, "Chinese Issues Rules to Limit E-mail and Web Content," *New York Times,* January 27, 2000; and Elisabeth Rosenthal, "China Tightens Controls on Internet Use," *New York Times,* January 26, 2000. These figures may actually be too low. On the other hand, Judy Chen has suggested that China's desire to attract foreign investors may create an incentive to overreport Internet use, thereby offering an impression of a technically advanced society. See Chen, "China Online," p. 26.

105. "China Clamps Secrecy Rules on the Internet," *New York Times,* January 26, 2000.

106. Rosenthal, "China Tightens Controls on Internet Use."

107. Weiguo Zhang, "Evading State Censorship," p. 25; and Chen, "China Online," p. 31.

108. Chen, "China Online," p. 30.

109. "China to Release New Regulations for Internet Service Providers," *Inside China Today,* January 10, 2000.

110. Harold Koh, U.S. Department of State On-the-Record Briefing upon Release of 1999 Human Rights Report, February 25, 2000, 20.

111. David Sanger, "A Deal That America Just Couldn't Refuse," *New York Times,* September 16, 1999, p. A10.

112. Liu Binyan, "China and the Lessons of Eastern Europe," *Journal of Democracy* 2, no. 2 (Spring 1991): 9.

113. Author interview with Louisa Coan, October 1999. Coan made this same observation in testimony before Congress in 1997. See U.S. Congress "U.S. Democracy Promotion Programs in Asia," p. 72.

114. Thurston, *Muddling Toward Democracy,* p. v.

Bibliography

Baron, Barnett F. "International Conference in Beijing Hails Emergence of Chinese NGOs." *Alliance* 4, no. 4 (December 1999): http://www.asiafoundation.org.

Boutros-Ghali, Boutros. *An Agenda for Democratization.* New York: United Nations, 1996.

Brook, Timothy, and B. Michael Frolic. *Civil Society in China.* Armonk, NY: M. E. Sharpe, 1997.

Chamberlain, Heath. "Civil Society with Chinese Characteristics?" *China Journal* no. 30 (January 1998): 69–81.

Chen, Judy. "China Online: Surfing into the Future." *China Rights Forum* (Fall 1998): 26–31.

Cook, John W., David M. Lampton, Kevin F. F. Quigly, Peter Riggs, William J. Van Ness Jr., M. Jon Vondracek, and Patricia D. Wright. *The Rise of Nongovernmental Organizations in China: Implications for Americans.* National Committee China Policy Series no. 8. National Committee on U.S.-China Relations, May 1994.

Diamond, Larry. "Rethinking Civil Society: Toward Democratic Consolidation." *Journal of Democracy* 5, no. 3 (1994): 9–17.

Ding, Yijiang. "Corporatism and Civil Society in China: An Overview of the Debate in Recent Years." *China Information* 12, no. 4 (Spring 1998): 44–67.

Forsythe, David. *Human Rights and U.S. Foreign Policy: Congress Reconsidered.* Gainsville: University of Florida Press, 1988.

He Baogang. *The Democratic Implications of Civil Society in China.* New York: St. Martin's Press, 1997.

Howell, Jude. "An Unholy Trinity? Civil Society, Economic Liberalization, and Democratization in Post-Mao China." *Government and Opposition* 33, no. 1 (Winter 1998): 56–80.

Human Rights in China. "Bound and Gagged: Freedom of Association in China Further Curtailed Under New Regulations." November 13, 1998.

Jones, Sidney. "The Three Freedoms in Asia: An Overview." In *Promoting Three Basic Freedoms: Towards Greater Freedom of Association, Assembly and Expression in Asia.* Human Rights Watch/Asia, September 1997.

Knup, Elizabeth. "Environmental NGOs in China: An Overview." China Environment Series, Working Group on Environment in U.S.-China Relations. Woodrow Wilson Center, pp. 9–15.

Ku Fong, ed. *2000 Directory of International NGOs Supporting Work in China.* Hong Kong: China Development Research Services, October 1999.

Liu Binyan. "China and the Lessons of Eastern Europe." *Journal of Democracy* 2, no. 2 (Spring 1991): 3–11.

Mathews, Jessica. "Power Shift." *Foreign Affairs* 76, no. 1 (January–February 1997): 50–66.

Moore, Rebecca R. "Globalization and the Future of U.S. Human Rights Policy." *Washington Quarterly* 21, no. 4 (August 1998): 193–212.

Pei, Minxin. "Chinese Civic Associations: An Empirical Analysis." *Modern China* 24, no. 3 (July 1998): 285–318.

———. "Is China Democratizing?" *Foreign Affairs* 77, no. 1 (January–February 1998): 68–82.

Saich, Tony. "Negotiating the State: The Development of Social Organizations in China." *China Quarterly* no. 161 (March 2000): 124–141.

Shi, Tianjian. "Village Committee Election in China: Institutionalist Tactics for Democracy." *World Politics* 51, no. 3 (April 1999): 385–412.

Thurston, Anne. *Muddling Toward Democracy: Political Change in Grassroots China.* Peaceworks no. 23. Washington, DC: United States Institute of Peace, August 1998.

Unger, Jonathan. "'Bridges': Private Business, the Chinese Government and the Rise of New Associations." *China Quarterly* no. 147 (September 1996): 795–819.

U.S. Congress. "U.S. Democracy Promotion Programs in Asia." Hearing Before the Subcommittee on Asia and the Pacific of the Committee on International Relations, U.S. House of Representatives, 105th Congress, 1st sess., September 17, 1997.

———. "U.S. Policy Options Toward China: Rule of Law and Democracy Programs." Hearing Before the Subcommittee on Asia and the Pacific of the Committee on International Relations, U.S. House of Representatives, 105th Congress, 2nd sess., April 30, 1998.

White, Gordon, Jude Howell, and Shang Xiaoyuan. *In Search of Civil Society: Market Reform and Social Change in Contemporary China.* Oxford: Clarendon Press, 1996.

Woodman, Sophia. "Less Dressed Up as More? Promoting Non-Profit-Making Organizations by Regulating Away Freedom of Association." *China Perspectives* no. 22 (March–April 1999): 17–27.

Yan, Ming Fu. "NGOs Are 'Inevitable Trend of the Times.'" *chinabrief* 2, no. 3 (August–November 1999): 21–23.

Young, Nick. "A Million Flowers Bloom: One Is Weeded Out." *chinabrief* 2, no. 4 (December 1999–March 2000): 11–18.

Zhang Weiguo. "Evading State Censorship: From the Bible to New Century Net." *China Rights Forum* (Fall 1998): 22–25.

7

Globalization and Human Rights for Workers in China

Convergence or Collision?

Dorothy J. Solinger

As globally au courant notions of human rights—and a swelling trend of promoting and fighting for them—buzz around the borders of mainland China, just as international economic firms and transnational agencies and organizations reach into the country, whether via the market, the media or the Web—or else in the person of foreign capitalists and external human-itarians—who or what is constructing a "universalism" there, and what is its content? Indeed, worldwide norms and values about rights are becoming as familiar to Chinese policymaking elites and to members of the ordinary populace as is the everyday reality of business and profit-seeking.

The query is difficult to answer. There is no obvious foreign pressure, since it is only quite recently (with China's accession to the World Trade Organization [WTO] in 2001) that any cross-border agents began forcing upon the Chinese the programs dear to the world of neoliberal business; nor are the Chinese people yet permitted openly to battle for the principles of fundamental birthrights. Thus, neither from the outside nor from "be-low" are there any discernible agents engaged in pushing new and foreign ideas or in promoting their acceptance in China. Nonetheless, in the 1990s and beyond there have clearly been concepts in the air that were novel in this country; there has also been brewing an incipient clash at work be-tween human rights and the steady incursion of global economic forces into China. Why a clash?

This chapter submits that there can be sharp disjunctures between the knowledge that rights exist and a rhetoric giving voice to them on the one hand, and their enshrinement and realization in practice by powerholders on the other. Also, the case of China demonstrates that there can be a significant lag between the initial entry of ideas and ideals from the outside into a country and their subsequent endorsement and enactment by those with the authority to make them safe for use.

Though leaders have become convinced that neoliberal formulas and international economic engagement will be good for growth, modern industrialization, wealth, and technological achievement for the nation as a whole (and for its external image), these leaders are still far from permitting the victims to announce their rights or to struggle for their compensation should they be compromised. Though leaders have embraced what they take to be universally valid claims about the beneficence of the market, they have not allowed their people to formulate their discomforts and hardships in the form of opposition parties, social movements, nongovernmental organizations, or even independent workers' unions.

So "universal" ideas (both about commerce and about constitutional justice for the individual) have entered China without any particular or explicit imposition; similarly, anger has simmered, but without an effective legal outlet. Globalization and the construction of universalism therefore occur neither from above nor from below. Thus, though the principles of global business have infiltrated and deeply transformed the once socialist Chinese economy, any spread of the language of rights into China has to date remained largely at the level of rhetoric. This story, as of the year 2002, is one that so far remains at odds with the bulk of cases presented in this volume, as well as with a significant portion of the literature on human rights-cum-globalization.

An important current in the study of globalization and its impacts holds that the spread of economic liberalism and of the concept of human rights globally have eventuated in new notions of citizenship.[1] What has been termed a "postnational" citizenship, granted "on the basis of personhood," has increasingly offered to immigrants the rights and privileges once granted just to nationals, in one scholar's view. Whether the mechanism at work is said to be principally ideational, as through "changes in the institutional and discursive order of rights at the global level,"[2] or ideational-cum-material, as, in the words of another author, through the dissemination of notions of social justice and human rights that accompany the spread of market relations, both domestically and internationally, this analysis claims to see under way a new "extension of rights to individuals who are not full members of the societies in which they reside."[3]

In another, similar formulation, the proliferation of international human rights law, which "recognizes the individual as an object of rights regardless of national affiliations or associations with a territorially-defined people," has meant, according to this view, that in recent years "states [have] had to take account of persons qua persons as opposed to limiting their responsibilities to their own citizens."[4] Whether or not these perspectives are valid, here I will argue, to the contrary, that globalization has probably done as much to *minimize* the granting of citizenship and membership rights and privileges to individuals as it has done to extend them.

China's Virtual Globalization in Comparative Perspective

Specifically, I propose that not just the Chinese case but others as well document that a political paradox lies at the core of globalization. By this I mean that globalization can be seen as a two-level, double-edged process: efforts at the level of the state to become accepted, included within the dominant, one might say hegemonic, global economic society have at the same time worked to *exclude* large numbers of immigrants and onetime citizens from genuine membership in the national community. I illustrate my analysis with a bit of material from France and Mexico, but principally focus upon the case of China.

Workers in and immigrants into all three countries have witnessed— and suffered from—burgeoning unemployment accompanying these states' joining, striving to join, or preparing to join the global economy more fully and becoming members of supranational economic organizations, the European Monetary System for France in 1979 and then the European Monetary Union, with its agreement to sign the Maastricht Treaty in 1992; the General Agreement on Trade and Tariffs (1986) and the North American Free Trade Agreement (NAFTA, 1994) for Mexico; and the World Trade Organization for China (in late 2001).[5] While seeming necessity and external economic pressures (most crucially, crushing foreign debt for Mexico, severe balance of trade problems for France)[6] pushed these countries to join those unions and to engineer massive turnarounds in their economic strategies, China's leaders scrapped much of its work force beginning in 1997 in the absence of any such direct exogenous goading.

Instead, they started to restructure their economy along market principles beginning in 1979 in part to gain new domestic legitimacy after the death of Mao Zedong and the misery of the Cultural Revolution and, also in large part, under the influence of a process I term "virtual globalization." According to this logic, a domestic economy mimics the effects presented among the major participants, *before,* but in the hope of, attaining full-scale global economic membership, and prior to becoming explicitly subject to its pressures, and so not primarily in response to the dictates of external material forces. Insofar as there are agents in the process, they are national leaders who have become persuaded that global economic affiliation is necessary for national greatness.[7]

Besides the various material foreign economic forces at work, virtual globalization also played a role in Mexico's economic liberalization: one writer remarks upon its eagerness for "membership in the rich countries' club."[8] Another scholar termed the French "policy paradigm" since the late 1950s as one that saw France's long-term national economic and security interests in solidarity within the European Community. In the 1980s, he states, "the economic component of this paradigm implied cooperation with the movement toward monetary integration and market deregulation."[9]

But in the case of China, with its lengthy merely partial "opening to the world" (at least up to the 1999 press for prompt WTO membership), the leadership *by choice* subjected the nation to the dynamic of globalization, without the usual concomitant constraints—foreign guest workers, economic stagnation and serious national indebtedness, negative trade imbalances, or even much menacing external competition.[10] And yet in China, the paradox of participation is if anything even more pronounced than elsewhere, because of the heritage there of specific socialist institutions.

And so in China the unemployment and downsizing, corporate mergers and bankruptcy promoted beginning in 1997 were mainly the result (at least initially) not of *foreign* debts so much as public enterprise indebtedness to *domestic* banks and to other Chinese firms, that is, internal arrears at the plant level were derived from competitive pressures and losses in state enterprises, and not (surely in the pre–Asian crisis period) so much from abroad as they were from nonstate firms in China itself.[11] Furthermore, the press of migrant labor in the cities has not been, as it was in parts of Western Europe in its heyday of growth or in the wealthier areas of the non-Western world, from foreign parts at all, but instead from China's countryside. Nor was its foreign trade even remotely in any difficulty at the time when economic liberalization was first put forward. And yet despite the relative lack of a direct material squeeze from outside forces, a case can be made that the world economy and its fashions—at a minimum at the level of ideas—were implicated nonetheless.

Thus globalization's reach is lengthier even than it appears at first glance. For its processes lure not just those places already more fully enmeshed in the world economy. As myth of modernity, metaphor for success, threat of extinction, inducement to acceptance, incentive to belong, globalization—along with its accompanying philosophy about the proper pathway to economic achievement—can also serve as a powerful idea enticing sites still in some ways on the periphery of the world marketplace to step deeper inside. And as they take this step, the workers in such places (plus the laborers these locales attract from outside) become subjected to ferocious competition (to promote exports, to attract investment) on an international scale, and its correlative search for "efficiency."

As this occurs, workers become pawns in this pursuit of advantage and supremacy, as the nations where they labor and the enterprises employing them "downsize" and "cut back"; and as "flexible" and "informal" forms of laboring restructure their working lives. Most starkly, increased unemployment and a reliance on migrant labor (and on types of labor typically filled by migrants) emerge as the twin answers to the national and corporate quests for ascendancy in the global marketplace. The persons who fill these roles—the jobless and the noncitizen worker—share a key characteristic: in critical ways they are outsiders, the excluded, nonmembers in the national community into which they were born (or migrated into and reside). Their growing presence and mounting numbers in much of the world today deprive the societies they inhabit of a fully participant population.

I proceed to sketch out the sense in which I am using the terms "globalization" and "membership" (or "citizenship"), indicating their interrelationship. I then present the background to and features of the Chinese adoption of the practices of globalization and the exclusionary consequences for many who dwell in that nation.

Globalization and Membership

Economic Globalization

Economic globalization entails the intensified connection between national economies in the late twentieth century, along with an attendant neoliberal economic ideology dictating deregulation and privatization. Its manifestations involve a mix of tightly interlinked phenomena. These include massive movements of capital, labor, and other factors of production on a worldwide scale; international hypercompetitiveness among firms, nations, and regions; monetarist management of the money supply, with the aims of cutting inflation, boosting exports, and attracting investment; and pressures on national governments to deregulate and liberalize financial markets, and to engineer low-deficit, low-debt, low-wage economies that win high credit ratings from financial institutions and attract foreign investment.[12]

At least two pivotal events set this chain of effects into motion among the nations pushed into the global race in the 1970s (of which China was not). The first of these was the collapse of the Bretton Woods fixed exchange rate mechanism of the early 1970s, which restored competition to the setting of interest and exchange rates. This event installed floating rates, which in turn promoted capital mobility and an expansion of financial markets. Relatedly, deregulation of financial markets followed within a decade, which, combined with deflationary measures to promote exports and cut inflation, ultimately produced massive speculation and an ever-present threat (and accelerating reality) of bankruptcy and takeover within these countries.[13]

The other pivotal event lies at the root of the inflation, whose reduction became the preoccupation of globally involved macroeconomic policy-makers in the 1970s, and even more so in the 1980s.[14] This was the double set of oil price shocks in 1973 and 1979. These called into question the several-decades-old Keynesian approach to demand management, which had privileged the solution of unemployment over concern with price rises in Western Europe, and, as it happened, within Mexico's statist economy as well, with its import substitution industrialization. These shocks brought in their wake crises for leading Western economies (and by a slightly different route, for the Mexican economy too, by 1981), quickly after which ensued recession, stagnation, and deficits. Elevated interest rates seemed the only antidote to remedy inflation; these rates went on to induce a reduction in investment, an increase in national indebtedness, and generalized fluctuations in demand. All of this summed up to the momentous replacement of Keynesianism with the policy of monetarism in the direction of national economies.[15]

Building upon and augmenting this approach to the conduct of domestic macromanagement in France and Mexico, respectively, were the regional free trade agreements of the early 1990s—Maastricht and NAFTA. These protocols, along with the mantra of international monetary, trade, and aid organizations, forced an intensified dismantling of trade barriers and demanded lowering both internal deficits and foreign debt. All of this lent an even more hectic pace to capital mobility, as the owners of investment capital perpetually sought out an ever more attractive environment for its (short-term) home.[16]

And so a race developed among the implicated nations, to balance budgets and cut back deficits. In the struggle to be at the forefront, governments drew upon the methods of monetarism to maintain low-inflation environments, the better to attract foreign investment and the better to push their own exports abroad via competitive prices. And all of this called for creating and sustaining competitive, low-cost labor markets composed of "flexible" workers—willing to work odd hours, for unpredictable periods, without safety or security. Such markets were "efficient," as they allowed firms rapidly to adapt to the persistent economic uncertainty.[17]

Yet another element was technological change. As higher technologies appeared and were applied to the workplace, service-sectoral employment increasingly replaced the labor-intensive, lower-skilled jobs of the past.[18] The overall result was a rebirth under high capitalism of the same sort of nonstandard, part-time or temporary, fixed-term contract or noncontract, low-paid, "downgraded," underentitled and unentitled, underprotected and unprotected work that marked this system's much earlier, lower-level version.[19]

Membership/Citizenship

In much of Western Europe, in the age of rapid postwar growth from the 1950s through the early 1970s, this low-tech niche had been supplied in large part by foreign migrant labor, the "guest workers" from the poorer countries to the east and south.[20] But with the onset of stagnation in the early 1970s, though the initial migrant labor's offspring remained in place, native workers either joined them in this niche or simply lost their jobs. A critical outcome was that the prolabor treatment of the preceding era, which had obtained for native workers, and increasingly for outsiders as well in many countries[21]—offering decent and safe working conditions and hours and welfare benefits—appeared to be too costly, uncompetitive, and "rigid," by contrast, too incapable of meeting the imperatives of the current juncture to keep inflation down, credit ratings up, and investment flowing inward.[22] Thus, as migrants' lot declined, locals' jobs were downgraded and the ranks of the unemployed mounted.

For in this overall climate in most of the countries of Western Europe and in Mexico, where the twin effects of global economic involvement and membership in regional free trade zones fostered these behavorial patterns, the drive for efficiency meant leaner firms with less costly operations, thus downsizing and a rise in unemployment.[23] That drive also eventuated in an expanding niche for migrant labor, which, with its powerlessness, is ideally suited for the vagaries of "flexible" employment.[24] These two expanding categories, the unemployed and migrants, came to share a critical trait: they both became the excluded, those outside the national community, those, that is, who cannot participate in it on anything approaching regular terms.[25] Katherine McFate, for instance, speaks of those forced into informal or illegal sectors of the economy by poor market conditions and discrimination as being "viewed as outside the boundaries of the political/ moral community."[26]

If we understand the concept of "citizenship" in the broad, social sense of membership and participation in all the dominant institutions of a particular community, we could make a claim that such people have been denied citizenship. This is to say that they are barred from receiving whatever social, economic, and political powers and privileges full members of the societies in which they are residing receive from the state and from dominant social institutions. Defined thus, only those who are fully members can be said to enjoy genuine citizenship or participation in the community. For, in the words of T. H. Marshall, who terms citizenship "a status bestowed on those who are full members of a community," a constitutive part of citizenship is the social dimension, which includes, "the whole range from the right to a modicum of economic welfare and security to the right to share to the full in the social heritage and to live the life of a civilized being according to the standards prevailing in the society. In the economic field the basic civil right is the right to work."[27] In a different vein, but bearing a parallel message, is Judith Shklar's characterization of U.S. citizenship, which grounds the notion in two essential features, the more typically cited equality of rights and also "the opportunity to work and to be paid an earned reward for one's labor."[28] She alleges that those without work are less than citizens, for they are not a part of the functioning community.

To pursue this line of thought, I take note here of a recent volume on social policy that highlights a direct connection between economic globalization, its behavioral manifestations, and the negative effects these practical embodiments have for citizenship, or membership, in domestic communities. Its authors link current economic crises in Europe to the deterioration of "social citizenship rights," as mass unemployment, pressures to reduce welfare benefits, and a decreased receptivity to migrant labor have spelt a marked restriction in social inclusion.[29] In Mexico, too, as a result of the austerity programs of the early 1980s onward—particularly following the onset of the debt crisis in 1982 and later the drop in the peso in 1994— unprecedented numbers became suddenly jobless.

In France, the unemployed, who with migrants make up the marginalized sector of society, are labeled, literally, the "excluded."[30] Similarly, in Mexico one scholar claimed that "a central characteristic of liberalization has been the vast *exclusion* of the population attempting to enter the formal economy," to say nothing of the disenfranchisement of the unemployed (emphasis added).[31]

The Chinese Case

A Limited Global Engagement

Unlike the member states of the European Union or a major Latin American player such as Mexico, which have all been at the center of the stage of global activity and vulnerable to its vagaries for nearly two decades in one way or another, up through 1999 China was a nation only partially (albeit increasingly) participant in the world economy. And yet its story demonstrates that the tenets of globalization and its seeming promise have become so enticing, and also so ineluctable, that a country not yet wholly subject to its actual dynamics and pressures may still fall virtually captive to its consequences by will.

After the Communist Party takeover of 1949, its leaders shunned or were shunned by much of the Western world, and its chief economic foreign partners were the Soviet Union and other socialist economies for its first decade in power. Once it split with the Soviets after 1960, China's principal ties were with the third world, and with a few individual capitalist countries. Its continuing isolation from the core of international economic activity in the early 1970s enabled it to escape the early onslaught of the more threatening aspects of globalization. For China was involved neither in the breakdown of Bretton Woods nor in the two oil price shocks of the decade.

Even at the end of 1978, when its own oil production reached a plateau, China did not suffer from the price increases affecting the rest of the world. The leadership simply suddenly discontinued a quite sizable planned and contracted importation of large-scale foreign plant projects, mainly because of the huge amounts of energy their operation would demand.[32] This peaking of oil production was one factor in China's shift to an outward-oriented, market strategy after 1978. For the country's embarkation then upon a massive manufacture of light industrial goods for export[33] conveniently meant less of a demand for energy.[34]

Beginning with this turn to exporting on a large scale in 1979, less than two and a half years after the 1976 death of the fiercely ideological Mao Zedong, the more pragmatic Deng Xiaoping ushered in China's much publicized "opening up" of its national economy, a move made possible by the discrediting of most of Mao's leftist policies upon his passing. Nonetheless, in several important respects this economy even long afterward remained less "globalized" than those of other countries with comparably developed economies. Even in the midst of the Asian financial crisis of 1997–1998, China, which had kept its currency nonconvertible on the capital account (the current account having become convertible in 1996), was less at the mercy of threatening international economic pressures than most other nations in East Asia. This owed much to the continuing nonconvertibility of its currency.

Too, its foreign debt—though by no means negligible—seemed to be quite manageable as of 1996, just before the crisis began, and surely did not act as a spur to revamping domestic economic arrangements. A 1997 World Bank report, in fact, speaks of China's "improved creditworthiness," which had made it "the main beneficiary of syndicated lending to developing countries." The report also notes that despite the steady increase in its external debt (at about U.S.$130 billion at year's end, 1996), the country's strong macroeconomic performance afforded it excellent debt indicators, at less than half the average among developing countries and, indeed, among the lowest in the entire region. Besides, its huge foreign exchange reserves, amounting to about U.S.$140 billion at the end of 1997, and its favorable international balance of payments, appeared to secure it further.[35]

Perhaps most importantly, China's longtime low-cost domestic consumer economy and accompanying relatively stable, low-wage structure has meant that ever since its leadership invited in foreign firms in 1979, until very recently, there has been negligible competition either from cheap foreign labor or even from foreign consumer products priced below those made in China. Indeed, on the eve of the Asian crisis China had already taken over the labor-intensive market for manufactured exports from South Korea, Taiwan, and Hong Kong.[36]

Moreover, through the end of the last century, China did not become a member of the WTO (in part because of its retention of some key features of a socialist economy, which included protection for state-owned enterprises, and in part because the United States in particular persistently demanded additional reforms before it would admit the country in). Thus, despite its steady elimination and reduction of tariffs,[37] it was relatively less subject than many other places to the more fully dismantled trade barriers driving a good deal of international competition. And the huge, underemployed rural work force available to fill the many niches for low-skill labor in this yet developing economy—as in simple construction, personal services, marketing, and assembly-line manufacture—obviated any need for foreign, immigrant workers.[38]

So in general, for the above reasons, China's leaders were under fewer constraints from abroad (at least until 1997 and the advent of the Asian financial crisis)—as compared with places where national debts appear insurmountable, competition from abroad fierce, and the pressure from international and regional associations to cut deficits inescapable—to balance budgets, reduce deficits, fight against inflation, install low-cost, competitive labor markets, and do battle in the market for export promotion and for outside investment. And yet these officials undertook these measures nonetheless, at least in part to qualify for global membership, to join the "globalized" elite.[39] As Long Yongtu, chief WTO negotiator, stated in an interview: "China . . . must secure its place in this economic united nations. . . . The days when China was chronically excluded from the mainstream of the world economy must come to an end."[40]

Thus for China the ideational component of globalization was at least as significant as the material one in propelling its policy choices. What for fifteen years seemed just an elusive vision, membership in the WTO—in large part for the prestige and acceptance it would bring,[41] even without actually joining—increasingly served for much of the Chinese political elite as an inducement to domestic change.[42] In short, at least until 1997, unlike in places such as France and Mexico, where external prods, in addition to the imagined promises of a more complete participation, operated to produce globalized behavior, for China material spurs from outside were not the motivating forces in the adoption of neoliberal policies. This is what I have labeled China's "virtual globalization": globalized conduct in the absence of a number of the key forms of global economic participation and pressure.

Parallel Symptoms with Fully Globalized Places but Different Causes

What has this virtually globalized economic conduct consisted in? In the first place, there is the selfsame search for developing flexible labor, competitive strategies, and efficiency.

Remarkably, even a known conservative such as China's then-premier Li Peng, speaking to the Ninth National People's Congress in March 1998, picked up the global jargon without a flaw. In various segments of his speech, he stated, "The government will encourage the establishment of large enterprise groups in order to increase their *competitiveness* in both domestic and foreign markets. . . . We should continue to implement . . . preferential policies that support enterprises when they carry out mergers and bankruptcies and try to increase *efficiency* through reducing staff size. . . . We should make sure that . . . small enterprises . . . can adapt themselves to the market in a more *flexible* way" (emphasis added).[43]

The management of Chinese labor has indeed become increasingly flexible, beginning with a 1986 Regulation on Labor Contracts. This ruling represented an initial move away from the permanent, full-employment system for urban workers that had obtained since the 1950s, as China moved further and further away from socialism. That measure was followed by a Regulation on the Employment of Staff and Workers, intended to reform the recruitment system away from the long-term socialist one that had been based upon administrative allocation of labor toward, instead, arrangements that would offer firms more autonomy in defining their own criteria for hiring; and a Regulation on Discharging Employees, for the first time giving the enterprises the power to dismiss workers.[44]

In July 1994 the Eighth Session of the Standing Committee of the Eighth National People's Congress passed a new Labor Law, which in Article 27 granted firms freedom to fire workers if near bankruptcy or in serious difficulty.[45] But none of these promulgations derived from compulsion from foreign investors; rather, they were part of the Chinese authorities' own political decision to move toward neoliberal strategies in running their economy.

Once China became a member of the WTO, the slashing of tariffs that the WTO demands (and the terms on which China entered it) will surely expose the country's producers to severely intensified international competition.[46] But the entry of au courant phrasing into leaders' language began at a time when this had not yet been the case. And yet the global climate enshrining market principles infected Chinese policymakers and, in turn, Chinese managers, as firms of all types took a stiffer stance toward labor under a much heightened pressure for profits.[47] In the late 1990s, however, when the official domestic media proclaimed that "market competition has forced state enterprises to discharge large numbers of workers,"[48] the principal rivals were not firms abroad. Indeed, domestic firms have actually been protected from international competition through the 1990s.[49] Until about 1993 or even 1996, largely out of a concern with maintaining urban stability, the regime continued to enforce a gradualist approach to tampering with the entitlements and security of the hallowed state sector.[50]

Instead, the old state-owned enterprises, which were made to perform as comprehensive welfare communities and as production entities through about 1997,[51] were forced since market reforms began in the early 1980s to face "collective," private, and foreign-invested firms within China, which are much less or not at all encumbered by welfare responsibilities.[52] Thus, over the years the state-owned sector's share of industrial output dropped from 80 percent in 1978 down to under 30 percent as of 1999, according to a leading Chinese economist.[53]

Another expanding source of homegrown rivalry, for city workers at least, are the rural migrant workers, who increasingly received permission to walk off the land for the first time in over two decades after 1983.[54] Once in the cities, as "flexible" as any foreign migrant laborers in other countries, they generally garner few if any benefits and in many cases labor under working conditions resembling those of early capitalism in the West.[55] And with the drive for high returns, such drudges appear increasingly attractive even to the management of state enterprise.[56]

Last, the campaign to attain efficiency, which intensified in the mid-1990s in China, could also have been a product of conforming to international stimuli, since external competition compels more efficient operations.[57] But the official Chinese commitment to "increase efficiency by downsizing staff," in order to prod firms to cut down on their losses,[58] is again a reference to internal considerations. As we will see below, enterprise losses have largely been the result of state policy,[59] not of competition from imports. For instance, the persisting "soft-budget constraint"[60] despite economic reforms allowed firms to distribute wage increases not commensurate with improvements in labor productivity.[61] Indeed, China's entire economic reform program, predicated on the notion that decentralizing management and financial authority to firms and local governments would spur economic growth, allowed enterprises to borrow from local bank branches with impunity, fueling a spree unstoppable for years of "over-consumption and over-investment."[62] Policymakers and enterprise managers have been hoping since 1996 to erase the resultant losses by dismissing workers.

Regardless of the domestic impetus for these moves—inspired more by foreign ideas, domestic economic and political considerations, and a yearning for external membership than by any sort of direct economic pressures from abroad—the consequences for the populace are in some ways similar to those in places more actually globalized. For instance, the textile sector—chosen by the State Council as the breakthrough point in a campaign to "reform" the state-owned sector—was ordered to slash 1.2 million jobs over the years 1998–2000, in the hopes of cutting losses and even generating profits.[63] In 1998, under the influence of this same impetus, Liaoning province decided to let 100 state firms go bankrupt or be merged while another 100 were to reduce their employees.[64] More broadly, this drive for competitiveness, flexibility, and efficiency has sparked a surge in enterprise bankruptcies since 1997.[65] But given policies to minister to the needs of workers from bankrupt firms—after the costs of the proceedings are paid off, the workers and retirees of a firm according to law have the first claim on any remnant assets of the firm[66]—the cases of de jure bankrupt firms have been kept artificially low in quantity, and so statistics reveal only a fraction of the story about the numbers of de facto bankruptcies.

More telling are the very inconclusive figures of unemployed and laid-off workers. Because of each firm's responsibility to see to the future of its own displaced workers, a range of disguised forms of unemployment have emerged under various names, including early "retirements" and long "holidays," often entailing drastic reductions in benefits and significant underpayment or nonpayment of wages, but without calling the worker "unemployed."[67] As of the end of 1997, some 11 to 12 million urban workers were said to be laid-off,[68] which amounted to double the figure for the registered unemployed.[69] But according to a mid-1999 report, government officials believed then that the real number of workers who should be counted as unemployed—including all those currently labeled as "waiting for work" but not included in the unemployed statistics—would be about 100 million.[70]

In China, most of these developments occurred during an era of generally rampant economic growth—between 1984 and 1995, China's real gross domestic product grew by an average of 10.2 percent annually, and in 1993, the year when the moves to lay off workers got under way with some vigor, was up 13.4 percent (with industry increasing at a rate of over 20 percent, according to official Chinese statistics).[71] True, China did experience two harsh austerity programs that set radical change in motion. But unlike in other, more truly globalized places, these were both the product of leadership decisions taken on domestic grounds, with political factors playing a heavy role.

The first of these two austerity programs was installed in 1988 after a spree of inflation that had been sparked by state policies; it was endorsed and intensified in the following year by the more reform-shy, conservative, proplanning faction in the wake of the Tiananmen denouement of 1989. For these politicians, briefly having the upper hand, understood the Tiananmen demonstrations as having been largely sparked by popular dissatisfaction with the inflation produced by a decade of market reforms.[72] And the second austerity episode was launched by then–vice premier (and premier, from March 1998 to 2003) Zhu Rongji in mid-1993. That time the cutbacks were undertaken in response to what for post-1949 China was deemed to be runaway inflation, the result of a stepped-up regimen of reforming and economic growth given impetus by then–preeminent leader Deng Xiaoping in early 1992.[73] Because of the stiff curtailment of access to guaranteed credit for state firms under both austerity programs, losses in state enterprises rose significantly.

In 1989 and 1990, total losses doubled each year;[74] after a 1991 relaxation and followed by 1992's progrowth prodding, the second program led to almost half the state firms showing operating losses in 1994 and 1995. By 1996, 45 percent of the state sector was operating at a loss; for the first time state firms collectively lost more money than they took in. Industrial operating losses in state-owned firms amounted then to 53 billion yuan,[75] up more than a third over the year before, with 12,000 enterprises the victim of long-standing deficits. At that point, about one-fifth of the business of banks consisted of uncollectible loans, the effect of the vulnerability of state bankers to continual requests by failing firms for operating capital.[76]

But given continuing high-level growth and excellent prospects in the global economy, leadership choices for heightened reliance on the market and attendant flexibility in the use of labor were by no means just the product of economic difficulties. Rather, these decisions derived from a determination among reform-minded politicians to push China ever further toward marketization and globalization, probably to appeal to foreign powers whose elites could endorse its bid to enter the WTO. Again, there is quite a contrast with the French or Mexican cases—where stagnation or only very low-level growth was the norm for the better part of two decades and where foreign economic difficulties or demands were often a definite prod.

Thus the impact of globalization on China's major shifts was in significant measure one of incentive, ideology, or paradigm for modernity. What China experienced, then, is more rightly labeled "virtual globalization," a largely internally generated set of effects fashioned after, but not itself directly generated by, external patterns. Still, the results for migrant labor and for employment, and thus for effective domestic membership and social citizenship, have been the same or even worse in the Chinese case.

Differences in Outcomes

I have argued that China's leadership was able largely to isolate the country from the world economy, with its encumbrances, imperatives, downslides, and perils for a number of decades after 1949 until Mao Zedong died; and that, even once the regime became partially connected to this economy after 1978, the direct effects for China's own domestic economy as a whole were usually not destructive nor even threatening. But this certainly does not mean that the outcomes for the work force have been salutary. As we have seen, though the causes have been different, the effects of China's urge to join the world economy—prompting its "virtual globalization"— have been similar to the effects for many workers who lost their jobs or saw working conditions grow insecure in places such as France and Mexico, where steps into the global economy were much more exogenously pressured and materially based.

In some ways, however, China's late and partial entry into the global market itself signals trouble. For the Chinese regime's old socialist values, alliances, and allegiances—the culture and politics of socialism—that in one way or another accounted for that tardiness have proven far stickier and harder to outgrow or discard than have the more material practices of the old planned economy. Ironically, the superstructure has outlived the base. Indeed, these socialist patterns serve only to enhance present-day impediments to workers' welfare introduced by the new market regime. These impediments, the residue of China's socialist past, make the plight of the disenfranchised even more serious in China than it is in the more fully globalized countries.

In particular, aftereffects from three of the central institutions the nation's rulers long ago installed for implementing their socialist system linger on, even as the institutions themselves weaken and atrophy. These legacies complicate the impact of China's imperfect global involvement, putting extra limits on the rights of membership, participation, and thus citizenship (in the special sense in which I am using the term) for its citizens. These three institutions are the socialist-era legal system, recently revamped to appear more predictable, procedural, and just, but still quite unreliable; a workplace-cum-welfare "unit" system (the *danwei*), which housed and nurtured, and also closely monitored the urban work force, though its welfare functions are now quickly slipping away; and a household registration system that from about 1961 until the early 1980s kept country people out of towns while grossly privileging only those born in cities and their own offspring (the *hukou*, or household registration, system). Whereas the freewheeling free-market economic practices that make for efficiency, competitiveness, and flexibility were quite easily incorporated into a still authoritarian regime, China's prior legal, management, and control systems have been much more difficult to dislodge and replace.

Under the reign of Mao Zedong, from 1949 to 1976, law was considered to be a "bourgeois" construct, inapplicable—at least in its Western incarnation—to a socialist society.[77] Nonetheless, China's often harsh socialist version was enshrined up until the Cultural Revolution, which began in 1966. With that movement, all legal institutions were dismantled for over a decade. Although with the onset of marketizing reforms in 1979 a myriad of new laws were written to suit an economy engaging in worldwide commercial relations,[78] even in the early years of the twenty-first century, the country continued to lack a legal system capable of governing a truly market-driven economy.[79] As noted above, a pervasive rhetoric of rights is rarely realized in practice, and defendants have generally lost their cases before they begin. Moreover, the right to strike is not protected, and the act of organizing a nonofficial union is illegal. Thus the chance to agitate in resistance to their second-class or sinking status is illicit for migrant labor and furloughed workers, and daring to test the law is perilous in the extreme.

Indeed, a prominent Western economist writing in 1997 adjudged that the "main [outstanding] issue" in the country's full integration into the world economy is "whether China will move toward a rule-based or law-based system."[80] And a legal scholar evaluating the state of the nation's legal arrangements in the mid-1990s opined that, notwithstanding the numerous laws that had been written onto the books in the preceding decade and a half, "The effectuation of many of the legal rules is, to say the least, problematic."[81] Even a book published quite recently held that while China may have in the years since 1978 put on the books a huge store of newly minted laws, it is yet to sustain a proper "legal system."[82] Accordingly, for laid-off workers and mistreated migrant laborers, all this means that the 1994 Labor Law and its promises of protection and inclusion are almost always honored only in the breach.[83] Thus, despite the attempt to bolster legality, authoritarian and lawless habits from the past persist.

The *danwei* system was China's version of the socialist propensity to combine welfare with control,[84] or as Janos Kornai framed it, solicitude paired with surveillance.[85] State-owned enterprises in the cities were variously equipped with a range of entitlements, at a minimum housing, pensions, and medical care, but at a maximum a large set of extracurricular privileges and facilities as well. The key point for our purposes here is that, given this purely enterprise-based provision, no larger-scale system was ever designed. With the coming of market society and the for-cost and increasingly expensive provision of what was once freely granted, the welfare role of the *danwei* is progressively falling into tatters, and there is nothing adequate to replace it.[86]

Although an unemployment insurance system was established in 1986, it was meant for the new "contract" workers, the only urban workers at that time whose positions could conceivably be terminated. It was rarely put into use (since firms were enjoined to redeploy their own workers if at all possible), even after it was extended to cover all urban workers in 1993. In 1994, 1.2 million workers were reported to have drawn benefits, a figure that labor organizer Han Dongfang estimated to amount to under a third even of the official registered figure of the unemployed as of that time;[87] but two years later the number served had risen to just 1.5 million, despite the big increase in the numbers laid off by then.[88]

Thus, even up to the present, China's former *danwei* system has so far obstructed the country's fashioning of a what one analyst has termed a workable "free-standing 'social safety net.'"[89] This means that, while the 1994 Labor Law promises in its third article that workers will possess the right to social insurance and welfare benefits,[90] a worker who left his/her job even in the late 1990s also lost any social security benefits once granted by the firm.[91] Moreover, as more and more firms fall into debt, they not only can no longer sustain their work forces, but they cannot even afford to pay into the pension and unemployment insurance funds set up in the cities.[92] In the words of a prominent Western specialist on Chinese law, "The futures of workers who are laid off have been held hostage to the resources of the enterprises that laid them off."[93]

Even official spokespersons have recognized and lamented the rudimentary level of succor available for workers in failing firms, especially those who have been laid off, whether temporarily or altogether. At a National Labor Work Conference held at the end of 1997, Vice Premier Wu Bangguo, who then concentrated on industry, called for "gradually establishing a social insurance system covering pension, medical, unemployment . . . and other aspects of a social insurance system."[94] By autumn of 1998, officials at the Ministry of Labor and Social Security admitted that it would be at least five years before the initial framework was in place; it would probably take until 2020 to put it totally into operation. And even that would be difficult once the capable then-premier Zhu Rongji had retired from the scene, they noted.[95] So, as two French scholars have concluded, "As for the unemployed, they are excluded from all social advantages and protection as they are jobless."[96]

The household registration system, or *hukou,* was initiated in the early 1950s, but did not become rigorous, serving as a nearly watertight barrier against peasant movement out of the countryside, until about 1961. The fully elaborated system granted steeply subsidized housing; dirt-cheap transportation; almost free medical care; rationed and underpriced food grains, water, and gas (along with many items of daily consumption); and gratis schooling to urban residents, all perquisites denied in whole or in large part to any rural people, should they be (almost always only temporarily) summoned into the cities to meet crash production targets. For, regime leaders reasoned, the collectively operated communes set up in the countryside in the late 1950s were charged with meeting peasants' needs (though they did so to a far more elementary degree than did the urban *danwei*); and in any event, resources were to be garnered for the cities, where potential popular discontent was deemed much more serious, and where a hope of building a modernized industry and economy seemed within reach, if only the numbers of population there could be kept within strict bounds.

After 1983, the rural communes having been eliminated, peasants received the right to go into cities in search of work, but they did so on distinctly inferior terms. Even as tentative reforms of this system were discussed once the early 1990s arrived, and even though market reforms themselves did a great deal to undermine the underpinnings of the system, the prejudicial boundary markers around and discrimination against peasants in the cities yet persisted.[97] Though many city-registered workers have now also lost their old benefits, the regime still attempts to cater to them in various ways, to the detriment of the peasants in town.[98]

The aspect of this issue relevant to my purposes here is twofold. First, as noted above, migrant rural labor makes up the great bulk of the work force in foreign-invested firms, especially those along the coast. There their willingness to toil under often seemingly intolerable circumstances effectively places these workers outside a welfare regime of any kind. And second, as urban managers even in Chinese state firms grew increasingly profit-conscious as the 1990s wore on, they increasingly turned to the recruitment of peasants migrating into town, people who could safely be hired with lesser—or often no—benefits and no particular security at all.[99]

As the numbers of laid-off and idle urbanites mounted, city officials bent on quietude clashed with firm managers hungry for cost-cutting measures, and demanded that local city labor be privileged over peasants when hiring and firing occurred,[100] much as foreign migrant workers were pushed out of Southeast Asian communities in the midst of the 1997–1998 financial crisis.[101] The manifestations of this bias are multifold: peasants in cities were not encompassed within the rules of the contract system for city labor; a regulation that applied to them alone, which specified a three-to-five-year contract as the norm, was far from fully honored,[102] with many contracts lasting under a year. Unemployment insurance is yet to apply to these workers,[103] nor does the national Reemployment Program aiming to place the furloughed.

Beginning in 1995, major cities such as Beijing and Shanghai began publicly requiring that certain occupations be reserved for city people (though repetitions of these demands a few years later raises questions about the extent of compliance they commanded).[104] Thus rural migrants' lack of an urban *hukou,* or household registration, an institution established under socialism, continues after more than forty years to mark them as excluded noncitizens when they work in cities.

A quick comparison with the situation in France and Mexico affords insight into the added layer of exclusion lent by the residue of China's bygone or fading socialist institutions. In those countries, political parties, no matter how predominant (such as Mexico's Institutional Revolutionary Party—the PRI) or how right-wing (such as France's National Front), must still—and do—court the votes of workers and even the unemployed. In both, the strike is today permitted, and is sometimes effective, such as in a Tijuana automobile assembly plant in 1997,[105] or in the French national transportation strike of 1995.[106] And in France, at least, substantial unemployment and welfare schemes sustain the unemployed.[107] This is not to argue that inclusion graces the lot of these excluded people, but only that exclusion has more or less tolerable degrees.

Conclusion

At first thought, it would appear that workers in China might have had a more auspicious prospect (at least until its 2001 formal entry into the WTO) than those caught in more globalized economies, given that neither their economy nor their rulers had fallen subject to an inexorable dynamic of difficult demands from abroad. Compared with places where regional trade regimes dismantled tariffs, thereby setting the conditions for threatening competition; where impending monetary unions called for erasing deficits; or where international lending institutions installed rigorous austerity programs to handle mammoth debts—all from the outside—those employed in the Chinese economy, where none of the above was present, ought to have been relatively privileged. For China did escape the externalities of global involvement altogether for a number of decades. And once it embraced the world economy, it came in as a welcome guest, with its vast and untapped market, its hunger for foreign technology, its preferential policies for foreign investors, and its cut-rate work force.

But the process of economic "globalization" contains more than a set of material practices. It is also an ideology, one might even say a culture, a metaphor for modernity and membership, but only at the level of the nation as a whole. Among the work force worldwide, whether its members be in places pulled into the nets of the global economy willy-nilly, or whether they live in locations where leaders can exercise more choice, onetime member citizens everywhere are seeing their participatory privileges shattered at home, as more and more of them find themselves among either the unemployed or else the migrants, but either way excluded from the community in which they are living and working.

In the case of China, virtual globalization presents even more perils for the people than true globalization does for many of those living in countries that have not been isolated in the past and that are not heirs to a legacy of socialist institutions—which, ironically, in their heyday provided a firm foundation and an inclusive community of belonging for most citizens, so long as they operated within the rules of the game, and remained where they were registered. For this virtual globalization came prematurely, before China had established a new institutional infrastructure commensurate to the social requirements of a humane market society: a working legal system, a dependable, public welfare system (at the very least for those who do have jobs), and citizenship rights for its own nationals, no matter where within the country they were born. Thus China's quest for membership, in serving as an extreme case, caricatures the paradox of participation that resides at the root of globalization: joining at the national level often entails exclusion at the individual level. And in the absence of these three critical institutions, China's aping of globalistic economic forms has particularly reduced—and will continue to reduce—the proportion of participants to overall residents within the Chinese nation.

So in China, for now, a strong case can be made that globalization and human rights are more on a collision course than they are converging. Moreover, the universalisms put into practice there are those of flexibility and efficiency, but not (except at the level of language) those of human rights. As for where to locate agency, it appears that through the 1990s it rested just with the Chinese leadership, and not with outside forces, above, demanding economic liberalization, nor with those below being pushed about by the logic of profits.

Notes

Adapted from "Globalization and the Paradox of Participation: The Chinese Case," from *Global Governance: A Review of Multilateralism and International Organizations*, Volume 7, Number 2. Copyright © 2001 by Lynn Rienner Publishers. Used with permission of the publisher.

1. For a small but critical segment of the literature on globalization in recent years, see Suzanne Berger and Ronald Dore, eds., *National Diversity and Global Capitalism* (Ithaca, NY: Cornell University Press, 1996); James H. Mittelman, ed., *Globalization: Critical Reflections* (Boulder, CO: Lynne Rienner, 1996); William Greider, *One World Ready or Not: The Manic Logic of Global Capitalism* (New York: Simon & Schuster, 1997); Philip Gummett, ed., *Globalization and Public Policy* (Cheltenham, UK: Edward Elgar, 1996); Dani Rodrik, *Has Globalization Gone Too Far?* (Washington, DC: Institute for International Economics, 1997); and David A. Smith and Jozsef Borocz, eds., *A New World Order? Global Transformations in the Late Twentieth Century* (Westport, CT: Greenwood Press, 1995).

2. Yasemin Nuhoglu Soysal, *Limits of Citizenship: Migrants and Postnational Membership in Europe* (Chicago: University of Chicago Press, 1994), pp. 3, 12.

3. James F. Hollifield, *Immigrants, Markets, and States: The Political Economy of Postwar Europe* (Cambridge: Harvard University Press, 1992), pp. 170,

216. A similar argument is made in Wayne A. Cornelius, Philip L. Martin, and James F. Hollifield, "Introduction: The Ambivalent Quest for Immigration Control," in Wayne A. Cornelius, Philip L. Martin, and James F. Hollifield, eds., *Controlling Immigration: A Global Perspective* (Stanford, CA: Stanford University Press, 1995), pp. 3–41.

4. David Jacobson, "New Border Customs: Migration and the Changing Role of the State," *UCLA Journal of International Law and Foreign Affairs* 3, no. 2 (Fall–Winter 1998–1999): 453. See also David Jacobson, *Rights Across Borders: Immigration and the Decline of Citizenship* (Baltimore: Johns Hopkins University Press, 1996).

5. See Gustavo V. del Castillo, "NAFTA and the Struggle for Neoliberalism: Mexico's Elusive Quest for First World Status," in Gerardo Otero, ed., *Neoliberalism Revisited: Economic Restructuring and Mexico's Political Future* (Boulder, CO: Westview Press, 1996), p. 28; and Richard Jackman, "The Impact of the European Union on Unemployment and Unemployment Policy," in David Hine and Hussein Kassim, eds., *Beyond the Market: The EU and National Social Policy* (London: Routledge, 1998), p. 69. On how France's joining first the European Coal and Steel Community, then the Common Market, and finally the European Monetary Union has dictated its domestic economic policies at different junctures, see Bernard H. Moss, "After the Auroux Laws: Employers, Industrial Relations, and the Right in France," *West European Politics* 11, no. 1 (January 1988): 71; and Anthony Daley, "The Steel Crisis and Labor Politics in France and the United States," in Miriam Golden and Jonas Pontusson, eds., *Bargaining for Change: Union Politics in North America and Europe* (Ithaca, NY: Cornell University Press, 1992), p. 175.

6. On the pressures on Mexico in 1982 and thereafter, see Peter Morici, "Grasping the Benefits of NAFTA," *Current History* no. 2 (1993): 49; Judith A. Teichman, *Privatization and Political Change in Mexico* (Pittsburgh, PA: University of Pittsburgh Press, 1995), p. 70; and Ruth Berins Collier, *The Contradictory Alliance: State-Labor Relations and Regime Change in Mexico,* Research Series no. 83 (Berkeley: International and Area Studies, University of California, 1992), chap. 5. For pressures on France beginning in the mid-1970s and intensifying by the early 1980s, see W. Rand Smith, "Unemployment and the Left Coalition in France and Spain," in Nancy Bermeo, ed., *Unemployment in Southern Europe: Coping with the Consequences* (London: Frank Cass, 2000), pp. 111–134; Jonah D. Levy, "France: Directing Adjustment," paper presented to the international research project on "The Adjustment of National Employment Policy and Social Policy to Internationalization," organized by Fritz Scharpf and Vivien Schmidt, Ringberg Castle, Germany, February 17–20, 1999 (preliminary draft); and Robert Boyer, "Wage Labor, Capital Accumulation, and the Crisis, 1968–82," in Mark Kesselman, ed., with the assistance of Guy Groux, *The French Workers' Movement: Economic Crisis and Political Change* (London: George Allen & Unwin, 1984), pp. 17–38.

7. See Lloyd Gruber, *Ruling the World: Power Politics and the Rise of Supranational Institutions* (Princeton, NJ: Princeton University Press, 2000) for a different, more economic analysis of this process.

8. James F. Rochlin, *Redefining Mexican "Security"* (Boulder, CO: Lynne Rienner, 1997), pp. 64, 179.

9. W. Rand Smith, "Industrial Crisis and the Left: Adjustment Strategies in Socialist France and Spain," *Comparative Politics,* October 1995, p. 18.

10. Until the Asian financial crisis, which began in late 1997, there was no competition to speak of.

11. In September 1997, at the Chinese Communist Party's Fifteenth Congress, a program calling for these measures was announced and the results were immediate. For coverage and official statements, see Summary of World Broadcasts (hereafter SWB), FE/3023, September 13, 1997, p. S1/1, from Chinese Central Television, September 12, 1997, and SWB, FE/3024, September 15, 1997, p. S2/18, from Xinhua [New China News Agency, the official Chinese news agency, hereafter XH], September 14, 1997. But the reforms enunciated then were in the works months before the Asian financial crisis broke, and so were not a result of it. At a January 1997 State Council National Work Conference on State Enterprise Staff and Workers' Reemployment, attendees were told that solving their firms' difficulties depended upon enterprise reform, system transformation, cutting staff, normalizing bankruptcies, and encouraging mergers. See Yang Yiyong et al., *Shiye chongji bo* [The shock wave of unemployment] (Beijing: Jinri Zhongguo Chubanshe [China Today Publishing], 1997), p. 220.

12. Vivien A. Schmidt, "Democracy at Risk? France, Great Britain, and Germany Between Globalization and Europeanization," in David A. Smith, Dorothy J. Solinger, and Steven Topik, eds., *States and Sovereignty in the Global Economy* (London: Routledge, 1999), pp. 172–192; Leo Panitch, "Rethinking the Role of the State," in Mittelman, *Globalization,* pp. 83–4; Robert Boyer and Daniel Drache, "Introduction," in Robert Boyer and Daniel Drache, *States Against Markets: The Limits of Globalization* (London: Routledge, 1997), pp. 1–27; and Ramesh Mishra, "The Welfare of Nations," in Boyer and Drache, *States Against Markets,* p. 316.

13. John Eatwell, "Unemployment on a World Scale," in John Eatwell, ed., *Global Unemployment: Loss of Jobs in the 1990's* (Armonk, NY: M. E. Sharpe, 1996), pp. 3–20; and Robert Boyer, "State and Market: A New Engagement for the Twenty-first Century?" in Boyer and Drache, *States Against Markets,* p. 91.

14. Valerie Symes, *Unemployment in Europe: Problems and Policies* (London: Routledge, 1995), pp. 4–5.

15. Robert Boyer, "Wage/Labour Relations, Growth, and Crisis: A Hidden Dialectic," in Robert Boyer, ed., *The Search for Labour Market Flexibility: The European Economies in Transition* (Oxford: Clarendon Press, 1988), p. 21; Harold Chorney, "Debts, Deficits, and Full Employment," in Boyer and Drache, *States Against Markets,* p. 363; and Eatwell, "Unemployment," p. 3.

16. Boyer and Drache, "Introduction," pp. 19, 20; Boyer, "State and Market," p. 85.

17. Boyer and Drache, "Introduction," pp. 1, 7–9, 19; Daniel Drache, "From Keynes to K-Mart: Competitiveness in a Corporate Age," in Boyer and Drache, *States Against Markets,* pp. 32, 42–43, 47–49; Symes, *Unemployment in Europe,* pp. 4–5, 21; Eatwell, "Unemployment," p. 4; Boyer, "State and Market," p. 87; Boyer, "Wage/Labour," p. 21; Pascal Petit, "Problems of the State in Dealing with the System of Wage/Labour Relations: The Case of France," in Boyer, *The Search,* p. 49; and Guy Standing, "Labor Insecurity Through Market Regulation: Legacy of the 1980s, Challenge for the 1990s," in Katherine McFate, Roger Lawson, William Julius Wilson, eds., *Poverty, Inequality, and the Future of Social Policy* (New York: Russell Sage, 1995), pp. 153, 164.

18. Saskia Sassen, *The Mobility of Labor and Capital* (Cambridge: Cambridge University Press, 1988), pp. 22–27; Standing, "Labor Insecurity," p. 164; Symes, *Unemployment in Europe,* p. 7; and Paul Krugman, "First, Do No Harm," *Foreign Affairs* 75, no. 4 (July–August 1996): 166.

19. Standing, "Labor Insecurity," pp. 153, 157, 163–168; Boyer and Drache, "Introduction," p. 18; Katherine McFate, "Introduction: Western States in the New World Order," in McFate, Lawson, and Wilson, *Poverty,* pp. 7–8; Boyer, "Growth and Crisis," p. 25; Petit, "Problems," p. 49; and Robert Boyer, "Division or Unity? Decline or Recovery?" in Boyer, *The Search,* p. 212.

20. Hollifield, *Immigrants;* and Ian Gordon, "The Impact of Economic Change on Minorities and Migrants in Westren Europe," in McFate, Lawson, and Wilson, *Poverty,* p. 525.

21. Jacobsen, *Rights Across Borders;* Soysal, *Limits of Citizenship;* and Hollifield, *Immigrants.*

22. Standing, "Labor Insecurity," p. 153; Gordon Betcherman, "Globalization, Labor Markets, and Public Policy," in Boyer and Drache, *States Against Markets,* p. 255; and Drache, "From Keynes," p. 31.

23. Standing, "Labor Insecurity," p. 164; Symes, *Unemployment in Europe,* pp. 4–5; Boyer, "State and Market," p. 91. By 1994, the numbers of the unemployed in OECD countries had risen from just over 10 million in 1974 to 35 million, according to Chorney, "Debts, Deficits," p. 373. By 1994, it could be said that unemployment within European Union member nations had risen "more or less continuously" for fifteen years; Symes, *Unemployment in Europe,* p. 1.

24. See Sassen, *The Mobility of Capital,* pp. 39, 47.

25. Gordon, "The Impact," pp. 521, 525, notes a "continuing perception that particular ethnic groups [in particular, the descendants of postwar labor migrants, who are seen as 'outsiders'] do not 'belong' and may appropriately be treated differently." Craig R. Whitney, "French Jobless Find the World Is Harsher," *New York Times,* March 19, 1998, p. A6, states, "Many of the longterm unemployed feel 'excluded,' a word that in French means being outside normal society and carries the connotation of alienation and poverty." See also Thomas Faist and Hartmut Haussermann, "Immigration, Social Citizenship, and Housing in Germany," *International Journal of Urban and Regional Research* 20, no. 1 (1996): 83–98, on the denial of welfare rights to migrants in Western Europe and North America since the mid-1970s.

26. McFate, "Introduction," p. 14.

27. T. H. Marshall, *Sociology at the Crossroads and Other Essays* (London: Heinemann, 1963), pp. 87, 73–77. For similar usages, Bryan S. Turner, "Contemporary Problems in the Theory of Citizenship," in Bryan S. Turner, ed., *Citizenship and Social Theory* (London: Sage, 1993), p. 2, defines "the modern question of citizenship" as being "structured by two issues": the nature of social membership and problems of the efficient and equal allocation of resources. See also Derek Heater, *Citizenship: The Civic Ideal in World History, Politics, and Education* (London: Longman, 1990); Bryan S. Turner, *Citizenship and Capitalism: The Debate Over Reformism* (London: Allen & Unwin, 1986); Rogers Brubaker, *Citizenship and Nationhood in France and Germany* (Cambridge: Harvard University Press, 1992); and J. M. Barbalet, *Citizenship: Rights, Struggle, and Class Inequality* (Milton Keynes: Open University Press, 1988), p. 2.

28. Judith N. Shklar, *American Citizenship: The Quest for Inclusion* (Cambridge: Harvard University Press, 1991), pp. 1–3.

29. McFate, "Introduction," p. 13; and Roger Lawson and William Julius Wilson, "Poverty, Social Rights, and the Quality of Citizenship," in McFate, Lawson, and Wilson, *Poverty,* p. 712.

30. Mark Kesselman, "Does the French Labor Movement Have a Future?" in John T. S. Keeler and Martin A. Schain, eds., *Chirac's Challenge: Liberalization, Europeanization, and Malaise in France* (New York: St. Martin's Press, 1996), p. 154.

31. Enrique Dussel Peters, "From Export-Oriented to Import-Oriented Industrialization: Changes in Mexico's Manufacturing Sector, 1988–1994," in Gerardo Otero, ed., *Neoliberalism Revisited: Economic Restructuring and Mexico's Political Future* (Boulder, CO: Westview Press, 1996), p. 80.

32. Shigeru Ishikawa, "Sino-Japanese Economic Cooperation," *China Quarterly* 109 (1987): 12.

33. Bruce Cumings, "The Political Economy of China's Turn Outward," in Samuel S. Kim, ed., *China and the World* (Boulder, CO: Westview Press, 1984), p. 242; and Dorothy J. Solinger, *From Lathes to Looms: China's Industrial Policy in Comparative Perspective* (Stanford, CA: Stanford University Press, 1991).

34. Dwight H. Perkins, *China: Asia's Next Economic Giant?* (Seattle: University of Washington Press, 1986), pp. 50–51.

35. SWB, FE/3168, March 6, 1998, p. S2/1, from XH, Mach 4, 1998.

36. Dwight Perkins, "Prospects for China's Integration into the Global Economy," in Joint Economic Committee, U.S. Congress, ed., *China's Economic Future: Challenges to U.S. Policy* (Armonk, NY: M. E. Sharpe, 1997), p. 35.

37. Peter Morici, "Barring Entry? China and the WTO," *Current History,* September 1997, p. 276. By August 1999 the average rate was 17 percent. See SWB, FE/3605, August 5, 1999, p. G/11, from XH, August 3, 1999.

38. At the Fifteenth Party Congress in September 1997, then–minister of labor Li Boyong referred to "approximately 130 million peasants" who had "become idle in the rural areas." See SWB, FE/3024, September 15, 1997, p. S2/18, from XH, September 14, 1997.

39. On this process, see Margaret M. Pearson, "China's Integration into the International Trade," in Elizabeth Economy and Michel Oksenberg, eds., *China Joins the World: Progress and Prospects* (New York: Council on Foreign Relations, 1999), pp. 161–205.

40. SWB, FE/3695, November 18, 1999, p. G/2, from Central Chinese TV, November 16, 1999.

41. The market access it would afford Chinese textiles and apparel and the competitive jolt it would provide to failing firms were also important factors.

42. Morici, "Barring Entry," pp. 274–77; and George D. Holliday, "China and the World Trade Organization," in Joint Economic Committee, *China's Economic Future.*

43. SWB, FE/3168, March 6, 1998, p. S1/9, from XH, March 5, 1998.

44. Lin Lean Lim and Gyorgy Sziraczki, "Employment, Social Security, and Enterprise Reforms in China," in Gregory K. Schoepfle, ed., *Changes in China's Labor Market: Implications for the Future* (Washington, DC: U.S. Department of Labor, Bureau of International Labor Affairs, 1996), p. 50.

45. Translated in U.S Foreign Broadcast Information Service (hereafter FBIS), July 19, 1994, pp. 18–26, from XH, July 5, 1994. See also James V. Feinerman, "The Past—and Future—of Labor Law in China," in Schoepfle, *Changes,* pp. 119–134.

46. Holliday, "China and the World Trade Organization," pp. 452, 467–468. See also Dorothy J. Solinger, "Jobs and Joining: What's the Effect of WTO for China's Urban Employment?" paper prepared for the conference "The Political and Economic Reforms of Mainland China in a Changing Global Society," sponsored by the College of Social Sciences, National Taiwan University, Taipei, April 25–27, 2002 (forthcoming).

47. Mary Gallagher, "An Unequal Battle: Why Labor Laws & Regulations Fail to Protect Workers," *China Rights Forum,* Summer 1997, p. 12. See also Minghua Zhao and Theo Nichols, "Management Control of Labour in State-Owned Enterprises: Cases from the Textile Industry," *China Journal* 36 (1996): 1–21; William A. Byrd, *The Market Mechanism and Economic Reforms in China* (Armonk, NY: M. E. Sharpe, 1991), pp. 112–119.

48. SWB, FE/3136, January 28, 1998, p. S/2, from *Liaowang* [Outlook], January 5, 1998.

49. Barry Naughton, "China's Emergence and Prospects as a Trading Nation," *Brookings Papers on Economic Activity* 2 (1996): 287.

50. From 1979 through the mid-1990s the practice was to succor on the original workers, via an array of disparate strategies over the years: first by retirements that permitted their own offspring to take their spots, then by the formation of "labor service companies" that provided job training and job creation, next by insisting that firms "redeploy" their redundant workers within their own firms by retraining them and/or by creating new affiliated enterprises (along with restrictions against dismissing workers, even if there was no work for them and little or no pay), and eventually, in 1995, by a national Reemployment Program, which offered tax and loan incentives for developing new avenues of work for surplus labor. See Naughton, "The Emergence," pp. 287, 289; Leonard J. Hausman and Barry J. Friedman, "Employment Creation: New and Old Methods" unpublished ms., n.d. (1996 or 1997), p. 43; Barry L. Friedman, "Employment and Social Protection Policies in China: Big Reforms and Limited Outcomes," in Schoepfle, *Changes,* pp. 151–166; Harry G. Broadman, "Reform of China's State-Owned Enterprises," in Schoepfle, *Changes;* Lim and Sziraczki, "Employment"; Loraine A. West, "The Changing Effects of Economic Reform on Rural and Urban Employment," paper presented at the conference "Unintended Social Consequences of Chinese Economic Reform," Harvard School of Public Health and the Fairbank Center for East Asian Studies, Harvard University, May 23–24, 1997 (draft); Feinerman, "The Past"; Hilary K. Josephs, "Labor Law Reflects New Realities," *China Rights Forum,* Fall 1996, p. 25; and Christine P. W. Wong, Christopher Heady, and Wing T. Woo, *Fiscal Management and Economic Reform in the People's Republic of China* (Hong Kong: Oxford University Press, 1995), p. 14.

51. Andrew G. Walder, *Communist Neo-Traditionalism: Work and Authority in Chinese Industry* (Berkeley: University of California Press, 1986), pp. 40–43, 56–68.

52. Antoine Kernen, "Surviving Reform in Shenyang: New Poverty in Pioneer City," *China Rights Forum,* Summer 1997, p. 11. See also Barry Naughton, "Im-

204 THE DYNAMICS AND COUNTERDYNAMICS OF GLOBALIZATION

plications of the State Monopoly over Industry and Its Relaxation," *Modern China* 18, no. 1 (1992): 14–41; and Broadman, "Reform," pp. 4–5. "Collective" firms are in name owned by neighborhoods or rural administrations, sometimes by groups of rural citizens.

53. Interview with Hu Angang in SWB, FE/3514, April 21, 1999, p. G/6, from *Gangao Jingji* [Lever Economics], April 1, 1999.

54. According to then–minister of labor Li Boyong, speaking in late 1997, these former peasants "may compete with urbanites for jobs." See SWB, FE/3024, September 15, 1997, p. S2/18, from XH, September 14, 1997; and Dorothy J. Solinger, *Contesting Citizenship in Urban China: Peasant Migrants, the State, and the Logic of the Market* (Berkeley: University of California Press, 1999).

55. Dorothy J. Solinger, "The Chinese Work Unit and Transient Labor in the Transition from Socialism," *Modern China* 21, no. 2 (1995): 155–183; and Anita Chan, *China's Workers Under Assault: The Exploitation of Labor in a Globalizing Economy* (Armonk, NY: M. E. Sharpe, 2001).

56. Sun Changmin, "Floating Population in Shanghai: A Perspective of Social Transformation in China," in Thomas Scharping, ed., *Floating Population and Migration in China: The Impact of Economic Reforms* (Hamburg: Institut fur Asienkunde, 1997), p. 210.

57. Holliday, "China and the World Trade Organization," pp. 452, 467–468.

58. For instance, SWB, FE/3104, December 14, 1997, p. S1/1, from *Renmin Ribao* [People's Daily] (Beijing), September 14, 1997.

59. Similarly, see Miriam A. Golden, Michael Wallerstein, and Peter Lange, "Postwar Trade-Union Organization and Industrial Relations in Twelve Countries," in Herbert Kitschelt, Peter Lange, Gary Marks, and John D. Stephens, eds., *Continuity and Change in Contemporary Capitalism* (New York: Cambridge University Press, 1998), p. 224, wherein the argument is made that state policy was the dominant influence in a sea change in the stance toward labor in the 1980s and 1990s in Britain and the United States.

60. This term was coined by Janos Kornai in *The Socialist System: The Political Economy of Communism* (Princeton: Princeton University Press, 1992).

61. See Stephen J. McGurk, review of Barry Naughton's book *Growing Out of the Plan, China Journal* 39 (1998): 126.

62. See Wing Thye Woo, "Crises and Institutional Evolution in China's Industrial Sector," in Joint Economic Committee, *China's Economic Future*, pp. 165, 167; and Edward S. Steinfeld, *Forging Reform in China: The Fate of State-Owned Industry* (Cambridge: Cambridge University Press, 1998).

63. SWB, FE/3135, January 27, 1998, p. S1/3, from XH, January 23, 1998; and SWB, FE/3111, December 29, 1997, p. S1/3, from XH, January 26, 1997.

64. SWB, FE/3143, February 5, 1998, p. G/3, from Sing Tao Jih Pao, February 4, 1998.

65. Into the 1990s only a scant number of bankruptcies were permitted to occur (see Hausman and Friedman, "Employment Creation," p. 36). But a sharp increase in numbers took place in 1996 and 1997, with over 9,000 firms reportedly applying for bankruptcy in September 1997, when the Communist Party's Fifteenth Congress announced an acceleration of reforms in state firms. See Hang-Sheng Cheng, "A Mid-Course Assessment of China's Economic Reform," in Joint Economic Committee, *China's Economic Future*, pp. 29–30; West, "The Changing

Effects," p. 6; and Lo Ping, "Wenjian toulou qigai xian pingjing" [Document reveals enterprises in a bottleneck] *Zheng Ming* [Contend] no. 12 (1997): 17. An official source claimed that 675 state enterprises were declared bankrupt and closed in China in 1997; SWB, FE/3168, March 6, 1998, p. S2/1, from XH, March 4, 1998.

66. West, "The Changing Effects," p. 8.

67. On this, see Andrew Watson, "Enterprise Reform and Employment Change in Shaanxi Province," paper presented at the annual meeting of the Association for Asian Studies, Washington, DC, March 28, 1998, pp. 15–16. See also Kernen, "Surviving Reform," p. 9; and Dorothy J. Solinger, "Why We Cannot Count the Unemployed," *China Quarterly* 167 (September 2001): 671–688.

68. According to *Ming Pao* [Bright Daily] (Hong Kong), December 20, 1997, p. A11, in SWB, FE/3109, December 23, 1997, p. S1/1, the State Statistical Bureau had offered a figure of about 11 million; *Liaowang,* January 5, 1998, in SWB, FE/3136, January 28, 1998, p. S1/2, states 13 million laid-off workers and staff as of the end of 1997, and *Ping Kuo Jih Pao* [Apple Daily] (Hong Kong), January 29, 1998, p. A15, in SWB, FE/3141, February 3, 1998, p. G/8, gives what it calls an "official figure" of 12 million. Chinese Academy of Social Science scholar Hu Angang claimed that the "actual urban jobless" numbered from 11 to 13 million, and that the actual unemployment rate was therefore about 7 percent, over twice the usual reported rate of around 3 percent. Hu's remarks are in *Ming Pao,* February 18, 1998, p. A13, reprinted in SWB, FE/3155, February 19, 1998, p. G/13.

69. Lim and Sziraczki, "Employment," p. 49, explain that only workers with an urban household registration who are not on forced leave are counted as registered.

70. William H. Overholt, "China in the Balance," Nomura Strategy Paper, Hong Kong, May 12, 1999.

71. Naughton, "The Emergence," pp. 285, 273; and Barry Naughton, *Growing Out of the Plan: Chinese Economic Reforms, 1978–1993* (New York: Cambridge University Press, 1995), p. 297.

72. Naughton, *Growing,* p. 286.

73. Naughton, "The Emergence," p. 294; and Wing, "Crisis," pp. 164–65. See also Naughton, *Growing,* pp. 274–300.

74. Naughton, *Growing,* pp. 286–87.

75. One Chinese yuan is equal to about U.S.12¢.

76. West, "The Changing Effects," p. 6. See also Lo, "Wenjian," p. 17.

77. Jerome Cohen, *The Criminal Process in the People's Republic of China, 1949–1963* (Cambridge: Harvard University Press, 1968).

78. Pitman B. Potter, "Riding the Tiger: Legitimacy and Legal Culture in Post-Mao China," *China Quarterly* 138 (1994): 325–358; and Pitman B. Potter, ed., *Domestic Law Reforms in Post-Mao China* (Armonk, NY: M. E. Sharpe, 1994).

79. Morici, "Barring Entry?" p. 275.

80. Dwight Perkins, "Prospects for China's Integration into the Global Economy," in Joint Economic Committee, *China's Economic Future,* p. 37.

81. Feinerman, "The Past," p. 119.

82. Stanley B. Lubman, *Bird in a Cage: Legal Reforms in China After Mao* (Stanford, CA: Stanford University Press, 1999).

83. This law was adopted on July 5, 1994, at the Eighth Session of the Stand-

ing Committee of the Eighth National People's Congress (translated in FBIS, July 19, 1994) and its implementation (supposedly) began in 1995; Josephs, "Labor Law."

84. See Walder, *Communist Neo-Traditionalism;* Gail E. Henderson and Myron S. Cohen, *The Chinese Hospital: A Socialist Work Unit* (New Haven, CT: Yale University Press, 1984); and Xiaobo Lu and Elizabeth J. Perry, eds., *Danwei: The Chinese Workunit in Historical and Comparative Perspective* (Armonk, NY: M. E. Sharpe, 1997).

85. Kornai, *The Socialist System,* p. 315.

86. See Lu and Perry, *Danwei.*

87. Barry L. Friedman, "Employment and Social Protection Policies in China: Big Reforms and Limited Outcomes," in Schoepfle, *Changes,* p. 157; Lim and Sziraczki, "Employment," p. 60; and Han Dongfang, "The Prospects of a Free Labor Movement in China," in Schoepfle, *Changes,* p. 167.

88. West, "The Changing Effects," p. 10.

89. Broadman, "Reform," p. 6.

90. FBIS, July 19, 1994, p. 19.

91. Lim and Sziraczki, "Employment," p. 52.

92. I wrote about the continuation of the work-unit basis for welfare even as failing work units disappear, in "Labor Market Reform and the Plight of the Laid-Off Proletariat," *China Quarterly* 170 (June 2002): 304–326.

93. Feinerman, "The Past," p. 129.

94. SWB, FE/3111, December 17, 1997, p. S1/4, from XH, December 1, 1997.

95. Author interview at the Employment Section of the Ministry of Labor and Social Security, Beijing, September 1, 1998.

96. Antoine Kernen and Jean-Louis Rocca, "The Reform of State-Owned Enterprises and Its Social Consequences in Shenyang and Liaoning," ms., 1999, p. 8.

97. Solinger, *Contesting Citizenship.*

98. Dorothy J. Solinger, "Clashes Between Reform and Opening: Labor Market Formation in Three Cities," in Chien-min Chao and Bruce Dickson, ed., *The Remaking of the Chinese State: Structure, Society, and Strategy* (London: Routledge, 2001), pp. 103–131.

99. Sun, "Floating Population," p. 211.

100. Cao Jingxing, "A Good Trend or a Reason for Worry?" *China Focus* 5, no. 8 (August 1997): 8; Lim and Sziraczki, "Employment," p. 53; and, for an official source, SWB, FE/3162, from Sing Tao Jih Pao, February 22, 1998, p. G/5, from XH, February 20, 1998.

101. See David Lamb, "Migrant Asians Now Out of Work," *Los Angeles Times,* March 3, 1998, pp. A3, A9; and Margot Cohen, "Deport and Deter," *Far Eastern Economic Review,* April 23, 1998, pp. 16–20.

102. "Provisions on Employing Contract Workers from Among the Peasants by State-Owned Enterprises," in *Zhonghua Renmin Gongheguo Guowuyuan Gongbao* [Bulletin of the State Council of the Chinese People's Republic] (Beijing) 28, no. 667 (October 18, 1991): 1001–1016.

103. A recent regulation, in "Shiye baoxian tiaoli" [Regulations on unemployment insurance], *Laodong Baozhang Tongxun* [Labor Social Security Bulletin] 2 (February 1999): 45–46, would make it appear as if rural migrants, if under very

restricted circumstances, might be eligible; it is quite unlikely that a firm would honor such a ruling in practice.

104. FBIS, February 23, 1995, p. 68; March 16, 1995, p. 33; and June 28, 1995, p. 81. See also West, "The Changing Effects," p. 11; and Xiao Lichun, "Shanghai shiye, xiagang renyuan xianzhuang ji fazhan qushi" [Shanghai unemployment, laid-off personnel's situation and development trend], *Zhongguo Renkou Kexue* [Chinese Population Science] 3 (March 1998): 26–37.

105. Sam Dillon, "Workers Win Showdown with Factory in Mexico," *New York Times,* December 14, 1997.

106. Craig R. Whitney, "Europeans Accept a Single Currency Despite Late Snag," *New York Times,* May 3, 1998.

107. Symes, *Unemployment in Europe.*

Bibliography

Barbalet, J. M. *Citizenship: Rights, Struggle, and Class Inequality.* Milton Keynes, UK: Open University Press, 1988.

Berger, Suzanne, and Ronald Dore, eds. *National Diversity and Global Capitalism.* Ithaca, NY: Cornell University Press, 1996.

Betcherman, Gordon. "Globalization, Labor Markets, and Public Policy." In Robert Boyer and Daniel Drache, eds., *States Against Markets: The Limits of Globalization.* London: Routledge, 1997, pp. 250–269.

Boyer, Robert. "Division or Unity? Decline or Recovery?" In Robert Boyer, ed., *The Search for Labour Market Flexibility.* Oxford: Clarendon Press, 1988, pp. 194–221.

———. "State and Market: A New Engagement for the Twenty-first Century?" In Robert Boyer and Daniel Drache, eds., *States Against Markets: The Limits of Globalization.* London: Routledge, 1997, pp. 84–114.

———. "Wage Labor, Capital Accumulation, and the Crisis, 1968–82." In Mark Kesselman, ed., with the assistance of Guy Groux, *The French Workers' Movement: Economic Crisis and Political Change.* London: George Allen & Unwin, 1984, pp. 17–38.

———. "Wage/Labour Relations, Growth, and Crisis: A Hidden Dialectic." In Robert Boyer, ed., *The Search for Labour Market Flexibility: The European Economies in Transition.* Oxford: Clarendon Press, 1988 pp. 1–25.

Boyer, Robert, and Daniel Drache, eds. *States Against Markets: The Limits of Globalization.* London: Routledge, 1997.

British Broadcasting Corporation. *Summary of World Broadcasts.* Selected issues.

Broadman, Harry G. "Reform of China's State-Owned Enterprises." In Gregory Schoepfle, ed., *Changes in China's Labor Market: Implications for the Future.* Washington, DC: U.S. Department of Labor, Bureau of International Labor Affairs, 1996, pp. 3–12.

Brubaker, Rogers. *Citizenship and Nationhood in France and Germany.* Cambridge: Harvard University Press, 1992.

Byrd, William A. *The Market Mechanism and Economic Reforms in China.* Armonk, NY: M. E. Sharpe, 1991.

Cao Jingxing. "A Good Trend or a Reason for Worry?" *China Focus* 5, no. 8 (1997): p. 8.

Castillo, Gustavo V. del. "NAFTA and the Struggle for Neoliberalism: Mexico's

Elusive Quest for First World Status." In Gerardo Otero, ed., *Neoliberalism Revisited: Economic Restructuring and Mexico's Political Future.* Boulder, CO: Westview Press, 1996, pp. 27–42.

Chan, Anita. *China's Workers Under Assault: The Exploitation of Labor in a Globalizing Economy.* Armonk, NY: M. E. Sharpe, 2001.

Cheng, Hang-Sheng. "A Mid-Course Assessment of China's Economic Reform." In Joint Economic Committee, U.S. Congress, ed., *China's Economic Future: Challenges to U.S. Policy.* Armonk, NY: M. E. Sharpe, 1997, pp. 24–33.

Chorney, Harold. "Debts, Deficits, and Full Employment." In Robert Boyer and Daniel Drache, eds., *States Against Markets: The Limits of Globalization.* London: Routledge, 1997, pp. 357–379.

Cohen, Jerome. *The Criminal Process in the People's Republic of China, 1949–1963.* Cambridge: Harvard University Press, 1968.

Cohen, Margot. "Deport and Deter." *Far Eastern Economic Review,* April 23, 1998, pp. 16–20.

Collier, Ruth Berins. *The Contradictory Alliance: State-Labor Relations and Regime Change in Mexico.* Research Series no 83. Berkeley: International and Area Studies, University of California, 1992.

Cornelius, Wayne A., Philip L. Martin, and James F. Hollifield. "Introduction: The Ambivalent Quest for Immigration Control." In Wayne A. Cornelius, Philip L. Martin, and James F. Hollifield, eds., *Controlling Immigration: A Global Perspective.* Stanford, CA: Stanford University Press, 1995, pp. 3–41.

Cumings, Bruce. "The Political Economy of China's Turn Outward." In Samuel S. Kim, ed., *China and the World.* Boulder, CO: Westview Press, 1984, pp. 235–265.

Daley, Anthony. "The Steel Crisis and Labor Politics in France and the United States." In Miriam Golden and Jonas Pontusson, eds., *Bargaining for Change: Union Politics in North America and Europe.* Ithaca, NY: Cornell University Press, 1992.

Dillon, Sam. "Workers Win Showdown with Factory in Mexico." *New York Times,* December 14, 1997.

Drache, Daniel. "From Keynes to K-Mart: Competitiveness in a Corporate Age." In Robert Boyer and Daniel Drache, eds., *States Against Markets: The Limits of Globalization.* London: Routledge, 1997, pp. 31–61.

Eatwell, John. "Unemployment on a World Scale." In John Eatwell, ed., *Global Unemployment: Loss of Jobs in the 1990's.* Armonk, NY: M. E. Sharpe, 1996, pp. 3–20.

Faist, Thomas, and Hartmut Haussermann. "Immigration, Social Citizenship, and Housing in Germany." *International Journal of Urban and Regional Research* 20, no. 1 (1996): 83–98.

Feinerman, James V. "The Past—and Future—of Labor Law in China." In Gregory Schoepfle, ed., *Changes in China's Labor Market: Implications for the Future.* Washington, DC: U.S. Department of Labor, Bureau of International Labor Affairs, 1996, pp. 119–134.

Friedman, Barry L. "Employment and Social Protection Policies in China: Big Reforms and Limited Outcomes." In Gregory Schoepfle, ed., *Changes in China's Labor Market: Implications for the Future.* Washington, DC: U.S. Department of Labor, Bureau of International Labor Affairs, 1996, pp. 151–166.

Gallagher, Mary. "An Unequal Battle: Why Labor Laws and Regulations Fail to Protect Workers." *China Rights Forum* (Summer 1997), pp. 12–15, 27.

Gordon, Ian. "The Impact of Economic Change on Minorities and Migrants in Western Europe." In Katherine McFate, Roger Lawson, and William Julius Wilson, eds., *Poverty, Inequality, and the Future of Social Policy.* New York: Russell Sage, 1995, pp. 521–542.

Grieder, William. *One World Ready or Not: The Manic Logic of Global Capitalism.* New York: Simon & Schuster, 1997.

Gruber, Lloyd. *Ruling the World: Power Politics and the Rise of Supranational Institutions.* Princeton: Princeton University Press, 2000.

Gummett, Philip, ed. *Globalization and Public Policy.* Cheltenham, UK: Edward Elgar, 1996.

Han, Dongfang. "The Prospects of a Free Labor Movement in China." In Gregory Schoepfle, ed., *Changes in China's Labor Market: Implications for the Future.* Washington, DC: U.S. Department of Labor, Bureau of International Labor Affairs, 1996, pp. 167–183.

Hausman, Leonard J., and Barry J. Friedman. "Employment Creation: New and Old Methods." Unpublished manuscript, n.d.

Heater, Derek. *Citizenship: The Civic Ideal in World History, Politics, and Education.* London: Longman, 1990.

Henderson, Gail E., and Myron S. Cohen. *The Chinese Hospital: A Socialist Work Unit.* New Haven, CT: Yale University Press, 1984.

Holliday, George D. "China and the World Trade Organization." In Joint Economic Committee, U.S. Congress, ed., *China's Economic Future: Challenges to U.S. Policy.* Armonk, NY: M. E. Sharpe, 1997.

Hollifield, James F. *Immigrants, Markets, and States: The Political Economy of Postwar Europe.* Cambridge: Harvard University Press, 1992.

Ishikawa Shigeru. "Sino-Japanese Economic Cooperation." *China Quarterly* 109 (1987): 1–21.

Jackman, Richard. "The Impact of the European Union on Unemployment and Unemployment Policy." In David Hine and Hussein Kassim, eds., *Beyond the Market: The EU and National Social Policy.* London: Routledge, 1998, pp. 60–78.

Jacobson, David. "New Border Customs: Migration and the Changing Role of the State." *UCLA Journal of International Law and Foreign Affairs* 3, no. 2 (Fall–Winter 1998–1999).

———. *Rights Across Borders: Immigration and the Decline of Citizenship.* Baltimore: Johns Hopkins University Press, 1996.

Josephs, Hilary K. "Labor Law Reflects New Realities." *China Rights Forum.*

Kernen, Antoine. "Surviving Reform in Shenyang: New Poverty in Pioneer City." *China Rights Forum,* Summer 1997.

Kernen, Antoine, and Jean-Louis Rocca. "The Reform of State-Owned Enterprises and Its Social Consequences in Shenyang and Liaoning." Ms., 1999.

Kesselman, Mark. "Does the French Labor Movement Have a Future?" In John T. S. Keeler and Martin A. Schain, eds., *Chirac's Challenge: Liberalization, Europeanization, and Malaise in France.* New York: St. Martin's Press, 1996, pp. 143–160.

Kornai, Janos. *The Socialist System: The Political Economy of Communism.* Princeton: Princeton University Press, 1992.

Krugman, Paul. "First, Do No Harm." *Foreign Affairs* 75, no. 4 (July–August 1996): 164–170.

Lamb, David. "Migrant Asians Now Out of Work." *Los Angeles Times,* March 3, 1998, pp. A3, A9.

Lawson, Roger, and William Julius Wilson. "Poverty, Social Rights, and the Quality of Citizenship." In Katherine McFate, Roger Lawson, and William Julius Wilson, eds., *Poverty, Inequality, and the Future of Social Policy.* New York: Russell Sage, 1995, pp. 693–714.

Levy, Jonah D. "France: Directing Adjustment." Paper presented to the international research project on "The Adjustment of National Employment Policy and Social Policy to Internationalization," organized by Fritz Scharpf and Vivien Schmidt, Ringberg Castle, Germany, February 17–20, 1999 (preliminary draft).

Lim, Lin Lean, and Gyorgy Sziraczki. "Employment, Social Security, and Enterprise Reforms in China." In Gregory K. Schoepfle, ed., *Changes in China's Labor Market: Implications for the Future.* Washington, DC: U.S. Department of Labor, Bureau of International Labor Affairs, 1996, pp. 45–87.

Lo, Ping. "Wenjian toulou qigai xian pingjing" [Document reveals enterprises in a bottleneck]. *Zheng Ming* [Contend] 12 (December 1997): pp. 17–19.

Lu, Xiaobo, and Elizabeth J. Perry, eds. *Danwei: The Chinese Workunit in Historical and Comparative Perspective.* Armonk, NY: M. E. Sharpe, 1997.

Lubman, Stanley B. *Bird in a Cage: Legal Reforms in China After Mao.* Stanford, CA: Stanford University Press, 1999.

Marshall, T. H. *Sociology at the Crossroads and Other Essays.* London: Heinemann, 1963.

McFate, Katherine. "Introduction: Western States in the New World Order." In Katherine McFate, Roger Lawson, and William Julius Wilson, eds., *Poverty, Inequality, and the Future of Social Policy.* New York: Russell Sage, 1995, pp. 1–26.

McGurk, Stephen J. Review of Barry Naughton's book *Growing Out of the Plan. China Journal* 39 (1998).

Mishra, Ramesh. "The Welfare of Nations." In Robert Boyer and Daniel Drache, eds., *States Against Markets: The Limits of Globalization.* London: Routledge, 1997, pp. 316–333.

Mittelman, James H., ed. *Globalization: Critical Reflections.* Boulder, CO: Lynne Rienner, 1996.

Morici, Peter. "Barring Entry? China and the WTO." *Current History* (1997).

———. "Grasping the Benefits of NAFTA." *Current History* no. 2 (1993): 49–54.

Moss, Bernard H. "After the Auroux Laws: Employers, Industrial Relations, and the Right in France." *West European Politics* 11, no. 1 (January 1988): 60–80.

Naughton, Barry. "China's Emergence and Prospects as a Trading Nation." *Brookings Papers on Economic Activity* 2 (1996).

———. *Growing Out of the Plan.* New York Cambridge University Press, 1995.

———. "Implications of the State Monopoly over Industry and Its Relaxation." *Modern China* 18, no. 1 (1992): 14–41.

Overholt, William H. "China in the Balance." Nomura Strategy Paper. Hong Kong, May 12, 1999.

Panitch, Leo. "Rethinking the Role of the State." In James H. Mittelman, ed., *Globalization: Critical Reflections.* Boulder, CO: Lynne Rienner, 1996, pp. 83–113.

Pearson, Margaret M. "China's Integration into the International Trade." In Elizabeth Economy and Michel Oksenberg, eds., *China Joins the World: Progress and Prospects.* New York: Council on Foreign Relations, 1999, pp. 161–205.

Perkins, Dwight H. *China: Asia's Next Economic Giant?* Seattle: University of Washington Press, 1986.

———. "Prospects for China's Integration into the Global Economy." In Joint Economic Committee, U.S. Congress, ed., *China's Economic Future: Challenges to U.S. Policy.* Armonk, NY: M. E. Sharpe, 1997.

Peters, Enrique Dussel. "From Export-Oriented to Import-Oriented Industrialization: Changes in Mexico's Manufacturing Sector, 1988–1994." In Gerardo Otero, ed., *Neoliberalism Revisited: Economic Restructuring and Mexico's Political Future.* Boulder, CO: Westview Press, 1996, pp. 63–83.

Petit, Pascal. "Problems of the State in Dealing with the System of Wage/Labour Relations: The Case of France." In Robert Boyer, ed., *The Search for Labour Market Flexibility: The European Economies in Transition.* Oxford: Clarendon Press, 1988, pp. 26–57.

Potter, Pitman B., ed. *Domestic Law Reforms in Post-Mao China.* Armonk, NY: M. E. Sharpe, 1994.

———. "Riding the Tiger: Legitimacy and Legal Culture in Post-Mao China." *China Quarterly* 138 (1994): 325–358.

"Provisions on Employing Contract Workers from Among the Peasants by State-Owned Enterprises." *Zhonghua Renmin Gongheguo Guowuyuan Gongbao* [Bulletin of the State Council of the Chinese People's Republic] (Beijing) 28, no. 667 (October 18, 1991): 1001–1016.

Rochlin, James F. *Redefining Mexican "Security."* Boulder, CO: Lynne Rienner, 1997.

Rodrik, Dani. *Has Globalization Gone Too Far?* Washington, DC: Institute for International Economics, 1997.

Sassen, Saskia. *The Mobility of Labor and Capital.* Cambridge: Cambridge University Press, 1988.

Schmidt, Vivien A. "Democracy at Risk? France, Great Britain, and Germany Between Globalization and Europeanization." In David A. Smith, Dorothy J. Solinger, and Steven Topik, eds., *States and Sovereignty in the Global Economy.* London: Routledge, 1999, pp. 172–192.

Shklar, Judith N. *American Citizenship: The Quest for Inclusion.* Cambridge: Harvard University Press, 1991.

Smith, David A., and Jozsef Borocz, eds. *A New World Order? Global Transformations in the Late Twentieth Century.* Westport, CT: Greenwood Press, 1995.

Smith, W. Rand. "Industrial Crisis and the Left: Adjustment Strategies in Socialist France and Spain." *Comparative Politics,* October 1995.

———. "Unemployment and the Left Coalition in France and Spain." In Nancy Bermeo, ed., *Unemployment in Southern Europe: Coping with the Consequences.* London: Frank Cass, 2000, pp. 111–134.

Solinger, Dorothy J. "The Chinese Work Unit and Transient Labor in the Transition from Socialism." *Modern China* 21, no. 2 (1995): 155–183.

———. "Clashes Between Reform and Opening: Labor Market Formation in Three Cities." In Chien-min Chao and Bruce Dickson, eds., *Remaking the Chinese*

State: Structure, Society, and Strategy. London, CO: Routledge, 2001, pp. 103–131.

———. *Contesting Citizenship in Urban China: Peasant Migrants, the State, and the Logic of the Market.* Berkeley: University of California Press, 1999.

———. *From Lathes to Looms: China's Industrial Policy in Comparative Perspective.* Stanford, CA: Stanford University Press, 1991.

———. "Jobs and Joining: What's the Effect of WTO for China's Urban Employment?" Paper prepared for the conference "The Political and Economic Reforms of Mainland China in a Changing Global Society," sponsored by the College of Social Sciences, National Taiwan University, Taipei, April 25–27, 2002 (forthcoming).

———. "Why We Cannot Count the Unemployed." *China Quarterly* 167 (September 2001): 671–688.

———. "The Plight of the Laid-Off Proletariat," *China Quarterly* 170 (June 2002): 304–326.

Soysol, Yasemin Nohuglu. *Limits of Citizenship: Migrants and Postnational Membership in Europe.* Chicago: University of Chicago Press, 1994.

Standing, Guy. "Labor Insecurity Through Market Regulation: Legacy of the 1980s, Challenge for the 1990s." In Katherine McFate, Roger Lawson, and William Julius Wilson, eds., *Poverty, Inequality, and the Future of Social Policy.* New York: Russell Sage, 1995, pp. 153–196.

Steinfeld, Edward S. *Forging Reform in China: The Fate of State-Owned Industry.* Cambridge: Cambridge University Press, 1998.

Sun, Changmin. "Floating Population in Shanghai: A Perspective of Social Transformation in China." In Thomas Scharping, ed., *Floating Population and Migration in China: The Impact of Economic Reforms.* Hamburg: Institut fur Asienkunde, 1997, pp. 201–215.

Symes, Valerie. *Unemployment in Europe: Problems and Policies.* London: Routledge, 1995.

Teichman, Judith A. *Privatization and Political Change in Mexico.* Pittsburgh, PA: University of Pittsburgh Press, 1995.

Turner, Bryan S. *Citizenship and Capitalism: The Debate over Reformism.* London: Allen & Unwin, 1986.

———. "Contemporary Problems in the Theory of Citizenship." In Bryan S. Turner, ed., *Citizenship and Social Theory.* London: Sage, 1993, pp. 1–18.

Walder, Andrew G. *Communist Neo-Traditionalism: Work and Authority in Chinese Industry.* Berkeley: University of California Press, 1986.

Watson, Andrew. "Enterprise Reform and Employment Change in Shaanxi Province." Paper presented at the annual meeting of the Association for Asian Studies, Washington, DC, March 1998.

West, Loraine A. "The Changing Effects of Economic Reform on Rural and Urban Employment." Paper presented at the conference "Unintended Social Consequences of Chinese Economic Reform," Harvard School of Public Health and the Fairbank Center for East Asian Studies, Harvard University, May 23–24, 1997 (draft).

Whitney, Craig R. "Europeans Accept a Single Currency Despite Late Snag." *New York Times,* May 3, 1998.

————. "French Jobless Find the World Is Harsher." *New York Times,* March 19, 1998, p. A6.

Wong, Christine P. W., Christopher Heady, and Wing T. Woo. *Fiscal Management and Economic Reform in the People's Republic of China.* Hong Kong: Oxford University Press, 1995.

Woo, Wing Thye. "Crises and Institutional Evolution in China's Industrial Sector." In Joint Economic Committee, U.S. Congress, ed., *China's Economic Future: Challenges to U.S. Policy.* Armonk, NY: M. E. Sharpe, 1997.

World Bank. *China 2020: China Engaged, Integration with the Global Economy.* Washington, DC: World Bank, 1997.

Xiao, Lichun. "Shanghai shiye, xiagang renyuan xianzhuang ji fazhan qushi" [Shanghai unemployment, laid-off personnel's situation, and development trend]. *Zhongguo Renkou Kexue* [Chinese Population Science] 3 (March 1998): 26–37.

Yang Yiyong et al. *Shiye chongji bo* [The shock wave of unemployment]. Beijing: Jinri Zhongguo Chubanshe [China Today Publishing], 1997.

Zhao, Minghua, and Theo Nichols. "Management Control of Labour in State-Owned Enterprises: Cases from the Textile Industry." *China Journal* 36 (1996): 1–21.

8

Localizing Human Rights in an Era of Globalization

The Case of Hong Kong

Linda Butenhoff

It's been a number of years since the term "globalization" was first heard. However, even though there have been volumes written on the topic, there is no clear consensus on the concept itself. Is it a process, a phenomenon, a state of being, what? International relations scholar Ian Clark has argued that "[b]y its very nature, globalization draws attention to the economic and technological aspects of life and to deep-seated change at the level of culture or identity. In all such cases, the very emphasis on the global highlights the integrative aspects of social life."[1] Despite definitions like Clark's that seek to get at economic and social aspects of globalization, most definitions end up explaining globalization as an economic and technological phenomenon. In this manner, globalization has meant that virtually every economy in the world has joined (or would like to join) the global capitalist market system. The penetration of the market is illustrated by the presence of multinational corporations (MNCs) around the world and the establishment of special economic zones from Latin America to Ghana and across Asia. Another frequently cited example of this type of globalization is the World Trade Organization, established through the Uruguay Round of the General Agreement on Tariffs and Trade (GATT), with its mission to spur capital flows, goods, and services across state borders. At the heart of this is what Thomas Friedman describes as a balance between nation-states and global markets:

> These global markets are made up of millions of investors moving money around the world with the click of a mouse. I call them the "Electronic

herd." They gather in key global financial centers, such as Frankfurt, Hong Kong, London, and New York—the "supermarkets." The United States can destroy you by dropping bombs and the supermarkets can destroy you by downgrading your bonds. Who ousted President Suharto in Indonesia? It was not another superpower, it was the supermarkets.[2]

This dominant and popular conceptualization of globalization is what Richard Falk refers to as "globalization from above." While Friedman applauds globalization, Falk cautions that the results of globalization from above have been the state's retreat from promoting holistic human rights, in particular, democratic participation and economic and social rights.[3] Furthermore, Falk and other scholars, such as Robert Cox, Immanuel Wallerstein, and Samir Amin, argue that along with the forces of globalization from above, there has been a corresponding phenomenon of "globalization from below," which represents the actions of social actors, such as grassroots nongovernmental organizations (NGOs), that join forces to address human rights abuses, inequality, and underdevelopment.[4] Indeed these forces of globalization from below have garnered headlines around the world for mobilizing around governmental meetings at various global financial institutions.

When taking these factors into consideration, it may be concluded that there has been a growing confrontation between the forces of globalization from above and from below, especially centering on human rights. For instance, in December 1999, the World Trade Organization's meeting in Seattle, Washington, became a virtual "battle zone" between these two forces. These networks of local and transnational social forces have mobilized around meetings of the World Bank, the International Monetary Fund, the G-8, and other international financial organizations, rallying around issues of workers' rights, sustainable development, and more democratic and transparent international institutions—representing a holistic notion of human rights. While the clashes in Seattle, and later in Washington, D.C., received international attention, they were actually activities developed over a number of years. For example, in August 1997, the World Bank meetings in Hong Kong provided an opportunity for many Asian organizations, through the coordination of Peoples' Platform for the Twenty-first Century (PP21), to draw attention to issues of worker rights, women's rights, and the state of the environment after major MNCs enter their country in order to promote economic development. Furthermore, for years The Other Economic Summit—(TOES) has been gathering at G-7/ Summit of 8 meetings to discuss issues not on the governments' agenda.

When reviewing the globalization literature it is apparent that it emphasizes globalization's role in challenging the sovereignty of the state. However, what does this mean for the promotion and implementation of human rights within and across states and peoples? In addition, while scholars and policymakers differ on the content of human rights (i.e., the "Asian values" debate), most agree that human rights are now promoted in virtually every society. Likewise then, current trends in the human rights literature have taken up this key issue of globalization and human rights. This growing body of literature emphasizes a systemic approach to globalization and the spread of international human rights norms. For instance, works by David Forsythe, Kathryn Sikkink, and Kurt Mills, to mention a few, have examined the emergence and growth of international human rights norms, global governance, and transnational movements.[5] While this approach allows us to examine macro forces of human rights, it opens a gap in the literature. Therefore, while not dismissing the much needed research on systemic and transnational factors that link globalization to human rights, I would argue that there is also a need to examine local social forces that contribute to our understanding of global human rights and the growing collective action of globalization from below.

Accordingly Hong Kong presents an interesting case to examine when considering the local effects of globalization and human rights. For instance, it could be argued that Hong Kong has been a global society ever since Great Britain established the colony in the nineteenth century after defeating China in the Opium Wars. The colony's trading base served as the key mechanism by which the British sought to integrate China into regional and international economies.[6]

Clearly today no one would dispute the role that Hong Kong plays in the globalized market economy, which ranges from multinational manufacturing companies to financial and telecommunication industries. Moreover, Hong Kong's human rights record, whether under British or Chinese rule, rarely has been criticized like the records of others in the region (i.e., mainland China, Singapore, Indonesia, Malaysia). On the surface, it would appear that Hong Kong is the quintessential modern (or even postmodern) society—characterized by a developed, hi-tech economy as well as respect for the rule of law and other international human rights norms. On the other hand, a deeper examination of Hong Kong's human rights situation reveals that Hong Kong symbolizes "the good and the bad" of globalization.

First, Hong Kong is often characterized as a society where the people are politically apathetic, care little about politics and political participation, and are really only interested in making money. And, there have been some public opinion surveys, conducted by scholars at Hong Kong Baptist University for instance, that seem to support this characterization.[7] Nonetheless, Hong Kong also has had a long history of challenging the local, dominant political and economic forces. For instance, strikes and boycotts of the early twentieth century shut down the colony for eighteen months in protest over unfair wages and working conditions as well as the lack of political participation in the colonial government.[8] Therefore, Hong Kong's economic success in the last fifty years should not be seen as a sign that Hong Kong is a paradise of productivity and wealth for all. Indeed the postcolonial Hong Kong government is facing a disgruntled civil service sector, which is being "corporatized,"[9] a democracy movement, which pressures for direct elections for the entire government (i.e., chief executive, legislative council, and municipal government), and a human rights community, which not only advocates for enhanced civil and political rights, but also pressures for children's rights, gender equality, workers' rights, immigrant's rights, continued public housing programs, and more money for education.

The case of postcolonial Hong Kong, Special Administrative Region (SAR) of the People's Republic of China (PRC), may be ideal for examining globalization and human rights. Indeed the PRC has become a central actor in the struggle to redefine the post–Cold War world order. Moreover, with the mainland's economic growth and international activity such as seeking membership in the World Trade Organization, Hong Kong's return to Chinese sovereignty raised questions about human rights in the SAR. Hong Kong's historical intermingling of cultures also provides a unique case for examining the relationship of globalization and human rights. Its blend of Western and Asian traditions poses a challenge to China's traditional and one-party notions of human rights. And, this has resulted in tensions between China and Hong Kong as well as between China and the international community. A recent manifestation of this tension is the pressure the Beijing government placed on the SAR government to monitor activities of Falun Gong.[10] These tensions have also led the SAR and Beijing governments to explain their actions to the UN Human Rights Commission.[11] These tensions are not new, however, they initially emerged once the British colonial government, in its waning days, instituted political reforms to protect human rights and develop democratic government institutions. China's response was to officially dismantle this political system on July 1, 1997. Now several years beyond the 1997 transfer of sovereignty to China, what are the human rights conditions in Hong Kong? On the one hand, even though Hong Kong went through the Asian economic crisis of 1997, it remains a stable, capitalist economy. On the other, tensions over political participation, the rule of law, and the right to free speech and public assembly have increased.

The chapter aims to examine human rights in Hong Kong in this period of globalization. In particular, it seeks to ask whether there is any relationship between local and global efforts to promote human rights. Thus this chapter examines the role that local social forces are playing in addressing problematic areas of Hong Kong's human rights record, focusing on political participation, the rule of law and autonomy, and economic and social rights. This chapter also seeks to determine if local social forces are linking up with regional and international movements. This activity, it may be argued, represents an effort not only to address the impact of globalization from above but also to develop solidarity networks that promote human rights, democracy, and human dignity for all peoples—that is, globalization from below.

This chapter begins with a discussion on human rights and the promotion of a holistic conceptualization of human rights. It then moves on to localizing human rights in Hong Kong, giving an overview of historical and contemporary human rights issues. Finally, the chapter concludes with a discussion of Hong Kong's role in the processes of globalization from below.

Conceptualizing Human Rights

The twentieth century has witnessed the emergence of human rights as a central issue in international affairs. Yet beyond that point there is considerable debate over the concept of human rights itself. Although the topic of human rights covers a broad spectrum, ranging from freedom of speech to the right to a clean environment, one of the most frequently debated issues is which rights, if any, should be given priority. Central to this is the debate between individual and collective rights and the role of culture in determining these rights. One side argues that human rights protect and promote the individual. Collective rights and cultural arguments, in this view, are too vague and flexible, giving states the opportunity to abuse human rights, whereas individual civil liberties are easier to implement because they merely require the absence of government intervention in people's lives. Moreover, proponents of civil and political rights argue that human rights are inherently independent of civil society, and individualistic, and that any implementation of collective rights would require a depreciation of an individual's liberty and equality.[12]

The other side argues that the community or collective needs are above individual needs, and without an emphasis on such basic needs as food, individuals have no need for the luxuries of political freedoms. This clash has been most evident between nations of the North and the developing countries of the South. It raises questions over whether or not human rights may be applied universally and if there is a global basis for a consensus on human rights as appears in the Universal Declaration of Human Rights, written immediately after World War II, when most current states were still colonies.

Nevertheless, most would agree that human rights are tools for defending the poor and the powerless. And, in order to build a foundation for human rights that goes beyond rhetoric and political manipulation, the UN's Universal Declaration and the international covenants and resolutions on human rights are a place to begin to build common ground as well as to acknowledge global human rights norms. Indeed they may be considered documents that help globalize human rights norms. Therefore a universal or holistic conception of human rights could be based on the Universal Declaration, the International Covenant on Civil and Political Rights (ICCPR), the International Covenant on Economic, Social, and Cultural Rights (ICESCR), and peoples or solidarity rights, which are rooted in the UN Charter, the 1976 Algiers Declaration (the Universal Declaration of the Rights of Peoples), and the Organization of African Unity's Banjul Charter on Human and Peoples Rights. Statements coming out of the Rio "Earth" Summit in 1992 and the UN Human Rights Conference in 1993 confirm this growing recognition of the need for holistic and comprehensive human rights promotion and implementation. In posthandover Hong Kong, several human rights controversies have emerged. In the following sections, this chapter reviews the historical context of human rights and then moves on to localizing current human rights concerns. Specifically, examples of human rights conditions, which represent a holistic framework, are highlighted. First, civil and political rights such as political participation, the rule of law and local autonomy, and the right to public assembly are examined. Then, cases of economic and social rights, drawn from workers' rights, social welfare issues, and public housing, are reviewed. Finally, selected cases of emerging peoples or solidarity rights, such as the right to a clean and healthy environment, identity, and local autonomy, as well as solidarity efforts, are explored. This final section, in particular, suggests that human rights in Hong Kong are indeed globalized.

Human Rights Controversies in Hong Kong

The century-and-a-half historical experience of British colonialism in Hong Kong illustrates an interesting case of human rights promotion and implementation. From the beginning, Great Britain's interest in Hong Kong was economic, not political or geostrategic. Thus, the evolution of colonial human rights practices reflects these interests. Great Britain established the British common law system in order to protect economic contracts and corporate interests in the territory—capitalist economies necessitate the enforcement of contracts. At the same time, the British also established typical British colonial political institutions. A government led by a British-appointed governor, an administrative service, and an appointed system of consultation in the executive and legislative councils. Although there were periodic episodes of rebellion and riots in the colony, Hong Kong elites were absorbed into the British political structure through indirect consultation. Thus no efforts were made to institute any sort of civil and political rights for the general population. Indeed, in order to maintain stability (i.e., control), the colonial government instituted measures such as the Public Order Ordinance, the Societies Ordinance, and the Education Ordinance (which prohibited the provision of civic education in schools) to limit political participation. Not only did the colonial government avoid involvement in social, economic, and cultural aspects of society, but it also limited the development of civil society. Ironically, as the United Nations was formed and human rights were enshrined in the Universal Declaration in 1948, followed by the covenants on civil and political rights and economic, social, and cultural rights (both signed by Great Britain in 1976), Hong Kong went without any mechanisms to implement these essential human rights. Even as Hong Kong industrialized and emerged as a newly industrialized economy in the 1960s and 1970s (and joined the processes of globalization), the protection and implementation of human rights were minimal.

For instance, while Great Britain was one of the first to sign both the ICCPR and the ICESCR, the British removed Hong Kong from the decolonization list and reserved most of the key articles in these documents from being implemented in the territory. Britain justified the reservations by stating that Hong Kong was not ready for self-rule, arguing that there was no real desire on the part of the population for democracy, due to their Confucian traditions.[13] Regardless of the colonial government's unwillingness to implement global human rights norms, the government began to face a more developed civil society, which demanded political reform.[14] The 1970s in fact are known as the "Golden Age" of social movement activity.[15]

Only after the initialing of the landmark Sino-British Joint Declaration, in 1984, did civil and political rights begin to be extended to the people of Hong Kong. The key point in the joint declaration was that on July 1,

1997, Hong Kong would become a Special Administrative Region of the People's Republic of China with a high degree of autonomy. Interestingly, Annex I, Section XIII, of the document stipulates that the provisions of the ICCPR and the ICESCR as applied to Hong Kong shall remain in force. At this time, it appeared that Hong Kong would have minimal human rights protection that even those on the mainland did not have. The colonial government also took steps to expand local representation in the political system, as a mechanism for preparing for self-rule as stipulated in the joint declaration. Great Britain decided at this point to institute political reforms and human rights protections. The initial reforms to the political process emphasized the development of direct elections for the local district boards.[16] In late 1984 the colonial government put forward the *Green Paper: On the Further Development of Representative Government in Hong Kong,* a proposal to expand direct elections to include members to the LegCo and the municipal councils (the UrbCo and RegCo) in the 1988 elections.[17] However, while public opinion polls showed local support for the elections, the government canceled them, claiming that there was "not enough support by the people" for the elections. Analysts and prodemocracy supporters instead point to pressure placed on the British by the Beijing government.[18]

In the years leading up to July 1997, reforms to expand political participation were made. On the one hand, human rights supporters argued that British common law established during colonial rule was the cornerstone for these political reforms and should be the foundation for protecting human rights. Thus the need to formally document human rights in Hong Kong law.[19] On the other hand, pro-China advocates argue that more attention should be given to continued economic prosperity, rather than Western-style civil and political rights.[20] Human rights activists in Hong Kong continued to argue, however, that human rights have always been poorly protected, whether they are individual or collective rights, and that there should be an effort made to comprehensively and holistically protect and promote human rights. They argued that despite political and economic advances, the ordinary Hong Kong person should be the measure by which reforms are instituted, not foreign investment.[21]

Human Rights Concerns in the Postcolonial SAR

The basis for civil and political rights in the SAR stems from the Basic Law, which was written by a committee composed mainly of mainland Chinese and Hong Kong businessmen and elites. The Basic Law serves as the SAR's mini-constitution, though it is not without its own amount of controversy. When it was initially drafted, the document was severely criticized by Hong Kongers for not upholding the Sino-British Joint Declaration's promise of the "Hong Kong people ruling Hong Kong." Even so, China's National People's Congress (NPC) approved it in 1990. This disappointment, coupled with the Tiananmen Square massacre, brought on a crisis in confidence in the territory and a movement to implement laws that would protect human rights and local autonomy. As a result, in 1991 the Bill of Rights Ordinance, which specifically applied the ICCPR, was passed into law.

Concerns over the state of civil and political rights continues in post-colonial Hong Kong, stemming from several key actions taken by the new SAR government. For instance, on July 1, 1997, the first act of the new SAR was to dismantle the existing government and in its place install a provisional one. The anticipation of the removal of the government led to a preoccupation with the formation of the new political system. As a result, there was a resurgence in the attention paid to civil and political rights. For instance, elections, free speech and media, the right to assemble, and the rule of law took center stage. Human rights and prodemocracy supporters believed these to be central to self-rule and local autonomy. Nonetheless, concerns were raised that civil and political rights were under attack by the SAR government and not just with the establishment of a provisional government. These complaints included eroding the rule of law, limiting popular participation, returning to old colonial laws, and silencing dissent and opposition groups.

Hong Kong is not a democracy and never was. To a large degree much of the concerns and controversies over human rights in Hong Kong today stem from a lack of direct political participation in the government. Thus the pace of "democratizing" Hong Kong and building an independent civil society is at the center of the contentious relationship between Hong Kong social forces, political parties, and the SAR government. While the British colonial government was willing to step up the pace of political reform in its last few years, the Beijing government has been unwilling to implement these reforms and indeed has rolled them back. Nonetheless, it is interesting to note that China did not ban elections in Hong Kong. Instead critics of the government point out that the posthandover system allows the mainland to control and influence the political process, without being directly involved.[22]

For instance, the first posthandover elections, in May 1998 and September 2000 for LegCo, consisted of three types of voting: twenty seats (twenty-four in 2000) from directly elected, geographical constituencies; thirty seats from functional constituency blocs; and ten seats (six in 2000) selected by the Electoral College.[23] While the prehandover elections were similar in construction, these elections were different in spirit. The elections were seen as a return to government by consultation of elites, not participation of the people. In preparation for the election, all voting rosters since the 1995 LegCo elections were redone. Moreover, while the prehandover functional constituency seats sought to broaden voter participation, the posthandover changes did the opposite. Redefinition of constituencies also contributed to a reduction in overall voter registration. In these elections, for instance, the number of eligible voters for the twenty-eight functional constituency seats was reduced from approximately 2.7 million in the 1995 elections to approximately 150,000 in 1998.[24] While technically these procedures conform to the Basic Law, in reality they appeared to limit authentic participation by the Hong Kong people and placed the mainland firmly in control of "democratizing" the political system. The 2000 elections were also controversial due to voter confusion, as the elections moved from single-member districts to proportional representation. However, despite changes in voting districts and requirements, the biggest surprise of the 1998 elections was in voter participation. Voter turnout increased considerably, the Hong Kong Transition Project reported a 53 percent voter turnout overall with a 61.8 percent voter increase (from 1995) in direct election seats and a 13.5 percent increase for both the geographic and the functional seats.[25] While explanations for the dramatic increase in voter turnout are still being debated, the same polls indicate that 62 percent of those planning to vote were dissatisfied with the current chief executive, Tung Chee-hwa.[26]

Moreover, along with continued criticisms about the method for constituting LegCo, its relationship with Tung remains tense. For instance, although the Democratic Party, the Frontier Party, and the Citizens' Party hold a majority of the directly elected seats in LegCo, they are prevented from challenging bills presented by the chief executive. Thus any attempt to balance the two branches of government has been thwarted. This has led such leading prodemocracy LegCo members like Christine Loh to leave office[27] while others, like Emily Lau and Lee Cheuk-yan, also work outside the LegCo to press for a greater respect for human rights and democratic governance.[28] In addition, the resignation and early departure of Anson Chan, from the office of chief secretary, has raised questions about her relationship with Tung. Hong Kong newspapers noted that as Chief Secretary Chan's approval ratings remained high and Tung's fell, a strained relationship developed between the two.[29]

The erosion of the rule of law in Hong Kong has become a focal point of concern. Thus criticisms over political rights and participation have been coupled with questions about the status of an independent judiciary in Hong Kong. In this regard, critics have pointed out that civil and political rights are returning to colonial practices instead of moving forward and respecting global standards. Questions about the legitimacy of the rule of law and an independent judiciary are based on the premise that under the Basic Law, Hong Kong's courts have independent jurisdiction. However, judicial decisions made after July 1, 1997, indicate that mainland laws and policies take precedence over Hong Kong laws, rendering Hong Kong's Court of Final Appeals incapable of interpreting the Basic Law itself.[30] Instead, the court must defer any final interpretation to the Standing Committee of the National People's Congress.[31]

Probably the most controversial of these decisions was Tung Chee-hwa's request for the National People's Congress to reinterpret the Basic Law. The issue at hand was the residency of mainland immigrants in Hong Kong.[32] Hong Kong's Court of Final Appeals interpreted the Basic Law residency requirements liberally in January 1999, and this meant that more rather than fewer immigrants would be allowed to reside in Hong Kong. After this decision was made public, Tung announced that his community "would be overrun with approximately 1.67 million mainlanders,"[33] and he overruled the decision, turning to the NPC for a reinterpretation of the Basic Law. Not only was this a local issue that was brought to Beijing, but it then became an international issue when local advocates turned to, among others, the United Nations, sympathetic governments, and bar associations across Europe and the United States, arguing that Hong Kong's "rule of law" was in jeopardy. Critics of Tung's decision argued that Hong Kong would lose its local autonomy and would not be able to determine for itself the legitimacy of laws and government behavior.[34] Indeed, it seemed to call into question the entire "one country, two systems" model developed by Deng Xiaoping. While recent law reviews have argued that it is too soon to tell, they do conclude that this was a troublesome act on the part of Tung and the SAR government.

Besides political rights, civil liberties were also redefined after the handover. It is rare to see a socialist government reinstate laws developed by their colonial predecessors, but soon after the transfer, Tung Chee-hwa announced the publication of the "Civil Liberties and Social Order Consultation Document," in which Tung targeted three existing laws for reform: the Bill of Rights Ordinance (BORO) as well as amendments made to both the Societies Ordinance and the Public Order Ordinance. The 1992 amendments to the Societies Ordinance that were targeted included the provision banning any connections with foreign political groups and the development of a new system based on notification rather than the registration of organizations. Tung's document stated that the 1995 amendments to the Public Order Ordinance, which allowed a system of seven-day notification for public processions with the permission of the police commissioner, would be rescinded.[35] In addition, Tung declared that the law must be based on striking a balance between personal freedom and social stability. Hong Kong human rights advocates, however, have argued that the intent of this "recolonization" of Hong Kong is to limit political participation and dissent. The NGO community, in particular, has been vocal in bringing to light the dangers of these laws. In the last year, challenges to this position have come from university students, who have raised their concerns about the right to assemble without fear of persecution. Throughout 2000, students in Hong Kong held meetings, marches, and demonstrations demanding that the Public Order Ordinance be reformed in line with international human rights standards.

In regards to the BORO, the Hong Kong Human Rights Commission pointed out that the effort to return to colonial laws lacks legal basis because the Sino-British Joint Declaration confirms the application of the ICCPR to Hong Kong, and the SAR government provided no solid evidence that the BORO "contravenes" the Basic Law.[36] Furthermore, the Human Rights Commission asserted that the definition of political organization was too broad. In sections of the current definition, a political organization is defined as such if the body is directly involved in politics or gives assistance to candidates running for office.[37] This is distressing to NGOs, a vital part of whose work is to support or criticize candidates' platforms as they relate to their own social issues. If, however, this activity defines NGOs as political organizations, it will have larger ramifications. For instance, being designated a political group will trigger the application of the Societies Ordinance and the Public Order Ordinance, and will subsequently limit their activities.

Thus while in the 1980s and early 1990s Hong Kong was developing an independent civil society capable of challenging the government and providing alternative avenues of political participation, the posthandover period has witnessed political and civil rights come under attack.[38]

Localizing Economic and Social Rights in Hong Kong

While the British, Chinese, and Hong Kong elite took every measure to ensure both political and economic stability, Hong Kong experienced difficulties in both areas after the transfer. As mentioned earlier, the government is stable but there is considerable disagreement over the pace of democratizing Hong Kong's political institutions. More important, however, was the impact that globalization from above had on Hong Kong when the economic crisis of 1997 hit. Friedman points out that the crisis helped bring down the corrupt Suharto government in Indonesia. In Hong Kong it meant that the government chipped away at economic and social provisions that had been in place for years (just as Falk cautions). Historically, the institutionalization and implementation of social and economic rights did not fare much better than civil and political rights in colonial Hong Kong. Because of the colonial government's laissez-faire style of management, social welfare was privatized. The responsibility for these concerns fell to either the Chinese community or the churches, through organizations like the Kaifong Associations, the Tung Wah Group of Hospitals, and the Hong Kong Council of Social Services. It was not until Hong Kong industrialized that the government established the Department of Social Welfare to coordinate the welfare activities, through its divisions of social security, family services, group and community work, probation and corrections, and rehabilitation.[39] Just as with the ICCPR, Britain signed the ICESCR in 1976 with reservations for its application to Hong Kong concerning issues of the right to equal pay to men and women for equal work in the private sector and the right of trade unions to establish national federations in Hong Kong.[40]

Did the return to Chinese sovereignty generate a renewed interest in furthering economic and social rights? Labor, education, housing, and women and children's rights are examples of important social and economic rights internationally and are demanded by the people of Hong Kong. Despite China being a socialist government, however, these rights remain minimal. In particular, workers' rights are not fully recognized. For instance, laws to protect collective bargaining and anti-union discrimination put forward by LegCo member, Lee Cheuk-yan have been removed. The Labour Advisory Board concluded that these actions were taken "in the overall interest of the community and take into account Hong Kong's socio-economic development."[41] Moreover, Hong Kong's labor laws do not allow the formation of union federations and full union activity due to limits placed on them by the Societies Ordinance,[42] and current labor laws allow employers to dismiss workers without reason.[43] Because of the government's failure to protect workers' rights, groups like the Christian Industrial Committee and the umbrella trade union organization, the Confederation of Trade Unions (CTU), are organizing workers to apply pressure on the government to protect their rights. Labor activists now insist that workers cannot trust the SAR because it is working only on behalf of corporate interests.[44]

As mentioned above, the "Asian economic flu" hit workers hard. According to leading labor activists, Apo Leong and Elizabeth Tang, Hong Kong is now experiencing the "worst of both [socialist and capitalist] worlds."[45] Because the laws do not protect workers, they are the first ones to be laid off in times of economic trouble and receive no protection from the government. Coupled with the economic crisis is the use of the labor importation scheme (another feature of globalization from above). This scheme allows companies to bring in low-wage workers instead of hiring locals.[46] Generally the workers are Chinese from across the border. While Hong Kong's labor movement wants to collaborate with Chinese workers on the mainland to improve conditions for all workers, the SAR forbids organizing across the border. Hong Kong's labor movement wonders why workers should not and cannot extend solidarity (and promote globalization from below), to workers on the mainland, much like businessmen have been doing for years.[47] Women workers, in particular, face several challenges in enjoying their rights. The SAR continues the colonial practice of allowing workplace gender discrimination. To compound the situation, women are overwhelmingly relegated to low-pay service-sector jobs and are the first to be laid off during economic instability.[48] Thus, while the Chinese Communist Party asserts that rights to development, including such collective rights as the right to work, have priority, in practice they are not fully implemented in Hong Kong.

Another criticism put forward by local activists emerged in response to the government's proposal to "corporatize" the civil service. While most people in Hong Kong would agree that the civil service was bloated, especially in terms of the economic downturn, there was also a sense that the civil service was one of the primary mechanisms for creating movement into the middle-class. As a result, Tung Chee-hwa's proposals have been met with action by civil servants, and labor, human rights, and social activists in Hong Kong. In response, they organized marches to protest the "breaking of the iron rice bowl." In May 1999, for three weeks in a row, thousands of civil servants, with spouses, children, and friends, marched in solidarity to protest the government's reforms. This activity continued into 2000 with a flurry of protests stemming from a dissatisfaction with the performance of Tung Chee-hwa. Clay Chandler commented in an *International Herald Tribune* article that Hong Kong has moved "from 'city of light' to 'city of protest.' "[49]

While social organizations, like the Society for Community Organizing (SoCO), have long promoted economic and social rights in Hong Kong, only in recent years has the government taken greater steps in this area. For example, for the 1998 budget Tung Chee-hwa unveiled the SAR's plan for enhanced social services (in particular, a retirement scheme). While the total costs for social welfare (including retirement and healthcare) increased by about 13.6 percent over the previous budget, its implementation was questioned. Housing, however, has been one area to receive consistent support by the government. From the time of the Shek Kip Mei fire in 1955, the government instituted one of the world's largest public housing programs. So although Hong Kong remains one of the most expensive cities in the world, roughly half the population receives some sort of housing subsidy. An interesting note and possible explanation for the government role in housing is that as Hong Kong emerged as a newly industrialized economy and welcomed foreign direct investment from MNCs, wages remained low and the labor movement remained weak.

In addition to housing costs and availability, education and, particularly, the language of instruction have become controversial in Hong Kong. Although Hong Kong is officially bilingual, in December 1997, the Department of Education determined that 300 out of 400 schools would have to use Chinese as the sole language of instruction.[50] Public opinion seems to be split on the issue. Polls, conducted by the Hong Kong Transition Project, found that 41 percent of respondents believe that English is the most important language of instruction. The poll also found that 38 percent believe the language of instruction should be Cantonese, while only 8 percent believe it should be Mandarin.[51] It may be gleaned from these polls that Hong Kongers see their city as an international society, one in which both English and Chinese should be utilized. While the SAR is not neglecting social and economic rights, neither is it emphasizing them.

The Search for Solidarity and Globalization from Below

In Hong Kong, peoples rights have been neither legally recognized nor implemented, and only recently have found any sort of general support. From the time of acquisition, the colonial government focused on economic development, and consequently, the right to development did not appear to be a vital issue in relationship to other developing countries. NGOs, however, have stated that Hong Kong has a severe problem of unequal distribution of wealth. In fact, the World Bank consistently reports Hong Kong as having one of the largest gaps between the wealthiest 20 percent of the population and the poorest 20 percent. Social activists assert that the people have the right to be treated justly and equitably, and they point to the global market economy as the root problem.[52] In September 1997 the World Bank's annual meeting was held in Hong Kong. Hong Kong and regional NGOs demonstrated in front of the meeting site, calling for global solidarity against efforts by the World Bank and the International

Monetary Fund to further promote privatization of economies at the expense of social welfare issues. At the conclusion of their activities, five of the activists were arrested. Despite the silencing of protests, time and again grassroots groups continue to point to Hong Kong's prosperity as being available only to the wealthy.[53]

Efforts to link up ward have led Hong Kong's Human Rights Commission to present its documentation on human rights problems to the UN Human Rights Commission and at regional human rights forums. Chairman Ho Hei-wah has taken an outspoken position on acknowledging the human rights situation at home and abroad.[54] Other groups like labor organizations, the Confederation of Trade Unions, China Labour Rights, and the Asia Monitor Resource Center also work locally, regionally, and internationally on promoting workers' rights. Yet another example of local groups linking up with other organizations is the Committee on Asian Women, whose work centers on local migrant women's issues. But in recognition that MNCs are transnational, the committee has developed networks with other women's and workers' organizations regionally and internationally.

The expression of other peoples rights, such as a sustainable global environment, is growing. The colonial government minimally supported the environmental movement with the creation in the late 1980s of a public education and awareness program to help combat waste and water pollution, even though raw sewage continues to be dumped directly into Hong Kong's harbor.[55] Since the transition, Hong Kong environmental NGOs like Green Power and Friends of the Earth (HK) are reevaluating the local green movement. They have expressed deep concern over the SAR's ability to respond to the concerns of Hong Kongers. Friends of the Earth (HK) has drawn its conclusions from the results of the Daya Bay Nuclear Power Plan campaign, in which the NGO gathered more than 1 million signatures and presented them to the government, only to have its efforts disregarded.[56] Thus a new strategy for creating solidarity with the mainland is being implemented.[57] For instance, Friends of the Earth (HK), working in cooperation with the PRC's State Environmental Protection Agency, helped train cadres on the mainland about various environmental issues. They believe that this campaign will not only raise public awareness, but also help to mobilize people on the mainland and subsequently support the Hong Kong environmental movement.[58] Likewise, Green Power undertook a fundraising campaign to collect $500,000 HK (U.S. $65,000) to support its Hong Kong agenda of not only building trails but also promoting solidarity with the mainland.[59] Although the green movement is young and the SAR has taken only limited action to either recognize or implement these rights, it is clear that environmental concerns are growing human rights concerns.[60]

Finally, self-determination and local autonomy remain an issue in Hong Kong. The collective right of the Hong Kong people to determine their future was violated by the process, which led to the signing of the Sino-British Joint Declaration. This process did not involve or consult the people. It was a bilateral process between the governments of China and Great Britain. Once the negotiations were settled, the agreement was signed and the deal was set to transfer approximately 6 million people to a new government. Nowhere in this process were the people allowed to participate or to determine for themselves what should happen with their society. In the absence of the protection and implementation of the right to self-determination, the people grew anxious over the 1997 transition and their future under the SAR government.[61] This anxiety was accompanied by an increasing number of NGOs that joined forces (such as July 1 Link), to bring greater awareness to the transition.

The right to protect and preserve their identity and thus local autonomy is a peoples right of particular importance to many Hong Kongers. In recent polls, 72 percent of Hong Kongers (as opposed to 22 percent of Chinese) identified themselves as either Hong Kong Chinese or Hong Kong people.[62] Choi Po-king argues that the reversion to Chinese sovereignty doesn't guarantee "political decolonization" or "cultural decolonization."[63] Rather he argues that there is a danger of an effort to build a unified homogeneous Chinese national identity, and of protecting Chinese national needs and interests. Hong Kongers are worried that their identity will be consumed by the Han culture and *putonghua* language. Choi contends that on the mainland there is disdain for the influence of Britain and Western culture in Hong Kong. Cultural purists state that Hong Kong has been contaminated by the West and does not follow Confucian *zhengtong*—"the orthodox way"—which is now linked to antiforeignist nationalism.[64] Indeed Hong Kong has grown a distinct identity. Capitalism and political and societal isolation from the mainland have influenced it, but Hong Kongers still maintain such Chinese traditions as the importance of the family. This culture and identity is illustrated through Hong Kong's language, music, films, and lifestyle.[65] As discussed above, in response to the desire to preserve the Hong Kong identity, a movement has emerged to preserve Cantonese and English in the schools and the government. Thus Choi's answer is to use public education to maintain local autonomy and promote civil society.[66]

Conclusion

What does the Hong Kong case illustrate? The anxiety created over the issue of democratic reform and self-rule has contributed to heightened tensions between politicians, government officials, and local social forces. On the one hand, public opinion polls seem to confirm the perception that certain groups are progovernment and thus pro-China (e.g., groups represented by political parties like the Democratic Alliance for the Betterment of Hong Kong [DAB] and the Liberal Party).[67] It is doubtful, however, that their positions are based solely on cultural or nationalistic arguments. For instance, in general the progovernment groups have not supported strong workers' rights and have agreed with the SAR's reinstatement of colonial laws. On the other hand, groups, such as the Frontier Party and the Democratic Party have encouraged the rapid development of civil and political rights. Interestingly, the perception of these groups does not seem to be anti-China but rather pro-Hong Kong.

Yet an alternative group of local activists, including the Human Rights Commission, the Hong Kong Human Rights Monitor, the Hong Kong Christian Institute, and SoCO, makes the case for both civil and political as well as economic and social rights.[68] These social activists argue that all human rights as designated by the Universal Declaration of Human Rights, UN covenants, and regional statements should be promoted and protected. Moreover, they assert that any divisions between the Asian and Western human rights policies tend to be cloaks that governments use for not granting greater political and social rights.[69] Despite statements made by the Beijing and Hong Kong governments that express a respect for international human rights norms, there is evidence that human rights are not fully respected or implemented. This is the challenge for local social forces seeking a greater respect for human rights locally, regionally, and globally.

In this manner it becomes clear that the case of Hong Kong highlights the interest in promoting and implementing both local and global human rights norms. What may be most interesting is the role that local social forces are playing in the promotion of human rights in terms of globalization from below. Additionally, this case highlights the need to incorporate both global and local considerations into any assessment of globalization and human rights. While globalization is not a new phenomenon for Hong Kong, it has facilitated the critique of human rights and democratic processes. Indeed, globalization has been a two-way street for human rights. The integration of local and global human rights issues has given local social forces a platform for pressing for a greater respect for all human rights in their society. Finally, it may be concluded that Hong Kong has been the location of an active network of local social forces (or citizen-based groups) promoting human rights locally, regionally, and internationally. In sum, this case demonstrates that the conventional wisdom about globalization needs to be broadened in order to include local actions and considerations of the processes that integrate the global and the local.

Notes

1. Ian Clark, *Globalization and International Relations Theory* (Cambridge: Oxford University Press, 1999), p. 2.

2. Thomas Friedman, "Dueling Globalizations," *Foreign Policy* (Fall 1999), http://web4.infortrac.galegroup.com/ . . . 560A56750484?swaep' stcloudmain (accessed January 15, 2001).

3. See, for instance, Richard Falk, *On Humane Governance: Toward a New Global Politics* (University Park: Pennsylvania State University Press, 1995); and Richard Falk, "Taking Human Rights Seriously at Home," *Political Quarterly,* 68, no. 2 (April–June 1997), 179.

4. See, for instance, Robert Cox, "Civil Society at the Turn of the Millennium: Prospects for an Alternative World Order," *Review of International Studies, 25* (1999), 3–28.

5. See, for instance, David Forsythe, *Internationalization of Human Rights* (Lexington, MA: Lexington Books, 1991); Jack Donnelly, *Universal Human Rights in Theory and Practice* (Ithaca, NY: Cornell University Press, 1989); and Louis Henkin, *The Age of Rights* (New York: Columbia University Press, 1996). Also of interest is William Korey, *NGOs and the Universal Declaration of Human Rights: A Curious Grapevine* (New York: St. Martin's Press, 1998).

6. Andre Gunder Frank's work presents an interesting analysis of the Asia-centered world. See A.G. Frank, *ReOrient: Global Economy in the Asian Age* (Berkeley: University of California Press, 1998).

7. For survey results, see the Hong Kong Transition Project website, http://www.hkbu.edu.hk.

8. See Linda Butenhoff, *Social Movements and Political Reform in Hong Kong* (Westport, CT: Praeger Press, 1999).

9. The process of "corporatizing" the civil service emerged as a response to the overbureaucratization of Hong Kong's administrative staff. Critics of the civil service argued that especially in economic turmoil, no one sector of the economy should enjoy special privileges. As a result, the government has been outsourcing various departments of the civil service. In 1999, the process began with the Departments of Housing and Water. Currently, the government is proposing to "corporatize" the Survey and Mapping Office of the Department of Lands. See Hong Kong, Special Administrative Region of the People's Republic of China, "Hong Kong Government Information Office," www.infor.gov.hk/gia/general/200006/05/06053223.htm (accessed June 2000).

10. See Hong Kong Voice of Democracy, "SAR Government Will Monitor

Falun Gong, Tung Said," www.democracy.org.hk//2001/feb/hr_04.htm (accessed February 6, 2001).

11. "UN Rights Commission in Hong Kong," http://news.bbc.co.uk/hi/english/world.pacific/newsid 1155000/1155056.st (accessed February 6, 2001).

12. See Maurice Cranston, *What Are Human Rights?* (London: Bodley Head, 1973); and Hugo Bedau, "Human Rights and Foreign Assistance Programs," in Peter Brown and Douglas MacLean, eds., *Human Rights and U.S. Foreign Policy* (Lexington, MA: Lexington Books, 1979).

13. It is believed that China and Britain made an agreement when the Chinese Communist Party came to power in 1949 that would keep Hong Kong a colony until the mainland was ready for its return.

14. Nihal Jayawickrama, "Hong Kong and the International Protection of Human Rights," in Raymond Wacks, ed., *Human Rights in Hong Kong* (Hong Kong: Oxford University Press, 1992), pp. 129–131.

15. See Butenhoff, *Social Movements.*

16. The district boards are Hong Kong's system of local representation. Their primary responsibility is to maintain the sanitation, recreation, and other local systems in Hong Kong.

17. *Green Paper: The Further Development of Representative Government in Hong Kong* (Hong Kong: Government Printer, 1984).

18. This point has been widely disputed, by the public opinion polls published in the local newspapers, which showed that there was considerable support for direct elections in 1988.

19. See Peter Wesley-Smith, "Protecting Human Rights in Hong Kong," in Wacks, *Human Rights in Hong Kong,* pp. 17–21.

20. Author interview with Tso Man-king, secretary-general of the Hong Kong Christian Council, summer 1994.

21. For instance, this is the position of the Hong Kong Human Rights Commission.

22. Author interview with Rev. Kwok, Hong Kong Christian Institute, May-June 1999.

23. Hong Kong Special Administrative Region of the People's Republic of China, Government Information Services website. www.hkinfo.gov.hk (accessed March 5, 1998).

24. See Angela Li, "Reduce Expectations for Functional Seats, Says Exco Man," *South China Morning Post,* January 6, 1998.

25. Hong Kong Transition Project, "Polarization: Election Politics and the Politicizing of Hong Kong," September 2000, www.hkbu.edu.hk/hktp, p. 72.

26. Ibid., tabs. 23, 25.

27. In public statements, Christine Loh expressed frustration with the government's failure to expand participatory politics. See *South China Morning Post,* April 12, 2000.

28. For a list of non-LegCo activities, see Frontier's website, www.frontier.org.hk.

29. Anson Chan's departure from the office of chief secretary raised some eyebrows. Several *South China Morning Post* articles in January 2001 speculated about the real reasons behind her early departure. They concluded that there may

have been tension between her and Tung. Chan's approval ratings have been consistently higher than Tung's for several years.

30. Cliff Buddle, "Two Systems in Peril Warns Judge," *South China Morning Post,* March 7, 1998.

31. See Hong Kong Human Rights Monitor, "Response to the Judgement of the Legality of the Provisional Legislative Council," July 30, 1997, Hong Kong Human Rights Monitor website http//www.freeway.org.hk/hkhrm (accessed February 22, 1998).

32. Author interview with academics and NGO leaders, Hong Kong, May-June 1999.

33. Author interview with Kwok Nai Wang, Hong Kong Christian Institute, June 1999.

34. See, for instance, Mark Elliott and Christopher Forsyth, "The Rule of Law in Hong Kong: Immigrant Children, the Court of Final Appeal, and the Standing Committee of the National People's Congress," *Asia Pacific Law Review* 8, no. 1 (2000), 53–75.

35. See Hong Kong Special Administrative Region of the People's Republic of China, "Civil Liberties and Social Order Document," February 1997, www.ceoffice.org.hk/press/ip970401.html (accessed March 13, 1998).

36. Hong Kong Human Rights Commission, "Commentary on Civil Liberties and Social Order Document," April 1997, www.hk.super.net/hkhrc/ (accessed February 22, 1998).

37. See Hong Kong Human Rights Monitor website, www.freeway.org.hk/hkhrm (accessed February 2, 1998).

38. See, for instance, reports in the *South China Morning Post.* Linda Choy and Andrea Li, "Ex-President Yang Avoids Protest," *South China Morning Post,* January 6, 1998, and May Sin-Mi Hon, "Activists Charged with Twenty-four Offences," *South China Morning Post,* November 12, 1997.

39. See *Social Welfare in Hong Kong* (Hong Kong: Government Printer, 1995).

40. Jayawickrama, "Hong Kong," pp. 139–141.

41. Sharon Cheung, "Exco Decides to Scrap Two out of Five Pre-Handover Labour Laws," *South China Morning Post,* October 1, 1997.

42. Elizabeth Tang and Apo Leong, "The Worst of Both Worlds: 1997 and the Hong Kong Labour Movement," *Asian Labour Update,* n. 24 (April–June 1997), 29.

43. Hong Kong Human Rights Commission, "Human Rights Now and Beyond 1997, Hong Kong: A Self-Published Report," pp. 10–12.

44. Tang and Leong, "Worst of Both Worlds."

45. Ibid.

46. Ibid., p. 28.

47. Ibid., p. 31.

48. Rose Wu, "1997 and the Destiny of Hong Kong People," 10.

49. Clay Chandler, "From 'City of Light' to 'City of Protest': Hong Kong's Middle Class Takes Its Argument to the Streets," *International Herald Tribune,* June 29, 2000, p. 7.

50. See Hong Kong Professional Teachers' Union, "Mother Tongue Education," www.hkptu.orc.hk (accessed March 5, 1998).

51. Hong Kong Transition Project, "Tomorrow Has Not Died," http://hkbu.edu.hk/hktp (accessed March 8, 1998).

52. See, for instance, the annual and special reports produced by SoCO and the Confederation of Trade Unions.

53. "Solidarity Against the World Bank/IMF!" *Asian Labour Update*, no. 25 (July-September 1997), 24.

54. See, for instance, Hong Kong Voice of Democracy, "HK Human Rights Group Said Government Official Creating White Terror," www.democracy.org.hk (accessed February 5, 2001).

55. Cecilia Chan and Peter Hills, *Limited Gains: Grassroots Mobilization and the Environment in Hong Kong* (Hong Kong: Centre of Urban Planning and Environmental Management, 1993), pp. 38–39.

56. Man Si-wai, "The Environment: A Cause Which Cuts Both Ways," in Romaniuk and Tong, 51.

57. See, for instance, the Friends of the Earth (HK) website, www.foe.org.hk..

58. Friends of the Earth (HK), "China Cadres Learn from FOE (HK)," *News, FOE Newsletter,* February 1998, www.foe.org.hk (accessed March 5, 1998).

59. Green Power, "Mission Statement," www.hk.linkage.net/green power (accessed March 5, 1998).

60. For instance, both the Chinese University of Hong Kong and Hong Kong University have active student groups. The students are replanting trees and rice paddies in the rural areas and are involved in public awareness campaigns to clean up the harbor and keep Hong Kong clean.

61. See Kwok Nai Wang, *Human Rights in Hong Kong* (Hong Kong: Swedish Mission Annual Report, 1990), p. 1.

62. Hong Kong Transition Project, September 2000, www.hkbu.edu/hktp (accessed December, 2000).

63. Choi Po-king, "1997 and Decolonization," in Romaniuk and Tong, p. 28.

64. See Paul C.K. Kwong, "Internationalization of Population and Globalization of Families," in Choi Po-king and Ho Lok-sang, eds., *The Other Hong Kong Report, 1993* (Hong Kong: The Chinese University Press, 1993).

65. Choi, "1997 and Decolonization," p. 29. Hong Kong's Canto Pop music and Jackie Chan films, along with Hong Kong's unique version of Cantonese, should be familiar to many.

66. Ibid., pp. 31–32.

67. Hong Kong Transition Project, September 2000, www.hkbu.edu.hk/~hktp, Tab. 122, 69–70.

68. Anxiety over these concerns has been manifested in NGOs taking a more cautious approach to their political activities. SoCO has made it clear that its mission is community development and not political development per se.

69. Author interview with Tso Man-king, summer 1994.

Part III

Setting the Terms of Debate
Pursuing Global Consensus

9

The Challenges to International Human Rights

Joanne Bauer

A commonly held notion among Western liberals is that Asian, African, and Arab perspectives on human rights are the greatest challenge to universality—the implication being that once the international human rights community reckons with the countries of these outlier regions, it will have eliminated the obstacle to universal human rights. This idea is mistaken. It ignores both the fact that even within the West, particularly in the United States, there are significant numbers of people who hold ideas of human rights that are in tension with the dominant liberal interpretation of international human rights, and the fact that within Asia, Africa, and the Arab world there are strong traditions that are consistent with it.

Sweeping characterizations of regions or civilizations have been widely discredited since Samuel Huntington's publication of *The Clash of Civilizations.*[1] The analysis has been accompanied by an "us" versus "them" rhetoric that reflects an unconscious but persistent failure to acknowledge that regions consist of diverse cultures and that all societies bear multiple and conflicting ethical perspectives. Careful observers know that any reference to an "Asian" perspective, for example, signals an ideological purpose: namely cultural nationalism, and likely a defensive reaction to Western pressure. To equate a region or society's human rights perspective with cultural nationalism is to neglect the efforts of many brave, highly committed people around the world struggling to promote support for human rights and take a stand against abuses in the settings they call home.

In this chapter I argue that conflicts over the meaning of human rights and the priority to accord to them occur within as well as across regions, reflecting their diversity. There is not only a need but also a basis, therefore, for resisting the temptation to view conflicts as occurring primarily across North-South or East-West lines. I begin by presenting a typology of the major ideological challenges to international human rights, drawing upon the work of Rhoda Howard, to support the point that the challenges are emanating from all parts of the globe, including the West. The empirical part of this chapter is devoted to a consideration of the human rights debates within three non-Western regions—Asia, the Arab world, and Africa—and in the United States. In all four settings I contrast the caricaturized version of the debates, which emanates from cultural nationalist agendas, with the debates among local activists and intellectuals. Two observations emerge: first, that genuine disagreement takes place not so much over human rights principles, but in their implementation and prioritization; and second, that Western human rights scholars must take their cue from scholars and activists in other parts of the world and shift their focus from a preoccupation with cultural relativism to the project of cultural legitimation.

Who Is Challenging "International Human Rights"?

Typically the scholarly debate over human rights is thought to take place between two opposing camps: the universalists and the cultural relativists. The universalists build their understanding of human rights upon the liberal tradition whereby rights are accorded to the individual by virtue of being human. Cultural relativists, on the other hand, argue that values are grounded in specific communities and that the communal group, not the individual, is the basic social unit. In reality, however, the ideological spectrum is much more complex; realizing that complexity can help point us to where the challenges to international human rights actually lie.

In *Human Rights and the Search for Community,* Rhoda Howard describes five contemporary ideological challenges to human rights.[2] Notably, each of these views is put forward within the North as well the South. "Radical capitalism," a view held by Western liberals, dismisses social and economic human rights as irrelevant and idealistic. To Howard, this view represents a "capitalist culture's rejection of economic rights" and confinement of rights to property rights and "the civil and political rights needed to carry out one's own affairs in peace."[3] The behavioral manifestation of radical capitalism, according to Howard, is "social minimalism": the belief in economic freedom without a corresponding recognition of the duty to assist those in need. The fact that social minimalism is so prevalent in the United States, a predominantly Christian society, underscores the fallacy of trying to characterize contemporary societies by their philosophical or religious roots. Clearly the conduct of American political life is not guided strictly by the principles of the "good Samaritan" or "do unto others," and often stands in contradiction to them.

The four other challenges to human rights that Howard identifies all overlap with what in the West is called "communitarianism." "Traditionalism" is adherence to the notion that international human rights conflict with traditional rules for orderly social behavior, and that within the confines of the group, the society protects the human rights of its members. It is this challenge that is usually presented under the guise of a distinctively "Asian," "African," or "Arab" perspective of human rights. "Reactionary conservatism" holds that the "excesses of contemporary freedom," such as women's liberation, homosexual rights, and so forth—in other words "excessive individualism"—are antithetical to social order. This view was inherent in the "Asian values" argument promoted by some Asian officials in the mid-1990s challenging the applicability of international human rights to Asia. It is also present in the West, where the argument resonated among large pockets of the population.

Howard's fourth category, "left collectivism," is a reaction against the West. Left collectivism holds that national self-determination and relief from Western imperialism and multinational corporations are the most important human rights. Adherents in the West can be found among ethno-religious minorities. Howard's final category is "status radicalism." Like the politics of identity, status radicalism is the belief that since rights are systematically denied to certain groups, one's group status and protection of that group's rights are more important than the protection of their individual rights. Many feminists and black activists in the Western world put forth this argument, demonstrating the failure of these societies "to incorporate all social groups in North America's heterogeneous environment."[4] Here again the rejection of the liberal human rights philosophy is not strictly a "third-world" perspective.

Missing from Howard's typology is religious fundamentalism, which while close to traditionalism, cannot be viewed as the same. Generally speaking, religious fundamentalism in its varied Islamic, Christian, and Jewish forms takes the notion of local norms much further than Howard's traditionalism does in that adherents believe that human rights are ordained by God alone. They recognize only the codification of those norms within the religious laws of Sharia, the Bible, and the Torah and dismiss other public, local, and international law, including international human rights. Howard's typology also does not specify the often heard critique of human rights that they conflict with societies and cultures—including many non-fundamentalist religious cultures—that place a greater emphasis on duties and obligations over rights and challenge the notion of equality, although this argument can be accommodated within traditionalism.

This typology helps us to see that challenges to international human rights principles are not isolated to particular regions; rather human rights have multiple and shifting meanings and their contestation appears to be universal. This observation weakens the notion that there can be one or two or three outlier countries or regions that stand in the way of universal human rights, and underscores the need for analysis that is locally situated, historical, and comparative. The rest of this chapter is devoted to an examination of rights discourses in both the non-West and the West in an effort to gain a better understanding of where genuine differences may lie.

Regional Perspectives of Human Rights

While there is no one Asian, African, Arab, or American perspective on human rights, it is possible to identify two broad types of perspectives within a given society: those wrapped up in cultural nationalism, which are often tied to and manipulated by the government; and what one might call the "activist-intellectual" perspective. The cultural nationalist perspective is easy to know: it can be found in government propaganda and policy statements aimed at both local and international audiences. The activist-intellectual perspective in many of these societies is less accessible, particularly since the people asking questions about and debating rights, governance, and social justice—intellectuals who tend to be also deeply involved in the activities of nongovernmental organizations (NGOs)—often must do so within a climate of repression.

But even in the case of politically open societies, such as the United States, the human rights perspectives of the many groups extending the liberal interpretation of human rights remain little known simply because they cannot command the attention of the mainstream media. For example, very few Americans are aware of the efforts of people like Clarice Friloux of Louisiana, Richard Murphy of North Carolina, Ramona Ortega of New York City, Cheri Honkala of Philadelphia, and Loretta Ross of Atlanta, Georgia, who are leading movements to fight for the recognition of economic and social rights—relating to the right to health, the right to a clean environment, the right to housing, and welfare rights—in the United States.[5]

Non-Western perspectives on human rights are being heavily shaped today by several overlapping trends: globalization, secularization, urbanization, and a resulting breaking down of community. These trends are also having their effect in the West. A major distinction between the discourses in the West and in the non-West is that in the non-West the social and economic dislocation resulting from globalization is coupled with another effect of globalization: exposure to the idea of human rights. The result has been a greater emphasis on economic and social rights in the South. A salient exception to this phenomenon is Latin America, where the human rights struggle has since its inception in the early 1970s been identified with the denunciation of violations and the defense of victims of authoritarian military dictatorships. Today, with so-called democratic consolidation in the region and the gross economic inequality and poverty that pervades, there is an active debate among human rights activists in these countries over whether to continue to prioritize civil and political rights or to move toward a new agenda that would include a much broader spectrum of rights.[6]

Activist-intellectuals from outside the West concerned with human rights in their societies tend to focus their energies in two areas: first, to look within their cultures for values and practices that resonate with the current human rights regime; and second, to attempt to enrich the current international rights regimes with values and practices from their cultures that may also resonate with Western ideas, but are not currently part of the international rights regime. The palavar political system of communal Africa, where the chiefs routinely consulted elders, as an argument for the right to political participation, is an example of the former; and promoting Confucian ideas about respect for the elderly, a notion that cannot be found in the existing UN international human rights documents, is an example of the latter.

A new attribute of the regional discourses among activist-intellectuals is that they have become integrated into a global discourse that includes the West. There are several recent examples of cross-cultural dialogues in Asia, spurred on by the Asian values debate (discussed below), most initiated by Western scholars.[7] Not only have the ideas generated from these dialogues begun to influence human rights debates locally, but they have also prompted serious reflection on the part of Western participants and observers about the validity of their own claims.[8]

Absent a catalyst like the Asian values argument, there has not been an engagement between Western and non-Western academics in Africa or the Middle East with the intensity of that between Westerners and Asians. But there has been a mixing of ideas of human rights through other means. Most notably, the major UN human rights conferences that began in the 1990s—Rio (environment), Vienna (human rights), Cairo (population), Copenhagen (social exclusion), Beijing (women's rights), Istanbul (human settlements), and Durban (racism)—have brought increasing opportunities for the integration of regional discourses with global discourses.

In what follows, I provide overviews of the contemporary human rights debates within four regions–Asia, the Arab world, Africa, and the United States—contrasting the cultural nationalist perspective with the intellectual perspective.[9]

Asia

The cultural nationalist perspective most closely associated with Asia can be found in the Asian values debate of the early to middle 1990s, which was sparked principally by the provocative writings and speeches of Singaporean senior minister Lee Kuan Yew and other senior Singaporean officials.[10] The thrust of the Asian values argument is that Asia can provide a countermodel to the "American model" or way of life, which has been overrun by civil society, shattered by excessive individualism, and has left the United States ridden with violent crime, drugs, guns, vagrancy, and immoral behavior. The countermodel, which relies on the strong hand of the wise and benevolent patriarch, can succeed by instilling respect for "Asian values"—obedience, thrift, industriousness, respect for elders and authority, an emphasis on family, and restraint of immediate gratification. Underlying all this is the claim that Asians prioritize economic and social rights over civil and political rights, the community over the individual, and social order and stability over democracy and individual freedom. It is important to note that these values are not so much "Asian" as they are those most often identified with Confucianism, which leaves out Asian countries throughout South Asia and parts of Southeast Asia without a Confucian past.[11] In this sense "Asian values" is a misnomer.

While maintaining the "traditionalist" position on human rights, Asian governments have come to see engaging in the international debate on human rights as a way of warding off Western influence. As Chinese legal scholar Xin Chunying explains in the case of China:

> Compared to Western societies, China places much less emphasis on individual rights and significantly more emphasis on the value of the individual in terms of his or her contribution to harmony in society. In fact, there is a strong reaction against the younger generation which thinks more about their "selfish" rights than the good of society. This is deeply rooted in Chinese culture. But today, in contrast to the past, human rights is not perceived as a threat to China's cultural identity. Rather, engaging in the international

human rights discourse is seen as a way of resisting foreign influence and keeping Chinese culture distinct.[12]

The Asian values rhetoric can thus be seen as a manifestation of this desire on the part of Asian governments to engage the international community in a debate on human rights while attempting to enjoin their people in an affirmation of the cultural nationalist perspective.

The primary target of Lee and his Singaporean colleagues was his home audience, and to some extent Western audiences. Yet his remarks were well received throughout Asia, notably even in the democratic (and non-Confucian) Philippines, where Lee gave a major speech on the subject. But many Asian activist-intellectuals remained unconvinced. For example, Japanese political philosopher Tatsuo Inoue argued that Asian values are an extension of Orientalism or what he terms "Asian Orientalism."[13] And as Singapore legal scholar Kevin Y. L. Tan noted at the height of the Asian values debate, "Asians appear to be speaking from a position of strength—strength drawn not from the merits of intellectual arguments but from their economic success."[14] The financial crisis that struck many of the East and Southeast Asian economies in the late 1990s put a hole in the argument that Asian economic success is due to the stability of the authoritarian and neoauthoritarian governments. But the unexpected recovery of the region just a few years later allowed the Asian values argument to regain some momentum.

Among Asian activist-intellectuals and human rights activists, two perspectives of human rights stand out. The first perspective is found in the NGO statement during the Bangkok regional preparatory conference leading up to the 1993 UN Conference on Human Rights in Vienna, which supports the universality and indivisibility of human rights: "We affirm our commitment to the principle of indivisibility and interdependence of human rights, be they economic, social and cultural, or civil and political rights. There must be a holistic and integrated approach to human rights. One set of rights cannot be used to bargain for another."[15] Support for the indivisibility of rights can also be found in the Bangkok Declaration, the statement crafted by Asian government officials at the conference, although it was not picked up within the official rhetoric once conference representatives returned home and received little attention within the ensuing "Asian values" debate.[16]

The second perspective put forth by Asian NGOs is that the Asian values argument should not be dismissed as cultural relativism, but rather that it is important to remain open to the possibility that justifications for human rights can be found in local traditions.[17] The project of cultural legitimation has been a primary endeavor of Asian activist-intellectuals in recent years, at times carried out together with their Western counterparts. An example is the work of the Malaysian women's group Sisters in Islam. This group advocates for the right of women to hold public office, protection of women from domestic violence, and other campaigns for women's rights that rely chiefly upon the technique of locating the justification for those rights in the Quran.[18]

The Arab World

Among the common misperceptions of the Middle East is that Islam is the only factor in the attitudes one finds toward human rights. The impression is fed by the manipulation of Islam by conservatives, who invoke Islam in denying the applicability of international human rights, much the same way the proponents of Asian values use Confucianism. As Ann Elizabeth Mayer writes, "The precepts of Islam, like those of Christianity, Hinduism, Judaism, and other major religions possessed of long and complex traditions, are susceptible to interpretations that can and do create conflicts between religious doctrine and human rights principles or that reconcile the two."[19]

A significant difference between the use of Islam in Arab rights discourses and the use of Confucianism in Asia is that whereas principally the governments of East Asia have used Confucianism in defense of their derogation of rights, in the Middle East and other parts of the Islamic world (including Southeast Asia, as seen in the example above) the NGO community invokes Islam in protesting repression by regimes. In fact, the debate over human rights within the Arab world is, in the most basic sense, between reformists (be they Islamists or secularists) and conservatives.

The discourse among Muslims in the Middle East can be summarized as follows. Globalization has revitalized cultural identity, but it has also helped the spread of ideas and information about other religious and cultural traditions. Overall, Muslims are concerned about losing their ability to control their own economies, their position in world power, and perhaps most importantly, their cultural assets. With respect to this set of issues, there are three identifiable perspectives: to Muslim conservatives, individual rights are immaterial to social justice; to Muslim liberals, the Muslim world must adjust to universal standards of human rights, an adjustment that requires a transformation in Islamic thinking; and to Muslim reformers, the revolution in information and communications technology, along with higher incomes and educational opportunities, offers new standards against which to assess progress toward the realization of human rights ideals.[20]

Contrary to popular belief, with a few exceptions, such as Afghanistan

and Saudi Arabia, modern Muslim politics has generally acquired a pragmatic dimension, and radical Islam has been relegated to the fringes of
Muslim societies.[21] Current reformist thinking in the Muslim world focuses
on tolerance, civil society, minority rights, women's rights, cultural identity, and social welfare. Women's struggles for freedom in the Middle East
have turned them into agents of modernization and globalization. Many
reform-minded women in Iran take their lines from the transnational
women's rights movement.

While the preceding discussion emphasizes the perspectives and dynamics among Muslims, it is important to note that Islam does not characterize
the entire Arab world. In Egypt, Syria, Lebanon, and Iraq, for example,
there are strong Christian populations, and in many cases it is the Christians
who are at the forefront of the local human rights movement.

Compared to Asia, there appears to be greater popular pressure on the
governments of the Middle East to change. Unlike in East Asia, where
economic success is closely correlated with a fairly equitable distribution
of educational and income opportunities, in the Middle East, failed economies and the rising gap between the rich and the poor have swelled the
ranks of the discontented. In particular, a growing middle class are demanding better jobs, housing, educational opportunities, political pluralism,
transparency, and accountability, especially in the context of a globalizing
world. Whereas Asians attribute their economic success to stable governments, in most Arab countries such stability today is hardly defined in
these terms; rather, people tend to speak of a crisis of governance. The
lack of consensus on modernization and social change in the Arab world
has resulted in a "cultural politics" that reflects an ongoing internal struggle
over who defines cultural meanings, symbols, and ideas.

Africa

The social and political concerns of Africans are shaped mainly by the
legacy of colonialism and postcolonial instability together with the severe
socioeconomic conditions the continent faces: staggering international debt,
the highest number of refugees in the world, widespread starvation, and
severe resource depletion. Despite this situation, the local African debate
on human rights today is not as active as either the Asian or Middle Eastern
debates. This is likely attributable to the fact that there are relatively few
locally based human rights NGOs in Africa. With the exception of a very
small number of activist organizations, most African NGOs are either
church-based or law-oriented, such as legal aid groups or bar associations.[22]

Foreign scholars of Africa and international human rights groups, therefore, generate much of the human rights activity and debate that takes place in Africa today. The few indigenous human rights groups that do exist, which are for the most part not membership-based organizations, are stigmatized within Africa as "elitist" and "out of touch." African social justice advocates, in particular, criticize them for their dependency on foreign funds and for having stronger ties with the international elite than with the common African people they claim to serve.

This critique has fueled the perception among Africans of the human rights regime as not just Western-inspired, but as something foreign and even imperialist. The support that Western powers gave over the years to Africa's dictators—perpetuators of massive violations of human rights—has raised suspicions about the intent of Western governments and NGOs in advocating for human rights. Some observers see the crisis of local legitimacy of the international human rights movement in Africa as stemming from its failure to build coalitions with the local human rights movement, thereby rendering the international movement (also known as "secondary activism") vulnerable to being hijacked by other political agendas.[23] The fact that in the 1990s the international human rights community was ineffective in stopping the genocide in Rwanda further discredited human rights in the region. But perhaps the greatest failing of the international human rights community, according to some Africans, is not exposing the human rights abuses of the imperialist system that Africa has long been subject to, and not promoting Africa's main human rights problem: the violation of the right to self-determination. It is this failing that has brought the human rights movement to the point of near irrelevance, according to a number of African critiques.[24]

Most recently, some scholars have argued that there was in Africa's past a vibrant rights discourse that has been lost in the contemporary debate on human rights, which if drawn upon can become the basis for a renewal of a genuinely local debate on human rights.[25] They point out that as early as the 1960s, when most African countries became independent, African leaders and activist-intellectuals from Nyerere of Tanzania to Nkrumah of Ghana were involved in a continentwide discussion about how to best guarantee human rights in their respective postcolonial states. In 1981, well before the Asian values debate gained currency in the West, the Organization of African Unity adopted the African Charter for Human and Peoples' Rights, which emphasized economic, social, and cultural rights, the rights of people to self-determination, and the right to existence, equality, and nondomination. According to human rights historian Bonny Ibhawoh, "At a time when the rest of the world was more concerned about civil and political rights, the African charter reflected the human rights concern about equality and non-domination of most Africans."[26]

To the extent that there remains a local debate about the possibilities of human rights, its characteristics are remarkably similar to those of the Asian values debate in several respects. Cultural nationalists arguing against the applicability of international human rights for Africa claim that the notion of the individual, upon which human rights rest, does not exist in Africa. Instead the individual's worth can only be found in the context of the community. Here again, primacy is placed on the communal nature of rights and social harmony, with an emphasis on duties and obligations over rights. Standing opposite the proponents of those claims are activist-intellectuals, such as Ibhawoh, Abdullahi An-Na'im, and Makau wa Mutua, who are seeking to identify a foundation for the legitimation of universal human rights in the African context and to inform the cross-fertilization of ideas between Africa and the rest of the world. A third prevalent argument made by some Africa scholars is that human rights in the West developed over a long period of struggle for democracy and that Africa has yet to go through these stages.

Also in Africa, as in other Southern Hemisphere contexts, the claim that economic and social rights should take priority over civil and political rights is prevalent. Yet, while many African activist-intellectuals hold the position that the two sets of rights are equally important, they tend not to dispute the claim as forcefully as their counterparts in other regions do. This attitude reflects the long-standing Marxist approach that still has many adherents in Africa today.

The United States

The split between the cultural nationalist perspective and the intellectual perspective of human rights is also found in the United States. The American rights debate centers around four main issues: what priority to accord economic, social, and cultural rights; the applicability of international human rights law to the United States; when, if ever, to use capital punishment; and most recently, whether there is justification for curtailing civil liberties in the interests of national security.

In one of his many recent writings on the human rights movement, Michael Ignatieff reminds his readers that the American vernacular of justice—civil liberties, civil rights, labor rights—is not the international language of human rights.[27] The fact that Americans and the international human rights movement based in the West have long equated human rights with civil liberties is precisely the cause of so much resistance to "international human rights" throughout the world. And when human rights advocates in the West rebuffed genuine efforts to promote a more expansive notion of rights, they only fueled this sentiment. Such was the response southern NGOs in Asia and elsewhere faced in the early 1990s when in the wake of the end of the Cold War they sought to fight the historical tendency—particularly strong in the United States—to delink civil and political from economic, social, and cultural rights. At that time, then–executive director of Human Rights Watch Aryeh Neier reportedly pointed out that "human rights activists in a number of Third World countries, especially Asia, have long held the view that both kinds of concerns are rights. Their argument has not proved persuasive in the West, however, and none of the leading international nongovernmental groups concerned with human rights has become an advocate of economic and social rights."[28] Much has changed in the last decade, however. Both Amnesty International and Human Rights Watch, the world's first and second largest human rights organizations headquartered in London and New York, respectively, have put major effort into thinking through and developing an effective strategy for championing economic, social, and cultural rights.[29] In addition, in the 1990s a new organization, the Center for Economic and Social Rights, which also houses the International Network for Economic, Social, and Cultural Rights, was established in New York, devoted entirely to promoting these so-called second-generation rights.

Americans are accustomed to thinking of human rights as a foreign policy issue, not as a matter of domestic concern. A minority group of left-leaning activists and intellectuals have long been pushing for the recognition of a broad range of rights for Americans, not only civil and political but also, increasingly, economic and social rights. Yet as in other domains of international affairs, American cultural nationalists resist the notion that international human rights rules should apply to the United States. The latter view appears to have won out in Washington, where the Senate has ratified few international laws and, most notoriously, has not ratified the Convention on the Rights of the Child—the most widely and rapidly ratified human rights treaty in history, with 191 participating nations—making the United States the only country not to do so.[30] Together with the efforts to reduce greenhouse gas emissions, the area in which American exceptionalism has most infuriated the international community has been in its refusal to support the International Criminal Court.[31]

One treaty upon which there has been recent action in the U.S. Congress is the Convention on the Elimination of All Forms of Discrimination Against Women, or CEDAW.[32] The debate on ratification of this treaty has touched a nerve among conservatives not unlike the reaction that has been taking place to the treaty in societies throughout the developing world. They have attacked the treaty, which the United States was instrumental in drafting and which President Carter signed in 1980, as "the work of international forces promoting abortion rights, sexual freedom, and promiscuity, while undermining motherhood" and "one more attempt to impose global norms on the U.S."[33] To date, the United States is the only industrialized nation that has not ratified the convention.

Another area of significant controversy is the use of the death penalty in the United States. Protests against the death penalty have been taking place since the U.S. Supreme Court reinstated capital punishment in 1976, after overturning the death penalty in 1972. In 1985, the Council of Europe adopted Protocol 6, which outlawed the death penalty during peacetime; in 1994 ratification of Protocol 6 was made a precondition for EU membership. In recent years activists have used the tactic of shaming the United States by drawing attention to the company it keeps in its liberal use of the death penalty. In 2001 the United States, along with China, Iran, and Saudi Arabia, accounted for 90 percent of the world's executions.[34] The United States has the dubious distinction of being the only developed country that still has and actively imposes the death penalty.[35]

The American perspective on human rights priorities is also becoming remarkably similar to that of nations the United States and the international human rights movement have long targeted in the arena of curtailing civil rights for the sake of national security. Such is the domestic fallout of the Bush administration's worldwide campaign against terrorism in the wake of the September 11, 2001, terrorist incident. Public criticism of the Bush administration and its measures to curtail civil liberties immediately following the World Trade Center attacks was limited to groups such as the American Civil Liberties Union, Human Rights Watch, Amnesty International, and other, smaller civil liberties organizations. In fact, the public tolerance for detention of terrorism suspects and open discussion of the merits of torture during interrogation in left-leaning publications, such as *The Atlantic Monthly,* shocked many American rights advocates. Pundits at all points on the political spectrum argue that the U.S. government's policies in the aftermath of September 11 reflect a necessary trade-off between freedom and security. Wire tapping of phone calls and e-mails is now acceptable; cable repairmen, truckers, and meter maids are encouraged, through the TIPS program, to report "suspicious activity" to a government hotline; and the Freedom of Information Act has been effectively thrown out with the issuance of Executive Order 13233, barring public access to presidential documents from the past four presidents. The justification for these measures resonates with arguments once heard only in places such as China and Singapore, which have long used public security as an excuse to limit individual rights. Similar claims to be protecting "more important rights" are being echoed in Malaysia's renewed usage of the Internal Security Act,[36] and in the campaign slogan "firm hand, large heart" of Álvaro Uribe, the newly elected president of Colombia, who sees greater state authority—not negotiations—as the first step toward resolving Colombia's crisis.[37]

Conclusion

In this brief overview of regional perspectives of human rights in four regions I have tried to show that conflicts over human rights are taking place across the board, not along civilizational lines and not primarily between North and South as so often assumed. The challenges to human rights, including the suspension of civil liberties, resisting economic and social rights, and the denial of rights to certain groups, are taking place in our own backyards. At the same time we see a creative borrowing of ideas and unplanned convergence of human rights debates worldwide among what I have been calling "activist-intellectuals."

Several lessons can be drawn. The first is the most obvious, but also one that bears repeating: while some regions are more diverse than others—the characterization of "Asian values" is a particularly big stretch—all regions consist of diverse cultures and carry differing viewpoints on human rights. Those views range from the assertion that local values are compatible with human rights principles; to the claim that human rights values are a product of Western culture—or in the case of American critics of CEDAW, liberal international forces—and therefore alien to the local culture; to in-between views that local values are not so much inimical to international human rights, but that in the application of rights they receive different priority. We need to recognize the diversity of human rights views existing within a society and avoid construing a government's human rights rhetoric as "the Asian," "the American," "the African," or "the Arab" perspective. To do so is to undermine the genuine debates on human rights happening within these cultures, and worse, to be complicit with states in silencing these voices.

Second, at the same time that we are seeing convergence of perspectives, different societies continue to have different human rights priorities that stem from their distinct histories and experiences. It is a mistake, however, to interpret the difference of priorities as a disagreement over norms. Investigations of rights discourses in different regions rarely turn up a conflict over principles. The death penalty and abortion—areas in which U.S. policy is heavily influenced by perspectives that go against the grain of the emerging international consensus—are two of the exceptions. Instead the area of difference almost always lies in the implementation and prioritization rights.

The third message is to scholars of human rights: cultural relativism is not where "the action" is. Rather than be sidetracked by the politically motivated statements of cultural nationalists, human rights scholars would do well to turn their attention to the projects of cultural legitimation that activist-intellectuals are engaging with in virtually every corner of the globe. Human rights advocates in the United States are among the newcomers. In 1997, with core support from the Ford Foundation, an initiative called "Human Rights USA" was started with the stated goal of demonstrating "that the Universal Declaration of Human Rights and other human rights documents are as relevant to life in the U.S. as they are to life in other countries, and to improve the protection of human rights in American communities by increasing Americans' awareness of these rights."[38] There is plenty of work to be done in this area, and focusing on cultural legitimation rather than cultural relativism is a surer way of meeting the many challenges to international human rights everywhere.

Notes

I would like to thank Jess Messer, Erin Mahoney, and Yesim Yemni, who provided valuable research assistance, and Bonny Ibhawoh, Jess Messer, Mahmood Monshipouri, Andrew Nathan, and Kavita Philip for their helpful comments. In 1999 I published with Daniel A. Bell a collection called *The East Asian Challenge for Human Rights* (New York: Cambridge, 1999). In the opening paragraph we explained that the preposition "for" in the title was used deliberately to indicate that we did not take the view that East Asia is a threat to international human rights; rather the book was an appeal to the human rights community to be receptive to the contributions East Asian intellectuals could make to the evolving rights regime. In this chapter's title, however, the preposition "to" does refer to the threats—perceived and real—to the idea of universal human rights.

1. Samuel Huntington, *The Clash of Civilizations and the Remaking of World Order* (New York: Simon and Schuster, 1996). For critiques, see contributions by Liu Binyan, "Civilization is Grafting; No Culture is an Island" (pp. 46–49), Jeanne Kirkpatrick, "Modernizing Imperative; Tradition and Change" (pp. 50–53) and Kishore Mahbubani, "The Dangers of Decadence; What the Rest Can Teach the West" (pp. 36–40) in *The Clash of Civilizations? The Debate,* A Foreign Affairs Reader (New York: Foreign Affairs, 1996); Fouad Ajami, "The Summoning," *Foreign Affairs*, September–October 1993 (Ajami's response to Huntington's first publication on the topic); Edward Said, "The Clash of Ignorance," *The Nation,* October 22, 2001; John Esposito, *Unholy War in the Name of Islam* (New York: Oxford

University Press, 2002); and Stanley Hoffman, "Clash of Globalizations," *Foreign Affairs,* July–August 2002.

2. Rhoda Howard, *Human Rights and the Search for Community* (Boulder, CO: Westview Press, 1995), pp. 3–5.

3. Page 3. This position and its prevalence in North America is Howard's main concern in this book.

4. Howard, *Human Rights and the Search for Community,* p. 212.

5. To learn more about these efforts, see *Human Rights Dialogue* ser. 2, nos. 1, 2, 6 (New York: Carnegie Council on Ethics and International Affairs). To learn about the work of Cheri Honkalu to promote welfare rights in the United States, see www.kwru.org.

6. See Eduardo Cáceres, "Building a Culture of Rights," and Carlos Bosombrío, "Looking Ahead: New Challenges for Human Rights Advocacy," both in *NACLA Report on the Americas* 34, no. 1 (July–August 2000): 6–8; and Carlos Bosombrío, "Crime: A Latin American Challenge for Human Rights," *Human Rights Dialogue* ser. 2, no. 1 (Winter 2000) (New York: Carnegie Council on Ethics and International Affairs).

7. These dialogues resulted in a number of book-length volumes including Joanne R. Bauer and Daniel A. Bell, eds., *The East Asian Challenge for Human Rights* (Cambridge: Cambridge University Press, 1999); Peter van Ness, ed., *Debating Human Rights: Critical Essays from the United States and Asia* (London: Routledge Press, 1999); William Theodore de Bary and Tu Wei Ming, *Confucianism and Human Rights* (New York: Columbia University Press, 1998); and James T. H. Tang, *Human Rights and International Relations in the Asia-Pacific Region* (New York: St. Martin's Press, 1995). In addition the *Korea Journal,* published jointly with the UN Educational, Scientific, and Cultural Organization (UNESCO) out of Paris, carried a debate recently on Asian values in its Summer, Autumn, and Winter 2001 issues that involved both Westerners and Asians.

8. See, for example, Roger T. Ames, "Continuing the Conversation on Chinese Human Rights," *Ethics & International Affairs* 11 (1997): 177–207.

9. For this section I have relied upon several texts, which are noted, as well as conversations with the following regional experts: Daniel A. Bell, Alex de Waal, Bonny Ibhawoh, Tony Lang, Mahmood Monshipouri, and Chidi Odinkalu.

10. See, for example, Kishore Mahbubani, "The United States: Go East, Young Man," *Washington Quarterly* 17, no. 2 (Spring 1994): 5–23; Kishore Mahbubani, "The Dangers of Decadence: What the Rest Can Teach the West," *Foreign Affairs,* September–October 1993; Fareed Zakaria, "Culture Is Destiny: A Conversation with Lee Kuan Yew," *Foreign Affairs,* March–April 1994; Bilahari Kausikan, "An East Asian Approach to Human Rights," *Buffalo Journal of International Law* 263 (1995–1996): 5–23; and Bilahari Kausikan, "Governance that Works," 8, *Democracy* (April 1997): 24–34. During the mid-1990s, there were also media reports of speeches on the topic given by Malaysian and Singaporean officials in both Western and Asian capitals. Examples accessible on the Internet include Malaysian prime minister Mahathir Bin Mohamad's speech at the Twenty-ninth International General Meeting of the Pacific Basin Economic Council, Washington, DC, April 21, 1996, www.smpke.jpm.my/website/webdb.nsf/?opendatabase; Anwar Bin Ibrahim's speech at the International Conference on Rethinking Human Rights, Kuala Lumpur, Malasia, July 12, 1994, www.smpke.jpm.my/482567bc00239b2c/0/

170b8f83285cec9f4825674f00115f5a?open; and a speech by Malaysian law professor Rohimi HJ Shapiee, "Third Generation Human Rights: Rights of the Third World—Conception and Policy Considerations," Dwan Bahasa dan Pustaka, Kuala Lumpur, Malaysia, 1994, as cited in Glyn Howells, "Which Way's South? Asian Values and Universal Human Rights," www.sfdonline.org/link%20pages/link%20folders/human%20rights/asianvalues1.html#kennett.

11. In fact, even the assertion that such values are "Confucian" has been subject to intense debate among Confucian scholars. See, for example, Daniel A. Bell and Hahm Chaibong, *Confucianism for the Modern World* (New York: Cambridge University Press, forthcoming); William Theodore de Bary and Tu Wei Ming, *Confucianism and Human Rights* (New York: Columbia University Press, 1997) and Theodore de Bary, *Asian Values and Human Rights* (Cambridge: Harvard University Press, 1998).

12. Xin Chunying, "A Brief History of the Modern Human Rights Discourse in China," *Human Rights Dialogue* ser. 1, no. 3 (December 1995) (New York: Carnegie Council on Ethics and International Affairs).

13. See Tatsuo Inoue, "Liberal Democracy and Asian Orientalism," in Bauer and Bell, *The East Asian Challenge for Human Rights,* pp. 27–59.

14. Kevin Y. L. Tan, "What Asian Think About the West's Response to the Human Rights Debate," *Human Rights Dialogue* ser. 1, no. 4 (March 1996) (New York: Carnegie Council on Ethics and International Affairs).

15. "Bangkok NGO Declaration on Human Rights and Plan of Action: Joint Statement of Several Human Rights and Development NGOs Presented at the Regional Meeting for the Asia-Pacific in Preparation for the UN World Conference on Human' Rights," March 29, 1993, www.ahrchk.net/hrsolid/mainfile.php/1993 vol03no02/2050 (accessed August 12, 2002).

16. "The Bangkok Declaration," adopted at the Asia Intergovernmental Meeting, Bangkok, March 29–April 2, 1993, in preparation for the Second UN World Conference on Human Rights, www.rwgmechanism.com/asia.html (accessed August 12, 2002). The Preamble reads: "Reiterating the interdependence and indivisibility of economic, social, cultural, civil and political rights, and the inherent interrelationship between development, democracy, universal enjoyment of all human rights, and social justice, which must be addressed in an integrated and balanced manner." Article 10 reads: "[The Ministers and representatives of Asian States . . .] Reaffirm the interdependence and indivisibility of economic, social, cultural, civil, and political rights and the need to give equal emphasis to all categories of human rights."

17. See comment by Philippines human rights activist Cecelia Jimenez in "Human Rights in the Post-Cold War Era: The Cases of North Korea, China, and Burma," *Human Rights Dialogue* ser. 1, no. 1 (May 1994) (New York: Carnegie Council on Ethics and International Affairs).

18. For a more detailed description of the advocacy activities of Sisters of Islam and examples of their arguments, see Norani Othman, "Grounding Human Rights Arguments in Non-Western Culture: Shari'a and the Citizenship Rights of Women in a Modern Islamic State," in Bauer and Bell, *The East Asian Challenge for Human Rights,* pp. 169–192. For another example of cultural legitimation in Asia, see the chapter by Suwanna Satha-Anand in Bauer and Bell, *The East Asian Challenge for Human Rights,* pp. 193–211.

19. Ann Elizabeth Mayer, *Islam and Human Rights: Tradition and Politics* (Boulder, CO: Westview Press, 1998), p. xi.

20. See Mahmood Monshipouri and Reza Motameni, "Globalization, Sacred Beliefs, and Defiance: Is Human Rights Discourse Relevant in the Muslim World?" *Journal of Church and State* 42, no. 4 (Autumn 2000): 709–736.

21. Ibid.

22. See Issa G. Shivji, *The Concept of Human Rights in Africa,* Codesria Book Series (London: Codeseria Book Series, 1989).

23. See Chidi Odinkalu, "Why More Africans Don't Use Human Rights Language," *Human Rights Dialogue* ser. 2, no. 1 (Winter 1999) (New York: Carnegie Council on Ethics and International Affairs).

24. Shivji, *The Concept of Human Rights.*

25. See Bonny Ibhawoh, "Human Rights and Cultural Relativism: Reconsidering the Africanist Discourse," *Netherlands Quarterly of Human Rights* 19, no. 1 (2001): 43–62; Mahmood Mamdani, *Citizen and Subject* (Princeton: Princeton University Press, 1996); Makau wa Mutua, "The Banjul Charter and the African Cultural Fingerprint: An Evaluation of the Language of Duties," *Virginia Journal of International Law* 35 (1995): 339–380; and Makau Wa Mutua, "Reformulating the Discourse of the Human Rights Movement," *East African Journal of Peace and Human Rights* 3, no. 2 (1996): pp. 317–324.

26. Author's e-mail exchange with Bonny Ibhawoh, August 8, 2002.

27. Michael Ignatieff, "The Rights Stuff," *New York Review of Books* 49, no. 10 (June 13, 2002): 18.

28. Cited by Chris Jochnick in "Human Rights for the Next Century," *Human Rights Dialogue* ser. 1, no. 10 (September 1997) (New York: Carnegie Council on Ethics and International Affairs) p. 6.

29. Today, Human Rights Watch's website reads: "Since its formation in 1978, Human Rights Watch has focused mainly on upholding civil and political rights, but in recent years we have increasingly addressed economic, social and cultural rights as well. We focus particularly on situations in which our methodology of investigation and reporting is most effective, such as when arbitrary or discriminatory governmental conduct lies behind an economic, social and cultural rights violation." www.hrw.org/esc (accessed August 21, 2002). How to "skill up" on economic, social, and cultural rights was a major agenda item at Amnesty International's 2002 general meeting. For a report of that meeting, see www.amnestyusa.org/events/agm2002/agmescr.html (accessed August 21, 2002).

30. Only two countries, Somalia and the United States, have not ratified this celebrated agreement. However, since Somalia currently does not have the governmental capacity to ratify a treaty, the United States stands alone as the only remaining nation that can ratify the convention.

31. In the eyes of the international community, the current U.S. administration has "launched an all-out effort not just to win an absolute exemption from the court's jurisdiction for Americans but, in the view of the court's supporters, to strangle it at birth" ("Tipping the Scales of Justice," *The Economist,* July 1, 2002, p. 1). Since the Bush administration on May 6, 2000, "unsigned" the treaty signed by President Clinton on the eve of his departure from office, the United States has been launching an aggressive campaign to exempt itself from prosecution by the

court. Most recently, this has manifested in the "Hague Invasion Act," which became law on August 3, 2002. Officially titled the American Service Members Protection Act of 2002, the law, according to some of its critics, is "intended to intimidate countries that ratify the treaty for the International Criminal Court (ICC)" and authorizes the use of military force to liberate any American or citizen of a U.S.-allied country being held by the court in the Hague.

32. On July 30, 2002, the treaty was favorably voted (12–7) out of the Senate Foreign Relations Committee. The convention was reported out of committee on a 13–5 vote in 1994 but was held by the full Senate and sent back to the committee with reservations. In 1995 the United States made a public commitment at the Fourth UN World Conference on Women in Beijing to ratify CEDAW by the year 2000. For more information on the history of American involvement with CEDAW and American groups supporting ratification, see www.crlp.org/pub_fac_cedaw. html (accessed August 27, 2002).

33. "Women's Treaty Revives Old Debates," *Christian Science Monitor*, July 30, 2002. For a discussion of reactions to CEDAW in Malaysia, see Norani Othman's chapter in Bauer and Bell, *The East Asian Challenge for Human Rights,* pp. 188–189.

34. "Worldwide Executions doubled in 2001," Amnesty USA press release, April 9, 2002, www.amnestyusa.org/news/2002/world04092002.html (accessed August 26, 2002).

35. Notably in 2001, Harold Hongju Koh, former assistant secretary of state for democracy, human rights, and labor, led a group of former ambassadors in a protest of the practice of some states of executing mentally retarded criminals. The memo, drafted by Koh and signed by a number of current and former ambassadors who had encountered outright hostility in their international travels, highlighted how the U.S. policy of executing people, particularly the mentally retarded, increasingly leads the United States into isolation internationally. More than half the countries in the world have abolished the death penalty, and, according to Koh, the United States is "completely isolated" in executing the mentally retarded. Recently, Koh has pointed out that this is a difficult position to be in while simultaneously trying to mobilize foreign opinion for the battle against terrorism. "Veteran U.S. Envoy Seeks End to U.S. Executions of Retarded," *New York Times,* June 10, 2001.

36. According to Elizabeth Wong, secretary-general of the National Human Rights Society (HAKAM), and member of the secretariat of Suara Rakyat, Malaysia (SUARAM): "Shortly following the September 11th attacks, government officials launched an aggressive promotion of the ISA against the backdrop of a growing anti-ISA movement and a popular campaign with the general population, arresting scores for their alleged 'terrorist' activities and links to Al-Qaeda. As a result of government propaganda, public support has dwindled alarmingly as the general population became increasingly subdued by the dubious arguments of 'human security' over 'human rights.' Even the chairman of the National Human Rights Commission publicly advocated that human rights have to take a backseat for the moment. While Malaysia's human rights record has its glaring blemishes, the events of September 11th have given an added impetus for the government to justify their own crackdowns on political dissidents and religious groups allegedly linked to opposition parties. Overnight, governments such as the United States and

Australia who were formerly critical of Malaysia's human rights record are now silent, providing tacit support for growing violations of civil liberties." Memo to the Carnegie Council, March 2002. See Wong's essay in "Public Security and Human Rights," *Human Rights Dialogue* ser. 2, no. 8 (Fall 2002–Winter 2003, forthcoming).

37. For a discussion of security and human rights in Uribe's Colombia, see Adam Isacson in "Public Security and Human Rights," *Human Rights Dialogue* ser. 2, no. 8 (Fall 2002–Winter 2003, forthcoming).

38. wwwserver.law.wits.ac.za/humanrts/160.94.193.60/Archive/vision.htm (accessed January 14, 2003).

10

Obstacles on the Road to an Overlapping Consensus on Human Rights

Charles Lockhart

Drawing on Mary Douglas and Aaron Wildavsky's "grid-group" theory, I argue that developing the unforced overlapping consensus on human rights for which Charles Taylor (1999) hopes may be much more difficult than he suggests. I contend that rival cultures (i.e., individualism, egalitarianism, and hierarchy) support distinctive ranges of human rights. Their disparate practices foster two sorts of complications to which Taylor devotes insufficient attention. First, the types of rights rival cultures support may conflict. For instance, individualistic support for property rights often raises claims incompatible with egalitarian and also hierarchical pursuit of economic rights through maximin economic redistribution. Second, the breadth of the social horizons within which rival cultures think it appropriate to apply those human rights they support vary sharply as do degrees of concern for supporting the dignity or limiting the suffering of those persons who fall beyond these horizons. Both of these complications pose significant obstacles on the road to the unforced overlapping consensus on human rights that Taylor envisions.

Scholars and statespersons argue over whether any human rights are universal, and if so, which ones and how they are universal. For instance, John Rawls expresses optimism that both liberal and what he calls "well-ordered" hierarchical states (1993, 60–63) might reach an unforced consensus on a limited range of human rights. While this view offers a useful benchmark for one sense of global justice, it fits poorly with the world as we know it, which is littered with hierarchical states that do not meet Rawls's demanding standards for well-orderedness and show little interest in realizing the rights that he sees as most capable of gaining consensus. In contrast, Daniel Bell (1998, 567–568) argues in favor of furthering worldwide realization of human dignity by working with distinctive local cultural traditions that support related rightlike entities. Yet Bell's suggestions draw a quick riposte from Evan Charney (1999, 841–842), who thinks that Western-style civil-political rights are the only universal human rights. Bell (1999, 850–851), in turn, adroitly reveals limitations on Charney's position.[1]

Taylor (1999) further develops a view similar to Bell's, contending that something more complicated than Rawls's unforced consensus (1993, 66–68) may be possible across societies with respect to human rights. Taylor is hopeful that similar practices that in effect support a range of human rights can be sustained by alternative but overlapping foundations (1999, 136). His principal example of an alternative foundation is the Buddhist commitment to nonviolence, which, he argues, "entails a nonpredatory stance toward the environment and calls also for the limitation of greed, one of the sources of anger and conflict" (134). In Taylor's view, this commitment can support some protective devices similar to those that have arisen in the West from the natural rights tradition. So, while Westerners and Asian Buddhists might continue to employ differing underlying bases for their views, they might nonetheless sustain related human-rights institutions. Taylor acknowledges that hierarchical perspectives, particularly influential in certain non-Western areas, pose difficulties for such a consensus by differentiating the suffering of some as more important than the suffering of others (139, 142). Yet he remains optimistic (124) that progress toward a consensus on an unspecified range of human rights can and will occur.

My argument in this chapter is directed at Taylor's because, among discussions about the universality of human rights, he offers a widely noticed and especially eloquent and influential view. Taylor's position is more subtle than efforts to impose a particular Western perspective universally—what Bell (1998, 568) calls "parochial universalism." What attracts many to Taylor's view is his acceptance of cultural difference, not only in acknowledging that cultures differ, but also in respecting the distinctive capacities of each for preserving human dignity and drawing on these varying capacities to achieve an unforced overlapping global consensus on human rights. Taylor's work thus represents a particularly sophisticated, attractive, and cautious example of a tendency among some Western scholars and political figures to speak of "universal human rights."

While the contemporary period evinces more interest in human rights than the past, I argue that specific types of rights (civil, political, economic, social, developmental, and cultural [United Nations 1966]) are the mani-festations of rival ways of life. So the rights supported by one culture are likely at least partially distinct from and may even involve contradictions with the rights supported by another culture. Thus while human rights may be increasingly universally supported, the same rights are not supported universally. There are not yet any "universal human rights," and their de-velopment would require something bordering on the global dominance of a particular culture.

Such dominance is, of course, entailed in one sense of "globalization." If the juggernaut of capitalist development penetrates sufficiently into even the villages of the developing world, the argument goes, then persons will come increasingly to adhere to a way of life that, following Mary Douglas and Aaron Wildavsky, I label individualistic, and support for civil and political rights will gradually become universal or nearly so. So by riding the triumph of this individualistic entrepreneurial orientation, some rights may become universal, but they may do so at the expense of other rights (e.g., economic, social, developmental, or cultural) that are among the in-stitutional expressions of other ways of life that will have succumbed to the triumph of this incompatible rival. For instance, while Chinese indi-vidualists would be encouraged by the civil-political rights this capitalistic conception of globalization fostered, other Chinese—who were devoted to socioeconomic rights—would be dismayed by this conception's likely de-struction of the human rights that they supported. Such a development, then, would represent a triumph for the advocates of some human rights but a disaster for the advocates of other human rights.

Associating different types of rights with rival ways of life alerts us to complexities to which Taylor's characterization of an unforced consensus on human rights is insufficiently sensitive. In contrast, Douglas-Wildavsky's "grid-group" theory, which has been used productively with respect to other political controversies (e.g., environmental issues [see Ellis and Thompson 1997]), offers a distinctive perspective that will help us to decipher human rights issues of this sort. Grid-group theory has not previously been deployed in examining conflicting conceptions of human rights, but it is ideal for the task since it identifies four cultures, each holding distinctive implications for human rights.

So with respect to the issues set out in the introduction to this volume, my argument in this chapter works from the following positions. First, various claims for human rights are socially constructed universals in the sense that, by supporting human dignity in distinctive ways, they each reduce specific forms of pain and suffering and facilitate various aspects of human agency wherever they are practiced. Second, while I touch on the various conceptions of globalization that the editors of this volume introduce, I emphasize the recent success of liberalism in both its political and its economic manifestations. Third, I see various types of human rights (e.g., civil-political, socioeconomic, developmental, and cultural) as the distinctive institutional products of rival cultures. While I recognize that at a high level of abstraction different types of rights exhibit shared concerns (e.g., supporting human dignity), I contend that in practical application their implications are often contradictory. So I do not concur with the view that various types of rights are naturally and thoroughly complementary. Nonetheless and fourth, I agree with many of my fellow contributors to this volume that social conditions cultivating considerable realization of, for instance, both civil-political and socioeconomic rights foster greater social justice than circumstances in which one of these types of rights is emphasized to the relative exclusion of the other. I think, however, that achieving this sort of mutual accommodation across rival categories of human rights is difficult and relatively rare.

General Human Rights Implications of Grid-Group Theory

Grid-group theory was conceived in sociology (Durkheim 1951), refined in cultural anthropology (Evans-Pritchard 1940; Douglas 1982), and recently advanced and applied in political science (Thompson, Ellis, and Wildavsky 1990; Ellis 1993). The theory explains how persons derive a limited range of answers to basic social questions such as (Wildavsky 1994): How does the world work, what are humans really like, and how do I hold others accountable to me? Grid-group theorists argue that persons' answers to these questions produce orientations toward two basic social dimensions: the legitimacy of external prescription (grid) and the strength of affiliation with others (group).[2] The theory thus fills a notorious void in the social sciences (Becker 1976, 133) by helping to explain how distinctive social relations preferences are formed as a consequence of various grid and group positions (Schwarz and Thompson 1990, 49). The range of actual social practice is constrained since only four general ways—each admitting some variations—of responding to these issues are socially viable.[3] Preferences with respect to various patterns of social relations prompt supporting justifications or cultural biases and vice versa. Together, the preferences and justifications create distinctive ways of life. For instance, where low tolerance for external prescription is reinforced by weak feelings of group membership, we find an individualistic way of life

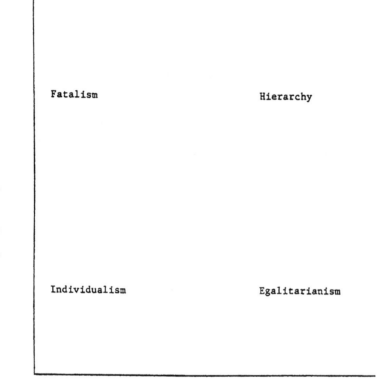

Increasingly strong feelings of group affiliation

organized largely by self-regulation among voluntary, shifting, contract-based networks of persons (see figure).

Promoting such a way of life among persons perceived as self-interested, with roughly equal broad competencies such as rationality, is one purpose of Smith's *Wealth of Nations*. Strong feelings of group affiliation together with weak prescription entail a way of life that grid-group theorists call egalitarian. From this perspective broadly equal humans, unmarred by natural flaws destructive of social harmony, ideally prefer to organize into small societies that reach collective decisions through discussions designed to produce consensus. This process is reminiscent of Rousseau's description of the social ideal in *The Social Contract*. High feelings of group affiliation in conjunction with perceptions legitimizing external prescription create a realm of hierarchy. In this view, unequal humans with various social shortcomings that require improvement through expert guidance are arrayed in vertical institutions. The ideal polis portrayed by Plato in *The Republic* illustrates this way of life. Finally, where weak feelings of group affiliation intersect with perceptions of inescapable external direction, grid-group theory locates fatalism. The unhappy combination of recognizing constraint by others but not feeling part of any broader social collective predisposes fatalists to social avoidance rather than varying forms of social interaction. One manifestation of avoidance is that fatalists rarely construct works of political theory; their social patterns have, however, been well portrayed by others (Banfield 1958; Turnbull 1972; Mars 1982).[4]

Scholars have conceived of culture differently and developed various theories of culture.[5] The conception of culture offered by grid-group theory is distinctive in several respects. First, in contrast to a convention by which cultures (sometimes allowing for multiple subcultures) are thought of as roughly coincident with societies (e.g., French, German, or Chinese culture), grid-group theorists argue that all four of their theory's global ways of life are present in varying proportions in all large-scale, long-lived societies (Grendstad 1999). Similar to the interaction of different amino acids in biological systems, each way of life provides services for the others that they cannot create for themselves. Societies are thus typically "multicultural" in this sense.

In part, grid-group theorists conceive of culture as beliefs about the natural and social environments that rest ultimately on experience (Douglas 1986). Distinctive conceptions of human nature follow from particular beliefs about the world. Together, these beliefs about humans and their world locate persons with respect to the grid and group dimensions, support characteristic value priorities, and spawn preferences for distinctive social institutions that are also indices of culture. Accordingly, a second distinctive feature of grid-group analysis is that the theory illuminates tighter, more specific relations between beliefs and values (i.e., cultural biases) and the institutions that embody them than do some other political culture theories (Ross 1997). Cultural biases and institutions require each other. Without specific institutions, adherents of rival cultural biases have no means for shaping social relations in accordance with their distinctive beliefs and values, and without relevant cultural biases, particular institutions have no justification in terms of beliefs and values.

Thus, third, grid-group theory is appropriately considered a theory of preference formation. It offers accounts of what persons want and why that, when coupled with an instrumental conception of rationality, create four rival, "thick" (Ferejohn 1991) or culturally constrained rationalities, each based on distinctive value clusters and holding constrained institutional (e.g., human rights) preferences (Lockhart and Coughlin 1992; Wildavsky 1994; Lockhart and Wildavsky 1998; Coughlin and Lockhart 1998; Lockhart 2001). Each of these culturally constrained rationalities is valid within particular ranges of human experience, and each is attractive in distinctive ways. We might reasonably be tempted to believe in more than one. For instance, we may think of humans as unequal in their capacities but equal in holding certain basic rights such as freedom from incarceration and torture for their political beliefs. Further, these rationalities have areas of overlap, but they are also separated by irreducible contradictions that arise from their distinctive ontologies and conceptions of human nature and that foster incompatible institutional preferences in support of action.

Individualism and Civil-Political Human Rights

In the instance of human rights, these disparate constrained institutional preferences translate into the adherents of grid-group theory's rival cultures supporting distinctive ranges of human rights. For instance, individualists perceive bountiful and resilient natural environments (Locke, *Second Treatise,* chap. 5) and social environments (Nozick 1974). They also view humans as motivated by egoistic hedonistic concerns and holding impressive and roughly equal broad capacities. These humans are thus properly motivated and sufficiently capable to master their own fates in a cornucopian world. This ontology accounts for individualists' preeminent value: a particular ("negative" [Berlin 1969]) conception of liberty. Accordingly, individualists prefer to rely primarily on self-regulation among persons, and a network of contractual (voluntary) relations that shifts over time as interests do is their preferred means of social coordination. For them, government—with its inherent coercion—should be limited in its domain and activity.

Especially across Western societies, classical liberal individualists' concern for respecting persons and tolerating individual differences, primarily by supporting this particular sense of liberty, has contributed much to the development of civil (including property) and political rights. But individualists have accommodated economic, social, developmental, and cultural rights only sparingly and grudgingly.

Egalitarianism's Uneven Support for a Range of Human Rights

Egalitarians, in contrast, see a fragile environment. Not only is the natural environment subject to depredation, but social contexts—the inner city—are easily perverted as well. Egalitarians believe that humans are naturally benign in their motives and broadly equal in both basic capacities and needs (Gewirth 1978), thus complementing this delicate context.[6] Yet humans are easy prey for social stratification that damages central egalitarian values of relatively equal interpersonal respect and material condition. Egalitarians believe that by undoing natural human equality, stratification creates arrogance in the dominant and resentment in the subordinated, perverting in the process the natural goodness of all. Accordingly, egalitarians prefer social relations among relatively small societies that share a limited material bounty fairly equally—exemplified by the aphorism "live simply so that others may simply live" or as E. F. Schumacher had it, "small is beautiful" (1973)—and that reach collective decisions through open discussion resulting in consensus (Downey 1986; Zisk 1992).[7]

In their ideal circumstances (i.e., small, relatively unstratified, Rousseauean communities), the collective yet individual-respecting motivational basis of egalitarians lends itself naturally to support for social rights (according all persons nearly equally high respect) and economic rights (maximin conceptions of material distributive justice [see Rae et al. 1981][8] rights). In advanced industrial societies, where the low-grid cultures are commonly well developed and frequently allied with one another on a variety of specific issues (e.g., alleviating ethnic and gender hierarchy), egalitarians routinely support political and some civil rights as well, although they do not emphasize various civil rights with the same vigor as individualists (Ellis 1998). The most obvious conflict between egalitarian and individualistic conceptions of rights lies in the claims that egalitarian maximin redistribution makes on individualists' conceptions of property rights. Egalitarians are eager to tax those who are relatively well off in order to fund public social programs that benefit broad segments of society by focusing on ordinary persons' vulnerabilities to various common vicissitudes of life.

Further, while egalitarians are reluctant to champion economic development as thoroughly as either individualists or hierarchists do, against the context of a world sharply divided into have and have-not societies, egalitarians generally support development rights for have-not societies designed to foster maximin redistribution cross-societally. Through such rights they understand most commonly the right of "a people" to develop free from exploitative constraints imposed by Western governments and the increasingly long fingers of global capitalism. Additional connotations of development rights often entail various obligations of advanced industrial societies to help to sustain indigenous, non-Western development efforts (Shue 1996). In this advanced industrial-developing, cross-societal context, egalitarians are also likely to support non-Western cultural rights to maintain distinctive patterns of social relations against incursions of the modern technologies (e.g., satellite television transmissions and the Internet) employed by international corporations. Both developmental and cultural rights are generally claimed by a "people," and in certain contexts below I refer to these inherently "high-group" rights as "sovereignty" rights.[9] Individualists are characteristically unsympathetic to these claims, which they see as constraining the desirable universality of civil-political rights. Indeed, they are generally reluctant at best to recognize the objects of such claims as human rights.

Hierarchy's Distinctive Differentiating Conception of Rights

Hierarchists believe in a more complex tolerant/perverse world. Both natural and social environments are sufficiently robust to support some exploitation, but if humans press too hard, disaster is apt to follow. Figuratively, humans live on mesas, not needing to worry about minor variations of the tabletop terrain, but having to stay clear of the encircling cliffs. This view of the human environment elicits a conception of humans that, in contrast to those of the low-grid cultures, attributes great importance to disparities of specific talents. Experts in various matters are required to discern crucial natural and social boundaries not equally evident to everyone as well as for ascertaining how humans should adjust their behavior in conformity with these limits. For hierarchists, then, many of the same obvious interpersonal differences that individualists and egalitarians believe to be inconsequential take on moral and social significance. This ontology focuses priority on the values of expertise as well as the social harmony and order that may be derived from expert knowledge. Accordingly, hierarchists prefer to organize society into vertically arrayed institutions with dual roles of education and social control. Experts guide these institutions, attempting to fill persons' lives with sanctioned activities. In this way the lives of less capable and more seriously flawed persons are improved and the social collective is simultaneously served by realizing a harmonious social order.

As Bismarck's much emulated, pioneering transformation of feudal rights to subsistence into modern social insurance programs suggests, hierarchists have commonly supported limited forms of economic rights. Hierarchists are naturally opposed to economic leveling, but their collective and dutiful motivation has routinely recognized an obligation on the part of societal elites to support certain crucial material needs of the less capable members of society, particularly against the onset of various social hazards that transcend individual responsibility. As Bismarck's example also illustrates, hierarchists frequently support a sense of social rights. If for no other reason than to foster national solidarity in the face of threatening international circumstances, Bismarck was anxious to have what he called "the working classes" feel included in German society. But hierarchically sponsored economic and social rights generally deviate from "human rights" in that they vary with social class. Inclusion of workers in German society did not entail for Bismarck any sense of social equality by which popular majorities might contribute importantly to shaping the character of public policy. Rather, hierarchical social rights grant different privileges to various social strata.

Yet among contemporary advanced industrial societies, in which the low-grid cultures are routinely well developed and thoroughly organized for political action, hierarchists have found it increasingly difficult to oppose civil-political rights. But they do not, as Republican resistance to "motor-voter" legislation in the United States suggests, advocate these rights as strenuously as the adherents of the low-grid cultures. Among non-Western and frequently less developed societies, in which the low-grid cultures are generally less thoroughly socially embedded and politically influential, hierarchists are characteristically hesitant about and frequently hostile toward civil and political rights. For instance, hierarchical Singaporese political elites have successfully resisted legal recognition of numerous civil rights despite extensive economic development (Englehart 2000).

Hierarchists may occasionally become involved in supporting a people's right to development, but as we shall see below, their support on these matters frequently arises from views distinct from those of egalitarians. The egalitarian notion of developmental rights rests on a conception of solidarity similar to that energizing the long-term practices of Swedish labor unions for moving wages of various categories of workers progressively toward a societal mean. In contrast, hierarchists are apt to claim a right to development in order achieve some advantage vis-à-vis a competing group or society. In this instance, the long-term goal is not fraternal solidarity, but rather relative dominance through competitive advantage. Hierarchists may also raise demands for cultural autonomy or "sovereignty" similar to those of their high-group egalitarian colleagues, but as we shall see below, in practice their applications of such rights are often based on conceptions of national or ethnic exceptionalism or superiority and do not fit the mold of human rights that are presumably held by all peoples.[10]

Implications

Taylor's argument and my own share areas of compatibility. I accept that, to the degree that Buddhists are aptly characterized by the quintessentially egalitarian portrayal that Taylor offers,[11] they are likely to sustain certain legal forms similar to some of the civil and political rights of the individualistic tradition of Western liberalism in spite of resting their support for these forms on distinctive grounds. So far, so good. But these two traditions are apt to have different priorities among civil rights (e.g., freedom of expression and property rights) and to differ in their support of various types of rights (e.g., social and economic versus civil and political) so that expanding individualistic influence would represent setbacks for some sorts of rights. Further, the most influential culture, especially among political elites, in much of the non-Western world is not egalitarianism, but hierarchy. Taylor himself (1999, 137–143) recognizes that this perspective poses difficulties for an uncoerced consensus on human rights. Overall, I see a more complicated situation than Taylor's suggestion of Buddhist egalitarians, Western liberal individualists, and unspecified additional traditions contributing to the near universal support of related legal forms from alternative foundations.

It may appear counterintuitive that grid-group theory's portrayal of societies as composed, in varying proportions, of versions of the same global cultures should be more pessimistic on the prospects for an uncoerced consensus on human rights than Taylor. If the adherents of each culture are favorably disposed toward some rights, should not societies composed of mixtures of these cultures find support of a broad range of human rights within their grasp? Especially favorable circumstances (examined below) may produce such results, but let me clarify why I think that this is not generally the case.

On one hand, grid-group theory portrays a world in which persons adhere to one of four rival global cultures, each with its own distinctive perspective on human rights.[12] Individualists in the United States and China, then, share support for civil-political rights and skepticism about the economic, social, and other rights integral to the perspectives of other cultures.[13] Shared support for civil-political rights will not obviate various conflicts of interest arising from concerns of relative advantage among American and Chinese individualistic entrepreneurs. Indeed, markets, whether domestic or international, cultivate such conflicts. Further, on the basis of ease (e.g., a common language) or familiarity (personal friendships) both Chinese and American individualists may prefer doing business with members of their own societies—whatever their (grid-group theory) culture—rather than across societal boundaries. But in spite of certain "nationalistic" preferences such as these, individualists in both societies will share support for civil-political rights, and they—as well as the adherents of other cultures—may develop transnational networks that advance universalistic claims.

On the other hand, persons live in societies that, while "multicultural" in this four-rival-cultures sense, act in ways that reflect the objectives of some cultures more than others. That is, while American society includes large numbers of egalitarians and hierarchists, U.S. public policy provides extensive support for civil-political rights, modest support (certainly in comparison to other advanced industrial societies) for socioeconomic rights, and only marginal support for developmental and cultural rights (e.g., exceptional status for the Navaho or Amish in some regards).

Cultures routinely act through formal public organizations (e.g., the U.S. Department of State, the World Bank) or private organizations (e.g., the Roman Catholic Church, Microsoft). Although organizations such as these frequently act in the name of multicultural entities (e.g., societies), they may be less "multicultural" themselves. Further, when organizations (or even persons) act, they characteristically have to choose the institutional designs of one culture over the conflicting designs of other cultures. For instance, in terms of perspective I am sympathetic to individualistic claims that candidates for various academic positions should be chosen on the basis of their professional qualifications as construed fairly narrowly, what James Fishkin (1983) calls "procedural fairness." But I also recognize the appropriateness of what Fishkin calls "equality of life chances." And since various persons have had vastly different opportunities for developing academic qualifications, I am sympathetic as well to egalitarian arguments for extending preferential treatment to candidates whose records are encouraging—though perhaps not strictly competitive—in spite of extremely limited prior opportunities. Yet if, as a public official, I acted to shape the societal institutions through which academic positions are allocated, the resulting institutions would either extend preferential treatment or not. Acting routinely—though perhaps not invariably—requires choosing the instruments of one culture over those of another.

So socioeconomic rights (e.g., the Confucian-based right to support from one's children in old age [Bell 1999, 853]) will not develop from, but be undercut by, the penetration of high-group societies by market institutions that are predisposed toward civil and perhaps political rights. The presence of adherents of the high-group cultures (e.g., hierarchy and egalitarianism) in the United States or of the low-grid cultures (e.g., individualism and egalitarianism) in China does not necessarily produce formal institutional support in these societies for the human rights these cultures favor, respectively. Such support is contingent on extensive political organization and a significant presence for the cultures in question among the society's political elite.

To recapitulate, I think Taylor underestimates the difficulties posed for a consensus on human rights by several circumstances. First, there are three ubiquitous socially interactive cultures: individualism, hierarchy, and egalitarianism. Across societies, egalitarians will share basic beliefs and values that distinguish them clearly from individualists and hierarchists. Second, one of the most socially important ways in which these cultures are distinguished is by building and maintaining disparate, frequently conflicting, institutions—including different conceptions of human rights—that realize their distinctive beliefs and values. Third, societies differ in the proportions of their populations—and particularly their political elites—that adhere to rival cultures.[14] Thus, fourth, a society whose elite is composed largely of hierarchists will likely support different rights or, minimally, support various rights differently than a society whose elite is composed largely of individualists. So while there may be nearly universal support for human rights, this support does not sustain the same rights universally. Rather, disparate, even conflicting, human rights are championed by the adherents of rival cultures socially embedded to different degrees in various societies.

Competition Between Low- and High-Group Human Rights

One central obstacle to developing an unforced overlapping consensus on human rights is that the rights pursued vigorously by individualists are distinct from and in some instances at odds with those strenuously advocated by adherents of the high-group cultures, particularly egalitarianism. While cross-societal differences in the relative support for specific human rights are frequently sharp, among similar societies practices with respect to related types of rights may vary only marginally. So, for instance, among Western European societies, in which hierarchically led, high-group cultural coalitions are often preeminent (e.g., the hierarchical-egalitarian coalitions of the Scandinavian societies), public officials regularly succeed in keeping various "state secrets" from the citizenry in ways that are sometimes legally challenged successfully in the United States. For example, in Western European societies the mass confiscation of daily newspapers occasionally occurs on grounds that are simply not accepted in the more individualistic United States, where civil rights against state authority are more firmly rooted.

Even among relatively similar societies, greater cross-societal variations in supporting human rights arise in those areas in which different rights come sharply into conflict. Historically, the preeminent example of such a situation has involved the property rights championed by individualism coming into conflict with various redistributive demands prompted by egalitarian or hierarchical claims of economic rights. This conflict has been not only an extremely potent and persistent issue of domestic political strife within many societies, but also a prominent basis for international disputes (e.g., aspects of the Cold War). The conflict is revealed as well in distinct UN covenants on civil and political as opposed to economic, social, and cultural rights (United Nations 1966) and the differing degrees of support various societies extend to these respective covenants. Wherever egalitarian claims for economic rights confront individualistic claims for property rights, the widespread support for human rights produces inherent competition between rival rights (and thus winners and losers) rather than support for universal human rights. Since these conflicts are deep, resting on contrasting conceptions of human nature and the human condition, they pose significant obstacles to the development of an overlapping consensus on rights among rival cultures.

Among advanced industrial societies a broad range of material resources are relatively abundant and all three of grid-group theory's socially interactive cultures generally have numerous organized adherents (Grendstad 1999). As Giovanni Sartori (1995) suggests, these factors help to "tame" politics (e.g., persons turned out of office are not severely mistreated). Under these exceptionally favorable circumstances, conflicts between individualistic conceptions of civil-political rights and egalitarian (or hierarchical) realizations of economic and social rights have experienced considerable accommodation (Marshall 1963). In the social democracies of Western Europe the precise point of compromise has moved toward the latter and then back in the direction of the former over the last half century via democratic procedures. Even in the more thoroughly individualistic United States some accommodation has been reached through democratic procedures, although adjectives such as "laggard" (Wilensky 1975) and "selective" (i.e., missing programs of national health insurance and child allowances [see Skocpol 1987]) routinely characterize American provision of socioeconomic rights.

So these exceptionally favorable circumstances produce accommodation across cultures with respect to human rights. But accommodation is distinct from Taylor's uncoerced consensus. For instance, while pretax income distributions among advanced industrial societies are fairly similar, posttax and public-transfer distributions differ a good deal (Birchfield and Crepaz

1998). Trying to gain acceptance for the limited American posttax and public-transfer redistributive results in Sweden, where the numerous and influential adherents of the high-group cultures are enthusiastic about socioeconomic rights, would produce sharp conflict. Similar conflict would arise from trying to gain acceptance for the much more extensive Swedish posttax and public-transfer redistributive results in the United States, where numerous and influential individualists are skeptical of socioeconomic rights. Moreover, adherents of the high-group cultures in the United States and Swedish individualists want more and less in the way of socioeconomic rights, respectively, but neither has the power to change existing public policy, which both likely view as coerced by a state in which their misguided cultural rivals are too influential.

Sharp differences in the realization of various types of rights often arise between Western and non-Western societies because the relative influence of rival cultures is characteristically quite different across these two categories. Consider recent disagreements between the United States and Singapore (Mahbubani 1998). The exceptionally individualistic United States has made the extension of particularly political and also civil rights an important foreign policy objective, but its policy eschews support of other forms of human rights. Indeed, for U.S. officials (at least in their public roles), human rights mean civil-political rights.

In contrast, hierarchical Singaporean officials have been relatively inclusive with regard to membership in society and the sharing of prosperity, supporting in the process social and economic rights. Yet they have been reluctant to open their society to the range and depth of civil-political rights advocated by the United States (Lee 1999). Many Singaporean political activists and possibly segments of the population generally support civil-political rights more ardently than do political leaders (Englehart 2000; Kelly and Reid 1998), but the influence of these cultures on Singapore's public policy is modest. Western public and corporate pressure for civil-political rights frequently runs into opposition from hierarchical elites across developing societies. However, these latter elites often support economic, social, and other rights. Yet the remarkably broad implications of contemporary Western conceptions of property rights, in particular, routinely run headlong into the beliefs and values with which the numerous adherents of high-group cultures in developing societies support these other types of rights.

Cross-societal differences in the realization of various types of human rights are attributable in essence to variation in the relative influence of rival cultures among societies. In "the West" (i.e., Western Europe, the Antipodes, and North America) adherents of both low-grid cultures are numerous (Grendstad 1999). Further, adherents of these cultures are often well organized politically into (classical) liberal individualistic and socialist egalitarian political parties (e.g., the German Free Democrats or the "Bush" wing of the American Republicans and various social democratic parties). Additionally, resources are abundant and, particularly under conditions of rapid economic growth, redistributive issues need not be zero-sum. So while the support of various types of human rights shifts somewhat across time with the alternation in power of various political parties, the influence of all three socially interactive cultures is sufficiently strong and persistent to produce relatively encouraging realization of civil, political, social, and economic rights. The United States appears exceptional among these societies in terms of the strength of its individualism, the weakness of its hierarchy (Lipset 1996, 1990), and the resulting dominance of civil-political over economic and social rights.

Among non-Western societies, most material resources are frequently in shorter supply, making redistribution more difficult. Additionally, the relative influence of rival cultures tends to be more asymmetrical with hierarchy—the least human rights supporting of grid-group theory's three socially interactive cultures—often holding a preeminent position. As Sartori (1995) suggests, under these conditions the taming of politics is more difficult, since political officials may cling to office out of fear for their lives. While hierarchy is dominant in a few Western European societies as well (e.g., Iceland [see Grendstad 1999]), the preeminence of hierarchy in much of the non-Western world is more pervasive. Not only is it frequently the most widely accepted culture, but it often holds a near monopoly on the practical political orientations of influential persons.

By this latter point I refer to something similar to the conflict in Western society between individualistic capitalism and egalitarian Christianity.[15] While many American businesspersons are arguably Christian in some nontrivial sense, their business practices likely embody the culture of individualism, exhibiting a concern for maximizing profits rather than sharing a limited bounty equally. Likewise, I think that while Thai or other political leaders may accept aspects of the egalitarian Buddhist orientation discussed by Taylor (1999), their political-economic practices are likely guided by hierarchical or individualistic tenets (Limanonda 1995; Englehart 1998). Such "bifocal" cultural orientations and the ensuing application of rival cultures to distinctive spheres of social life are neither unusual (Hochschild 1981; Walzer 1983; Free and Cantril 1967) nor unreasonable.[16] Different spheres of social life (e.g., the family, the labor market, and the battlefield) may sensibly elicit distinctive orientations. The world does not work the same way in all places and times, and the support for civil-political rights that is so prominent among Western societies is muted in the more thoroughly hierarchical social environments of non-Western societies, in which other types of rights—which frequently conflict with civil-political rights—are the logical expressions of hierarchical orientations. So while support for human rights is found widely across societies, even societies differing as sharply as advanced industrial and developing ones, this support is frequently not for the same types of human rights.

Thus I think that the path to an uncoerced consensus on human rights is vastly more difficult than Taylor (1999) imagines; indeed I think that it fades out entirely in the swirling sands of cross-cultural disagreement about which human rights are appropriate. The situation is simply more complex than he suggests. It is not that important points that he makes are inaccurate. Buddhist egalitarians and Western individualists might reasonably come to support some related legal forms (e.g., most likely a range of civil-political rights) from their alternative foundations. But that would not be the end of the matter. These two cultures are apt to disagree about economic, social, and other rights, and support for distinctive types of human rights by rival cultures dominant in different societies is more likely to produce conflicting rights than mutually supportive efforts to achieve complementary objectives. As I mentioned above, exceptionally favorable circumstances help to elicit more complementary achievement and less ferocious conflict, but these circumstances are nowhere in sight across much of the non-Western world. Under current circumstances the rights most clearly associated with largely Western-initiated efforts at various conceptions of globalization tend to appear as new forms of imperialism having the effect, if not the intention, of exacerbating various forms of oppression (e.g., through the destruction of economic, social, developmental, and cultural rights) with respect to weak and vulnerable persons and peoples rather than "arming" them against various infringements on their autonomy as civil-political rights have historically done for a socioeconomic elite in the Western tradition of "protective" or liberal democracy (Held 1987).

Rival Cultures' Varying Horizons on Human Rights Concerns

Taylor also underestimates a second set of obstacles, posed particularly by certain societally dominant hierarchical cultures, to an uncoerced consensus on human rights. Taylor (1999, 137–143) and others (Donnelly 1989, 49–65; 1982; Howard and Donnelly 1986; see also Margalit 1996; Cornell 1998; and Nussbaum 1997) point out that human rights of varying sorts embody broad principles, such as supporting human dignity, that transcend specific categories of rights. That is, while civil-political and socioeconomic rights offer different and sometimes conflicting means for supporting human dignity, they both share this concern. So these scholars argue that stressing such vague transcendental principles, rather than specific means of realizing them, may facilitate a consensus in favor of various practices, including human rights.

Yet both the varying breadth and disparate nature of the social horizons of rival cultural perspectives make it difficult for these broad principles to foster an unforced consensus on human rights. For instance, Thomas Jefferson, arguably the most influential egalitarian in American political history, did not include women and slaves among the humans he perceived as equal. Certainly Jefferson's society offered little support for broadly inclusive perspectives on human equality. Nonetheless, it seems remarkable that the person who penned the famous statement of Lockean claims in the Declaration of Independence, a statement that has subsequently provided inspiration for repeated waves of low-grid (i.e., egalitarian and individualistic) civil and political rights reformers in the United States, should have been so constrained about extending his conception of human equality to such extensive segments of humanity. Similarly Andrew Jackson, another prominent American egalitarian, was a major practitioner of ethnic cleansing with respect to Native Americans, who simply stood outside the horizons of his egalitarian perspective. The perspectives of the high-group cultures emphasize group boundaries, and these boundaries are often drawn sufficiently narrow that many persons are excluded.

Probably the greatest difficulties in this regard come from hierarchists whose high-group perspectives facilitate sharp group boundaries and whose high-grid perspectives encourage viewing persons as sharply unequal. That is, whereas subsequent egalitarian reformers with broader social horizons for the application of their culture than Jefferson have helped to extend civil-political and other human rights increasingly throughout the American population,[17] hierarchists find similar expansions of the social horizons within which the rights they support are applicable to be more difficult. Hierarchists' high-group horizons are not only typically narrow like Jefferson's, they are as well explicitly marked by high-grid perceptions of inequality. So for hierarchists it is particularly easy to view persons with different ethnic, gender, social-class, or other distinctions as having varying worth. Thus various sorts of hierarchical nationalistic and ethnic identities justify treating outsiders sharply differently than group members, and the social horizons beyond which persons are perceived as outsiders can be quite narrow.

Consider the relatively routine practices of Serbian nationalism during the 1990s in Bosnia and Kosovo. Nationalistic or ethnic purity concerns on this order create states that are truly rogue entities with regard to the universality of human rights. The conflict between property and socioeconomic rights discussed in the previous section was a struggle over which human rights would triumph over others. In contrast, the nature of the group boundaries perceived by some virulently hierarchical states or ethnicities poses a conflict between select persons with some rights and others to whom these select persons grant no rights at all. The persons who have guided Serbia (and some other states) in the recent past have shown no respect during the course of their state-expansion activities for any sorts of rights beyond extremely narrow ethnic, gender, and class horizons. In their state-expansion efforts, leaders of these groups have simply refused to accept that any but a narrow circle of persons merit dignity-supporting or suffering-limiting practices.

I suggest that these terrible activities represent unusually severe examples of a practice of drawing social horizons of concern in which many adherents of various cultures engage. For instance, Henry Shue (1996) contends that, with respect to facilitating the provision of various "primary goods," persons in advanced industrial societies owe persons in developing societies greater redistributive efforts than the former's social horizons generally support.[18] Similarly, Rawls (1971) argues that we need to expand our social horizons in terms of time to reduce our proclivity for squandering limited resources that later generations will need.

Yet the adherents of rival cultural biases draw these horizons of concern with varying degrees of narrowness and sharpness. On one end of the spectrum, individualists, while supporting only a specific range of human rights, tend—as we might anticipate of a culture with low-group consciousness—to see less distinct horizons to the practice of these rights than adherents of the high-group cultures perceive on the distinctive human rights that they support. Indeed, Hobbes and Locke have often been criticized by later philosophers (e.g., Hume) and contemporary high-group theorists (Macpherson 1973, chap. 5) for, among other matters, their insensitivity to limitations on the range of appropriate social application of their ideals. Individualists are, for instance, generally much less concerned with immigrants "polluting the Volk" than are the adherents of the high-group cultures. Individualists are inclined to view immigrants as sources of innovative ideas and practices.

Between the high-group cultures, hierarchists are more likely to violate the human rights they support outside group boundaries, because they are more apt to view persons outside these boundaries as inferior and thus meriting less, if indeed any, dignity-supporting activity than persons within their group.[19] Since human inequality is a foundational principle for hierarchists, we cannot generally expect them to engage in a gradual broadening of group horizons similar to that which has characterized succeeding generations of American "Jeffersonians." (See Chapter 2 for a more optimistic view.) Hierarchy is surely the most prevalent culture among political leaders in developing societies, and given the extraordinary dominance of hierarchy across human experience, it seems unlikely that it will soon fade sharply in practical social influence. So I view the prospects of a progressively more thoroughly overlapping consensus on human rights, prompted by principles such as supporting human dignity or limiting human suffering, more pessimistically than does Taylor. For hierarchists in particular, rights are generally accorded only to specific types of humans.

Hierarchists' penchants for honoring rights only within narrow national or ethnic communities poses two distinct contrasts with Taylor's vision (1999) of an unforced consensus on human rights. First, both the Western natural rights tradition and the Buddhist commitment to nonviolence are routinely expressed as universals. That is, their advocates aspire to see them practiced universally. Further, all individuals have to do to become members of these contrasting "faiths" is to adopt their respective ideals. Clearly, rights claimed by Serbs or similar national or ethnic identity groups are not universal in this sense. These latter rights could contribute to an unforced consensus on human rights only if the various nationalities or ethnicities that claim them practiced them broadly within their communities and minimized their contact and thus conflict with other peoples. Yet, second, this is not how hierarchists often employ such rights. Rather they frequently use them as rallying cries for national expansion and ethnic cleansing activities that inherently deny similar rights to "outsiders" living within or proximate to these communities. Thus common acts of claiming these rights require treating others with little or no regard to supporting their dignity or limiting suffering

Globalization and Human Rights

I have employed the term "globalization" in two senses common among political scientists.[20] First, I have referred to the progressive expansion of a global market by which increasing portions of economies worldwide fall under a single set of impersonal, economic forces, and second, I have mentioned the recent worldwide trend toward democracy. (See also Chapter 2.) Both of these senses of globalization support a similar, relatively narrow range of human rights. The capitalist juggernaut emphasizes civil—

especially property—rights incorporated in a rule of law rather than men; while democratization emphasizes political and, frequently less prominently, civil rights. Much good might come from the greater global success of this range of human rights, but implanting such rights increasingly firmly around the world also carries a price in terms of the deleterious consequences for rival cultures and the distinctive rights (especially economic and social) that they support.[21]

While some overlapping of rights concerns is possible across the adherents of grid-group theory's three socially interactive cultures, significant rifts in support for various types of human rights separate individualists from both egalitarians and hierarchists. I have focused on two examples of common rights conflicts between low-grid, low-group individualists and the others: the competition between individualistic property rights and egalitarian—and often hierarchical—pursuit of socioeconomic rights through maximin economic redistribution, and the greater narrowness of the social horizons of the high-group cultures as well as the frequent willingness of hierarchists in particular to act without regard for supporting human dignity or limiting human suffering beyond these horizons. Arguably, the economic development and growing affluence, which some analysts see as inevitable consequences of the increasingly global reach of a single market, might ameliorate some instances of these conflicts and prompt greater support for a broader range of human rights among non-Western societies.

Such a process has already occurred in advanced industrial societies by fostering the growth and progressive institutionalization of both low-grid cultures vis-à-vis hierarchy and taming politics in the process (Inglehart 1997). Yet even if—as many following Martin Lipset (1961) argue—development brings democracy, Fareed Zakaria (1994) and Bell and others (1995) contend that the democracies that develop in social environments lacking an individualistic, civil rights tradition are frequently illiberal or intolerant of interpersonal differences.[22] Moreover, capitalistic support for civil rights is sometimes narrow, centering on property rights. The vision of developing societies as illiberal democracies that secure the property rights of (largely foreign) investors suggests that the human rights support available through either of the senses of globalization employed in this chapter might be limited.

Yet four factors lead me to think that such a vision is more realistic than Taylor's relatively optimistic scenario. First, each of grid-group theory's socially interactive cultures supports or emphasizes a distinct portion of the full gamut of human rights recognized in various UN declarations and covenants as well as other attempts to specify the complete range of such rights (Center for the Study of Human Rights 1994). Second, rival cultures differ in the breadth of the social horizons within which they seek to support those rights they recognize. Civil-political rights are currently the subject of a global campaign in part because the individualistic culture employs broader horizons on the sphere of application of those rights it recognizes than do the high-group cultures, and in part because the United States, a highly individualistic society, enjoys considerable global influence as the single remaining superpower.

Third, the adherents of other cultures are not incorrect in perceiving a form of imperialism in U.S. support for civil-political rights in other societies. However well intentioned this imperialism may be and in spite of some undeniable salutary consequences of extending civil–political rights across societies, aspects of these rights also undercut other types of human rights that rival cultures support. Thus, fourth, the development of "universal human rights" would represent both gains and losses. It would require the global dominance of a particular culture (the individualism of global capitalism currently appears to be the most likely bet) and would entail the extension of a particular swath of human rights to an extensive population. In the process it might frequently constrain the capacities of certain assertive and currently regionally dominant hierarchical cultures to commit the sorts of exceptionally egregious travesties associated with recent Serbian or Indonesian nationalism. But the global dominance of this culture would mean attenuated influence for rival cultures and thus reduced support for the institutions they seek to foster, including other types of human rights. The damage to socioeconomic rights—for instance, the Confucian-based right to support from one's children in old-age (Bell 1999, 853)—among numerous highly vulnerable persons around the world, especially in developing societies, represents a particularly alarming prospect.

Notes

This paper draws on my experience in a 1999 National Endowment for the Humanities Summer Seminar: "Cultural Difference and Values: Human Rights and the Challenge of Relativism." I am grateful to Andrew J. Nathan, the seminar director, and to my seminar colleagues, particularly Neil Englehart, Mahmood Monshipouri, and Kavita Philip, for comments on previous drafts of this chapter.

1. For a related argument on the difficulties for achieving universal recognition of moral views similar to those that Charney holds (e.g., the "seven deadly sins"), see Lockhart and Franzwa 1994. (See Chapter 12 in this volume for a more optimistic view.)

2. By "legitimacy of external prescription" I refer to the varying ease with which persons accept that other persons' judgments are valid for and binding on

them. For a career enlisted person in a military service, for instance, this legitimacy is apt to be high, since she or he will have chosen a life that routinely involves accepting with few questions the orders of officers. So think of grid as the legitimacy of some making decisions binding on others. Group, in contrast, involves feelings of belonging to a multiperson collectivity clearly distinguished from outsiders.

3. This claim in controversial but less limiting than the widely accepted idea that variations on only two ways of life—hierarchy and individualism—are socially viable; see Lindblom 1977. Also, Alan Fiske (1993), Magoroh Maruyama (1980), Mark Lichbach (1995), and B. Guy Peters (1996) have derived similar typologies, and considerable empirical research supports this claim; see Evans-Pritchard 1940; Dumont 1980; Strathern 1971; and Uchendu 1965. Additionally, grid-group theory includes a fifth nonsocially interactive way of life—the hermit's—which I do not consider here; see Thompson 1982.

4. There are exceptions to fatalists' reticence. See *Ecclesiastes* 9:11 and Schopenhauer's *The World as Will and Representation.*

5. Even within political science a broad range of cultural approaches contend. Ruth Lane (1992) and Marc Ross (1997) provide fine surveys of this variation. Prominent examples of various approaches to cultural analysis include Inglehart 1997; Lipset 1996, 1990; Putnam with Leonardi and Nanetti 1993; Huntington 1996; Almond and Verba 1963; Verba et al. 1987; Verba, Nie, and Kim 1978; and Laitin 1986.

6. Thus, if Taylor's interpretation of a particular Buddhist tradition is correct, these Buddhists are clearly within the egalitarian fold. Yet while Buddhism is clearly a high-group culture, there are bases for considering Buddhists as much hierarchical as egalitarian. See Limanonda 1995.

7. Each of the low-grid cultures (i.e., individualism and egalitarianism) frequently form coalitions with hierarchy in order to better project aspects of their ways of life into society at large. Thus varying forms of limited government and social democracy are adopted by individualists and egalitarians, respectively.

8. Redistributive concerns with a maximin emphasis focus on upgrading the allotments of crucial goods among the least well-off. In practice, then, such efforts attempt to improve what it means to be poor in a particular society by, for instance, developing public social programs that provide free access to education and medical care and possibly ensure as well a minimum household income, particularly for the elderly and the disabled. Thus the practical implications of such an emphasis might differ from those of a concern with minimizing the distance between the top and the bottom of a society's socieconomic ladder or with a "minimax" emphasis that would cap the income and/or wealth of society's most well heeled members.

9. Falk (1999, 164–165) makes a similar suggestion with his idea of "statist backlash."

10. The relatively low levels of social interaction sustained by fatalists lead me to reduce the attention accorded to them from here on in this chapter. Briefly, fatalists perceive context as random and humans, fittingly, as capricious. Accordingly, they attempt to reduce their social relations to essentials, staying out of harm's way by minimizing their interaction with unpredictable, uncontrollable forces. Thus fatalists are rarely enthusiastic supporters of any sort of human rights, although they may claim a right of "privacy" for themselves.

11. See note 6 above.

12. Some persons hold "bifocal" cultural biases, practicing individualism in the workplace and egalitarianism in the family, for instance (Lockhart 2001, chap. 3). Since I think that these "bifocals" do not alter the situation I portray in this chapter, I do not generally complicate matters by including them in the analysis, but see the discussion of p. 274–275 in text.

13. Even within societies, some intracultural differences are not uncommon. For example, contemporary German egalitarians are divided between the Social Democrats (SPD) and the Greens. Whereas the SPD has historically made reducing certain social class differences its primary concern, the Greens have focused more on reducing the social implications of gender differences.

14. This is because different societal experiences elicit distinctive cultural orientations. For a more detailed explanation as to why this is so, see Lockhart 2001, chap. 1.

15. By egalitarian Christianity, I refer to the character of much of the text of the New Testament, not to the character of organized religious practice, much of which is clearly hierarchical (e.g., Roman Catholicism).

16. See note 12 above on "bifocal" cultural biases. Additionally, available evidence (e.g., Hochschild 1981; Walzer 1983; Free and Cantril 1967) suggests that persons with bifocal cultural biases apply particular cultural "lenses" persistently to distinct domains of social life.

17. Some contemporary egalitarians, for instance, have exceptionally broad horizons, including not only all humans, but also other living creatures (e.g., animal rightists [Singer 1975]).

18. Primary goods are those that are requisite to any rational life plan (e.g., medical care, basic education). See Rawls 1971.

19. Others have suggested that egalitarians' penchants for systematically abusing the human rights of those beyond a narrow circle are as great or perhaps even greater than hierarchists'. See Pye 1988 and Jackson 1989.

20. For broader conceptions, see Jameson and Miyoshi 1998 and Castells 1998.

21. Falk (1999, 161, 163, 166; 1998, 264) also argues that globalization in these senses favors civil-political over socioeconomic rights.

22. Daniel Bell and Kanishka Jayasuriya (1995) do a particularly good job of contrasting core values of liberal and illiberal democracies—equality, freedom, and pluralism as opposed to inequality, orderliness, and substantive moral consensus, respectively—that contribute to distinctive conceptions of human flourishing.

References

Almond, Gabriel A., and Sidney Verba. 1963. *The Civic Culture: Political Attitudes and Democracy in Five Nations.* Princeton: Princeton University Press.

Banfield, Edward C. 1958. *The Moral Basis for a Backward Society.* Glencoe, IL: Free Press.

Becker, Gary S. 1976. *The Economic Approach to Human Behavior.* Chicago: University of Chicago Press.

Bell, Daniel A. 1998. "The Limits of Liberal Justice." *Political Theory* 26, no. 4 (August): 557–82.

————. 1999. "Which Rights Are Universal?" *Political Theory* 27, no. 6 (December): 849–856.

Bell, Daniel A., David Brown, Kanishka Jayasuriya, and David Martin Jones. 1995. *Towards Illiberal Democracy in Pacific Asia.* New York: St. Martin's Press.

Bell, Daniel A., and Kanishka Jayasuriya. 1995. "Understanding Illiberal Democracy: A Framework." In Daniel A. Bell, David Brown, Kanishka Jayasuriya, and David Martin Jones, *Towards Illiberal Democracy in Pacific Asia.* New York: St. Martin's Press, 1–16.

Berlin, Isaiah. 1969. "Two Concepts of Liberty." In Isaiah Berlin, *Four Essays on Liberty.* Oxford: Oxford University Press, 118–172.

Birchfield, Vicki, and Markus M. L. Crepaz. 1998. "The Impact of Constitutional Structures and Collective and Competitive Veto Points on Income Inequality in Industrialized Democracies." *European Journal of Political Research* 34: 175–200.

Castells, Manuel. 1998. *End of Millennium.* London: Basil Blackwell.

Center for the Study of Human Rights. 1994. *Twenty-five Human Rights Documents.* New York: Center for the Study of Human Rights, Columbia University.

Charney, Evan. 1999. "Cultural Interpretation and Universal Human Rights: A Response to Daniel A. Bell." *Political Theory* 27, no. 6 (December): 840–848.

Cornell, Drucilla. 1998. *At the Heart of Freedom: Feminism, Sex, and Equality.* Princeton: Princeton University Press.

Coughlin, Richard M., and Charles Lockhart. 1998. "Grid-Group Theory and Ideology: A Consideration of Their Relative Strengths and Weaknesses for Explaining the Structure of Mass Belief Systems." *Journal of Theoretical Politics* 10, no. 1 (January): 33–58.

Donnelly, Jack. 1982. "Human Rights and Human Dignity: An Analytic Critique of Non-Western Human Rights Conceptions." *American Political Science Review* 76, no. 2 (June): 303–316.

————. 1989. *Universal Human Rights in Theory and Practice.* Ithaca, NY: Cornell University Press.

Douglas, Mary, ed. 1982. *Essays in the Sociology of Perception.* London: Routledge and Kegan Paul.

————. 1986. *How Institutions Think.* Syracuse, NY: Syracuse University Press.

Downey, Gary L. 1986. "Ideology and the Clamshell Identity: Organizational Dilemmas in the Anti-Nuclear Movement." *Social Problems* 33, no. 3 (September): 357–373.

Dumont, Louis. 1980. *Homo Hierarchicus: The Caste System and Its Implications.* Mark Sainsbury, Louis Dumont, and Basia Gulati, trans. Chicago: University of Chicago Press.

Durkheim, Emile. 1951 [1897]. *Suicide: A Study in Sociology.* John A. Spaulding and George Simpson, trans. Glencoe, IL: Free Press.

Ellis, Richard J. 1993. *American Political Cultures.* New York: Oxford University Press.

————. 1998. *The Dark Side of the Left: Illiberal Egalitarianism in America.* Lawrence: University Press of Kansas.

Ellis, Richard J., and Fred Thompson. 1997. "Culture and the Environment in the Pacific Northwest." *American Political Science Review* 91, no. 4 (December): 885–897.

Englehart, Neil A. 1998. "The Political Economy of Deforestation in Thailand and Indonesia." Paper presented at the 1998 annual meeting of the Midwest Political Science Association, Chicago, IL.

―――. 2000. "Rights and Culture in the Asian Values Argument: The Rise and Fall of Confucian Ethics in Singapore." *Human Rights Quarterly* 22, no. 2 (May): 548–568.

Evans-Pritchard, E. E. 1940. *The Nuer: A Description of the Modes of Livelihood and Political Institutions of the Nilotic People.* Oxford: Oxford University Press.

Falk, Richard. 1998. "A Half Century of Human Rights." *Australian Journal of International Affairs* 52, no. 3: 255–272.

―――. 1999. "The Quest for Human Rights in an Era of Globalization." In Michael G. Schechter, eds., *Future Multilateralism: The Political and Social Framework.* New York: St. Martin's Press, 153–178.

Ferejohn, John. 1991. "Rationality and Interpretation: Parliamentary Elections in Early Stuart England." In Kristen Renwick Monroe, ed., *The Economic Approach to Politics: A Critical Reassessment of the Theory of Rational Action.* New York: HarperCollins, 279–305.

Fishkin, James S. 1983. *Justice, Equal Opportunity, and the Family.* New Haven, CT: Yale University Press.

Fiske, Alan. 1993. *Structures of Social Life: The Four Elementary Forms of Human Relations.* New York: Free Press.

Free, Lloyd A., and Hadley Cantril. 1967. *The Political Beliefs of Americans: A Study of Public Opinion.* New Brunswick, NJ: Rutgers University Press.

Gewirth, Alan. 1978. *Reason and Morality.* Chicago: University of Chicago Press.

Grendstad, Gunnar. 1999. "A Political Cultural Map of Europe: A Survey Approach." *Geojournal* 47, no. 3: 463–475.

Held, David. 1987. *Models of Democracy.* Stanford, CA: Stanford University Press.

Hochschild, Jennifer L. 1981. *What's Fair: American Beliefs About Distributive Justice.* Cambridge: Harvard University Press.

Howard, Rhoda E., and Jack Donnelly. 1986. "Human Dignity, Human Rights, and Political Regimes." *American Political Science Review* 80, no. 3 (September): 801–817.

Huntington, Samuel P. 1996. *The Clash of Civilizations and the Remaking of World Order.* New York: Simon and Schuster.

Inglehart, Ronald. 1997. *Modernization and Postmodernization: Cultural, Economic, and Political Change in 43 Societies.* Princeton: Princeton University Press.

Jackson, Karl D., ed. 1989. *Cambodia: Rendezvous with Death.* Princeton: Princeton University Press.

Jameson, Fredric, and Masao Miyoshi, eds. 1998. *The Cultures of Globalization.* Durham, NC: Duke University Press.

Kelly, David, and Anthony Reid, eds. 1998. *Asian Freedoms: The Idea of Freedom in East and Southeast Asia.* New York: Cambridge University Press.

Laitin, David D. 1986. *Hegemony and Culture: Politics and Religious Change Among the Yoruba.* Chicago: University of Chicago Press.

Lane, Ruth. 1992. "Political Culture: Residual Category or General Theory?" *Comparative Political Studies* 25, no. 3 (October): 362–387.

Lee, Kuan Yew. 1999. *The Singapore Story: Memoirs of Lee Kuan Yew.* New York: Prentice-Hall.

Lichbach, Mark Irving. 1995. *The Rebel's Dilemma.* Ann Arbor: University of Michigan Press.

Limanonda, Bhassorn. 1995. "Families in Thailand: Beliefs and Realities." *Journal of Comparative Family Studies* 26, no. 1 (spring): 67–82.

Lindblom, Charles E. 1977. *Politics and Markets: The World's Political-Economic Systems.* New York: Basic Books.

Lipset, Seymour Martin. 1960. *Political Man: The Social Bases of Politics.* Garden City, NY: Doubleday.

———. 1990. *Continental Divide: Values and Institutions in the United States and Canada.* New York: Routledge.

———. 1996. *American Exceptionalism: A Double-Edged Sword.* New York: Norton.

Lockhart, Charles. 2001. *Protecting the Elderly: How Culture Shapes Social Policy.* University Park: Pennsylvania State University Press.

Lockhart, Charles, and Richard M. Coughlin. 1992. "Building Better Comparative Social Theory Through Alternative Conceptions of Rationality." *Western Political Quarterly* 45, no. 3 (September): 793–809.

Lockhart, Charles, and Gregg Franzwa. 1994. "Cultural Theory and the Problem of Moral Relativism." In Dennis J. Coyle and Richard J. Ellis, eds., *Politics, Policy, and Culture.* Boulder, CO: Westview Press, 175–189.

Lockhart, Charles, and Aaron Wildavsky. 1998. "The Social Construction of Cooperation: Egalitarian, Hierarchical, and Individualistic Faces of Altruism." In Sun-Ki Chai and Brendon Swedlow, eds., *Aaron Wildavsky's Culture and Social Theory.* New Brunswick, NJ: Transaction, 113–131.

Macpherson, C. B. 1973. *Democratic Theory: Essays in Retrieval.* Oxford: Oxford University Press.

Mahbubani, Kishore. 1998. *Can Asians Think?* Singapore: Times Editions.

Margalit, Aavishai. 1996. *The Decent Society.* Naomi Goldblum, trans. New York: Cambridge University Press.

Mars, Gerald. 1982. *Cheats at Work: An Anthropology of Workplace Crime.* London: Allen and Unwin.

Marshall, T. H. 1963 [1949]. "Citizenship and Social Class." In T. H. Marshall, *Sociology at the Crossroads and Other Essays.* London: Heinemann.

Maruyama, Magoroh, 1980. "Mindscapes and Science Theories." *Current Anthropology* 21, no. 5 (October): 589–600.

Nozick, Robert. 1974. *Anarchy, State, and Utopia.* New York: Basic Books.

Nussbaum, Martha. 1997. *Cultivating Humanity: A Classical Defense of Reform in Liberal Education.* Cambridge: Harvard University Press.

Peters, B. Guy. 1996. *The Future of Governing: Four Emerging Models.* Lawrence: University Press of Kansas.

Putnam, Robert D., with Robert Leonardi and Raffaella Y. Nanetti. 1993. *Making Democracy Work: Civic Traditions in Modern Italy.* Princeton: Princeton University Press.

Pye, Lucian W. 1988. *The Mandarin and the Cadre: China's Political Cultures.* Ann Arbor: Center for Chinese Studies, University of Michigan.

Rae, Douglas, Douglas Yates, Jennifer Hochschild, Joseph Morone, and Carol Fessler. 1981. *Equalities*. Cambridge: Harvard University Press.

Rawls, John. 1971. *A Theory of Justice*. Cambridge: Harvard University Press.

———. 1993. "The Law of Peoples." In Stephen Shute and Susan Hurley, eds., *On Human Rights: The Oxford Amnesty Lectures 1993*. New York: Basic Books, 41–82.

Ross, Marc Howard. 1997. "Culture and Identity in Comparative Political Analysis." In Mark Irving Lichbach and Alan S. Zuckerman, eds., *Comparative Politics: Rationality, Culture, and Structure*. New York: Cambridge University Press, 42–80.

Sartori, Giovanni. 1995. "How Far Can Free Government Travel?" *Journal of Democracy* 6, no. 4 (October): 101–111.

Schumacher, E. F. 1973. *Small Is Beautiful: Economics As If People Mattered*. New York: Harper and Row.

Schwarz, Michiel, and Michael Thompson. 1990. *Divided We Stand: Redefining Politics, Technology, and Social Change*. Philadelphia: University of Pennsylvania Press.

Shue, Henry. 1996. *Basic Rights: Subsistence, Affluence, and U.S. Foreign Policy*. Princeton: Princeton University Press.

Singer, Peter. 1975. *Animal Liberation: A New Ethics for Our Treatment of Animals*. New York: Random House.

Skocpol, Theda. 1987. "America's Incomplete Welfare State." In Martin Rein, Gosta Esping-Andersen, and Lee Rainwater, eds., *Stagnation and Renewal in Social Policy*. Armonk, NY: M. E. Sharpe, 35–58.

Strathern, Andrew. 1971. *The Rope of Moka: Big-Men and Ceremonial Exchange in Mount Hagen, New Guinea*. Cambridge: Cambridge University Press.

Taylor, Charles. 1999. "Conditions of an Unforced Consensus on Human Rights." In Joanne R. Bauer and Daniel A. Bell, eds., *The East Asian Challenge for Human Rights*. New York: Cambridge University Press, 124–144.

Thompson, Michael. 1982. "The Problem of the Center: An Autonomous Cosmology." In Mary Douglas, ed., *Essays in the Sociology of Perception*. London: Routledge and Kegan Paul, 302–327.

Thompson, Michael, Richard Ellis, and Aaron Wildavsky. 1990. *Cultural Theory*. Boulder, CO: Westview Press.

Turnbull, Colin. 1972. *The Mountain People*. New York: Simon and Schuster.

Uchendu, Victor C. 1965. *The Igbo of Southeast Nigeria*. New York: Holt, Rinehart, and Winston.

United Nations. 1966. "International Covenant on Economic, Social, and Cultural Rights and International Covenant on Civil and Political Rights." United Nations General Assembly Resolution 2200 (XXI), A/6316, December 16.

Verba, Sidney, Steven Kelman, Gray R. Orren, Ichiro Miyake, Joji Watanuki, Ikue Kabashima, and G. Donald Ferree Jr. 1987. *Elites and the Idea of Equality: A Comparison of Japan, Sweden, and the United States*. Cambridge: Harvard University Press.

Verba, Sidney, Norman H. Nie, and Jae-on Kim. 1978. *Participation and Political Equality: A Seven Nation Comparison*. New York: Cambridge University Press.

Walzer, Michael. 1983. *Spheres of Justice: A Defense of Pluralism and Equality*. New York: Basic Books.

Wildavsky, Aaron. 1994. "Why Self-Interest Means Less Outside of a Social Context: Cultural Contributions to a Theory of Rational Choices." *Journal of Theoretical Politics* 6, no. 2 (April): 131–159.

Wilensky, Harold L. 1975. *The Welfare State and Equality: The Structural and Ideological Roots of Public Expenditures.* Berkeley: University of California Press.

Zakaria, Fareed. 1994. "Culture Is Destiny: A Conversation with Lee Kuan Yew." *Foreign Affairs* 73, no. 2 (March/April): 109–126.

Zisk, Betty. 1992. *The Politics of Transformation: Local Activism in the Peace and Environmental Movements.* New York: Praeger.

11

Globalizing Cultural Values

International Human Rights Discourse as Moral Persuasion

Chenyang Li

In this chapter I argue that the ultimate goal of the international human rights discourse is to promote certain moral values through persuasion; it should not be merely forcing people to change their behavior, but rather convincing people to accept certain moral values that they have not embraced or to embrace certain moral values as more important than they previously have held. I say "is" in the sense we say that the president's job is to provide leadership; it does not necessarily mean that the person in office is actually providing leadership: he or she may lack the leadership that the job requires. Thus "is" used in this way is normative. In the current international human rights discourse, broadly speaking, persuasion has already taken place, along with other means such as threat, coercion, and even military intervention. The purpose of my argument here is to clearly define and clarify such a goal. I will first support this understanding of the international human rights discourse as moral persuasion by examining the global background of the international human rights discourse process, and then examine various alternatives to this approach as well as various ways of persuasion. Finally, I will draw conclusions on the limits of the human rights movement if we accept this discourse as a process of moral persuasion.

My task is to provide a philosophy on the nature of international human rights discourse, not to provide a human rights worker's manual. I will not argue for a position as to which international human rights document should be used as the starting point for moral persuasion. In principle, my view is that any legitimate and effective document has to be a means or a result of moral persuasion, has to possess persuasive force, and has to be subject to future revisions in an ongoing persuasion process.

A Historical Perspective

Let me start with the relation between moral values and community. By moral values I mean preferences on which one builds decisions for action that have ethical implications. It could be argued that, in the end, every preference has ethical implications (e.g., a strict utilitarian approach), but it is also true that some values are more directly morally relevant than others. In this chapter I am primarily concerned with values that have direct moral relevance.

As human beings we live in communities. A community is a group of people who share more or less similar morals and values. The degree of this similarity may vary and shared values may change. We may say that there are different levels of communities and that communities overlap and change. But clearly, individuals who share absolutely no common values and who are not involved in shaping these values cannot be members of the same community in the moral sense. Because evaluative activities are intrinsic to the very existence of a community, without shared morals and values, no community can operate. The fact that a society has different value systems (see Chapter 10) does not preclude that different cultures and societies have had more or less different moral codes and hence different prevalent moral values. In ancient Greece, the Athenians and the Spartans were evidently two different communities with different moral codes, even though neither was entirely homogeneous. In ancient China, there were the Zhou and the Chu.[1] These moral codes reflect different values. Naturally one feels more comfortable in dealing with people with similar values and moral codes, and feels less comfortable with people with different values and moral codes. There was no major problem with different values across societies in preindustrial ages, because there was little communication and exchange of ethical ideas between societies. It was easy and natural for one to believe that all other cultures were barbarian simply because they did not conform to one's own "tested" morals. The Greeks certainly thought this way, and so did the Chinese. It is arguable that, in those old days, all peoples were ethical universalists, not because they saw universally accepted or practiced morals—which certainly did not exist—but because they believed that their own morals were the only right ones and all other peoples, in order to be civilized, must adopt these morals. In retrospect, one can hardly make a case for any single civilization's claim to the only right way—all others being wrong. But because of isolation there was no practical need for people to contemplate whether it was possible for moral values different from one's own to be valid.[2]

Modern technology has changed the world and has brought us an entirely different environment. It has made it possible for us to communicate, trade, and travel across societies to a greater extent than ever before. Our televisions show happenings from all over the world instantly. People in different countries can log on to the Internet and see what people in other parts of the world are doing. In this way, modern technology puts the entire world in front of us. It has reduced, though not eliminated, the distance between societies. Technology has brought us into a global village, and now forces us to face one another in a global community in an inevitable way.

Unlike a natural community, into which members have evolved or been born, the global village is in a sense an artificial community that was created in a relatively short period of time; it includes members of vastly different cultural and ethical backgrounds.[3] Just as we need some common monetary currencies for our economic life in the global economy, in order to live meaningfully with one another within the international community, we also need to have some kind of similar morals and values on matters that are important to members' visions of the good life. It is pointless and unproductive to condemn or praise one another with moral languages coded with moral values that have no collective meaning. Some kind of common moral language is needed in our international community in addition to our "local" or traditional languages. In other words, common values are like common currencies. The question is, whose or which morals and values are to become the common currency? When people identify some of their own values as being worthy candidates, they need to persuade others to accept that these values are worthy throughout the entire global community. They need to persuade others to accept these values as their own. This, I maintain, is the nature of the international human rights discourse.

In the international human rights movement, both persuasion and coercion have played a role. It is hard to deny the usefulness of coercion, which sometimes is certainly justified and necessary. However, persuasion, rather than coercion, is the most effective way to spread moral values. First, moral coercion usually does not work. One may be coerced to act a certain way for a variety of reasons. But one cannot be forced to *accept* a value, that is, to turn a value into one's own, unless one is convinced that the value is worthwhile. Coerced behavior lasts only as coercion continues. In the long run, moral order in the world cannot be maintained by coercion.

Second, even if sometimes a value can be imposed on someone through coercion, there is a high moral risk involved: the imposer may turn out to be wrong, as history has repeatedly evidenced. For the moral person who wants to make other people moral as well, this would be the worst outcome possible. Moral persuasion reduces the chance of such grave mistakes. Third, international human rights norms, whether in the form of international laws or covenants, have to be enforced through sovereign nations. That makes them different from domestic law, which is enforced on citizens who are without individual legal sovereignty. For all these reasons, moral persuasion is the best way to establish long-term consensus on human rights. If the international human rights movement aims at long-lasting solutions rather than short-term remedies, it has to persuade people to accept the fundamental values of human rights.

Let me suggest that the adoption of human rights as a predominant currency for international moral discourse is a historically contingent but not accidental fact. It is historically contingent because the industrial revolution took place in the West and thus is largely responsible for making the West the dominant world power today. The industrial revolution could have happened some place other than the West *if* similar factors had obtained (there was neither metaphysical nor logical necessity that these factors had to obtain in the West). Had that happened, then today the dominant world force would be a non-Western one. Just as the U.S. dollar has become a predominant monetary currency in world trade (i.e., it has recognizable economic power in the world) largely because of the economic power of the United States, the concept of human rights has become a predominant moral currency largely because of the political and possibly moral power of the West. If the United States and a third-world country, say India, were today transposed in economic power, we would probably be using among others the Indian rupee instead of the U.S. dollar as a world currency. Similarly, if India were the dominant world political force today, we would be talking about internationalizing *dharma* ("duty," "right action"); if China were the dominant world force today, we would be talking about internationalizing *ren* ("humanity," "benevolence"). Then, whatever concepts of moral ideals we would be using today would have been laden with new implications that serve today's societal needs; our international moral discourse would include such issues as how much room *dharma* requires us to leave the individual or how human dignity implied in *ren* (especially in Mencius's thought) demands others to respect the individual's autonomy in addition to its implication of treating others kindly. The difference is that India or China would claim primary authority in defining and interpreting these concepts; they would have more authority in judging whether a country's practice meets the standards of *dharma* or *ren*.

That the West has become the dominant world force is a historically contingent fact, but it is not accidental that the idea of human rights, rather than any other Western value concepts, has become a central moral-political currency, given that the pool of ideas in Western traditions has been large. The West did not just arbitrarily pick a value from its cultural pool. "Human rights" has been chosen because it has merit that other Western concepts lack. It has a strong appeal: it is more forceful than some other moral concepts such as "love" and "charity" and it serves some urgent needs in the industrialized state society. Just as the U.S. dollar serves a positive function in the world economy today by providing a common currency, the concept of human rights also serves a positive function in today's world by providing a common language for international moral-political communication. The danger, however, is that some human rights advocates forget that the idea of human rights is a value concept (i.e., it reflects certain values), and that dealing with people with different values is much more complicated than dealing with people with different commercial goods. They fail to understand that persuasion, instead of economic and political coercion, should be the ultimate means to unite people under the values clustered on human rights.

To be sure, sometimes human rights discourse is mainly a fight between human rights advocates on the one hand and authoritarian regimes or human rights abusers on the other. In such cases there appears to be a relatively clear line between right and wrong. But international human rights issues often involve disagreement between people in different cultures with different values. Human rights discourse involves fundamentally different beliefs in value. For example, even though totalitarian governments have their own hidden agendas in the "Asian values" debate, it would be simpleminded to assume that the battle is merely between human rights advocates on the one hand and a handful evil totalitarians on the other. It does involve innocent people with different beliefs and different values. For example, while one may argue that the Chinese leaders have their own interest in using prison labor, such a practice is not a moral wrong nor a human rights violation judged by the values of the general Chinese population. In fact, many Chinese think it ridiculous that prisoners in many states of the United States do not have to labor during their sentence, and that they can just sit idly watching cable television most of the time. Rightly or wrongly, the general population in China tends to see a connection between inmates' "leisure" life and the high crime rate in the United States. In cases like forced prison labor, the fight is not simply between international human rights advocates on the one side and a repressive regime on the other. If human rights advocates are convinced that it is morally wrong to force prisoners to labor, they will have to convince the Chinese people before they can win the fight with the regime.

In order to reach some kind of consensus on important human rights issues, persuasion is necessary. Even with authoritarian leadership, who may not be labeled appropriately as mere "evil," persuasion should be the chief means to achieve the ultimate goal of human rights movements.

The Misguided Debate Between Value Universalism and Relativism

In the international human rights discourse one important issue has been whether certain values are universal or relative. In his celebrated book *The Age of Rights,* Louis Henkin writes:

> Human rights are universal: They belong to every human being in every human society. They do not differ with geography or history, culture or ideology, political or economic system, or stage of societal development. To call them "human" implies that all human beings have them, equally and in equal measure, by virtue of their humanity—regardless of sex, race, age; regardless of high or low "birth," social class, national origin, ethnic or tribal affiliation; regardless of wealth or poverty, occupation, talent, merit, religion, ideology, or other commitment. (Henkin 1990, 2–3)

In other words, human rights are universal in that each and every human being possesses the same rights.

Universalists fall into three categories. In the first group, human rights are held to be universal in the sense that certain values are accepted universally. Let us call this position the de facto universalism of human rights. De facto universalists believe that human rights have been already universally accepted as a universal value in the same way that the belief that bank robbery is wrong has been accepted as a universal value. Even though there is still bank robbery, it is only that the bank robbers are wrong; similarly, even though human rights violations occur, it is simply that the violators are wrong. Another kind of universalism is the belief that human rights are a universal natural property that every human being possesses naturally, even though some people have not realized it as a reality, in the sense that even though the earth is round, some people still believe it to be flat: they are ignorant and need to be educated of the factual truth. Accordingly, the goal of the international human rights movement is to promote an awareness of the existence of human rights as reality. This position may be called universal realism of human rights. Still others claim that, although the values of human rights are not a matter of fact, nor have they been accepted universally, they ought to be accepted universally. Let us call this group the de jure universalists. All three kinds of universalism oppose the relativist position on human rights. Relativists hold that human rights are values, and because values are culture-specific, human rights are also culture-specific; therefore, there are no universal human rights.

Though philosophically meaningful, the debate between universalists and relativists on human rights, I believe, is misguided. Moral or value relativists claim that peoples of different cultures have different values (they may not deny at the same time that there are values shared more or less by peoples across cultures).[4] Even if they are right on this claim, this reality does not tell us whether people ought to hold on to different values. After all, values change. Even within the same culture, values have evolved. Most of us like to think that our own values are by and large not only better than those of other cultures, but also better than those of our forebears. Therefore, even though a culture has values different from the values advocated by the human rights movement, the fact that it has different values or that its values have changed does not say anything about whether these people should change their values. Value relativism provides no answer to the question of whether one ought to adopt values foreign to one's traditional culture. It may provide reasons for not changing one's values, but there are good reasons for trying to change others' values, as I will show later in this chapter.

From the fact that a large number of nations have signed various international human rights covenants, de facto universalists argue that certain values are universal. This approach does have some merit. If a government has signed a covenant to protect the freedom of religion, for example, that government is vulnerable to accusations of inconsistencies between its words and its practice if it represses religious freedom. If the fact of covenant violations is clear, that government has some explaining to do to the international community. However, these international covenants are subject to different interpretations. For example, is forced prison labor a form of slavery or not? While in the West many consider forced prison labor a form of slavery, in some other countries it is considered a legitimate form of reforming inmates (this fact, of course, says nothing about whether this practice is morally right or wrong). Some countries will only sign an agreement against slavery because it does not specify, for example, that forced prison labor is slavery. Without specifications, an international agreement against slavery has little force in dealing with forced prison labor. Different interpretations of international covenants create a gray area, which can make de facto universalism forceless.

Another weakness of de facto universalism concerns the question of how to deal with nations that refuse to sign international human rights covenants. The United States, for example, has refused to sign or ratify a number of these covenants. De facto universalists have little resort in such cases. Furthermore, even if some governments accept an international human rights covenant in word, it does not mean that they will follow it through in practice. Louis Henkin maintains that hypocrisy is the homage that vice pays to virtue; even if some governments do not really subscribe to the values of human rights, they nevertheless accept these values nominally (Henkin 1990, x). Henkin's comment may make human rights activists feel good; after all, it is better for the vice to pay homage than not to. But a nominal victory of this sort is hardly worth celebrating. The real question is: How do we bring these governments into the international human rights regime?

The problem with universal realists of human rights is twofold. First, there is no convincing way to prove that there exists such a natural property of human rights. After all, saying that human rights exist is different from saying that the earth is round, which can be proven by scientific facts. Second, even if such a natural property exists in the world, we still need to convince people to value human rights. Natural existence does not imply valuation. Human rights, whether natural or not, will not be effective unless people actually value these rights.

Unlike de facto universalists, de jure universalists do not deny that certain human rights values have not been accepted universally; they argue, however, that these values ought to be accepted and practiced universally. They recognize the fact that values are different from culture to culture and from time to time. Nevertheless, they hold that there are certain important values that are "correct" or superior, which we all ought to embrace. The difficulty with this approach, however, is that there is simply no objective basis to justify some select values that ought to be universal. Besides, who is to select these "universal values"?

The debate between value universalism and value relativism may never be resolvable. My argument in this chapter attempts to go beyond this debate. Universalists, de facto, de jure, or realist, seem to take human rights values as fixed standards, which, once determined or discovered, must be applied to every corner of the world. Some universalists are often "self-righteous" fighters, with self-endowed absolute truths in their hand. But to others, these universalists often evoke images of religious crusaders, with God always on their side. Relativists, on the other hand, seem to assume that, because some people have different values, it is always legitimate for them to uphold these values. Some relativists promote "overlapping consensus." They take the morals of different peoples to be absolutely their own business and hope to find some overlapping values. It appears that neither side considers values as products of a continuous process in which human beings make and remake their own existence. I suggest that people are beings with values and beings who renew themselves by reshaping, refining, and re-creating their values. One important way of undertaking this process is through dialogue and communication, which allow one to rethink and reexamine existing values and make adjustments to form and reform those that one is most at home with. The international human rights discourse is such a process, in which some people attempt to persuade others to accept certain values. Therefore, my argument does not require morality to be relative or to be absolute; it only relies on an empirical fact that people can and do change their values and that people influence one another in their values.

Moral Persuasion Without Universalistic Foundation

Some people may worry that without moral universalism the human rights movement will lose legitimacy; after all, much of the human rights movement so far has been grounded on the claim of moral universalism. To many, it just feels more justified to promote values that are deemed universally valid. Indeed, they would not feel justified if these values were not claimed to be universally valid. If we regard the human rights discourse primarily as moral persuasion, on what ground can we justify it? In other words, can we justify human rights persuasion without a universalistic foundation? Can one counter some human rights advocates' move toward moral universalism without relying on moral relativism?

I think that there are good reasons to support the promotion of human rights values. First, as human beings, we all have our own values and we hold on to these values because we believe they are good values. Second, we also have concerns for others. We care about others and want others also to have good values. Third, we usually feel more comfortable with others who feel the same way, and uncomfortable with our moral opponents. This is so because approving a moral value entails opposing actions to its contrary. When bad things happen due to other people's conscious choices, we feel the urge to find the source and correct them. Therefore, when we believe that some of our own values can benefit others who do not yet possess them, we feel the need to persuade them to accept these values. Thus one may say that this felt need for moral persuasion is based on both altruism and self-interest.

I do not believe that moral persuasion should aim at reaching an absolute consensus on values. Nor do I believe that we are finally approaching the "end of history," when humankind finally concludes its journey for moral values and reaches the ultimate universal consensus.[5] I see the formation of moral values through persuasion as a process rather than a finished product. In other words, the fruitfulness of moral persuasion yields in the continuing process. We should have patience with different values. Indeed, it is quite amazing how much closer various cultures have become in the past half century (e.g., on issues such as national independence and democracy). The result deserves celebration. Nevertheless, consensus is not ultimate because moral consensus is always reached within a particular historical setting and human history continues to evolve. Rhoda E. Howard has forcefully argued that "human rights are a modern concept now universally applicable in principle because of the social evolution of the entire world toward state societies. . . . [It is] one particular conception of human dignity and social justice. It is not synonymous, despite their joining in the Universal Declaration of Human Rights, with human dignity" (Howard 1991, 81, 99). We have no assurance that the type of society we have today will remain forever, and we have no assurance of the type of human society that awaits us in the future. As society evolves, moral values (or at least the priorities of various moral values) cannot but change too.

This is one area in which I disagree with such authors as Abdullahi A. An-Na'im. An-Na'im makes a strong case for the approach through internal cultural discourse and cross-cultural dialogue in order to promote human rights values, which I believe to be very important for the moral persuasion of human rights. But he bases his approach on an essentialism of cross-cultural universal values. He writes "[My] approach is based on the belief that, despite their apparent peculiarities and diversity, human beings and societies share certain fundamental interests, concerns, qualities, traits, and values that can be identified and articulated as the framework for a common 'culture' of universal human rights" (1992, 21). He calls such a common culture "*genuinely universal* human rights" (1992, 5, italics are original). I disagree with essentialism or universalism of moral values. First of all, moral values evolve. What appears as a universal human right may not be so in the future. Today, the right of reproduction is widely accepted as a basic human right. But if the human population continues to expand against the earth's capacity to sustain it, such a right may be suspect. If some animal rights advocates turn out to be correct about animal rights, the concept of human rights may be fundamentally inadequate. Second, even if we humans do share certain fundamental common interests and concerns, it does not follow that they can be formulated only in the same way or articulated only in the human rights language. Different societies and social circumstances may assign different priorities to the same moral values. Third, in my view, consensus is to be broken and remade as both the human race and our morals evolve. But the endless process is not in vain: in it are human satisfaction, happiness, and flourishing.

Admittedly, this conception of human rights discourse as moral persuasion is in a sense a "weaker" one compared with the universalist approach. It leaves little or no room for hegemony, which is usually based on universalism. But this should not be perceived as a defect. Under the banner of moral universalism, humans have done tremendous atrocities to one another. With a firm belief of having absolute truth in their own hand, or with God on their side, self-righteous people have forced themselves on others again and again, resulting in disaster after disaster. On my approach, moral persuaders do not have a mandate from any absolute source. They do not have a God locked in their own pocket. They cannot take their moral superiority for granted. They have to approach the persons being persuaded as equals.

On the other hand, the moral persuasion approach is stronger than merely looking for "overlapping consensus." Charles Taylor (1999), for example, distinguishes two levels of issues with human rights discourse: norms of conduct and their underlying justification. Sensitive to fundamental differences between cultures, Taylor sees the international human rights discourse as a process searching for "overlapping consensus" on norms of conduct that comply with human rights, while leaving room for fundamental cultural differences. It is not clear how moral values fit onto Taylor's two levels. Moral values are reflected in the norms of conduct, but they cannot be reduced to norms. If values belong to the level of justification, then my approach goes further than Taylor's. Mine strives beyond existing cultural values and attempts to change at least some of them. The persuasion approach is a forward-looking one, not a static approach. It does not accept what can be found in the existing culture as the last word. To the moral persuader, saying that a certain culture has not had human rights values is no longer a legitimate excuse not to accept such values, because the persuader's purpose is precisely to convince others to accept new values. If a culture does not have human rights values, this approach tries to help introduce or produce them.

The moral persuader differentiates a people from a culture, even though the two are closely related. The so-called Asian values are nothing inherently or uniquely Asian. They are just those values that have been held by most Asians for a long time. Non-Asians could also hold these values, and Asians could discard these values. Being Chinese (e.g., Chinese-American) does not necessarily imply possessing traditional Chinese values, even though the word "Chinese" is often used to mean "having traditional Chinese values" (e.g., "She is very Chinese"). Similarly, the Chinese people would remain Chinese even if they were to abandon Confucian, Daoist, or Buddhist values. To say that Chinese cannot be un-Confucian is analytically not true, and it is empirically false. Of course, whether Chinese being un-Confucian is a good thing is entirely another matter. It is up to the Chinese to decide whether to remain Confucian. Introducing new values to a culture can be both a blessing and a curse: the culture may gain some good and lose some good.[6]

Persuasion is based on reasonableness instead of hegemony. The need for successful persuasion requires the persuader to achieve one's goal by ways acceptable to the person being persuaded. This does not only require the persuader to examine one's own ideas and reasons for holding certain values, but also requires the persuader to take seriously what the persons being persuaded have to say and their specific situations.

Persuasion may seem to be a one-directional process, that is, one party trying to change another party's mind. But it does not have to be that way; a reasonable persuader should be prepared to change or modify one's own position in the process of persuading others. This sounds paradoxical: one wants to persuade another of something that oneself might abandon. But there is no hypocrisy here as long as one still sincerely believes in it. A reasonable person usually does not lack such experience: starting out trying to convince other people but only to be convinced otherwise in the end. It happens, and a reasonable person must be open to various possibilities. One of my firmest beliefs is that the computer I used to type this chapter is mine. I can hardly imagine otherwise. It is my firmly believed truth. But suppose an FBI agent comes to my house with an FBI report that this computer has been replaced without my knowledge for an important national security operation, and the agent shows me the documented evidence. I may need to be cautious in reviewing the document, but it would be unreasonable for me to reject the agent's account simply because I have formed a firm belief and feel quite comfortable with it. If a person can change one's mind on a believed fact, so can one change believed values. This has nothing to do with moral relativism or absolutism. The fact is that people can and do change their moral beliefs. Reasonable people must be reasonable in upholding and reconsidering their own moral beliefs.

If one sees the human rights discourse as moral persuasion, one needs to exercise humility. One needs to realize that one does not have absolute truth, and that one could be mistaken. History is the best witness. Many once "self-evident" truths turned out to be nontruths. What we see as "self-evident" today may turn out not to be so tomorrow. Often our own values appear to us to be so "self-evident" that we just cannot imagine otherwise. We cannot overestimate the power of a value commitment. Today in the United States, it is obvious to anti-abortionists that abortion is one of the worst human rights violations; it is just as obvious to pro-choicers (or anti-anti-abortionists) that a ban on abortion would be one of the worst human rights violations. Neither side can imagine otherwise. Convicted murderers of a German business executive and his family were sentenced to death recently in China. The German government protested against the death sentence (*CND-Global,* July 17, 2000, GL00-088). The same report said that the relatives of the victims also did not wish the convicted murderers to be put to death. There is little doubt that this death penalty sentence would have been on the U.S. government's international human rights agenda had it been widely accepted as a violation of human rights in the United States. We are often extremely stubborn with our own values. Values can make us blind.

In moral persuasion, the persuader needs to invite others to think together, to look for agreement. This, I claim, is a basic requirement for being morally reasonable. In this volume, John Downey (Chapter 12) has argued that the experience of suffering brings us together. Empathy enhances communication. After communicating with others, sometimes one may find that one's own position needs rethinking. Or one may find from others important aspects of the issue that one has not taken into account. When this occurs, a reasonable person must be willing to adjust one's own position. This is a main difference between moral persuasion and coercion.

One may say that my own position is still universalistic: I am still taking some values (e.g., persuasion over coercion) to be universal. However, it should be clear that my position is not based on, nor does it support, de facto universalism, de jure universalism, or universal realism. I am not opposed to convincing more and more people to accept certain values through persuasion, even though these values may change in the future. I believe my position is coherent and can be established without begging the question. I start the thesis of moral persuasion and certain values (e.g., persuasion over coercion) with myself. Then by persuasion I get my readers and listeners to agree with me on these values. Furthermore, I expand the circle of these moral persuaders through more persuasion. After a person has been persuaded, he or she has come to share certain values with me. These shared values between us are not universal values; they are values established through persuasion.

Applying Human Rights Moral Persuasion

The goal of human rights moral persuasion is twofold. First, it is to persuade people to accept certain moral values that have been alien to their cultural traditions. For example, intrinsic to the concept of human rights is that every human being, per one's being a member of the species *Homo sapiens,* has certain equal inherent rights. Jack Donnelly, for example, includes this element of human rights as "the standard sense of 'human rights' in contemporary international discourse" (Donnelly 1999, 62). Some societies have lacked this value. In the mainstream Chinese tradition, for example, a person acquires moral worth by being a member of the moral community, not by merely being a member of the biological species. In Confucian language, "humanity" is a social and moral, not biological, concept. In other words, Confucianism may be a humanism but not a "speciesism" (the belief that the species *Homo sapiens* as a whole, including each and every one of its members, is superior and deserves special consideration—to borrow Peter Singer's terminology [1990]). This tradition itself does not possess the value of all *Homo sapiens* being equipped with equal human rights.[7] If human rights advocates want to sell this value into the Chinese culture, they need to persuade the Chinese people to accept it.

Sometimes a society may only appear to have accepted a value because of ambiguities of words. A verbal agreement on certain values can be just that, a verbal one; it may not be substantive. As Andrew Nathan has forcefully pointed out,

> much of the apparent new agreement on value is merely verbal, and disappears when broad concepts like development, democracy, or human rights are analyzed more closely for their specific meanings within different cultures. Similarly, many apparent universalistic values describing such economic or political "system outputs" as welfare, security, equity, freedom, or justice are not understood or ranked the same way in different societies. In many areas, such as the proper limits of state power or the role of law, the differences between the two cultures' preferences are too obvious to be papered over by any formula. Thus the problem remains, because in many respects the values of the two societies remain different, even if they no longer seem to be as different as they once were. (Nathan 1997, 203)

My earlier example of whether forced prison labor constitutes slavery is an issue in point. A country signed to the covenant against slavery may outright reject that forced prison labor is slavery. If the human rights advocates believe it is a form of slavery, they need to sell that value through persuasion.

The second aspect of human rights moral persuasion is to persuade people to accept certain moral values as more important than they have held previously. Sometimes a culture already possesses certain human rights values, but it does not give such values the kind of priority that human rights advocates believe they deserve. The Bangkok Declaration reaffirms "the interdependence and indivisibility of economic, social, cultural, civil and political rights, and the need to give equal emphasis to all categories of human rights." But there is no such thing as "equal emphasis." In the end, one always has to give some values (rights) more priority than others. For example, people may agree that citizens have a privacy right and that the police should not unnecessarily intrude on citizens' privacy. But they may interpret "necessary" and "unnecessary" very differently than do some human rights advocates; they may see some sacrifice of privacy as necessary to ensure that their neighborhood is free of illegal drugs, for example.

Human rights are freedoms. As Isaiah Berlin pointed out, freedoms may conflict:

> One freedom may abort another; one freedom may obstruct or fail to create conditions which make other freedoms, or a larger degree of freedom, or freedom for more persons, possible; positive and negative freedom may collide; the freedom of the individual or the group may not be fully compatible with a full degree of participation in a common life, with its demands for co-operation, solidarity, fraternity. (Berlin 1969, lvi)

The issue of priority can even arise with some "hard" human rights categories. Sometimes violations of human rights may be justifiable because of different priorities. For example, it is virtually universally held that torture is a violation of human rights. But if torturing a bomb maker is the only way to save New York City from a devastating terrorist attack, should it be justified? (Some may say even in this case torture is still not justified; I, and probably the majority of New York City residents, disagree.) It may be argued that here there is a conflict between the New York City people's right to life and the terrorist's right not to be tortured; the question is which right overrides which. As cruel as it sounds, the New York City people's right to life is greater than the latter. One may feel this example is irrelevant to the human rights discourse: after all, hardly any case of torture today is like that. But this rebuttal misses the point. The issue here is not whether we should tolerate torture when a terrorist is going to bomb New York City, but that, if one agrees that in such a case torture would be justified, one has agreed that *under certain circumstances* extreme cruelty like torture, which is universally regarded a violation of human rights, can be justified; one has rejected the position that torture is *never* justified. Then the issue has become not whether torture can be justified—which now has been decided—but under what circumstances torture can be justified. For the latter, unfortunately no international covenants specify. In cases like that, international covenants that outlaw torture entirely would have to be suspended for legitimate reasons. Issues of this kind complicate human rights in practice. Merely possessing human rights values in a culture does not solve problems of human rights violations. Under the name of different priorities of human rights, violations occur. Human rights advocates need to prevent a regime from giving priority to, say, a citizen's right to the safety of one's own car over a thief's right not to be tortured. They need to persuade others to give adequate priority to human rights values.

Elements of Value Formation

By now it should be clear that my thesis of human rights discourse as moral persuasion is a kind of discourse ethics. It seeks agreement through discourse, dialogue, and communication. Jürgen Habermas distinguishes between communicative and strategic action:

> Whereas in strategic action one actor seeks to *influence* the behavior of another by means of the threat of sanctions or the prospect of gratification in order to *cause* the interaction to continue as the first actor desires, in communicative action one actor seeks *rationally* to *motivate* another by relying on the illocutionary binding/bonding effect of the offer contained in his speech act. (Habermas 1990, 58, italics are original)

Moral persuasion is a kind of "communicative" rather than "strategic" action. My thesis, however, is different from Habermas's communicative theory. Whereas his theory solely relies on rationality, rationality is just one of several elements in moral persuasion in my thesis.

If we regard the international human rights discourse as moral persuasion, as a process of changing people's moral values, we need to examine how human values are formed and reformed. Philosophers have argued that morals are formed (or should be formed) in at least three ways. Rationalists argue that reason is the foundation of morals. Immanuel Kant maintains that if one is rational, one will be able to form morals on the sole basis of reason (Kant, 1959). That rationalism contains at least a grain of truth can be seen in the fact that we often reason with ourselves and with one another to determine the moral path. The rational approach to moral values may be found in many cultures. The golden rule is an example. (Perhaps emotions are also involved in the practicing of the golden rule. But the golden rule primarily relies on reason to figure out the appropriate action to take.) One may be inclined to do one thing, but deliberation on the golden rule may lead one to do another. One philosopher once told me that, after reading Peter Singer's powerful argument on animal liberation, she had to quit eating meat. The power of reason in moral value formation is evident. Sentimentalists, on the other hand, argue that our sentiments or feelings determine our moral values. David Hume, for example, argues that ultimately it is how we feel that determines the moral right and wrong (Hume, 1957). Sentimentalism can find its support as one reflects on one's own morals: often we follow our instinctive feelings in making moral decisions. One example is the issue of abortion. The rational approach rarely works in leading one to change positions on the issue of abortion. In the end it is how one feels that determines one's position. The philosopher who quit eating meat because of Peter Singer's argument also told me that she had to take her children to a slaughter house to change their minds on eating meat. Moreover, traditionalists believe that our morals are formed within traditions. Alasdair MacIntyre argues that, without the tradition, one would not be able to determine the moral right and wrong (MacIntyre, 1984). Traditionalists insist that both reason and sentiment are shaped by tradition.

The truth may be that human values are shaped and reshaped by all three: reason, sentiment, and tradition. We reason with people to make them realize that certain things are more important than others; we react to a situation according to how we feel about it; and living within a tradition, we inherit values from earlier generations. Joel Kupperman speaks of ethics as "a patchwork of questions and judgements of a variety of kinds" (1999, 4). Similarly, it is arguable that a person's values, though changing over time, are a result of all three processes. I agree with James Griffin when he writes that, in practice, "[p]urely moral considerations often leave us well short of determinate standards for action, and other considerations, for example, social agreement or convergence or tradition, have to be brought in to fill the gap" (Griffin 1996, 117). In such a process, moral persuasion will include reasoning, feeling, and accommodating traditions. If the international human rights discourse is a process of moral persuasion, we need to look into how each of the approaches works in the process.

It appears that human rights movements tend to use the rationalist approach to rationalize certain moral values as universal, while human rights contenders (those who dispute the human rights agenda and defend their own human rights records) tend to use the traditionalist approach to formulate how values vary from culture to culture. Both sides have appealed to sentimentalism from time to time, partly because people are prone to emotional influence and partly because modern technology (e.g., television) has made the means for emotional manipulation easily available.

Let me suggest that the moral persuasion approach on human rights is more feasible today than ever because of the available technology. Along with the rapid development of global economy, more and more people are connected through newspapers, radio, television, and even the Internet. These means of communication are also means of moral persuasion. They open an increasingly broader door for human rights persuaders to communicate their message to the entire world.

Conclusion

If we accept that the ultimate goal of human rights discourse is to promote certain moral values through moral persuasion, what implications can we draw from it? First, with this goal in mind, we need to make strategies suitable for this purpose. It is counterproductive to do things that result in turning people away from embracing certain values advocated by human rights activists. In this regard, it is particularly important to understand the power of internal cultural discourse in introducing new values into a culture, which in turn demands our studying and understanding of respective cultures. Second, as we promote human rights values, we must realize that we are trying to change others' values in accordance with our own. Even though we firmly believe that our values are better than others', we do not have absolute assurance of that. Therefore, we need to reserve the possibility, no matter how slim it seems, that we might be wrong and might need to change our own beliefs and values. Finally, along this line of thinking, we need to understand that there is no higher goal in people's lives than a good life. Value changes should aim at improving people's lives. The justice and injustice of promoting certain values have to be measured ultimately by whether they result in improving people's lives, not the kind of life we think desirable, but the kind of life that the people affected by the values deem desirable.

Notes

I would like to thank the following individuals for their comments, critiques, suggestions, and encouragement on this chapter: Neil Englehart, Yong Huang, Joel Kupperman, Mahmood Monshipouri, Andrew Nathan, Kavita Philip, Linda Radzik, Matthew McGrath, Michael Launius, and Hong Xiao. Earlier versions of this chapter were presented at the Eighth East-West Philosophers Conference in Honolulu, January 2000; the Fifty-second Northwest Conference on Philosophy, at Pacific University, Forest Grove, Oregon, November 10–11, 2000; and the Philosophy Colloquium at Central Washington University, January 2001. I benefited from discussions with the audience.

1. See Sandra Wawrytko, "Prudery and Prurience: Historical Roots of the Confucian Conundrum Concerning Women, Sexuality, and Power," in Li 2000, 163–197.

2. Here the matter has nothing to do with whether these cultures were good or bad, these values valid or invalid, whatever that means; or whether traditionalism or universalism of morals is true. I simply make reference to the historical background of today's international human rights discourse.

3. Both "natural" and "artificial" are relative terms. There is probably no sharp distinction between a natural community and an artificial one. One may argue that all communities are artificial. But there is clearly a difference between, say, a primitive tribe on the one hand and New York City on the other. One may have to deal with different value issues than the other.

4. By "different societies having different values" I include the fact that various societies do not give the same priority to shared values.

5. Fukuyama 1989. For my discussion of the "end of history," see Li 1999, chap. 7.

6. For my discussion of the incompatibility of Confucian values and democratic values, see Li 1999.

7. It may be argued that in the Chinese categorization of "heaven, earth, and people" (*tian, di, ren*), "people" refers to all human beings and therefore all humans have the same status. This is debatable. The Confucian poet Tao Yuanming (365–427 C.E.) sent a servant to his son with a letter stating, "This is also someone's son, [you] should treat him well [*ci yi ren zi ye, dang shan yu zhi*]," instead of simply stating that the servant was also a human being. Evidently, in raising a family, a father is an established moral person and hence being a father's son carried more weight than simply being a (young) human oneself. Quoted from Yu Yingshi (1998, 408).

References

An-Na'im, Abdullahi Ahmed, ed. 1991. *Human Rights in Cross-Cultural Perspectives: A Quest for Consensus.* Philadelphia: University of Pennsylvania Press.

Bauer, Joanne R., and Daniel A. Bell, eds. 1999. *The East Asian Challenge for Human Rights.* Cambridge: Cambridge University Press.

Berlin, Isaiah. 1969. *Four Essays on Liberty.* New York: Oxford University Press.

Donnelly, Jack. 1985. *The Concept of Human Rights.* New York: St. Martin's Press.
———. 1989. *Universal Human Rights in Theory and Practice.* Ithaca, NY: Cornell University Press.
———. 1993. *International Human Rights.* Boulder, CO: Westview Press.
———. 1999. "Human Rights and Asian Values: A Defense of 'Western' Universalism," in Bauer and Bell, 1999, 60-87.
Dworkin, Ronald. 1977. *Taking Rights Seriously.* Cambridge: Harvard University Press.
Fukuyama, Francis. 1989. "The End of History?" *National Interest* 16: 3–18.
Griffin, James. 1996. *Value Judgement: Improving Our Ethical Beliefs.* New York: Oxford University Press.
Habermas, Jürgen. 1990. *Moral Consciousness and Communicative Action.* Cambridge: MIT Press
Henkin, Louis. 1990. *The Age of Rights.* New York: Columbia University Press.
Howard, Rhoda E. 1991. "Dignity, Community, and Human Rights." In Abdullahi A. An-Na'im 1991, 81–102.
Hume, David. 1957. *An Inquiry Concerning the Principles of Morals.* New York: the Bobbs-Merrill Company, Inc. Originally published in 1751.
Kant, Immanuel. 1959. *Foundations of the Metaphysics of Morals.* Trans. Lewis White Beck, New York: the Bobbs-Merrill Company, Inc. Originally published in German in 1785.
Kupperman, Joel J. 1999. *Value . . . and What Follows.* New York: Oxford University Press.
Li, Chenyang. 1999. *The Tao Encounters the West: Explorations in Comparative Philosophy.* Albany: State University of New York Press.
———, ed. 2000. *The Sage and the Second Sex: Confucianism, Ethics, and Gender.* Chicago: Open Court, 2000.
MacInyre, Alasdair. 1984. *After Virtue,* second edition. Notre Dame, Indiana: University of Notre Dame Press.
Nathan, Andrew J. 1997. *China's Transition.* New York: Columbia University Press.
Singer, Peter. 1990. *Animal Liberation.* New York: HarperCollins Publishers.
Taylor, Charles. 1999. "Conditions of an Unforced Consensus on Human Rights." In Joanne R. Bauer and Daniel A. Bell, eds., *The East Asian Challenge for Human Rights.* Cambridge: Cambridge University Press, 1999, 124–144.
Yu, Yingshi. 1998. "The Modern Meaning of Chinese Culture Seen from the Value System" [*cong jiazhi jitong kan zhongguo wenhua de xiandai yiyi*], in Wang Yuanhua, Hu Xiaoming, and Fu Jie, eds., *Interpreting China,* vol. 1. Shanghai: Shanghai Literature Publishers, 387–445.

12

Suffering as Common Ground

John K. Downey

Talking about human rights is talking about universals. If we cannot talk across cultural, social, gender, and political particulars—across our difference and otherness—we cannot talk about human rights. But talking across these borders has proven risks: conversation may become monologue, local knowledge may masquerade as common knowledge, a hermeneutic of acknowledgment may fade before a hermeneutic of domination. We must talk about universals and yet we must honor the particulars of globalization. In this volume my colleagues have inoculated the conversation on human rights with questions that reveal both the complexity and the hope of human rights talk. I want to add one more safeguard: I want to suggest a critical and constructive common authority. And I want to use the technical discussions of another intellectual discipline, theology, as a guide.

In a world that celebrates pluralism and grounds understanding in context, the missionary (and by extension Christianity) has become shorthand for the mistakes of a passé classical empire. But this notion is itself passé. A glance at recent writing in missiology or theology will show a genuine care for the foundational character of cultures and a turn to hopes of a local enculturation that eschews social or economic colonization.[1] Modern and postmodern theologians are committed to globalization, quite critical of the cultural hegemony of past missionary positions, and concerned with cultural integrity.

Christianity knows how to survive: it enters and uses the dominant culture while at the same time preserving its own traditional identity. Theologians, the facilitators of this balancing act, may disagree as to what counts as balance, but not as to the basic task.[2] This tactic has become a hallmark of theological method. As David Tracy's work has shown,[3] honest intellectual conversation within our pluralistic times requires a methodologically self-consciousness navigation of sources, cultures, and identities.[4] Belief—religious or any other sort—is always a function of culture.[5] Religious intellectuals are not unaware of the realities of hermeneutic, contextual relativism, and the social bedrock of meaning. Entering and learning from these social critiques distinguishes recent liberation and political theologies from many more traditional mainstream metaphysical or existential approaches.[6]

The most useful theological conversation partner on the issues of globalization and universals will be the subdiscipline of fundamental or philosophical theology: This branch of the theological enterprise concerns itself less with particular doctrines than with the rules for any theological discourse. It addresses methodological issues and asks how the diverse sources and situations of theology can talk to each other. It takes as its task finding common frameworks for public conversations about religion. Such a public theology can contribute to the pubic academic discussion because it appeals to common human experiences as articulated in the methods and explanations of other disciplines.[7] One of the newer fundamental theologies—a reorientation to social roots called political theology—can help by suggesting some common criteria for a conversation that respects the paradox of globalization.

Conversation in the Paradox of Globalization

Globalization razes the walls that divided us, that blocked our vision, and that cushioned our impact on each other. Globalization fosters a new cultural grammar for self-understanding and action. New amalgams emerge within and across established borders. Within a widening net of ambiguity and pluralism, modernity and postmodernity loosen our innocent metaphysical grasp of nation, "race," class, and way of life. In one sense globalization infects us with postmodern worry, relativity, and pluralism, and yet we cannot surrender modernity's pleading for the dignity of the person, for the test of freedom, and for hope in our common humanity. We live confidently—if ironically—in a world known to be a socially constructed, contingent weave. We have the technological means to know and appreciate variety, we are committed to honoring differences, and yet simultaneously our diversity has become threatened.

Roland Robertson aptly describes this new dialectic as an ongoing presence of "the two-fold process involving the universalization of particularism and the particularization of universalism."[8] The very fact of our conversations shows there are commonalities, yet these must emerge in particular settings. Globalization exists as a tensive interplay between the global and the local, a situation Italians have begun to call *glocale.*

Like the religious conversation with cultures, the conversation over human rights must be credible, but not credulous. One must be vigilant lest the conversation shift to a monologue. Similarly, a global awareness that notices differences certainly can function as a "discourse of hegemony" to suppress those differences.[9] Students of the religion debate have learned that persons, groups, and nations can use the mantle of their communal tradition to cloak a pathology of power, fear, wealth, or myopia; one strand of the tradition's dialogue with cultures—for example, the dialogue with Aristotle's philosophy so essential to credibility in the middle ages— becomes uncritically identical to the tradition.

So also in the political realm, the simple fact that, say, China and Singapore assert their cultural difference—their Asian values—does not make that difference accurate, contrary, or essential.[10] Neil Englehart discovered that when the government of Singapore attempted to engage its people in reclaiming their supposed Confucian ethics, they weren't much interested.[11] Instead of presuming that differing cultural language games are absolutely incommensurate, one could draw points of contact for guiding discussions from within Chinese culture as, for example, philosopher Chenyang Li suggests. The local and the global touch and they need not always collide. Globalization itself presents resources that transform the simplistic apocalyptic notion of the "West and the rest."[12]

The human rights discussion surely developed in Western categories,[13] but that fact does not a priori mean that it cannot, mutatis mutandis, function in other cultures. Similarly, it is possible to learn global lessons, however tentative or partial, from a particular tradition, voice, or idiom. I want to look at one example of contemporary intellectual discourse—political theology—that accepts globalization and yet seeks common criteria for conversation.[14] From it we might glean points of contact and expectations useful in the global human rights discussion. One way to preserve a particular identity while engaging the claims of universality is to measure our work by a strategic commitment to honor the "other," to value the different one, the stranger. Sensitivity to these others may be the most practical way to enflesh universal connections within particular borderlands.

Of fundamental concern is the authority that might be invoked in this conversation. I argue here that we turn to the authority of suffering and solidarity. Since one cannot argue outside of some particular point of view—there is no view from nowhere—I begin within Christian and Western thought, but without any claim to exclusivity. This perspective is the start of a conversation, not its end. Within the paradoxes of globalization, solutions will only emerge from particular stories striving for wider resonance. My question is this: Can political conversation be grounded in mutual respect for the suffering of others?

Awakening to the Other: Political Theology

Political theology is a major strand of contemporary Christian thought. Accepting all the issues of historicity and contextuality, it moves to the praxis mode for its truth criterion. It is not a new list of doctrines but a new fundamental theology, that is, a new way to construe the foundations—the rules—for theologizing. It is a corrective to notions of religion as a private affair. Johann Baptist Metz, founder of this new political theology,[15] insists that Christianity is both mystical and political. Not only do theologians admit religious experience, but they see that experience as intertwined with the social, political, economic agenda of all human enterprises. This new political theology insists on turning our attention to particulars and highlighting the baggage hidden in culture, science, and society. This attention calls us to remember who we human beings are by evoking our past suffering and recalling our future possibilities. And this remembering expects appropriate action.

A political theology seeks to be a theology of this world. Far from being a calming opium or a path of escape, this theology connects humankind through disruption and dissension: It names evils and calls on human beings to change the world. It is an antidote to the shift of religion into the private sphere. A theology that abstracts from concrete human lives, that pretends to be situation-free, is naive. In response to Enlightenment reason, Christianity downplayed its controversial social dimension and reduced its heritage to the realm of private, intimate, apolitical decision. But the Enlightenment itself implies the political: If, as Kant said, human beings must be free to use their reason publicly, then it follows that they must also construct social situations in which these reasoning people can flourish. There is no theology, then, that can ignore concrete social settings; political theology is pleonastic.

Metz's actual strategy is to acknowledge "the other."[16] The universalism suggested here is a universalism of responsibility for other human beings. Attending to unreasonable human suffering, especially to others' suffering, provides direction for reasonable human praxis. The memory of suffering and the acknowledgment of the other have a practical intent.

Political theology focuses on hearing the voices of the marginal, those who have disappeared behind the projection of universal essences. Metz uses this memory as an interruption that honors otherness. In this way the victims of structures and policies are not erased from the conversation. Metz cautions against living off a "bread of domination"[17] that disconnects people: subjugation does not give lives their value. Christian discipleship offers human solidarity rather than domination as its hope. All human beings are called to be subjects, that is, to be agents of human value in the world, actors who declare human value in their action.

Remembering this call to act humanly as well as remembering the suffering from particular actions and structures can be dangerous. These dangerous memories of our hope and our grief position us to build a humane future. These memories shape a resistance and an agenda that spring not from a theoretical naiveté but from memory and narratives of pain, suffering, and invisibility. Noticing and norming by concrete human suffering brings an anthropological revolution. The memory of suffering makes concrete the value of the other and helps one resist the culture's homogenizing amnesia.

Metz's focus on suffering decenters the controlling ego: "I begin not with the question 'What happens to me when I suffer, when I die?' but rather with, 'What happens to you when you suffer, when you die?'" The classical question of theodicy, of how to justify God in the face of human suffering, should not be a question about our own sufferings. Again one sees the same decentering in Metz's insistence that true hope must be a messianic in-break, not an endorsement of the future we have already laid out for ourselves. The claim of the other exposes the illusion of the controlling autonomous ego.[18]

It is important to bring victims into the foundations of knowing and acting. The usual story must be interrupted by connecting with others in a strategic love that sides against human agony. Metz wants to interrupt the ordinary by bringing the faces of the victims to mind. Narratives about the suffering of others, including Jesus, work to highlight and disable dehumanizing structures and behaviors. "We have a duty to face these catastrophes and remember them with a practical-political intention so that they might never be repeated."[19] Theological investigations and constructions done before the eyes of the victims will value difference.

For example, Metz integrates unity and diversity in the polycentric global culture by calling for all enculturations of Christianity to be locally generated but guided by two fundamental tracks from the Christian biblical inheritance: the commitment to seeking freedom and justice for all, and the acknowledgment of others in their otherness. These imperatives could spin out various faithful reinterpretations of the Christian story in sundry situations. Metz also argues that a hindrance to this joining of unity and diversity is the epistemological assumption that only like knows like. Rather, it is better to say that "only unlike can know unlike—in mutual acknowledgment."[20] The focus on the other, then, interrupts our fascination with the camouflage of sameness. For Metz, this interruption reorients the hope for a new life and a new world. The drive for justice, for the dignity of the other as other, is the heart of any version of Christianity. The world emerges in difference, difference that the theological enterprise has habitually overlooked. These are irreducible themes of the Christian narrative that mark and judge all dimensions of theology. They put a face on "human being": the call of other can only be heard from particular persons. This limited, concrete face-to-face is the universal starting point. It is founded on a hope that the human heart will naturally turn outward.

Jesus followed his Jewish tradition by joining the love of God and the love of neighbor. His parables of the Last Judgment (Matthew 25:31–46) and the Good Samaritan (Luke 10:30–36) shape this tradition into the authority of others' suffering. In Matthew's parable we discover that "sheep go to heaven and goats go to hell" largely because they do or do not care for others, for those different ones: the hungry, the thirsty, the sick, those in need of clothing, prisoners, and strangers. Luke's story of the man who helped the stranger who had been robbed and thrown into a ditch argues that one may not delimit who counts as a neighbor. The obligation is universal.

It is not just remembering one's own suffering that matters but, as Metz points out, remembering the suffering of others, *even the suffering of one's enemies*. Jesus focuses not on the sin of others, but on the suffering of others. Sin is "a refusal to participate in the suffering of others, a refusal to see beyond one's own history of suffering. Sin is, as Augustine put it, turning the heart inward."[21]

Metz offers this awareness of others' suffering as common ground that survives in the midst of pluralism and as an antidote to any totalitarianism of rights. In addition, the memory of suffering—or as Metz calls it, *memoria passionis*—might be a control on the negative aspects of fundamentalism. For him the dominating subtext of these discussions could be modulated by refusing to separate the authority of God from the authority of others' suffering.[22] Xenophobia, ethnocentrism, and religious arrogance generate human misery. Various religions and cultures might come together to resist the sources of unjust suffering in the world. This call to memory and to resistance would function as the criterion for judging moral visions and their concrete tactics.

This *memoria passionis*—the memory of others' suffering—jars people's amnesia and awakens them to a universal responsibility for others. This interruption necessarily reshapes the political imagination.

Human Rights and the Authority of Suffering

One's picture of the "subject," of the human person, is also foundational for the conversation on human rights. The discussion of human rights is a discussion about the political means for honoring humanity. When Jack Donnelly and Rhoda Howard distinguish between human rights and human dignity, they are pointing to the same sort of differing layers in the human rights discussion.[23] Though certainly not allied with the Donnelly-Howard camp, Chandra Muzaffar likewise writes that human rights notions are embedded in specific cultural worldviews that norm the picture of the human being, human relationships, and the good society. After excoriating the West for its deteriorating human rights standards, he asks for some universal vision of human dignity: "Without a larger spiritual and moral framework, which endows human endeavor with meaning and purpose, with coherence and unity, wouldn't the emphasis on rights *per se* lead to moral chaos and confusion?"[24] The human rights discussion will be equivocal until some common criteria emerge.

Continuing a conversation within the paradoxes of globalization still implies a common authority. In order to be credible, such common ground must honor differences; it must seek the universal while attending to the other. The theoretical phrase "human dignity" could become a cover story for other commitments to communication, political structures, or economic theories. But are there roots down beneath these various techniques? Isn't the authority of human suffering a sort of bedrock? The particular story of Christianity may highlight some strategies.

Metz proposes a new type of reason for the post-Enlightenment age: reason endowed with the power of memory. "The Enlightenment has never overcome a deeply rooted prejudice in the model of reason that it developed: the prejudice against memory. The Enlightenment promotes discourse and consensus, but—in its abstract, totalizing critique of traditions—underestimates the intelligible and critical power of memory."[25] Thinking critically is more than logical coherence, instrumental reason, or following procedures: it includes remembering others and their suffering. This socially oriented reason focuses on not forgetting (anamnesia) and on actions of recollection or remembrance. This epistemological mediation of human suffering is practical in that it responds in ways that prevent abstract ideas of freedom or peace from erasing the concrete history of others' suffering. Anamnestic reason recovers memory as a resource for critical thought and political life. "Remembrance allows later generations to enter into solidarity with the dead in the act of recollection that brings the suffering of the past to light today."[26] This solidarity then becomes a resistance that transforms the world.

Reason endowed with the power of memory, a *memoria passionis* rooted in the memory of someone else's suffering, demands more than mere assent. This reason is not just a feeling, not simply compassion, but also a claim on us: it is a call to responsibility. The solidarity encouraged by our memories and hopes entails an impulse to action. After all, Christianity and Christian theology are practical at the core: "Ultimately, it is of the very essence of Christian faith to be believed in such a way that it is never just believed, but rather—in the messianic praxis of discipleship—enacted."[27] It is so simple to merely believe in compassion—who can be against that great virtue?—but anamnestic reason asks for more.

Prior to every theory, prior to every relationship of exchange and competition should be the metapolitical turn to the other. The best way to effect this turn concretely is through contact with the suffering of others. (Perhaps this was one benefit of the South African truth commissions.) In this way the whisper of human suffering keeps the political imagination alive in the face of the giants of technology and economics. The point of solidarity is not just to remember suffering but to enforce the changes needed to end it. "The catastrophes must be remembered with a practical-political intention so that this historical experience does not turn to tragedy and thus bid the history of freedom farewell. That is a great seduction: to face these catastrophes and then end up with a kind of tragic consciousness."[28]

The West has, for example, the dangerous memory of Auschwitz as a warning. Its ignominy teaches that compassion without any entailed action cultivates the disconnectedness that allows Christians to go on untroubled "believing and praying with our backs to Auschwitz." Christians, as Dietrich Bonhoeffer put it, were able "to go on singing Gregorian chant during the persecution of Jews without at the same time feeling the need to cry out in their behalf."[29]

Concrete dangerous memories, memories of real suffering and hope, are key. They are anamnestic: they interrupt in order to awaken people, to reorient them. "With its creed—'suffered under Pontius Pilate'—[Christianity] is and remains bound to concrete history, to that history in which people have cried and loved, but also hated, tortured, crucified, and massacred."[30] Political theology points to a common ground for intercultural and interreligious collaboration. This common ground is found not in a theory or policy but rather in the common human response to others' suffering. This response-ability is a human imperative confirmed, demanded, and maybe enhanced by Christian hope. It is specific—though not exclusive—to Christian identity.[31]

This conversation calls us to act on our hope and memory by changing damaging social structures of domination.[32] Political discourse needs a shock, an interruption that reorients: it needs to touch the authority of suffering. Putting people in contact with the suffering of others may generate new ways of acting, thinking, and living. Here is a common criterion that at the same time can be internal to particular cultures. "Articulating others' suffering is the presupposition of all universalist claims."[33]

This turn to suffering does not turn on a fixed "norm"; it is not a defined theoretical or metaphysical essence but rather a contextually normed imperative that honors particular settings. In current discourses the turn to interpretation and to the social roots of human constructions undermines the pretensions of any so-called pure, disconnected essence. The sensitivities of the academy—hermeneutic, social sciences, ethnography, postmodernity—have raised suspicions about the clear and distinct knowing of some "already-out-there-now-real." But one could speak descriptively of culturally diverse yet overlapping discussions about humane behaviors and postures. One might, with Ludwig Wittgenstein, speak not of sharply defined borders and essences but of "family resemblances" that crisscross in our discussions.[34] Such a socially described commonality can enable a global discussion of human rights and human suffering. Anthropologist Ann-Belinda S. Preis seems open to this move when she argues: "Human rights increasingly form part of a wider network of perspectives which are shared and exchanged between North and South, centers and peripheries, in multiple, creative, and sometimes conflict-ridden ways. Human rights have become 'universalized' as values subject to interpretation, negotiation, and accommodation. They have become 'culture.'"[35] Human rights talk does not revive the decontextualized assertions of Enlightenment foundational reason, but operates as a highly contextual description of diverse family resemblances. Universals aren't what they used to be.

An appeal to the authority of suffering, especially the "unreasonable" suffering of the innocent, is both universal and particular. Of course, talk about such suffering has its full meaning only within a particular context, within the practices of a particular group, within an actual language game or setting, yet that linguistic use also has meaning across these borders. Cultures, horizons of difference, and local language games can be context-specific and still overlap. They may be, to use Michael Walzer's phrase, "thick and thin." Thick meanings are culturally resonant and richly referential, locked into local symbols and detailed networks. Thin are not. Thin meanings are notions of the rules: they assume the thick meanings and yet lack their richness and texture. I know what you mean by suffering or torture because we both use those words to do similar work in our differing cultural contexts. I can see how you use it, and I can relate that to my own thick weave of life. We have then deeply particular roots that also lend themselves to an accurate but thin commonality.[36] Language games may overlap without being congruent.

Political theology offers talk about human rights rooted in the "family resemblance" of *memoria passionis* and in the practice of anamnestic reason. This authority is not the authority of a particular interpretative community, but of those who suffer. The common ground is our mutual responsibility rather than individual rights.

Rules of the Game: Talking About Human Rights

Fear of a hidden cultural hegemony troubles human rights discussions today. To discuss humanity and rights across cultural lines risks denying difference.[37] Talk of universals is suspect since many so-called universals simply impose one local practice on many others. At the same time, the actual international discussion of human rights has never been more universal.[38] Differing discourses may overlap and cultural borders are often permeable. Acknowledging a cultural situatedness does not mean that unique persons and communities cannot understand or influence one another. Nor does it imply that they cannot agree on some things that harm the person enduring them. They can, they have. As Michael Perry puts it: "No one believes that rape, or slicing off breasts, or ripping out wombs, or decapitating a child in front of its mother (who has just been raped), or castrating a prisoner (or forcing another prisoner to do so), or throwing a prisoner into hot oil—no one believes that such acts are or might be good for them on whom the horror is inflicted."[39] The authority of others' suffering implies negative critique, not any alternative theory or political system, as a valid starting point.[40]

Metz's political theology is not arguing for a global ethic but for a global touchstone. With this we can build a constellation of values and ultimately specific tactical policies. The common ground for conversing on human rights lies deeper than marking "human capabilities" (Martha Nussbaum) or agreeing on a "global ethic" (Hans Küng).[41] While these proposals do value empathy and compassion, they do not concretize these in the practical memory of suffering. Nussbaum and Küng function on the penultimate level of seeking consensus on mediating principles of human action. Metz addresses the further question: How is the consensus—whether on ethics or capabilities—itself to be grounded?

In the shifting particulars and shady borderlands of globalization, the human rights discussion must be dialectical and dynamic. It functions within family resemblances and shifting contexts. Thus it is mistaken to take universal and permanent closure on issues as the only measure of success in the human rights conversation: such expectations hark back to a preglobalized world. But the conversation on human rights could at least function as an interruption prodding communities to improve human life on the planet.[42] One way talk about human rights improves lives is to function as an anamnesis: it keeps the faces of suffering people before our eyes. Posing questions about human rights and responsibilities is more basic than agreement on answers. The dialogue itself challenges personal apathy and disrupts social amnesia.

Remembering not just one's own or one's people's suffering but also the suffering of others becomes a local criterion for global political dialogue. Political theology voices a common human call to respond, to connect, and to imagine new political relations, a new πολις. It calls for an interruption that promotes the imagination of new possibilities. Discussing human rights is similarly disruptive. The radical goal of human rights talk is to change the vision. Human rights discourse has a protest character: the conversation itself is a strategy of protest as well as a preemptive strike aimed at changing the weave of life.[43] Appealing to an anamnestic reason that faces others' suffering protects the integrity and mutuality of the conversation. Here lie the foundations; here "our spade is turned."

To talk about human rights, then, is to talk at once about three interlocking planes. While the conversation cannot be reduced to pragmatic political and legal questions, attention to the common authority of human suffering or basic principles of action will not create an actual culture of human rights. On the first level, conversing about human rights must look at human suffering and human responsibility. The second level would develop "bridge values"—global ethics, consensus, moral persuasion—to provide principles and a context for concrete action. The third level produces actual strategies: Which political images and actions will produce concrete results in a particular situation? Rights derive from responsibility: they are attempts to answer the authoritative claims of the suffering. Neither the authority of suffering nor the spinning out of general ethical guidelines from this suffering denies the need for debate over various actual rights and policies.[44] Concrete human rights strategies and tactics give strength to the authority of the suffering. Policy and structure, law and political will—rights—project our commitments into the real world. "Without rights, there are insufficient means for engendering and enforcing human responsibility. 'Care' and 'respect' and the voluntarism of sound civil society [are] too little and too episodic to address systemic issues fairly and justly."[45]

We need to name human suffering, we need to be in solidarity with those who suffer, and we need to grieve. But these practices are not enough to change the world. Human beings also need expectations. They need hope. A solidarity that feels the claim of the other and responds in the real world provides not just empathy or identity with the past but a chance to transform the future. When the memory of suffering is merely the memory of one's own or one's people's suffering, it can be harmful, as in the former Yugoslavia. The suffering of others must be acknowledged in political negotiations. There is no place for silence, no place for turning away the *memoria passionis*. The authority of suffering interrupts our banality, our control, and our egocentrism. It calls for a political imagination that trusts in the future, that has expectations, that transforms societal structures accordingly. "There can be no peace without hope."[46]

The human rights discussion is not grounded finally in a consensus about definitions, laws, ethics, or rights. Rather, those arguments must be anchored to something prior to any consensus: suffering. The authority of those who suffer is both universal and particular: universal without falling into abstract idealism and particular without being myopically egocentric or ethnocentric. It grounds a realistic hope, one that hopes in the face of the radical denial of humanity in Auschwitz and other places.[47]

The universal starting point offered by political theology is not a particular human rights formulation but the experience of the authority of those who suffer. Metz offers a starting point in the way our humanity is empathically lured toward humanity in pain and the claims that the other's suffering makes on us. "Is there any suffering at all in the world of which we might say that it does not concern us all? Is there a single cry of suffering that is not meant for every ear?"[48] Human rights after globalization should be, in the phrase of Ronald Dworkin, "political trumps" that outrank sovereignty, laws, or cultures.[49] And when the authority of suffering trumps these human rights, we can converse.

Notes

1. For example, Robert J. Schreiter, *Constructing Local Theologies* (Maryknoll, NY: Orbis Books, 1985). For an update and discussion of models for relating faith and culture, see Robert J. Schreiter, "Faith and Cultures: Challenges to a World Church," *Theological Studies* 50, no. 4 (December 1989): 744–760. For an astute integration of globalization and Christianity, see T. Howland Sanks, "Glob-

alization and the Church's Social Mission," *Theological Studies* 60, no. 4 (December 1999): 625–651.

2. History tells us that religions that fail to engage the larger culture or that stress local practice over forging a "grand tradition" are doomed to shrink from the ranks of world religions into curious local devotions good for a tourist's snapshot. Historian of religions Robert Ellwood argues this well in *The History and Future of Faith: Religion Past, Present, and to Come* (New York: Crossroads, 1988).

3. David Tracy, *Blessed Rage for Order: The New Pluralism in Theology* (New York: Seabury Press, 1975), esp. pp. 3–21. See also his dialogue with deconstruction and linguistic analysis in *Pluralism and Ambiguity: Hermeneutics, Religion, Hope* (San Francisco: Harper & Row, 1987).

4. So, for example, Tracy defines theology as a correlation of the meanings present in the "Christian fact" with those we find in our "common human experience." Tracy, *Blessed Rage,* pp. 43–63. This notion of beginning with cultural dialogue derives from Paul Tillich, *Systematic Theology,* vol. 1 (Chicago: University of Chicago Press, 1973), esp. pp. 3–66. Philosopher Bernard Lonergan, one of the major architects of the paradigm shift in theology, claims that "a theology mediates between a cultural matrix and the significance and role of a religion in that matrix." Bernard Lonergan, *Method in Theology* (New York: Herder and Herder, 1972), p. xi. Theology, like Christianity, appropriates various cultural forms and yet supposes that it can maintain its identity.

5. Bernard Lonergan, "Belief: Today's Issue" and "Theology in Its New Context," in William Ryan and Bernard Tyrrell, eds., *A Second Collection* (Philadelphia: Westminster Press, 1974), pp. 87–99, 57–67.

6. For a sense of the terrain, see John K. Downey, *Beginning at the Beginning: Wittgenstein and Theological Conversation* (Lanham, MD: University Press of America, 1986), esp. pp. 1–26. Liberation theologies arose from the work of Latin American theologians such as the Peruvian Gustavo Gutierrez and have found expression in Asian, African, and feminist idioms. For examples, see Curt Cadorette, Marie Giblin, Marilyn Legge, and Mary Snyder, eds., *Liberation Theology: An Introductory Reader* (Maryknoll, NY: Orbis Press, 1992). Political theologies address social issues from a different context, class, and culture, but no less aggressively. This theological approach arose in affluent West Germany in late 1960s with the work of Johann Baptist Metz, Jürgen Moltmann, and Dorothee Sölle. For recent examples, see Johann Baptist Metz and Jürgen Moltmann, *Faith and the Future: Essays on Theology, Solidarity, and Modernity* (Maryknoll, NY: Orbis Press, 1995) and Dorothee Sölle, *Theology for Skeptics: Reflections on God* (Minneapolis, MN: Fortress Press, 1995).

7. Contemporary theologies seek to augment the notions of "human being" already proposed with rational and critical arguments—not with special pleading or authoritarian imperatives. Hence Michael Perry has no trouble reaching out to theologians from the disciplines of law and political science. See, for example, his discussion of religion and politics, "American Catholics and American Politics," *Catholic Theological Society of America Proceedings* 55 (June 2000): 55–82.

8. Roland Robertson, *Globalization: Social Theory and Global Culture* (London: Sage, 1992). 100. It is not a matter of *either* universal *or* particular. Globalization cannot be reduced to economic mechanics, but should be treated as a

cultural, political, and religious dynamic. Robertson sketches his concept of *glocalization* and applies it to religions in "Globalization and the Future of 'Traditional Religion,'" in Max L. Stackhouse and Peter J. Paris, eds., *God and Globalization: Religion and the Powers of the Common Life* (Harrisburg, PA: Trinity Press International, 2000), pp. 53–68. For an example of this dialectical blending, see the study of Iran by Mahmood Monshipouri in this volume (Chapter 5).

9. See Nikhil Aziz, "The Human Rights Debate in an Era of Globalization," in Peter Van Ness, ed., *Debating Human Rights: Critical Essays from the United States and Asia* (London: Routledge, 1999), pp. 32–55.

10. The Asian values debate helps to focus the issues. An excellent collection with which to begin is Joanne R. Bauer and Daniel A. Bell, *The East Asian Challenge for Human Rights* (Cambridge: Cambridge University Press, 1999). A good supplement to these approaches is Van Ness, *Debating Human Rights*. See also the stimulating essays by Singapore's ambassador to the United Nations, Kishore Mahbubani, *Can Asians Think?* (Singapore: Times Books International, 1998). The dialogue with Islamic cultures also incorporates traditional cultural articulations. See Ann Elizabeth Mayer, *Islam and Human Rights: Tradition and Politics,* 2nd ed. (Boulder, CO: Westview Press, 1995).

11. Neil A. Englehart, "Rights and Culture in the Asian Values Argument: The Rise and Fall of Confucian Ethics in Singapore," *Human Rights Quarterly* 22, no. 2 (May 2000): 548–68. See also Andrew J. Nathan, "Is Chinese Culture Distinctive?" *Journal of Asian Studies* 52, no. 4 (November 1993): 923–936.

12. Samuel Huntington, *The Clash of Civilizations and the Remaking of World Order* (New York: Simon & Schuster, 1996), esp. pp. 183–206, 301–321. Though much debated, this blunt formulation indicates a continuing shadow over the human rights debate. One informed antidote is the sort offered by Edward Friedman in "Asia as a Font of Universal Human Rights," in Van Ness, *Debating Human Rights,* pp. 56–79. See also Chenyang Li, *The Tao Encounters the West: Explorations in Comparative Philosophy* (Albany: State University of New York Press, 1999), esp. pp. 163–89. Cultures are not monolithic. For a clear statement on the use of internal criteria of legitimacy in arguing for universal human rights in a particular culture, see Abdullahi Ahmed An-Na'im, "Toward a Cross-Cultural Approach to Defining International Standards of Human Rights: The Meaning of Cruel, Inhuman, or Degrading Treatment or Punishment," in Abdullahi A. An-Na'im, ed., *Human Rights in Cross-Cultural Perspectives: A Quest for Consensus* (Philadelphia: University of Pennsylvania Press, 1992), pp. 19–43.

13. See Jack Donnelly, "Human Rights and Asian Values: A Defense of 'Western' Universalism," in Bauer and Bell, *East Asian Challenge,* pp. 60–87.

14. I do not wish to argue here that human rights imply religious justifications. That case is made in an interesting way by Michael Perry in *The Idea of Human Rights: Four Inquiries* (New York: Oxford University Press, 1998), pp. 11–41. See also Max L. Stackhouse, "Human Rights and Public Theology: The Basic Validation of Human Rights," in Carrie Gustafson and Peter Juviler, eds., *Religion and Human Rights: Competing Claims?* (Armonk, NY: M. E. Sharpe, 1999), pp. 12–30.

15. Johann Baptist Metz (b. 1928) is a Roman Catholic diocesan priest from Bavaria. He holds degrees in both theology and philosophy and is Ordinary Professor of Fundamental Theology, Emeritus, at Westphalian Wilhelms University in

Münster. He has also been Visiting Lecturer in Politics and Religion at the Institute for Philosophy at the University of Vienna. Metz has consistently sought to view theological and philosophical problems through the lens of human suffering. His political theology should not be confused with that of Nazi legal theorist Carl Schmitt, who sought to justify the political as polemical.

16. While Metz does not rely on Jacques Derrida and Emmanuel Levinas, their postmodern philosophies express a strikingly similar turn. A relevant overview of Derrida and Levinas can be found in Richard Kearney, "Desire of God," in John D. Caputo and Michael Scanlon, eds., *God, the Gift, and Postmodernism* (Bloomington: Indiana University Press, 1999), pp. 112–145.

17. Friedrich Nietzsche, *Thus Spoke Zarathustra* (New York: Viking Press, 1966), p. 171: "I am Zarathustra, the godless: I still cook every chance in my pot. And only when it has been cooked through there do I welcome it as my food. And verily, many a chance came to me domineeringly; but my will spoke to it still more domineeringly–and immediately it lay imploringly on its knees." The human will to power remains the great philosophical challenge for any call to dialogue or to otherwise trust our humanity. For essays that address the danger of domination inherent in globalization, see Fredric Jameson and Masao Miyoshi, eds., *The Cultures of Globalization* (Durham: Duke University Press, 1998).

18. Johann Metz, "Communicating a Dangerous Memory," in Fred Lawrence, ed., *Communicating a Dangerous Memory* (Atlanta: Scholars Press, 1987), pp. 37–53. For an introductory collection of articles, see J. B. Metz and J. Moltmann, *Faith and the Future: Essays on Theology, Solidarity, and Modernity* (Maryknoll, NY: Orbis Books, 1995).

19. Metz, "Communicating," p. 42.

20. Johann Metz, "Unity and Diversity: Problems and Prospects for Inculturation," in Metz and Moltmann, *Faith and the Future,* pp. 57–65.

21. Johann Metz, "In the Pluralism of Religious and Cultural Worlds: Notes Toward a Theological and Political Program," *Cross Currents* 49, no. 2 (Summer 1999): 230.

22. Ibid., pp. 233–335.

23. Jack Donnelly and Rhoda E. Howard, "Human Dignity, Human Rights, and Political Regimes," in Jack Donnelly, ed., *Universal Human Rights in Theory and Practice* (Ithaca, NY: Cornell University Press, 1989), pp. 66–87. On the theological side, see political theologian Jürgen Moltmann's "Human Rights, Rights of Humanity, Rights of Nature," in Metz and Moltmann, *Faith and the Future,* pp. 178–193.

24. Chandra Muzaffar, "From Human Rights to Human Dignity," in Van Ness, *Debating Human Rights,* pp. 28–29. Muzaffar believes that all "people of faith" need to begin a dialogue on human life and living. Hans Küng makes the point that there will be no world peace without dialogue among the world's religions, in *A Global Ethic for Global Politics and Economics* (New York: Oxford University), pp. 114–154. See also the interdisciplinary essays in Stackhouse and Paris, *God and Globalization.*

25. Johann Metz, "Religion and Politics on Modernity's Ground," in J. Matthew Ashley, trans., *A Passion for God: The Mystical-Political Dimension of Christianity* (New York: Paulist Press, 1998), p. 142. Ashley notes that the word for

"remembering," or more accurately "remembrancing," used by Metz *(Eingedenken)* implies "doing in remembrance of" (p. 181).

26. Marsha Hewitt, "The Redemptive Power of Memory: Walter Benjamin and Elisabeth Schüssler Fiorenza," *Journal of Feminist Studies in Religion* 10, no. 1 (Spring 1994): 77.

27. Johann Metz, "Christians and Jews After Auschwitz," in John K. Downey, ed., *Love's Strategy: The Political Theology of Johann Baptist Metz* (Philadelphia: Trinity Press, 1999), p. 47.

28. Metz, "Communicating," p. 42.

29. Metz, "Christians and Jews," p. 48. The horrors of the Holocaust challenged Enlightenment confidence and yet were a major factor in generating the hopeful Universal Declaration of Human Rights in the United Nations. See Johannes Morsink, *The Universal Declaration of Human Rights: Origins, Drafting, and Intent* (Philadelphia: University of Pennsylvania Press, 1999), pp. 36–91.

30. Johann Metz, "The 'One World': A Challenge to Western Christianity," *First Hunthausen Lecture,* Saint Martin's College, Lacey, WA, October 9, 1989; unpublished typescript, p. 6.

31. See, for example, the general but still informative survey by Keith Soko in "Human Rights and the Poor in the World Religions," *Horizons* 26, no. 1 (Spring 1999): 31–53.

32. Johann Metz, "Messianic or 'Bourgeois'?" in Metz and Moltmann, *Faith and the Future,* pp. 17–29.

33. Johann Metz, "Monotheism and Democracy: Religion and Politics on Modernity's Ground," in Ashley, *Passion for God,* p. 145. Richard Falk makes a similar suggestion in "Cultural Foundations for the International Protection of Human Rights," in An-Na'im, *Human Rights,* pp. 44–63. Falk states that "taking suffering seriously is the Archimedes point for intermediation between the universal claim and the particular practice when it comes to resolving antagonisms between widely endorsed human rights norms and culturally ordained patterns of behavior" (p. 49).

34. Ludwig Wittgenstein, *Philosophical Investigations* (New York: Macmillan, 1966). Paragraphs 66–67 reveal Wittgenstein asking what is common to all games. He shows that while there is no invariable core to the word "game," there are overlapping and crisscrossing similarities. He calls these similarities "family resemblances" because in a family, "build, features, colour of eyes, gait, temperament, etc., etc., overlay and criss-cross in the same way—and I shall say: 'games form a family.'" No tightly patrolled concept defining an essence allows us to communicate exactly, but rather patterns of use and usage in the stream of life. "Human rights" gathers its meaning from this practiced weave in overlapping language games.

35. Ann-Belinda S. Preis, "Human Rights as Cultural Practice," *Human Rights Quarterly* 18, no. 2 (May 2000): 290. This article shows a sensitivity to epistemological and hermeneutical developments and discusses three field studies as examples. Michael J. Perry, "Are Human Rights Universals? The Relativist Challenge and Related Matters," *Human Rights Quarterly* 19, no. 3 (August 1997): 461–509.

36. Michael Walzer, *Thick and Thin: Moral Argument at Home and Abroad* (Notre Dame, IN: University of Notre Dame Press, 1994), pp. xi–21.

37. For a sense of this economic and cultural jeopardy, see the studies by Caren Irr and Rebecca Moore in this volume (Chapters 1 and 6).

38. While this paper argues that our human rights conversation must be more than a conversation about tactical formulations, it is certainly noteworthy that at the World Conference on Human Rights, sponsored by the United Nations in June 1993, 171 nations affirmed by consensus the "universal nature" of those "fundamental freedoms" and "human rights" articulated in the Universal Declaration of Human Rights. In 1948 the declaration was approved forty-six to zero with eight abstentions. For a good discussion of what this practical fact says to postmodern challenges, see José A. Lindgren Alves, "The Declaration of Human Rights in Postmodernity," *Human Rights Quarterly* 22, no. 2 (May 2000): 478–500.

39. Perry, *The Idea of Human Rights,* p. 71. He continues in pp. 71–86 to explode what he calls the myth of anthropological relativism, that is, the illogical jump from the contextual anchor of meaning to the impossibility of naming any common human good.

40. If all these things are so spontaneously horrible, one may ask how people can do them. There is, of course, pathology. But psychologists have also noted the ordinary human drive to reduce any dissonance between actions and values. See, for example, James E. Waller, "Perpetrators of the Holocaust: Divided and Unitary Self Conceptions in Evildoing," *Holocaust and Genocide Studies* 10, no. 1 (Spring 1996): 11–33. Waller argues that the need to form a unitary self-concept brings those who act inhumanely eventually to adjust their thinking about themselves and their victims. "The evildoing becomes justified or rationalized when its effects, however atrocious, are no longer empathically considered by the evildoer" (p. 18).

41. See the striking work of Martha C. Nussbaum in *Women and Human Development: The Capabilities Approach* (Cambridge: Cambridge University Press, 2000). Nussbaum's "capabilities approach" flows from a picture of human potential (see esp. pp. 70–86). She develops, with help from Aristotle and Marx, a theory of what a human being ought to be and from that calculates a list to mediate this notion for our concrete public political arrangements. "The aim of the project as a whole is to provide the philosophical underpinning for an account of basic constitutional principles that should be respected and implemented by the governments of all nations, as a bare minimum of what respect for human dignity requires" (p. 5). Also note her earlier piece in Martha C. Nussbaum and Jonathan Glover, eds., *Women, Culture, and Development: A Study of Human Capabilities* (Oxford: Clarendon Press, 1995), esp. pp. 63–69. See Hans Küng's proposal for a basic global consensus in Küng, *A Global Ethic.*

42. Donnelley's idea that human rights are always at root extralegal challenges to existing practices and institutions (*Universal Human Rights,* p. 14) might support this.

43. How we see suffering tells us about our humanity. Marianne Heimbach-Steins discusses the relationship of human suffering to notions of the person in society and uses the interesting example of the disabled in "Das Menschenrechtsethos vor der Realität des Leidens," in Gerhard Hover, ed., *Leiden* (Münster, Germany: Lit Verlag, 1997), pp. 229–257.

44. Conversation on the levels of consensus and concrete rights is complex and embedded. Charles Lockhart's application of group-grid theory in this volume

(Chapter 10) warns that rival cultural visions (individual, egalitarian, and hierarchical) direct the inevitable range and limits for evidence, arguments, and lists of rights. While human rights may be increasingly universally supported, the same rights are not supported universally.

45. Larry Rasmussen, "Human Environmental Rights and/or Biotic Rights," in Gustafson and Juviler, *Religion and Human Rights,* p. 47.

46. Albert Camus, *The Plague* (New York: Random House, 1948) p. 263. It is not an easy task to turn real political discussions toward the memory of suffering. And hope in human responsibility remains controversial. For an example of the sort of indirect denial of the primacy of suffering, often trivialized as "humanitarian concerns" in global politics, see Joseph S. Nye Jr., "Refining the National Interest," *Foreign Affairs* 78, no. 4 (July–August 1999): 22–35.

47. Metz's whole approach calls for facing the negativity in human history. "Only a few people make the connection between Auschwitz and the present crisis in the humanities: a growing numbness regarding universal and 'high' norms and values, the decline of solidarity, a clever readiness to make ourselves small in order to adapt to any situation, a growing refusal to endow the human self with any moral perspective, and so forth. Are not all of these votes of no confidence in the human person?" Ekkehard Schuster and Reinhold Boschert-Kimming, eds., *Hope Against Hope: Johann Baptist Metz and Elie Wiessel Speak Out on the Holocaust* (New York: Paulist Press, 1999), p. 18.

48. Johann Metz, "The Last Universalists," in Miroslav Volf, Carmen Krieg, and Thomas Kucharz, eds., *The Future of Theology: Essays in Honor of Jürgen Moltmann* (Grand Rapids, MI: William B. Eerdmans, 1996), p. 51.

49. Ronald Dworkin, *Taking Rights Seriously* (Cambridge: Harvard University Press, 1977), p. xi.

Bibliography

Alves, José A. "The Declaration of Human Rights in Postmodernity." *Human Rights Quarterly* 22, no. 2 (May 2000): 478–500.

An-Na'im, Abdullahi A., ed. *Human Rights in Cross-Cultural Perspectives: A Quest for Consensus.* Philadelphia: University of Pennsylvania, 1992.

Bauer, Joanne R. and Daniel A. Bell. *The East Asian Challenge for Human Rights.* Cambridge: Cambridge University Press, 1999.

Camus, Albert. *The Plague.* Trans. Stuart Gilbert. New York: Modern Library, 1948.

Downey, John K., ed. *Love's Strategy: The Political Theology of Johann Baptist Metz.* Harrisburg, PA: Trinity Press International, 1999.

———. *Wittgenstein and Theological Conversation.* Lanham, MD: University Press of America, 1983.

Donnelly, Jack. *International Human Rights.* Boulder, CO: Westview Press, 1998.

———. *Universal Human Rights in Theory and Practice.* Ithaca, NY: Cornell University Press, 1989.

Englehart, Neil A. "Rights and Culture in the Asian Values Argument: The Rise and Fall of Confucian Ethics in Singapore." *Human Rights Quarterly* 22, no. 4 (May 2000): 548–68.

Friedman, Thomas L. *The Lexus and the Olive Tree.* New York: Random House, 2000.

Hewitt, Marsha. "The Redemptive Power of Memory: Walter Benjamin and Elisabeth Schüssler Fiorenza." *Journal of Feminist Studies in Religion* 10, no. 1 (Spring 1994): 73-89.

Huntington, Samuel. *The Clash of Civilizations and the Remaking of World Order.* New York: Simon & Schuster, 1996.

Jameson, Fredric and Masao Miyoshi, eds. *The Cultures of Globalization.* Durham: Duke University Press, 1998.

Küng, Hans. *A Global Ethic for Global Politics and Economics.* New York: Oxford University Press, 1998.

Li, Chenyang. *The Tao Encounters the West: Explorations in Comparative Philosophy.* Albany: State University of New York Press, 1999.

Mahbubani, Kishore. *Can Asians Think?* Singapore: Times Books International, 1998.

Manemann, Jürgen. "Kritik als zentrales Moment des Glaubens: Zur gesellschaftskritischen Dimension der Fundamentaltheologie." In Klaus Müller, ed., *Fundamentaltheologie: Fluchtlinen und gegewärtige Herausforderungen.* Regensburg: Verlag Friedrich Pustet, 1998, pp. 217–241.

Metz, Johann Baptist. Trans. J. Matthew Ashley. *A Passion for God: The Mystical-Political Dimension of Christianity.* New York: Paulist Press, 1998.

———. "Communicating a Dangerous Memory." In Fred Lawrence, ed., *Communicating a Dangerous Memory.* Atlanta: Scholars Press, 1987.

———. "In the Pluralism of Religious and Cultural Worlds: Notes Toward a Theological and Political Program. *Cross Currents* 49, no. 2 (Summer 1999): 227–236.

———. "The 'One World': A Challenge to Western Christianity." *First Hunthausen Lecture*, Saint Martin's College, Lacey, WA, October 9, 1989. Unpublished typescript.

———. *Zum Begriff der neuen Politishchen Theologie, 1967–1997.* Mainz: Grünewald, 1997.

Metz, Johann Baptist and Jürgen Moltmann. *Faith and the Future: Essays on Theology, Solidarity, and Modernity.* Maryknoll, NY: Orbis Books, 1995.

Morsink, Johannes. *The Universal Declaration of Human Rights: Origins, Drafting, and Intent.* Philadelphia: University of Pennsylvania Press, 1999.

Ogden, Schubert M. *Doing Theology Today.* Valley Forge, PA: Trinity Press International, 1996.

Perry, Michael. *The Idea of Human Rights: Four Inquiries.* New York: Oxford University Press, 1998.

Preis, Belinda S. "Human Rights as Cultural Practice: An Anthropological Critique." *Human Rights Quarterly* 18, no. 2 (May 1996): 286–315.

Robertson, Roland. *Globalization: Social Theory and Global Culture.* London: Sage Press, 1992.

Rosaldo, Renato. *Culture and Truth: The Remaking of Social Analysis.* Boston: Beacon Press, 1993.

Sanks, T. Howland. "Globalization and the Church's Social Mission." *Theological Studies* 60, no. 4 (December 1999): 625–651.

Schreiter, Robert J. *Constructing Local Theologies*. Maryknoll, NY: Orbis Books, 1985.

———. *The New Catholicity: Theology Between the Global and the Local*. Maryknoll, NY: Orbis Books, 1997.

Soko, Keith. "Human Rights and the Poor in the World Religions." *Horizons* 26, no. 1 (Spring 1999): 31–53.

Stackhouse, Max L. and Peter J. Paris, eds. *God and Globalization: Religion and the Powers of the Common Life*. Harrisburg, PA: Trinity Press International, 2000.

Tracy, David. *Blessed Rage for Order: The New Pluralism in Theology*. New York: Seabury Press, 1975.

———. *Plurality and Ambiguity: Hermeneutics, Religion, Hope*. San Francisco: Harper & Row, 1987.

Van Ness, Peter and Nikhil Aziz, eds. *Debating Human Rights: Critical Essays from the United States and Asia*. London: Routledge, 1999.

Volf, Miroslav, Carmen Krieg and Thomas Kushcarz. *The Future of Theology: Essays in Honor of Jürgen Moltmann*. Grand Rapids, MI: Eerdmans, 1996.

Walzer, Michael. *Thick and Thin: Moral Argument at Home and Abroad*. Notre Dame, IN: Notre Dame University Press, 1994.

Wittgenstein, Ludwig. Trans. G. E. M. Anscombe. *Philosophical Investigations*. New York: Macmillan, 1969.

Conclusion

Reconstructing Human Rights in the Global Society

Andrew J. Nathan, Mahmood Monshipouri,
Neil A. Englehart, and Kavita Philip

The debate over the impact of globalization has raised profound questions for students and proponents of human rights. Have globalization theorists been proven right in their prognosis that globalization would improve the prospects for human rights in political communities across the world? Does globalization presage a power shift from national governments to evolving systems of regional and global governance that will give more effective protection to human rights? The answers to these questions lie in part in the nature of the globalization process itself and partly in the changed structural context in which globalizing forces operate (Held and McGrew 2000; Linklater 2001; McGrew 2000). To the extent that globalization embodies a broad range of competing and often contradictory values (Clark 2001; Cox 1996; Falk 1999), no conceptual framework or theoretical position can be either fully adopted or entirely dismissed. Our studies in this book suggest that there is no single answer to these questions, and that globalization's effects on human rights have been for both good and ill, depending upon the context.

Understanding the complex relations between globalization and human rights requires an examination of the contemporary context of the post–Cold War order within which such relations occur. Whether globalization is the defining feature of this order remains a subject of debate. A broad consensus, however, holds that globalization both contributed to the demise of the Cold War and is a basic feature of the contemporary order (Clark 2001). A study of the post–Cold War period, however, yields mixed results. It demonstrates flaws in overly optimistic theories of globalization, but also underscores the rise and importance of transnational cooperation and global civil society (Falk 2000; Scholte 2000).

The post–Cold War era has not brought the global peace and stability that many observers hoped for. History did not, as optimists expected, "end" (Fukuyama 1992). Instead, it has given rise to surprising turbulence, shocking violence, and intense controversy that have damaged human rights (Rosenau 1990). The optimists were correct to foresee that globalization would intensify, if we measure its expansion by faster communications, greater interdependence within the world economy, and accelerated flows of people, goods, and ideas across borders. They were also right to foresee the expansion of international regimes intended to regulate finance and trade, migration, aviation, weapons proliferation, and of course human rights, among many other issues. These two developments—intensified technical, economic, and social globalization, and the expansion of pro-market and prodemocracy interstate regimes—were precisely the sorts of trends toward a more secure and prosperous world that many human rights advocates in the West (and some elsewhere) looked forward to as the Cold War ended.

Yet both developments have by now revealed darker sides that even their proponents must acknowledge. Although some economists argue that globalization has reduced global inequality (Dollar and Kraay 2002), others contend that globalization has worsened inequality and increased the vulnerability of large populations to economic instability (Peterson, Wunder, and Mueller 1999; Mittelman 2000; Thompson 2000; Lorenz 2001; Rodrik 2001). The debate turns on how global inequality is conceptualized. David Dollar and Aart Kraay (2002) are probably correct that the rapid economic growth of large and formerly poor countries like China, India, and Vietnam has diminished inequality measured as the distribution of income among individuals worldwide. The critics argue, however, that it is equally true that inequality has increased when measured both country-to-country and within developing countries individual-to-individual. Moreover, as shown by surging inequality within China and India, just because economic growth raises the income of the poor does not mean that it lessens inequality (Pitts 2002). This apparent contradiction is explained by the fact that China and India are so huge demographically that their growth has brought hundreds of millions of individuals out of poverty at the same time that a wealth gap has widened between those persons living at the poverty line and entrepreneurs at the top of the wealth pyramid.

Also at the same time, poverty has deepened in the countries that have adapted less well to globalization, but since they are demographically smaller, their problems are not reflected in Dollar and Kraay's aggregate findings. Dani Rodrik (2001) points out that the best results—economically and even more so socially and politically—have been generated by countries that refused to play by globalization's purported rules and that instead implemented strong defensive policies to mitigate and control its effects. In short, the early faith has dissipated that deep, rapid trade and monetary liberalization would deliver both fast and fair economic growth.

Aside from its pure economic effects, it is clear that globalization has generated profound social disruption and cultural resistance, and has at least indirectly contributed to some of the devastating outbreaks of interstate war, civil war, terrorism, refugee flows and illegal migration, and even genocide that have marred the post–Cold War period. In the era of globalization, states find themselves more vulnerable than ever to the impacts of one another's internal economic, social, political, and even cultural instabilities. This has produced stronger motives for mutual intervention, thus fundamentally challenging the relatively stable old-world order of formally equal sovereign states. In addition, the increasing reach under globalization of such international financial institutions as the World Bank and the International Monetary Fund, and of international legal regimes for trade and investment like the World Trade Organization, has created new dilemmas of fairness—whose interests should these regimes serve?—and new struggles over the ability to control international trade standards and regimes (Stiglitz 2002).

As recounted in the introduction to this book, the move toward a more robust international human rights regime has been one of the most striking developments of the post–Cold War era. In its relations with globalization, the human rights regime typifies the complex dynamics and multilayered ethical implications of the new era. Interdependence has created stronger motives for states to try collectively to regulate some aspects of one another's internal behavior, while at the same time globalization has enlarged the information base for the international community to take an interest in the internal affairs of states. The rise of regimes in other functional areas, especially those relating to economic interactions, has made it seem more natural and even more necessary that states should also join conventions and treaties relating to human rights. And if globalization has helped to spread and legitimize the human rights idea, so too the human rights idea with its impulse to level differences and open markets has helped prepare the ground for globalization.

Despite its often benevolent effects, the growth of the international human rights regime has not been exempt from the dilemmas and paradoxes that attend other aspects of globalization and international regime formation. While the same reactions against cultural subversion and the devaluation of local identities that confront human rights also confront other features of globalization, the same ethical questions that confront the human rights regime also confront other international regimes. Whom does the system serve? And who should shape its development?

Rather than leading to the harmonious cosmopolitan order envisioned by the drafters of the Universal Declaration of Human Rights (UDHR), the notion of universal rights stimulates conflict and generates its own opposition. Often this notion is framed in correspondingly universal terms and institutions, claiming universal validity. Although their advocates might often argue that their validity stems from a universally true foundation of ontological givens, we see these ideas and institutions, rather, as constructed approaches. Competing approaches do not need to rest on axiomatic foundational transcultural truths; rather, they draw their power from the specific cultural and political contexts in which they are constructed.

Contributors to this book have focused on these dilemmas of and resistances to the new globalization-era human rights regime, not out of antagonism to human rights as an idea, but from a recognition of the problems inherent in creating a firm global basis for human rights in the new era. This explains the title of the book. The human rights system that may now, we hope, be coming into its own must nonetheless construct a firm foundation for itself under more challenging conditions than most advocates had previously anticipated.

The chapters in the book have addressed three attributes of the international human rights regime in particular that link its fate to issues central to globalization. Our investigations suggest that these are key issues that the human rights community must confront honestly in constructing human rights in the age of the globalization. First, the emerging international human rights regime is linked to and conspicuously serves the interests of dominant Western liberal states. Second, it is associated largely with Western culture and identity. Third, promoting human rights also tends to promote the conditions for globalization writ large. In making these points, we are not suggesting that the idea does not serve the interests of the weak and poor whom it is ostensibly designed to protect. No doubt it frequently does so. Our intervention is a friendly one, aimed at helping the regime stabilize itself ethically and politically in the stormier atmosphere that it confronts today. Proponents of the international human rights regime cannot credibly claim that it is purely altruistic or that it is neutral as regards economic, political—and more controversially social and cultural—systems. Stronger legitimation and broader effectiveness must be built on a foundation of intellectual honesty.

Facing such challenges, in what ways will human rights—as an idea, and as an institutional system—have to change to remain relevant and to grow in authority? One answer to the challenge of strengthening the human rights regime focuses on culture and values, and has been widely vetted in recent years. This is the idea that the human rights idea needs to break the bonds of cultural particularity—of its rootedness in the Western tradition—and needs to regroup itself on a multicultural basis, or even on several overlapping multicultural bases. On the other hand, certain complexities confront this program. One is that the struggle between globalizers and localizers, both claiming roots in local traditions and both, paradoxically, claiming some kind of universal validity for their positions, will be fought out over a long period of time. To be sure, it is inconclusive at this stage. Another is the difficulty of linking broad cultural values that may indeed overlap—fairness, for example, or justice—with specific provisions in international human rights law, such as freedom of speech or equal education for women.

While Charles Lockhart (Chapter 10) argues that finding the overlapping consensus is a vastly more difficult task in practice than in prospect, other contributors, such as Joanne Bauer and Chenyang Li (Chapters and 11), note that different regions have varying human rights priorities that stem from their own history and experience with human rights, but that it is a mistake to interpret the differentiation of priorities as a disagreement over norms. Similarly, John K. Downey (Chapter 12) argues that the global conversation on human rights may find a common ground in the authority of those who suffer. This simple recognition of the claims made on human beings by the suffering of other human beings provides criteria for tactical moves to principles, ethics, and rights. In the end, just keeping such a conversation on human rights going constitutes also a contribution.

Yet developing "bridge values" and global consensus is facilitated by a phenomenon noted in several of these chapters, that of globalization from below. In very diverse contexts Neil Englehart, Mahmood Monshipouri, Rebecca Moore, and Linda Butenhoff (Chapters 2, 5, 6, and 8) demonstrate how internal dynamics lead to transnational, globalizing linkages between local activist and international actors. This offers a second answer to the problem of how best to construct a human rights regime: let it emerge as a by-product of the increasing global circulation of ideas and resources, and the increasing homogenization of cultures, economies, and political institutions. Limits to globalization, however, must be acknowledged. As Dorothy J. Solinger (Chapter 7) reminds us, in China, for now, a strong case can be made that globalization and human rights are more on a collision course than they are converging. Moreover, the global standards put into practice there are more those of flexibility and efficiency than (except at the level of language) those of human rights.

A third answer to the problem of how to construct human rights in the age of globalization has been to insist that human rights are no longer grounded in any particular cultural setting but have shifted to a basis in international positive law. This is not to deny that the idea of human rights originated in the West. But by now, the obligations of states to comply with international human rights norms are rooted in a series of treaties and conventions that they have signed, most notably the International Covenant on Civil and Political Rights and the International Covenant on Economic, Social, and Cultural Rights. This is a crucial growth frontier for human rights in the current age. As human rights becomes entrenched in international and domestic law, institutions arise designed to support and promote it. Even if these are relatively weak, they command certain personnel and resources, they create relentless pressure at both the international and national levels for human rights improvements, and they have the potential to grow in influence.

But these chapters suggest that such institutions can have unintended practical as well as ethical consequences. Human rights changes as it spreads. As it becomes universal, it becomes a terrain of struggle among groups with competing interests and goals. These groups resourcefully use human rights—qua discourse, qua institutions, qua legitimation, and qua a language of communication—to press their very different, often diametrically opposed, goals and values. As such, the discourse and institutions of human rights that originally had a fairly specific meaning become stretched and altered, and they come to accommodate some surprising things.

Consider, for example, the struggles over intellectual property as a human right (Caren Irr, Chapter 1). Many in the developing world have argued that traditional and communal modes of ownership can serve as the best safeguards against transnational corporations controlling intellectual property in seeds, genetic information, and agricultural techniques. Further, more and more of what has historically been considered basically "human" or part of a "common heritage of mankind" is now treated as the intellectual property of individual authors. The advocates of peoples' rights challenge the foundational premises of intellectual private property. While private property is forcefully installed around the world as part of economic globalization, communal and collective forms of ownership establish themselves in response to that process. The ownership of culture as such appears to be less amenable to the norm of universality than it is presumed under the Universal Declaration of Human Rights. Likewise, as Kavita Philip (Chapter 3) argues, when a product patent increases the price of a resource (e.g., the neem tree in India) that was previously free and integral to the life of a villager, political ecologists would argue that we cannot separate economic rights from environmental rights, nor analyze human rights in isolation from the context of the global power differentials within which transnationals operate in dispersed locations and with scattered accountability.

Even the process of drafting the UDHR exemplifies this. Faced with competing conceptions of human rights—that is, civil-political rights and socioeconomic and cultural rights—the authors of the UDHR edged more toward a liberal than a socialist conception of the rights. Canadian international lawyer John P. Humphrey, who served as head of the UN Human Rights Division of the Secretariat throughout the drafting process, admitted that the influence of English-speaking sources and the democratic West on drafting of the declaration was obvious. A small working group headed by French delegate René Cassin, undertook the responsibility of converting Humphrey's outline into a draft declaration (Winston 2001, 932). Since the core decisions regarding the content of the declaration were made at the drafting-committee stage, conception of the rights came primarily from the philosophical traditions and historical experiences of the North American, European, and British Commonwealth members of the drafting committee and secretariat.

Moreover, because the declaration had a nonbinding character, many states voted in favor of the UN General Assembly resolution, despite their strong ideological objections to and profound disagreement with its content. They were seemingly convinced that it would not create obligations for them in the future. In the end, although the draft attempted to combine aspects of liberalism and social democracy, its balance as a whole was unmistakably Western (Poole 1999, 62–63). Michael Ignatieff, albeit from a different perspective, argues that the moral consensus, which sustained the Universal Declaration in 1948, has over time increasingly splintered (2001, 93). There is, Ignatieff continues, no evidence that economic globalization entails moral globalization. In fact, as economies have integrated their business practices, ownership, languages, and networks of communication, a countermovement has developed to maintain the integrity of national communities, national cultures, religions, and indigenous ways of life.

The end of the Cold War and the processes of globalization in the sense of post-1989 developments have accelerated that process of transformation. In a sense, this book has presented a series of studies of this process. The processes of struggle we are describing—struggle over globalization within the human rights terrain—are by no means equal. Surely conspicuous among the losers—or those who benefit less, who are less able to use the human rights lingo to serve their ends—are small indigenous populations as well as the large populations of the poor and the powerless. Thus in building the new legal order, we need to be more attentive to the unintended consequences. Whose interests are really served? Which forces are taking advantage?

Despite the advance of globalization, we are still constructing human rights. The task in a sense has become harder than before because the stronger the regime, the more complex the political and normative struggles among the many interests who would make use of it to their own ends. In human rights as in globalization, the liberal/capitalist Western society stands to gain more than the rest (Donnelly 1998; Forsythe 2000; Risse, Ropp, and Sikkink 1999). From a different perspective, Ellen Freeberg (Chapter 4) defends a version of liberal feminism in this volume, arguing that religious law—be it Sharia or any other religious edicts—cannot supersede women's capacity for agency altogether. She makes a compelling case for sustaining universal women's rights; but while she expects regard for agency to ground general protections for women, she also expects it to enhance mechanisms that allow women's voices to shape and reshape their future in their own settings.

Likewise, the various forms of global and regional fundamentalism can arguably exploit different aspects and problems associated with globalization, including the disillusionment resulting from the prevailing identity crisis, poverty, and social injustice (Castells 1997; Lechner 2000). In a world where certain forms of injustice are progressively worsening, human rights continues to be just one of the instruments of amelioration. Human rights must be continuously rethought and reconstructed in response to emerging global transformations if they are to be a cure for rather than a cause of discord among and within different societies and cultures. It may be the case that no simple or coherent blueprint can serve to construct the best human rights regime for the age of globalization. In confronting this conundrum, we hope we have demonstrated here, however, the value of eschewing grand theory in favor of close attention to the particular impacts of the human rights regime in local settings.

References

Castells, Manuel. 1997. *The Power of Identity: The Information Age—Economy, Society, and Culture.* Vol. 2. Malden, MA: Blackwell.
Clark, Ian. 2001. "Globalization and the Post-Cold War Order." In John Baylis

and Steve Smith, eds., *The Globalization of World Politics: An Introduction to International Relations.* Oxford: Oxford University Press, 634–647.

Cox, Robert W. 1996. "A Perspective on Globalization." In James H. Mittelman, ed., *Globalization: Critical Reflections.* Boulder, CO: Lynne Rienner, 21–30.

Dollar, David, and Aart Kraay. 2002. "Spreading the Wealth." *Foreign Affairs* 81, no. 1 (January–February): 120–133.

Donnelly, Jack. 1998. *International Human Rights.* 2nd ed. Boulder, CO: Westview Press.

Falk, Richard A. 1999. *Predatory Globalization: A Critique.* London: Polity Press.

———. 2000. *Human Rights Horizons: The Pursuit of Justice in a Globalizing World.* New York: Routledge.

Forsythe, David P. 2000. *Human Rights in International Relations.* Cambridge: Cambridge University Press.

Fukuyama, Francis. 1992. *The End of History and the Last Man.* London: Hamish Hamilton.

Held, David, and Anthony McGrew. 2000. *The Global Transformations Reader: An Introduction to the Globalization Debate.* London: Polity Press.

Ignatieff, Michael, K. Anthony Appiah, David A. Hollinger, Thomas W. Laqueur, and Diane F. Orentlicher. 2001. "Human Rights as Idolatry." In *Human Rights as Politics and Idolatry.* Princeton: Princeton University Press.

Lechner, Frank J. 2000. "Global Fundamentalism." In Frank J. Lechner and John Boli, eds., *The Globalization Reader.* London: Blackwell, 338–341.

Linklater, Andrew. 2001. "Globalization and the Transformation of the Political Community." In John Baylis and Steve Smith, eds., *The Globalization of World Politics: An Introduction to International Relations.* Oxford: Oxford University Press, 617–633.

Lorenz, Edward C. 2001. *Defining Global Justice: The History of U.S. International Labor Standards Policy.* Notre Dame, IN: Notre Dame University Press.

McGrew, Anthony. 2000. "Power Shift: From National Government to Global Governance?" In David Held, ed., *A Globalizing World? Culture, Economics, Politics.* London: Open University, 127–167.

Mittelman, James H. 2000. *The Globalization Syndrome: Transformation and Resistance.* Princeton: Princeton University Press.

Peterson, R. Dean, Delores F. Wunder, and Harlan L. Mueller. 1999. *Social Problems: Globalization in the Twenty-first Century.* Upper Saddle River, NJ: Prentice Hall.

Pitts, Joe W., III. 2002. "Inequality Is No Myth." *Foreign Affairs* 81, no. 4 (July–August): 179–180.

Poole, Hilary, ed. 1999. *Human Rights: The Essential Reference.* Phoenix, AZ: Oryx Press.

Risse, Thomas, Stephen C. Ropp, and Kathryn Sikkink. 1999. *The Power of Human Rights: International Norms and Domestic Change.* Cambridge: Cambridge University Press.

Rodrik, Dani. 2001. "Trading in Illusions." *Foreign Policy* 123 (March–April): 54–62.

Rosenau, James N. 1990. *Turbulence in World Politics: A Theory of Change and Continuity.* Princeton: Princeton University Press.

Scholte, Jan Aart. 2000. *Globalization: A Critical Introduction.* New York: St. Martin's Press.

Stiglitz, Joseph E. 2002. *Globalization and Its Discontents.* New York: W. W. Norton.

Thompson, Grahame. 2000. "Economic Globalization?" In David Held, ed., *A Globalizing World? Culture, Economics, and Politics.* London: Open University, 85–126.

Winston, Morton E. 2001. "Universal Declaration of Human Rights." In James R. Lewis and Carl Skutsch, eds., *The Human Rights Encyclopedia,* vol. 3. Armonk, NY: M. E. Sharpe, 926–934.

About the Contributors

Joanne Bauer is director of studies at the Carnegie Council on Ethics and International Affairs. In 1993 she founded the Carnegie Council's Human Rights Initiative and is editor in Chief of the publication, *Human Rights Dialogue*. She is also the director of a multiyear comparative study of values in environmental policy in the United States, Japan, India, and China, funded by the National Science Foundation, the U.S.-Japan Foundation, and the Henry Luce Foundation. Bauer is coeditor with Daniel A. Bell of *The East Asian Challenge for Human Rights* (1999).

Linda Butenhoff is Director of the International Relations Program and Associate Professor in the Political Science Department at St. Cloud State University. Among her publications is *Social Movements and Political Reform in Hong Kong* (1999). She is currently working on *Taking Sides: Controversial Issues in Global Human Rights* (forthcoming).

John K. Downey is Professor of Religious Studies at Gonzaga University in Spokane, Washington. A former Director of the Coolidge Research Colloquium, his recent articles and translations have appeared in *Horizons*, *Cross Currents*, and *Philosophy and Theology*. He is the editor of *Love's Strategy: The Political Theology of Johann Baptist Metz* (1999).

Neil A. Englehart holds a Ph.D. from the University of California, San Diego. He is currently on leave from the Department of Government and

Law at Lafayette College, in Easton, Pennsylvania, and is a Member of the Institute for Advanced Studies in Princeton, New Jersey. His research focuses on the origins, spread, and consequences of the institutions of the modern state.

Ellen M. Freeberg holds a Ph.D. from Johns Hopkins University. She serves as Director of Academic Affairs and teaches as Affiliated Faculty in Political Science at the Graduate Faculty of New School University. She is author of *Regarding Equality: Rethinking Contemporary Theories of Citizenship, Freedom, and the Limits of Moral Pluralism* (2002). Her current research focuses on feminist interpretations of mothering and on public policies related to family and work.

Caren Irr is Associate Professor of English at Brandeis University. She is the author of *The Suburb of Dissent: Cultural Politics in the United States and Canada* (1998) and the co-editor of *Rethinking the Frankfurt School: Alternative Legacies of Cultural Critique* (2002). Her current research concerns gender and intellectual property in the context of globalization.

Chenyang Li is Chair and Professor of Philosophy of Anhui University, China, and Professor and Chair of the Department of Philosophy at Central Washington University, USA. He holds a Ph.D. from the University of Connecticut. He is author of *The Tao Encounters the West: Explorations in Comparative Philosophy* (1999) and editor of *The Sage and the Second Sex: Confucianism, Ethics, and Gender* (2000). His most recent articles have appeared in *International Philosophical Quarterly*, *Philosophia*, *Journal of Applied Philosophy*, *Journal of Chinese Philosophy*, and *Philosophy East & West*. He served as the first President of the Association of Chinese Philosophers in America, Inc., during 1995-1997. Currently, he is Secretary of the International Society for Chinese Philosophy.

Charles Lockhart is professor of political science at Texas Christian University. In recent years he has combined his interests in theories of distributive justice and comparative social policy to focus on the contributions that variation in societies' political cultures makes to explaining cross-societal social program differences. He has published a number of articles and several books on this topic. His most recent book is *The Roots of American Exceptionalism: Institutions, Culture and Policies* (forthcoming).

Mahmood Monshipouri is Chair and Professor of Political Science at Quinnipiac University, Hamden, Connecticut. He is author of *Democratization, Liberalization, and Human Rights in the Third World* (1995), and *Islamism, Secularism, and Human Rights in the Middle East* (1998). His most recent articles have appeared in *Yale Human Rights & Development Law Journal, Human Rights Quarterly, Middle East Policy,* and *Journal of Church and State.* Currently, he is the executive director of the Center for the Iranian Research and Analysis in the United States.

Rebecca R. Moore is Associate Professor of Political Science at Concordia College, Moorhead, Minnesota. Currently, she holds a NATO Fellowship and is writing a book on the evolution of NATO's political dimension since the end of the Cold War. Her research on the topics of democracy promotion, U.S. human rights policy, and NATO has appeared in academic and policy journals such as *Washington Quarterly.*

Andrew J. Nathan is Class of 1919 Professor of Political Science and former Director of the East Asian Institute at Columbia University. His publications include *Chinese Democracy* (1985); *Human Rights in Contemporary China,* with R. Randle Edwards and Louis Henkin (1986); *The Tiananmen Papers,* edited with Perry Link (2001); *Negotiating Culture and Human Rights: Beyond Universalism and Relativism,* co-edited with Lynda S. Bell and Ilan Peleg (2001), and *China's New Rulers: The Secret Files,* with Bruce Gilley (2002). His current research involves collaborative survey-based studies of political culture and political participation in mainland China, Taiwan, Hong Kong, and other Asian societies.

Kavita Philip received her doctorate in Science and Technology Studies from Cornell University, and is Associate Professor at Georgia Institute of Technology, Atlanta, Georgia. She teaches in Georgia Tech's undergraduate programs in Science, Technology and Culture, and Women, Science and Technology, and the graduate program in Information Design and Technology. Her current research interests are in environmental history; postcolonial and feminist science studies; globalization, law, and human rights; and new media technologies. She is author of *Civilizing Natures: Race and Resources in Colonial South India* (2003), and the co-author of *Going Native: Postcolonialism and Cyberculture* (with Terry Harpold, forthcoming). Her articles have appeared in the *Cultural Studies, Postmodern Culture, Irish Studies Review,* and *Environment and History.*

Dorothy J. Solinger is Professor of Political Science at the University of California, Irvine and Adjunct Senior Research Scholar at the East Asian Institute, Columbia University. Her most recent book is *Contesting Citizenship in Urban China: Peasant Migrants, the State and the Logic of the Market* (1999). She has co-edited a volume, *States and Sovereignty in the Global Economy* (1999).

Index

Abortion, 131, 251, 252–53, 300, 304
Activist-intellectuals, 242, 243, 245, 249, 252
African Charter on Human on People's Rights. *See* Banjul Charter
Agency: capacity for, 336; freedom of, 98, 100; human, 261; importance of, 90; and irrational behaviors, 102; practice-bound, 104, 105; and religion, 105, 106–7
Age of adulthood, 132
Age of Rights, The (Henkin), 293
Aghajari, Hashem, 119
Albright, Madeleine, 146–47
Alien Tort Claims Act (U.S.), 69–70, 84n41
Alston, Philip, 60
American Bar Association, 158–59
American Civil Liberties Union, 251
Amin, Samir, 215
Amnesty International, 44, 250, 251
Anghie, Anthony, 79–80
Animal rights, 297–98
An-Na'im, Abdullahi A., 249, 297
Anticolonialism, 11, 12–13, 15
Antiessentialists, 97, 98
Asia Foundation, 149, 155–56, 157–58, 164

Asian financial crisis, 186, 187–88, 196, 226–27, 245
Asian Orientalism, 245
Asian values debate: and culture, 298–99; and diversity, 252; and human rights, 216, 292; and nationalism, 244; and the West, 243, 310
Atrinafard, Saeed, 121
Auschwitz, 315, 319
Authors, rights of, 9–10, 13, 20, 24
Autonomy, 100–101, 102, 103

Bahbahani, Simin, 137
Bangkok Declaration on Human Rights: and civil rights, 44, 47; Preamble to, 255n16; values in, 245, 302; wording of, 49–50n11
Banjul Charter (African Charter on Human on People's Rights), 19–21, 59, 71, 219, 248–49
Baradaran, Monireh, 137
Baron, Barnett, 157, 164
Bauer, Joanne, 239–53, 333
Bazargan, Medhi, 125
Bell, Daniel, 260
Berlin, Isaiah, 302
Biases, cultural, 264
Bill of Rights Ordinance (BORO), 225

CPSIA information can be obtained
at www.ICGtesting.com
Printed in the USA
LVHW031743111219
640174LV00012B/979/P

9 780765 611383